Network Virtualization

Victor Moreno, CCIE 6908.
Kumar Reddy

Cisco Press

800 East 96th Street
Indianapolis, Indiana 46240 USA

Network Virtualization

Victor Moreno, Kumar Reddy

Copyright © 2006 Cisco Systems, Inc.

Cisco Press logo is a trademark of Cisco Systems, Inc.

Published by:
Cisco Press
800 East 96th Street
Indianapolis, IN 46240 USA

Printed in the United States of America 1 2 3 4 5 6 7 8 9 0

First Printing   July 2006

Library of Congress Cataloging-in-Publication Number: 2005926713

ISBN: 1-58705-248-2

Trademark Acknowledgments

Warning and Disclaimer

Corporate and Government Sales

Cisco Press offers excellent discounts on this book when ordered in quantity for bulk purchases or special sales.

For more information please contact: **U.S. Corporate and Government Sales**   1-800-382-3419
corpsales@pearsontechgroup.com

For sales outside the U.S. please contact: **International Sales**   international@pearsoned.com

Feedback Information

At Cisco Press, our goal is to create in-depth technical books of the highest quality and value. Each book is crafted with care and precision, undergoing rigorous development that involves the unique expertise of members from the professional technical community.

Readers' feedback is a natural continuation of this process. If you have any comments regarding how we could improve the quality of this book, or otherwise alter it to better suit your needs, you can contact us through email at feedback@ciscopress.com. Please make sure to include the book title and ISBN in your message.

We greatly appreciate your assistance.

Publisher	John Wait
Editor-in-Chief	John Kane
Cisco Representative	Anthony Wolfenden
Cisco Press Program Manager	Jeff Brady
Executive Editor	Brett Bartow
Production Manager	Patrick Kanouse
Development Editor	Deadline Driven Publishing
Project Editor	Kelly Maish
Copy Editor	Keith Cline
Technical Editor(s)	Zahir Aziz, Khalil Jabr, Marcus Phipps
Team Coordinator	Raina Han
Book Designer	Louisa Adair
Cover Designer	Louisa Adair
Composition	Interactive Composition Corporation
Indexer	Ken Johnson

CISCO SYSTEMS

Corporate Headquarters
Cisco Systems, Inc.
170 West Tasman Drive
San Jose, CA 95134-1706
USA
www.cisco.com
Tel: 408 526-4000
    800 553-NETS (6387)
Fax: 408 526-4100

European Headquarters
Cisco Systems International BV
Haarlerbergpark
Haarlerbergweg 13-19
1101 CH Amsterdam
The Netherlands
www-europe.cisco.com
Tel: 31 0 20 357 1000
Fax: 31 0 20 357 1100

Americas Headquarters
Cisco Systems, Inc.
170 West Tasman Drive
San Jose, CA 95134-1706
USA
www.cisco.com
Tel: 408 526-7660
Fax: 408 527-0883

Asia Pacific Headquarters
Cisco Systems, Inc.
Capital Tower
168 Robinson Road
#22-01 to #29-01
Singapore 068912
www.cisco.com
Tel: +65 6317 7777
Fax: +65 6317 7799

Cisco Systems has more than 200 offices in the following countries and regions. Addresses, phone numbers, and fax numbers are listed on the
Cisco.com Web site at www.cisco.com/go/offices.

Argentina • Australia • Austria • Belgium • Brazil • Bulgaria • Canada • Chile • China PRC • Colombia • Costa Rica • Croatia • Czech Republic
Denmark • Dubai, UAE • Finland • France • Germany • Greece • Hong Kong SAR • Hungary • India • Indonesia • Ireland • Israel • Italy
Japan • Korea • Luxembourg • Malaysia • Mexico • The Netherlands • New Zealand • Norway • Peru • Philippines • Poland • Portugal
Puerto Rico • Romania • Russia • Saudi Arabia • Scotland • Singapore • Slovakia • Slovenia • South Africa • Spain • Sweden
Switzerland • Taiwan • Thailand • Turkey • Ukraine • United Kingdom • United States • Venezuela • Vietnam • Zimbabwe

About the Author(s)

Kumar Reddy is a Manager of Technical Marketing Engineering at Cisco Systems. Kumar has more than 15 years of industry experience. He has held a variety of technical roles at Cisco, including working with service provider customers as a systems engineer, as a technical specialist for both *digital subscriber line* (DSL) and Ethernet products and technology and, most recently, designing end-to-end systems for small and medium-size businesses.

Before joining Cisco, Kumar taught unsuspecting engineering students in Paris and worked as a programmer in Tokyo. Kumar has a degree in Computer Engineering from Trinity College, Dublin, Ireland.

Victor Moreno, CCIE No. 6908, is a Technical Marketing Engineer at Cisco Systems. Victor is a Cisco Certified Internetworking Expert (CCIE) and has more than 10 years of industry experience, of which the past 5 he has spent at Cisco involved in enterprise network design and architecture. Victor is a recognized expert in the field of virtual enterprise networks and has been involved with enterprise network virtualization since 2001. He has worked directly with major customers and designs, both in the United States and internationally, and has done extensive research in this domain, working with internal engineering and marketing teams on new product features and direction. Victor has a degree in electrical engineering from the Simón Bolívar University in Caracas, Venezuela, and a Master degree from the University of York, England, and specializations from Stanford University.

About the Technical Reviewers

Zaheer Aziz, CCIE No. 4127, is a co-author of the Cisco Press title *Troubleshooting IP Routing Protocols and currently works as a Technical Leader in SP Solutions group focusing on Multiprotocol Label Switching* (MPLS) *virtual private networks* (VPNs). Prior to this role, Zaheer worked in the Cisco Customer Advocacy group providing dedicated consulting and support to large Internet service providers, specializing in IP networks using MPLS, *Border Gateway Protocol* (BGP), *Open Shortest Path First* (OSPF), and *Intermediate System-to-Intermediate System* (IS-IS). Zaheer presents at Cisco seminars and customer events, including APRICOT and Networkers, and is a frequent contributor to Cisco Packet Magazine. He holds Bachelor of Science and Master of Science degrees in Electrical Engineering from Wichita State University, is married with two children, and enjoys playing cricket and Ping-Pong.

Khalil Jabr, CCIE No. 3260, is a Cisco Distinguished Systems Engineer who is focused on advanced enterprise routing architectures. He has worked with some of the largest enterprise networks in the areas of MPLS and routing architectures. He is also involved in multiple development projects that will affect the future of enterprise networking. Khalil has been with Cisco for more than 10 years.

Dedications

Victor: To Cesar, Olga and Aquilino. Thanks for the music, the colors, and the laughter.

Kumar: To my parents.

Acknowledgments

Victor: The biggest thank you goes to Shannon for her support throughout this project. Thanks for understanding, keeping me balanced, and always seeing beyond what is perceptible.

The ideas here contained have been inspired throughout the years by many of our colleagues. There are too many names to mention here; thanks to all.

I would like to acknowledge the seminal contribution of pioneers in this field such as Gerd Pflueger, Patrice Bellagamba, and Guenter Honisch.

I would like to thank my co-author, Kumar Reddy. Kumar has been an extraordinary guide during my tenure at Cisco, and the writing of this book would not have been possible or enjoyable without him.

Kumar: First and foremost, I would like to thank Julia, Chloe, Emma, and Isabelle, who put up with me writing another book and being busy or absent during too many weekends, evenings, and holidays. It is a small part of our great adventure together.

Thanks are due to my co-author, Victor Moreno, as nice and as smart a coconspirator as one could ever hope to find. The vision in this book is very much his.

I would also like to acknowledge the many extraordinary people I have been fortunate to work with at Cisco, both now and in previous teams. I have learned a lot from them, and this book would be much poorer without their influence over the years.

Speaking of years, I want to conclude by thanking my boss, Stephane Lamarre, for his long-standing support and his friendship.

Both: our technical reviewers were wonderful. They were generous with their suggestions, exacting with their standards, and detailed in their correction. They are true experts in their fields.

A big "thank you" goes out to the production team for this book. Brett Bartow, Ginny Munroe, and Christopher Cleveland have been incredibly professional and a pleasure to work with. We could not have asked for a finer team.

This Book Is Safari Enabled

The Safari Enabled icon on the cover of your favorite technology book means the book is available through Safari Bookshelf. When you buy this book, you get free access to the online edition for 45 days.

Safari Bookshelf is an electronic reference library that lets you easily search thousands of technical books, find code samples, download chapters, and access technical information whenever and wherever you need it.

To gain 45-day Safari Enabled access to this book:

- Go to http://www.ciscopress.com/safarienabled
- Complete the brief registration form
- Enter the coupon code F3F4-YDHG-WZQL-KGGZ-RLVS

If you have difficulty registering on Safari Bookshelf or accessing the online edition, please e-mail customer-service@safaribooksonline.com.

Contents at a Glance

Table of Contents

Introduction xviii

Part I A Network Architecture for the Virtual Enterprise 3

Chapter 1 Business Drivers Behind Enterprise Network Virtualization 5

Why Virtualize? 5
- Visitors, Partners, Contractors, and Quarantine Areas 7
- Regulatory Compliance 8
- Secure Service Areas 9
- Network Consolidation 10
- Acquisitions and Mergers 11
- Multitenant Enterprises 11
- Virtual Project Environment: Next-Generation Business Processes 12

Business Requirements Drive Technical Requirements 14

Summary 15

Chapter 2 Designing Scalable Enterprise Networks 17

Hierarchical Campus Design 17

Virtualizing the Campus 22

WAN Design 22
- WAN Provider Service Offerings 23
- WAN Architecture 25
- WAN Resiliency 27
- WAN Routing Considerations 29
- Securing the WAN 31
- WAN Virtualization 32

Summary 33

Chapter 3 Basic Virtualized Enterprise 35

The Virtual Enterprise 37

Transport Virtualization—VNs 40
- VLANs and Scalability 42
- Virtualizing the Routed Core 43
  - Policy-Based Segmentation 43
  - Control-Plane-Based Virtualization 45
- The LAN Edge: Authentication and Authorization 47

Icons Used in This Book

Command Syntax Conventions

The conventions used to present command syntax in this book are the same conventions used in the IOS Command Reference. The Command Reference describes these conventions as follows:

- **Boldface** indicates commands and keywords that are entered literally as shown. In actual configuration examples and output (not general command syntax), boldface indicates commands that are manually input by the user (such as a **show** command).

- *Italics* indicate arguments for which you supply actual values.

- Vertical bars (I) separate alternative, mutually exclusive elements.

- Square brackets [ ] indicate optional elements.

- Braces { } indicate a required choice.

- Braces within brackets [{ }] indicate a required choice within an optional element.

Introduction

The rapidly changing demands of the modern business require a flexible and highly adaptable IT infrastructure. The virtualization of resources plays a key role in achieving the required degree of adaptability. Therefore, the term *virtualization* is heard in many areas, including the virtualization of servers, applications, storage devices, security appliances, and, not surprisingly, the network infrastructure. This book attempts to illustrate the landscape of virtualization architectures, technologies, and techniques pertinent to the network infrastructure.

Goals and Methods

The overall goal of this book is to provide the reader with an understanding of what network virtualization is, which problems it can solve, and what techniques are currently available to virtualize the network. The concepts are covered both from a theoretical and practical point of view.

One important goal of this book is to provide an architectural framework for the problem of network virtualization. This framework should allow the reader to better understand the different network virtualization technologies and architectures.

Based on the architectural framework, many technologies are discussed and illustrated through network design examples. The goal of this discussion is to provide the reader with enough information about the technologies and techniques to either use them as presented or creatively implement variations of the proposed designs.

Who Should Read This Book?

This book has been written primarily for enterprise network designers, planners, architects, operators, and support personnel. These are the people responsible for the support, design, and deployment of network services; and they will find the topic, scope, and level of detail beneficial, whether they are looking at understanding virtualization's effect on enterprise networks, deploying segmented networks, shared services or just migrating from a legacy transport infrastructure, such as Frame Relay or ATM.

This book is also of interest to the user and purchaser of enterprise networks, including IT and telecom consultants and directors and CIOs or CTOs in small, medium-size, and large enterprises and network engineers and support staff. Technical sales personnel both at network vendors and their integration partners will also greatly benefit from this book.

How This Book Is Organized

Although this book could be read cover to cover, it is designed to be flexible and allow you to easily move between chapters and sections of chapters to cover just the material that you need more work with. The book is organized into three sections. Part I reviews the business imperatives driving network virtualization, reviews enterprise network design best practices, and introduces the basic technology and architectures used in virtualized networks today. Part II is the core of the book and discusses how to design virtualized networks in the core, across the WAN, in the data center, and in the access layer.

Part III is the appendix section, which has supplemental information for topics that might be less familiar to readers with an enterprise background and a collection of reference material.

- **Chapter 1, "Business Drivers Behind Enterprise Network Virtualization"**—The nature of business continues to evolve, and in great part, this evolution depends on the advent of new technologies that allow unprecedented levels of communication and collaboration. This chapter takes a close look at how virtualized networks can support optimized business processes to the extent of enabling revolutionary process changes, which would have been costly and difficult to implement without the appropriate enabling technology.

- **Chapter 2, "Designing Scalable Enterprise Networks"**—This chapter describes the fundamental principles on which highly available, scalable enterprise networks are designed. These principles are the foundation of good network design and must be maintained as the network is virtualized.

- **Chapter 3, "A Basic Virtualized Enterprise"**—In this chapter, the basic elements of a virtualized enterprise network are introduced. An architectural framework is proposed to break down the problem of virtualization. The framework is made of functional areas that are the building blocks of a virtualized network architecture.

- **Chapter 4, "A Virtualization Technologies Primer: Theory"**—There are different levels of virtualization: device, data path, and control plane. There are different constructs and protocols to implement each of these, depending on the problem to be solved. This chapter covers the technology used to build virtualized networks, including virtual partitions on routers and switches and protocol extensions.

- **Chapter 5, "Infrastructure Segmentation Architectures: Theory"**—This chapter brings together the technologies introduced in the previous chapter in several architectures for network virtualization. The alternatives covered are tunnel overlay for Layer 2 and Layer 3 transport, RFC 2547, and hierarchical Layer 3 VPN.

- **Chapter 6, "Infrastructure Segmentation Architectures: Practice"**—The concepts discussed in the previous chapters are put in practice in this chapter. The subtleties of the implementation of the different technologies and architectures are analyzed in the context of the campus and
metropolitan-area network.

- **Chapter 7, "Extending the Virtualized Enterprise over the WAN"**—The use of the virtualization technologies and architectures in the WAN poses unique challenges. In this chapter, we explore the challeneges and best practices for the extension of virtualized networks over the WAN.

- **Chapter 8, "Traffic Steering and Service Centralization"**—In this chapter, we explore the different methods for sharing and centralizing services among different virtual networks.

- **Chapter 9, "Multicast in a Virtualized Environment"**—A virtualized enterprise network is fully capable of carrying multicast traffic. This chapter discusses how to carry multicast data in a virtualized network environment. There are two main transport architectures: point-to-point and multicast VPN. We examine each in turn, with a discussion of the design trade-offs and an example to show the basic configuration steps involved.

- **Chapter 10, "Quality of Service in a Virtualized Environment"**—This chapter focuses on quality of service mechanisms available in virtualized networks and discusses deployment considerations. This chapter discusses the traditional enterprise QoS model, but also MPLS traffic engineering and differentiated services-aware traffic engineering, which are two powerful applications available on virtualized networks.

- **Chapter 11, "The Virtualized Access Layer"**—This chapter covers virtualized access layer design. The major impact of virtualization concerns authentication and authorization, and this chapter discusses clientless and client-based methods, notably 802.1x. A design example is provided to show how to implement network policy at the access layer and how to interact with the rest of the virtualized network.

- **Appendix A, "L2TPv3 Expanded Coverage"**—Additional information on the *Layer 2 Tunnel Protocol Version 3* (L2TPv3), introduced in Chapter 4.

- **Appendix B, "MPLS QoS, TE, and Guaranteed Bandwidth"**—In-depth explanation of MPLS QoS mechanisms and MPLS traffic engineering and MPLS guaranteed bandwidth. This appendix is additional content for Chapter 10.

- **Appendix C, "Recommended Reading"**—This appendix lists documents used during the preparation of this book and additional sources of information for the interested reader.

- **Appendix D, "RFCs and Internet Drafts"**—Relevant RFC and Internet drafts for the technologies and architectures covered in this book.

PART I

A Network Architecture for the Virtual Enterprise

CHAPTER 1

Business Drivers Behind Enterprise Network Virtualization

Today's enterprises service diverse groups of users, each with specific needs. The different business needs of these groups translate into varying network requirements. In some enterprises, these requirements can be so dissimilar that the different groups must be treated as totally separate customers by the enterprise's IT department.

Network virtualization is an architectural approach to providing a separate logical networking environment for each group within the enterprise. These logical environments are created over a single shared network infrastructure. Each logical network provides the corresponding user group with full network services similar to those provided by a traditional nonvirtualized network. The experience from the end-user perspective is that of having access to a dedicated network with dedicated resources and independent security policies. Thus, the virtualization of the network involves the logical segmentation of the network transport, the network devices, and all the network services.

Because the diverse logical networks share a common network infrastructure and a common, often centralized, set of service appliances and servers, user groups can collaborate with enhanced flexibility and manageability. This enhanced collaboration enables new business processes that would not be possible (or even imaginable) over a traditional network. Throughout this chapter, you will see examples of enterprises that rely on the virtualization of their network to modify their processes and operations. You will see how some enterprises can transform their network into a revenue-generating asset or increment the volume of operations possible at a specific facility or even open new streams of revenue by exploiting otherwise idle resources in creative ways.

Why Virtualize?

Consider the diverse networking needs of different enterprises. At one end of the spectrum is the enterprise that might require the separation of a single user group from the rest of the network for security purposes. For this enterprise, segmenting traffic seems easy to address by means of proper cabling and firewall positioning. For example, guests at a company site would be expected to access the network only from certain areas, such as lobbies or guest meeting rooms, where they can be easily isolated from the rest of the network through the use of firewalls. This setup works relatively well for separating guests from employees, provided that guest physical access to the enterprise network is strictly restricted. However, the separation becomes more complex when it is not possible to confine specific users to specific areas in the network, or when the number of user groups increases beyond just guests and employees. When this occurs, the physical positioning of firewalls can no longer address the problem in a scalable manner (not to mention the huge management challenge that this scenario represents).

At the other end of the spectrum are enterprises in which a common campus is home to many different and often competing customers. Multitenant campuses such as technology incubators, universities, airports, and even cooperatives fall under this category. Such enterprises leverage their high-capacity intelligent networking infrastructure to provide connectivity and network services for many groups and in many cases transform the IT department into a profit center providing billable services. For instance, different airlines could share the airport network and use it as a billable service. This arrangement accelerates the return on network infrastructure investment, optimizes network operations and operational expenses through economies of scale, and can ultimately help transform the business model of the different groups on the network by providing an enhanced collaboration environment that enables new business processes and efficiencies. For an airline, being able to easily create virtual communication environments for each flight removes a lot of the overhead and delay present in the current flight-launch process, allowing more flights per day, but also allowing the airline to seamlessly change gates or even terminals. We take a detailed look at the alteration of business processes in a later section.

Many business drivers are behind the virtualization of enterprise networks, including the following:

- Productivity gains derived from providing visitors with access to the Internet so that they can connect to their own private networks.

- Increasing network availability by quarantining hosts that are infected by viruses or not compliant with the enterprise security policies.

- A business model that involves the services of in-house consultants, partners, or even contractors requires the enterprise to provide this personnel connectivity to the Internet and select internal resources.

- Legal/regulatory compliance. Acts such as HIPAA and Sarbanes-Oxley define privacy and integrity standards for health and financial data.

- Creation of secure network areas that are partially or totally isolated.

- Consolidation of multiple networks onto a single infrastructure.

- Collocation of diverse competing customers on a shared infrastructure.

- Integration of subsidiaries and acquisitions.

- Next-generation business models aimed at improving efficiencies, reducing costs, and generating new streams of revenue. For instance, the IT department could become a revenue-generating service provider, or the airlines could optimize their use of shared services such as baggage handling.

Visitors, Partners, Contractors, and Quarantine Areas

It is important for today's enterprise to provide network access for groups of users who are not members of the enterprise. Visitors bring much more business benefit if they have access to the Internet and can get their information dynamically while they visit. Having this connectivity could make the difference between concluding business in one visit or having to schedule a follow-up meeting because some information was not readily available at the time of the meeting. Because these users are not part of the enterprise, they should be able to access only specific resources, and their connectivity should resemble that of a network that is separate from the main enterprise network.

Guest access should be limited to the Internet, and enterprises should ensure that guests cannot connect to any internal network resources. Enterprises could easily provide such limited access by deploying a totally separate network just for guests to access the Internet. However, owning a separate network solely for the purposes of providing guests with Internet access is not a viable alternative. The goal is to leverage the existing network infrastructure and the existing Internet access services to provide guest access as if guests had a dedicated network to connect them solely to the Internet.

One coarse way to achieve this is to define physical locations in the campus as guest-access locations (conference rooms, lobbies, cafeterias, and so on) and isolate them using firewalls. The guest locations become small dedicated networks for visitors. Even employees would be restricted to accessing the Internet only when connected at these locations. The success of this scheme relies heavily on the effectiveness of the physical-access restriction mechanisms in place at the enterprise facilities. If a visitor enters an employee-only area, there is the potential for guests accessing the internal network unless the appropriate security mechanisms are in place. A pervasive mechanism is required to create a guest virtual network segment that can be accessed by guests from anywhere in the enterprise.

A dynamic mechanism for authenticating guests and employees and authorizing and restricting them to the appropriate *virtual network* (VN) segment is required. A network-based authentication and authorization mechanism removes the dependency on physical-access restriction for securing the network. Dynamic authentication also allows users from different groups to work in the same room while still connected to their appropriate VN. Thus, visitors and employees can attend the same meeting and enjoy network connectivity levels in accordance with their roles.

Network admission control mechanisms call for the creation of a quarantine network segment to isolate devices that are found to be either infected with a virus or simply do not comply with the enterprise security policies. In either case, these devices must be isolated and fixed. The isolation of the devices calls for the creation of a quarantine VN segment. Because infected or noncompliant hosts can connect anywhere in the network, the quarantine VN must be accessible from any port in the enterprise. Hence, rudimentary solutions based on physical network segmentation, such as that proposed for guest access, are not viable.

Providing access for in-house partners or consultants is also an interesting scenario that calls for the virtualization of the infrastructure. In-house consultants generally require access to the Internet plus a few select internal resources. These internal resources can be distributed across the enterprise, making the connectivity requirements for partners slightly more sophisticated than those imposed by guests.

Both guest access and quarantine VN segments provide access to a single resource for many users. In the case of guest access, the single resource is the Internet, whereas the quarantine segment provides access to a remediation server only. This defines a many-to-one connectivity requirement easily serviced by a simple hub-and-spoke topology. Meanwhile, partners require connectivity to several resources, which are not necessarily located at a single site. Therefore, partners present a many-to-few requirement that is better served by an overlay of several hub-and-spoke topologies, in which case it might be easier to deploy an any-to-any topology. It is important to highlight this distinction because the business requirements will clearly determine the viability of different virtualization technologies and the complexity of the solution that is required.

When we separate guests from employees and these from contractors, we are basically creating user groups based on their roles. A dramatic example of the value of creating groups based on roles and actually providing virtual environments for each group is seen in the separation of contractors and employees. Contractors and employees have different types of benefits, different levels of compensation, and overall their relation with their employer is governed by different laws. In a recent lawsuit, a large group of contractors claimed full employee rights based on the fact that their work environment was no different from that of an employee. This work environment largely involved the network. With this precedent in place, enterprises are making sure that a clear differentiation exists in the connectivity provided to a contractor from that provided to a full-time employee.

Regulatory Compliance

Data security and integrity is the subject of tight controls. Some of these controls are imposed by internal policies, whereas others are required by law and specified in a detailed regulatory framework. This regulatory framework is captured in acts such as the *Health Insurance Portability and Accountability Act* (HIPAA) and the Sarbanes-Oxley Act. Although these acts do not explicitly call for specific security features or functionality, they do require that appropriate controls contain and detect fraud. Furthermore, these controls must be part of the periodic reporting process and must be endorsed by the CFO and CEO of the company, who are directly responsible for the integrity of the data in question.

Network virtualization is instrumental in achieving compliance with many of these regulations in a cost-effective manner. Because one VN cannot communicate with another unless the security policies are explicitly opened, the virtualization of the network adds an extra layer of security that restricts the number of users who have access to critical resources and thus simplifies the necessary controls and makes them more effective.

Often, enterprise user groups are defined by departments or roles. In this scenario, users are grouped according to their role in the enterprise. For example, an engineering firm may be interested in keeping the finance personnel and resources on a VN separate from that devoted to engineering contractors. This separation keeps the financial information out of the reach of curious computer-savvy engineers, while all engineering traffic is also kept away from the administrative personnel. The Sarbanes-Oxley Act regulates the protection of financial data in the enterprise. Many technical measures must be taken to comply with these regulations, and the virtualization of the network is one tool to be considered.

Secure Service Areas

Many enterprises converge services onto their IP network. Some examples of services that are typically converged onto an IP network include telephony, surveillance systems, badge readers, and energy-efficiency systems for intelligent buildings. Enterprises that own a production line also converge their production robots and controllers (such as *Programmable Logic Controllers* [PLC]) onto the IP network.

This convergence brings a special type of endpoint onto the network. These endpoints do not require connectivity to the Internet and are not subject to the broad variety of network traffic a user PC would be subject to. These endpoints are part of closed systems with a task that is static in terms of the type of traffic they handle. Therefore, each one of these systems can be isolated in its own VN segment. This isolation provides the systems and services with protection from the Internet or even viruses that spread from hosts in the internal network.

Many of the systems already mentioned (PLCs, PCs, and so on) are business critical; therefore, it is important to provide the maximum amount of protection possible to them. Furthermore, many of the systems leverage mainstream operating systems such as Windows or Linux and are therefore susceptible to common network attacks. However, most of these systems cannot be fixed rapidly, and an infected station could be rendered unusable and beyond repair by such an attack.

A sample scenario is that of a car manufacturer in which the assembly line consists of robots and PLCs that are all interconnected by an IP network. Because the assembly line is located in a specific physical plant and does not really require external connectivity, it is tempting to physically isolate the network in the plant from the rest of the enterprise. This approach is not cost-effective because two separate infrastructures would need to be maintained, increasing both the operational and capital costs. Furthermore, most plants are collocated with administrative offices, and the demarcation is blurry to say the least. Many employees actually require network access from within the plant. This brings to the table the requirement to dynamically and pervasively virtualize the network to provide the appropriate access to users, while maintaining the isolation of the production line. In this specific scenario, the robots on the assembly line had a long *mean time to repair* (MTTR) in the case of a virus attack. Hence, the preferred policy was to avoid attacks at all costs. Given that the assembly line did not require any type of Internet, intranet, data-center connectivity, or even human intervention, the assembly line was kept isolated. The necessary isolation can be achieved by creating a VN segment for the assembly line robots and PLCs, instead of deploying a separate physical network for the assembly line.

Network Consolidation

Because of their operations and the way in which they have grown, many enterprises maintain multiple physical networks. The operational cost associated with the ownership of this multitude of networks is extremely high. Therefore, it is desirable for the enterprise to consolidate the multiple networks onto a single infrastructure. The value of an infrastructure capable of supporting VNs is evident because consolidating the networks does not necessarily mean that the security boundaries between the networks are to disappear with the consolidation. Thus, each physical network will usually be migrated onto a VN in the consolidated infrastructure.

We use the example of airports to discuss the subject of network consolidation.

Airports run separate physical networks for each airline serviced. Imagine a fully meshed network of fiber deployed for each airline. Not only is this expensive, it is also hard to maintain and provides little to no flexibility when it comes to moving airlines around the airport. The reason for these separate physical networks is to preserve the privacy and security of the individual airlines. In these networks, the fiber runs only to specific places, so certain sectors of the airport are dedicated to certain airlines. Airports also run all their internal operations over their LAN. Baggage services, air traffic control, maintenance, and governmental agencies controlling immigration and security—all require LAN services and privacy. The ability to virtualize the network infrastructure allows enterprises to converge these separate physical networks onto a shared infrastructure and still preserve the privacy of the different groups.

The degree of sophistication in the virtualization technology to be used is determined by the enterprise business processes. For some enterprises, the business processes are such that failure of a single network would halt the entire operation. In this case, maintaining separate networks does not increase the availability of the business, and the benefit to consolidating the networks is clear. For other enterprises, the use of multiple networks is aimed at increasing the resiliency of the business that could continue to partially function in case of a failed network. In the latter case, sophisticated virtualization technologies involving the use of separate memory spaces and even separate processors are required so that the different networks can be consolidated while still maintaining the availability benefits of physically separate networks.

The financial results of multinetwork consolidation are capital investment savings and reduced operational expenses. The maintenance of a single network is much cheaper than maintaining separate networks. Note that policies that previously had to be applied in a distributed and complex manner can now be centralized and simplified.

Acquisitions and Mergers

IT departments often have to integrate the network infrastructure and resources of an acquired company into the existing network. A similar scenario is presented when two companies merge.

After an agreement has been reached to acquire or merge with another company, IT must start the process of integrating the network resources. However, a time lag occurs between the time when the acquisition is agreed upon and when all regulatory clearances have been granted by governing bodies (for example, the *Federal Communications Commission* [FCC] in the United States). IT departments require a way of laying out the foundations for the integration to enable connectivity in a phased manner as the regulatory clearances are granted. By laying out the foundation for the integration ahead of time, the integration of acquired companies is expected to be as nondisruptive as possible.

One significant way to avoid operational disruption is to preserve the network structure of the acquired company. The creation of VNs accommodates the integration of acquisitions by creating a separate environment to interface with the acquired infrastructure. In this way, the acquired network does not have to change basic things, such as its IP addressing scheme or its routing protocols, which can be independently supported within its assigned VN. Communication between the VN for the acquired network and the VNs containing the traffic for the parent (acquiring) network can be gradually opened as the regulatory clearances are obtained.

Multitenant Enterprises

Business centers provide office space to many different companies within a physical space that is equivalent to a campus. The companies lease the physical space and the network infrastructure along with voice, video, surveillance, and paging services. In some cases, even server farms are available for lease. Deploying a dedicated data center for each customer can be extremely expensive because of the intelligence necessary at the data center front end. Many customers require only a small server farm, which makes the expense of deploying a dedicated data center per customer even more difficult to justify. Therefore, a high-performance network that can be virtualized to provide private services to the different customers is desirable.

Similarly, universities host many faculties that need to be kept separate. Universities are also home to numerous research groups (often privately funded). It is usually a requirement of the funding institution that the project's network be isolated, while still being able to access all the university's network resources. Furthermore, the funding institution often requires that the network section on campus be directly connected to their corporate network, thus extending their enterprise into the university campus and raising the bar in terms of security and routing requirements. This arrangement becomes expensive when the university has to deploy separate physical networks with dedicated firewall and routing appliances. Therefore, a virtualized shared infrastructure is desired.

Virtual Project Environment: Next-Generation Business Processes

The speed and dynamic nature of today's business environment calls for the frequent creation of virtual teams. These teams include individuals from many groups inside and outside of a company. The virtual teams are usually formed to complete a specific project. For some enterprises, these projects are long term; other enterprises start and finish projects in a single day. Whichever the case, the interactions within each of these virtual teams can be enhanced by the creation of a virtual environment that provides an optimal set of resources, communication, and security policies for each virtual team to complete its project. A virtual project environment allows the virtual team to work in an environment customized for their mission, making communications much more efficient.

A significant challenge in the creation of a virtual project environment is that of managing the policies and connectivity between members of the virtual team. The creation of a VN for each project greatly simplifies this task, with users being assigned to project networks as required. The policies associated with the VN are inherited by any user who is allowed access to the VN. This scenario reduces the problem to the creation of a policy for each project (instead of having to maintain a set of policies for each user and resource).

Let's take a closer look at how the creation of virtual project environments can impact the business process.

Most personnel in the enterprise have a relatively well-defined role. As part of their role, they must carry out certain tasks. Tasks and roles are defined to support different processes. Therefore, by enhancing communications, through the creation of virtual work environments, it is possible to modify the tasks that are carried out by certain personnel (making these tasks easier, faster, or sometimes even automating them and eliminating the need for human intervention). Taken to the extreme, the modification of tasks will alter the roles of the personnel. More importantly, the added flexibility in the definition of tasks impacts the business process directly. This flexibility allows for the implementation of new models and processes that were impractical over a nonvirtualized infrastructure.

So far, we have defined a *process* as a group of tasks that are carried out by different personnel in their corresponding roles. When these roles meet to get the process rolling, they are part of a *project*. Projects are governed by the existing business processes, which, as discussed, depend directly on the different type of tasks possible within the organization.

An intelligent network can dynamically create groups of users and resources on a per-project basis. In the airport example, a typical example of a project is a specific flight. To launch a flight, many instances (roles) within the airline and the airport operations need to come together in a common project and use certain resources in a dedicated manner during a well-defined time window. By creating virtual groups (or what some call an "extended enterprise"), the users involved in the project of launching a flight have secure access to their private resources and those shared resources that are common to the project.

A sample project group for a flight launch would include runway personnel, traffic control, baggage handling personnel, ground crew, maintenance technicians from vendor A (vendor B, C, and so on), load calculation resources, maintenance manuals, procedure manuals, overhead paging systems, announcement boards, and so forth. These resources need to work closely together while the specific flight is being launched. After the flight has launched, these resources must be able to dynamically be liberated and assigned to another flight (project). Having the resources "on the same page" eliminates communication delays that were implicit with the use of technologies such as fax, telex, and even phone conversations.

This type of connectivity allows for communication efficiencies that translate into faster operations and opens the potential for new forms of revenue. A salient consequence for the air transportation industry is that such increased efficiencies allow for faster loading and reloading of cargo on a passenger plane. In the past, the speed of the processes related to load-distribution recalculations drastically limited the amount of cargo that could be transported on passenger planes. By creating virtual project environments, it is possible to redesign the business operations and ultimately allow the airlines to tap into new sources of revenue, such as an increased cargo allowance, a higher number of flights per day, and perhaps a lower cost per flight in terms of man-hours. From the airport's perspective, the dynamic creation of these virtual environments allows resources (gates, for instance) that used to be dedicated to a certain airline to be shared by different airlines, thus maximizing the utilization of the resource and servicing more customers with fewer resources, which clearly leads to considerable operational expense reduction.

The creation of virtual project groups is also necessary in university environments, where expensive resources could be shared by many groups. Some examples include electronic microscopes, particle accelerators, and clean rooms. Although we use universities as an example, these requirements are typical of any campus hosting research groups, including technology incubators and shared business parks. In an industry setting, it is not uncommon to find different companies developing competing products in parallel with a common technology provider while being collocated in the same campus. The security requirements of such interactions are demanding, and even though they could become complex, the virtualization of the network allows for their simplification.

Business Requirements Drive Technical Requirements

Enterprises face many technical challenges when attempting to fulfill the requirements described so far, including the following:

- Guarantee total privacy between groups
- Assign users to their appropriate group based on some sort of authentication
- Enforce independent security policies for each group
- Enable secure collaboration mechanisms between groups
- Provide basic networking services for the different groups
- Provide independent routing domains and address spaces to each group
- Provide group extensibility over the WAN
- Implement billing and accounting mechanisms for each group
- Enforce the previous policies regardless of the physical location of the user in the network

Many technologies could be used to solve the problems listed; some are perceived as simple, whereas others are perceived as complex. Different business requirements will call for different degrees of connectivity and a different subset of the functionality described previously. Fulfilling the subsets of functionality will in turn demand varying degrees of technological sophistication. In general, an overlap of diverse business drivers will result in increased technological sophistication. For simple business requirements, simple technologies suffice. As the requirements become more complex or numerous, however, simple technologies cease to scale or even provide adequate connectivity.

A simple example of how business requirements drive the use of different technologies can be seen when we compare the connectivity requirements for simple guest access against the connectivity needed when supporting a secure service area. Guest access requires many-to-one connectivity (many guests to one Internet access point), whereas a secure service area will most likely require any-to-any connectivity. When providing many-to-one connectivity, the technology used could be as simple as *access control lists* (ACLs) or a mesh of tunnels that connect to a head end. However, providing any-to-any connectivity with either ACLs or a static mesh of tunnels is highly impractical. Therefore, more sophisticated *virtual private networking* (VPN) technologies, such as those discussed throughout this book, are necessary.

Summary

Modern enterprises can benefit in many ways from the creation of VNs and the virtualization of network services. Network virtualization capabilities must be considered as a key network service when defining the network strategy for an enterprise.

Existing business pressures and the potential to enable change in business processes make network virtualization relevant in the agenda of any IT discussion. This chapter has explored some of the business requirements that are driving the virtualization of the network, including the following:

- Support for visitors (guests, partners, and contractors)
- Quarantining of infected servers
- Isolation of critical resources such as assembly line robots
- Consolidation of separate networks
- Regulatory compliance
- Infrastructure integration for mergers and acquisitions
- Dynamic creation of virtual project groups

VNs can be created in a number of ways. The sophistication of the technique used directly correlates with the complexity of the business requirements.

CHAPTER 2

Designing Scalable Enterprise Networks

Modern enterprise network design focuses on achieving high availability, security, and scalability. The modern enterprise follows a certain design methodology to achieve these objectives. This methodology is the product of years of experience, careful feature development, and detailed protocol optimization. Any technology introduced into an enterprise network must not interfere with these principles and mechanisms.

When a network is virtualized, it must continue to meet the resiliency, security, and scalability levels that modern enterprises demand. To continue to deliver the appropriate connectivity level, a virtualized enterprise must follow the same design principles that have traditionally provided the desired resiliency, security, and scalability in campus-, metropolitan-, and wide-area networks.

This chapter presents the network design principles used to achieve enterprise resiliency and scalability objectives. As previously mentioned, these principles should continue to apply to a virtualized network. Resiliency and scalability support is seamless with some virtualization technologies, but you must be careful with certain other techniques because of their potential impact on the resiliency and scalability characteristics of the network. This chapter presents the basic design principles that serve as the framework for the discussion throughout this book. In many cases, the choice of *virtual private networking* (VPN) technologies is based on the extent of their impact on resiliency.

Hierarchical Campus Design

The recommended approach to designing campus networks is one that is both hierarchical and modular. This hybrid approach makes the campus network highly resilient, scalable, and easy to maintain.

As shown in Figure 2-1, traffic is aggregated hierarchically from an access layer into a layer of distribution switches and finally onto the network core. At each layer of this hierarchical topology, redundant components connect in a redundant topology. This redundancy of links and components provides the campus network with resilient and symmetric traffic paths. These symmetric traffic paths provide network-level resiliency and optimize the convergence of networking protocols. For instance, routing protocols will benefit from symmetric paths by having multiple equal-cost paths to a destination, which allow for virtually immediate failover.

Figure 2-1 *Hierarchical/Modular Campus Network*

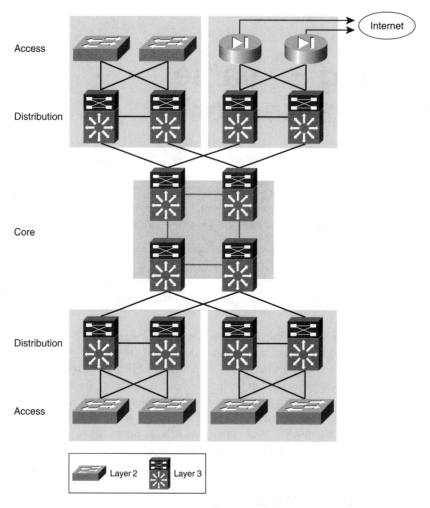

Modularity is achieved by pairing distribution switches to aggregate a group of access switches and thus provide resilient access to the core for entire physical network areas. These network areas can include an entire building or several floors in a large building. A distribution module can also be used to connect WAN aggregation routers, Internet access routers, or a data center to the campus core.

You can add or remove distribution modules to or from the network with minimal or no impact to other modules. As these modules are added, symmetric paths to all other modules are automatically created. However, a greater benefit of a modular and hierarchical architecture is that failures are intrinsically isolated. This isolation occurs at many levels, the first of which is the isolation of broadcasts by the termination of all access VLANs onto a routed distribution. The presence of a routed distribution and core minimizes the size of the Layer 2 broadcast domains and isolates them from the rest of the network by preventing the spread of broadcasts beyond the domain. Within the Layer 3 core and distribution layers, the use of a hierarchy, by means of summarization and area creation, prevents a change in one portion of the network from causing the reconvergence of the entire routed domain. Let's discuss these isolation mechanisms in more detail.

The different layers of the campus network must fulfill certain roles, which require specific features and functionality. For instance, a distribution switch simultaneously has the roles of a *Spanning Tree Protocol* (STP) root bridge, a first-hop router, and a *quality of service* (QoS) policing enforcement point. In contrast, an access switch does not require routing or even that it be an STP root candidate. However, it does require many features related to the connectivity of hosts into the network such as in-line power, QoS trust functionality, authentication mechanisms, and so on. A key component of enterprise network scalability is the use of Layer 3 (routed) technologies at the core and distribution layers of the network, while using Layer 2 (switched) connectivity to aggregate the access switches into the distribution layer, as shown in Figure 2-1. This model is the most common practice today because it minimizes the size of Layer 2 failure domains while keeping the deployment of routing protocols simple. A failure in a Layer 2 domain usually propagates over the entire Layer 2 domain; this model restricts the propagation of failures by terminating the Layer 2 domain at the distribution layer. Some examples of failures that can cause broadcast storms include STP loops and jabbering *network interface cards* (NICs).

In this topology, a failure might affect an entire module but should not be able to propagate into the core. Preventing the propagation of failures depends not only on the hierarchical nature of the network topology and the termination of Layer 2 domains, but it also depends on the hierarchical deployment of the networking protocols used. Therefore, an *interior gateway protocol* (IGP) deployment that uses a hierarchical routing structure to present the core with a summary of the prefixes present in every distribution module will be less likely to face a global reconvergence than a deployment without any hierarchical routing considerations.

It is important to emphasize that the hierarchy and symmetry of the physical topology actually allows the campus architect to fully exploit the benefits of the network protocols, not only by creating a hierarchy capable of containing the effect of network changes, but also by creating symmetrical paths that allow the networking protocols to leverage equal-cost paths in their calculations. The use of equal-cost paths enables extremely fast failover times, which do not depend on protocol reconvergence. This is a classic example of how a well-designed topology allows for the best use of the networking protocols and how a good use of the networking protocols exploits the benefits of a resilient and hierarchical topology.

As shown in Figure 2-2, deploying Layer 3 switching all the way to the access layer also represents a viable solution. However, this design choice could create added challenges when attempting to virtualize the network transport. These challenges will become evident as we analyze the different virtualization technologies for the campus in Chapter 6, "Infrastructure Segmentation Architectures: Practice."

Alternatively, the extension of Layer 2 VLANs throughout the access and distribution layers could be considered. This might be attractive to network architects seeking the virtualization of the network transport, because VLANs actually achieve such virtualization at Layer 2. However, the extension of switched domains requires extreme caution in its implementation because strict failure-isolation mechanisms must be put in place to protect the core from a now-extended failure domain. Furthermore, by reducing the size of the Layer 3 domain in the core, you lose many of the benefits of a Layer 3 area. Some of the lost functionality includes load balancing or even traffic engineering over symmetric paths and most of the fault isolation a hierarchical Layer 3 core/distribution can provide, not to mention the added complexity of maintaining larger Layer 2 domains and the required spanning tree. In general, the extension of failure domains is not recommended.

Figure 2-2 *Extension of Failure Domains*

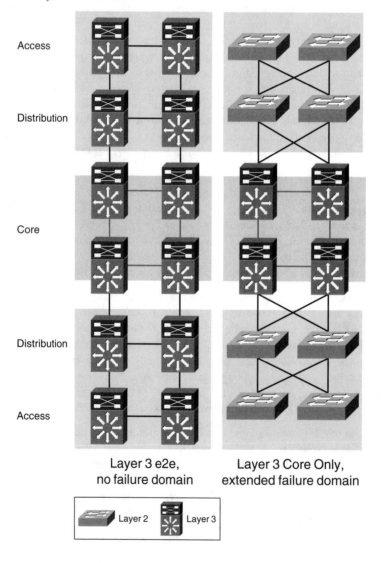

Similarly, as the extension of Layer 2 and Layer 3 domains can vary for different networks, so can the roles of access and distribution or core and distribution. For example, they can be collapsed together onto a single layer of switches.

In a network where the distribution and access are collapsed, the distribution switches also act as access switches (as shown in Figure 2-3). Collapsing network layers in this manner limits the port densities that can be handled by the network and thus its scalability. Therefore, this solution is normally chosen for networks of limited size that expect little growth.

Figure 2-3 *Collapsed Network Roles*

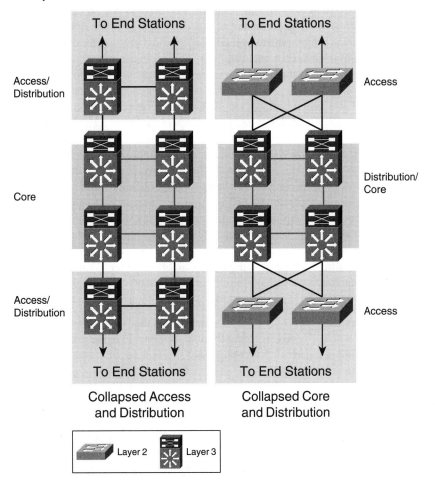

In the specific example where the distribution and core are collapsed, the core is directly exposed to failures in the access. This type of design calls for specific failure-isolation features to improve the required level of availability in the network. Even though they offer an improvement, features such as storm suppression and sophisticated spanning tree cannot deliver the same level of resiliency achieved by a hierarchical architecture leveraging a multilayer routed core. The limitations of this reduced Layer 3 core are the same as those already discussed for an extended failure domain: loss of load balancing, limited scalability, and lack of fault containment.

Virtualizing the Campus

The design principles discussed so far must be preserved as we virtualize the campus. To preserve the hierarchy and path symmetry provided by a multilayer routed core, this routed core must be kept in place. It is tempting for the network architect to associate the concept of *virtual networks* (VNs) with that of VLANs. Although a VLAN is a form of a VN, it is not by itself a hierarchical or modular VN and therefore does not preserve all the characteristics of resiliency and scalability desired in the enterprise. VLANs are an important component of a VN because they allow the virtualization of the Layer 2 portion of the network. However, to preserve the desired scalability and resiliency, a routed core is necessary. Therefore, the VLANs in the Layer 2 access must be combined with Layer 3 VPNs in the routed core. By combining VLANs with Layer 3 VPNs, you can create an end-to-end hierarchical VN in the campus. Therefore, an overlay of VPNs must be added to the routed core to virtualize it. The choice of VPN technology to use depends significantly on how well the VPN technology accommodates a hierarchical routing structure, the efficient use of redundant paths for load balancing, and failover and support for the different types of traffic present in the enterprise. The technologies available to create such an overlay and the subtleties of their deployment in the enterprise campus are discussed in Chapters 4 through 6. Chapter 4, "A Virtualization Technologies Primer: Theory," discusses the technologies in detail. Chapter 5, "Infrastructure Segmentation Architectures: Theory," discusses the different VPN architectures available. Chapter 6 "Infrastructure Segmentation Architectures: Practice" explains the caveats and best practices for the successful application of these virtualization techniques in the enterprise campus and metropolitan-area network.

Another important part of an enterprise network is the wide-area network. The design of the WAN has also evolved significantly over the years to achieve the desired level of resiliency and modularity. The remainder of this chapter discusses the general guidelines for designing a WAN.

WAN Design

The WAN provides connectivity between the different sites of an enterprise. In general, WAN design involves the aggregation of many branch sites into one headend site in a hub-and-spoke fashion. The headend site is usually located at the main enterprise campus where key computing resources can be accessed at a data center. Large enterprises often have several headend sites that service diverse branches according to geographic proximity. Figure 2-4 shows a typical WAN distribution of headend sites and branches. These headend sites must also be interconnected, thus we breakdown the problem of the WAN in two: Branch Aggregation and Site Interconnection.

Figure 2-4   *WAN*

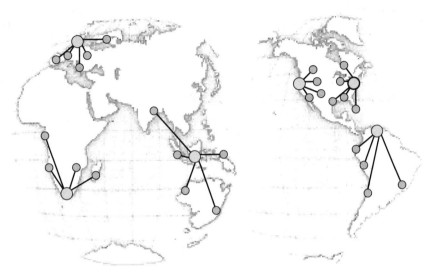

WAN Provider Service Offerings

Because the WAN uses connectivity services from a service provider, many variations exist as to traffic aggregation and security. The different types of wide-area services can be broadly categorized as private services or public services, providing either point-to-point or point-to-cloud connectivity, as shown in Figure 2-5.

Figure 2-5   *WAN Service Types. Point-to-Point vs. Point-to-Cloud Connectivity*

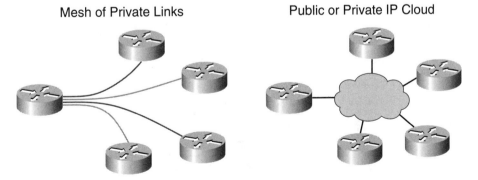

Mesh of Private Links   Public or Private IP Cloud

Examples of private services providing point-to-point connectivity are traditional services such as leased lines (PPP, *High-Level Data Link Control* [HDLC]), Frame Relay, and ATM. Meanwhile, the Internet is an example of a service that is publicly shared and allows multipoint connectivity (because each point is connected to an IP cloud).

In general, private point-to-point services are perceived as secure and not requiring encryption. In contrast, public services such as the Internet require an overlay of encrypted logical circuits to form VPNs on the shared WAN.

Depending on the WAN service, the enterprise network may be a mesh of physical or logical circuits. To successfully scale the mesh of circuits, a hub-and-spoke topology, such as that shown in Figure 2-6, is used. This can be a static topology in which the hub acts as the headend for the network. In this scenario, all traffic traverses the headend, including spoke-to-spoke traffic.

Figure 2-6 *Tunnel Overlay on a Shared Cloud—Hub-and-Spoke Topology*

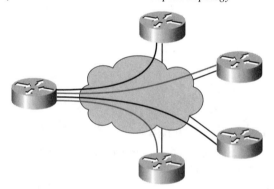

Alternatively, techniques such as *dynamic multipoint VPN* (DMVPN) allow for the dynamic creation of circuits to allow direct spoke-to-spoke connectivity. Such techniques require an IP-based WAN service capable of providing point-to-cloud (or multipoint) connectivity. Figure 2-7 illustrates the dynamic creation of circuits in a DMVPN WAN.

Figure 2-7 *Dynamic Spoke-to-Spoke Overlay Connectivity*

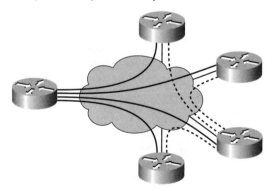

Aside from the Internet, service providers are increasingly providing private IP-based WAN services that allow private point-to-cloud connectivity. This type of service is known as *IP VPN*. In theory, an IP VPN service should not require encryption. However, many customers think IP VPNs are not as secure as private virtual circuits and therefore call for an encryption overlay that renders a static or dynamic hub-and-spoke topology similar to that discussed for the Internet.

Regardless of the WAN service purchased or the circuit overlay implemented in the WAN, certain principles must be followed in architecting the WAN. Namely, the WAN must be hierarchical, modular, and resilient. The following section discusses these architectural design principles.

WAN Architecture

The WAN architecture should provide hierarchy, modularity, and resiliency. Similar to the campus architecture principle of hierarchy, the different devices in the WAN have different roles depending on the hierarchy they occupy. The hierarchical network layers in the WAN are similar to those proposed for campus networks: access, distribution, and core (as shown in Figure 2-8). However, the roles and functionality of the devices at each layer differ from those that are required in the campus.

Figure 2-8 *WAN Hierarchical Architecture*

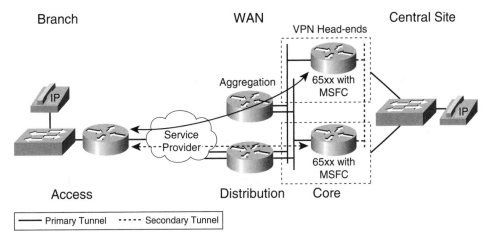

The branch-end routers at the access layer provide the branches access to the WAN, and all traffic from the access layer devices is aggregated by the WAN aggregation routers at the distribution layer. The aggregation routers connect into the network core, which provides connectivity between the aggregation routers, the VPN headend devices, and the campus core.

In the hub-and-spoke topology, the branch routers represent the access layer. These routers, known as *branch-end routers*, terminate the WAN interfaces to the service provider, connect to the local-branch LAN segment, and provide IPsec and *generic routing encapsulation* (GRE) tunnel termination when necessary.

The distribution layer is implemented with pairs of WAN aggregation routers. All traffic from the access layer devices is aggregated by the WAN aggregation routers. In an implementation over a Layer 3 service provider providing point-to-cloud connectivity (*Internet service provider* [ISP]), these routers would have a high-speed WAN interface and one or more high-speed Ethernet interfaces. They would typically be *external Border Gateway Protocol* (eBGP) peers with the ISP's edge routers and would peer via *internal Border Gateway Protocol* (iBGP) between all WAN aggregation routers. This Layer 3 peering provides the single connection to the cloud required to aggregate WAN traffic from a point-to-cloud service such as an ISP or IP VPN provider.

In an implementation with a Frame Relay service provider or point-to-point network, the distribution layer WAN aggregation routers have one or more high-speed WAN interfaces and hundreds of subinterfaces/DLCIs (*data-link connection identifiers*), one for each branch. In this scenario, each WAN aggregation router must maintain a separate circuit for each branch.

The core layer is implemented with pairs of high-performance multilayer switches such as the Catalyst 6500. These switches provide connectivity to the network core and provide redundant Layer 2 and Layer 3 connectivity between the WAN aggregation routers and the IPsec/GRE headend routers. Thus, different devices at different network layers aggregate traffic and terminate IPsec/GRE tunnels.

The IPsec/GRE headend routers terminate the IPsec peers and the IP GRE tunnels. They advertise the branch subnets learned through the tunnel interfaces to the core switches.

Dedicating routers for a specific function at the network core provides several advantages:

- The performance characteristics of the IPsec/GRE headend might dramatically differ from those of a WAN aggregation router.

- Separating the two functions allows different ratios between IPsec/GRE headends and WAN aggregation: Two WAN aggregation routers might be sufficient for four IPsec/GRE headends.

- WAN aggregation routers require a lower average CPU busy percentage to accommodate CPU spikes.

- WAN aggregation routers running *Border Gateway Protocol* (BGP) might experience considerable CPU spikes during network instability because of link flaps, for example.

- In addition, the separation of roles allows different versions of Cisco IOS Software to be run at different locations in the network topology. For example, the WAN aggregation router can run a *General Deployment* (GD) release of 12.0 mainline, whereas the IPsec/GRE headend routers may need an *Early Deployment* (ED) release to support a new hardware encryption accelerator.

The advantages and flexibility of this design outweigh the additional capital costs involved in separating the WAN aggregation from the IPsec/GRE headend.

WAN Resiliency

When using a point-to-point service, it is recommended to provision two circuits out of each branch-end router, connecting the branch to both headend routers. As Figure 2-9 shows, this setup involves the provisioning of a *permanent virtual circuit* (PVC) for each branch at the headend routers and the provisioning of two PVCs at each branch-end router to connect with the redundant headend points. In this model, load balancing and failover are achieved via the routing protocol enabled between the branch routers and the core routers.

Figure 2-9   *Dual-Circuit Resiliency*

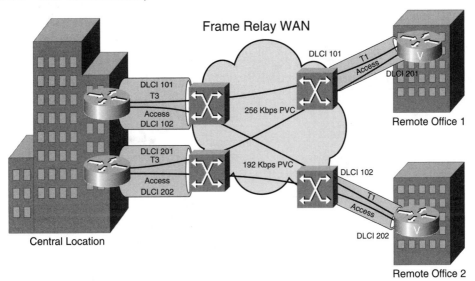

An alternative to deploying dual PVCs is to provide ISDN dialup connections as backup links. Figure 2-10 shows this resiliency mechanism.

Figure 2-10 *ISDN Backup*

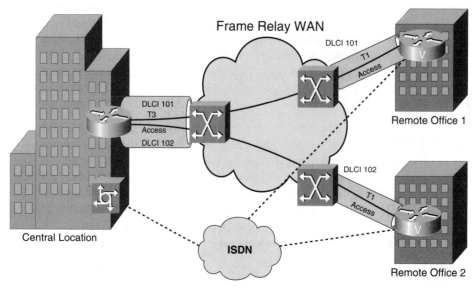

When IPsec or GRE tunnels are overlaid onto the WAN, resiliency must be provided for the tunnels (as shown in Figure 2-11). Each branch router can provide two IP GRE tunnels, one to each pair of IPsec/GRE headend routers. This setup provides for an alternate path in the event a headend router is taken out of service.

Figure 2-11 *Resilient Tunnel Overlay*

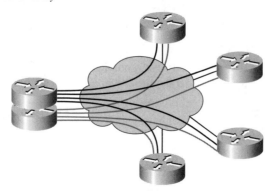

Alternatively, IPsec/GRE stateful resiliency mechanisms can be used to avoid the use of dual tunnels to the headend site. As shown in Figure 2-12, with IPsec/GRE stateful resiliency, the headend site is seen as a single router site by the branches, allowing the establishment of a single tunnel between each branch and the redundant pair of headend routers while still preserving the required headend resiliency.

Figure 2-12   *Stateful Resiliency for IPsec/GRE*

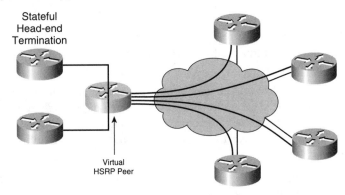

WAN Routing Considerations
==========================

Depending on the type of WAN service purchased, different routing challenges must be considered.

For an IP service (point-to-cloud), exchange of routes between the enterprise and the provider cloud is necessary. This is usually achieved by using eBGP between the enterprise routers and the service provider (some providers support the use of IGPs for *provider edge-to-customer edge* (PE-CE) integration of IP VPN services). Figure 2-13 shows the routing adjacencies necessary to connect to a point-to-cloud type of service.

Figure 2-13   *Point-to-Cloud IP Service Routing Adjacencies*

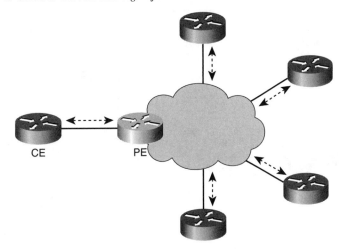

It is common to overlay a mesh of IPsec/GRE tunnels to provide encryption over an IP service. In this case, two types of routing information must be present:

- Routes for the endpoints to reach each other and establish the tunnels
- Routes for the traffic at the sites to use the encrypted tunnels to reach remote destinations

These routes are all part of the same control plane. Therefore, to ensure that traffic between sites uses the tunnels, the traffic must be engineered based on its source and destination. You can do so by tweaking the routing protocols to use the tunnels for inter-site communication, or you can use policy-based routing to inject traffic into the tunnels as needed.

When virtualizing the network, you can use the same mesh of IPsec/GRE tunnels to create IP VPNs over an IP service. In this scenario, the tunnel interfaces are assigned to a routing table that differs from that used to establish the tunnels. Thus, the tunnel overlay forms VPNs that require a routing overlay additional to the routing used to provide connectivity into the IP cloud and between the tunnel endpoints. As depicted in Figure 2-14, two routing control planes will be active in an IP cloud supporting VPNs, one global control plane providing connectivity between all branch and headend routers and a VPN-specific control plane that transports routing updates for the different VPNs. The routing overlay for the VPNs will benefit from similar best practices as those described for point-to-point services, which are discussed next.

NOTE This model and many others for creating VPNs in the WAN are explored in detail in Chapter 7, "Extending the Virtualized Enterprise over the WAN."

Figure 2-14 *IP Service with VPN Overlay Routing Adjacencies*

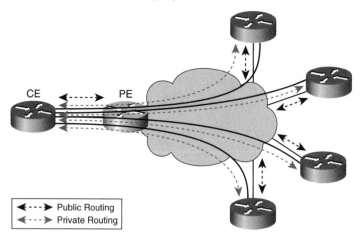

For point-to-point services, no route exchange occurs between provider and enterprise. Routing adjacencies for the enterprise's IGP are established over the overlay of point-to-point tunnels. For these routing adjacencies, it is advisable to summarize the routes from the branches into the core.

NOTE	The summarization of routes allows a single IP prefix to represent many subnets in the branch. A failure in one of the subnets will not alter the advertised route and therefore will not cause any sort of reconvergence.

Advertising default routes from the core (headend) into the branches greatly simplifies the routing overlay and reduces the size and number of routing updates necessary. By choosing an IP addressing scheme capable of accommodating such use of the IP address space, you can reduce the burden on the routing protocols and thus accelerate convergence times and minimize potential network reconvergence by creating a simple routing hierarchy that isolates failures. Figure 2-15 shows these routing recommendations.

Figure 2-15 *Point-to-Point Service Routing*

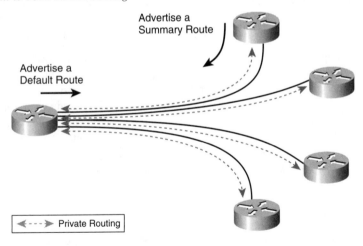

Securing the WAN

Securing the WAN involves two main tasks: protecting the perimeter and securing the transport.

The protection of the perimeter involves the use of firewall functionality at the branch-end routers and at the headend.

The most widely used mechanism to secure the transport in the WAN is IPsec encryption. Because IPsec is a point-to-point technology, its use can alter the logical topology of the WAN. If the logical topology is altered, chances are that resiliency is also affected. Therefore, it is necessary to be able to support routing protocol adjacencies over the tunnels created by the IPsec overlay. Many IGPs use multicast to maintain communications between routers. Multicast is not natively supported by IPsec, and therefore an auxiliary tunneling mechanism is required to transport the multicast and still be able to encrypt the traffic (achieved by combining IPsec with GRE encapsulation). The main principle is that of encapsulating all traffic, including the multicast, in a GRE tunnel and then encrypting the contents of the GRE tunnel. Not all enterprises require support for multicast as their resiliency models may not rely on routing protocols. However, a resiliency model based on routing protocols has proven to deliver the best results and is therefore recommended.

The combination of IPsec and GRE tunnels leads to several deployment scenarios depending on the dynamic or static nature of the tunnels.

The simplest scenario is that in which plain IPsec encapsulation is used. As previously discussed, IPsec alone will not support multicast and, therefore, IGP updates. Plain IPsec designs require resiliency mechanisms such as stateful IPsec failover at the headend, which basically eliminates the need to provision dual tunnels from the branch to the headend while still providing headend resiliency. Because routing updates are not able to traverse the IPsec overlay, this solution must rely on static routing or unicast-based routing protocols such as BGP. This solution lacks support for any type of multicast traffic or any non-IP protocol.

When support for an IGP across the IPsec overlay is required, and this is a common requirement when virtualizing networks, it is necessary to combine GRE tunneling with IPsec encryption. You can establish the GRE tunnel mesh in many ways, including static point-to-point GRE, dynamic point-to-point GRE, and dynamic multipoint GRE. All of these tunnel meshes support IPsec encryption, but the most flexible combination is provided by DMVPN, which combines dynamic multipoint GRE with the dynamic creation of IPsec tunnels. Chapter 5 "Infrastructure Segmentation Architectures: Theory" discusses this technology and other relevant technologies in detail.

WAN Virtualization

The challenge of virtualizing the WAN is in preserving the required hierarchy and resiliency while deploying an increased number of VPNs over the WAN in a cost-effective manner. Doing so may lead to the creation of VPNs or tunnels within provider VPNs. The proliferation of VPNs in the WAN brings with it the challenge of managing a more-complex logical topology and sets higher expectations for a processing hierarchy that will scale to support the increased number of VPNs.

Chapter 5 "Infrastructure Segmentation Architectures: Theory" discusses the different techniques available for the creation of VPNs in the WAN, based on the foundation technologies introduced in Chapter 4 "A Virtualization Technologies Primer: Theory."

Chapter 7 "Extending the Virtualized Enterprise over the WAN" discusses in detail the design recommendations and best practices an enterprise must follow when virtualizing the WAN.

Summary

Enterprise network design has evolved throughout the years. A hierarchical approach to network design has proven to deliver the best results in terms of optimizing scalability, improving manageability, and maximizing network availability. When virtualizing the enterprise network, you must maintain all these characteristics. Therefore, the model you use to virtualize the network should follow the basic principles of hierarchy and modularity, described in this chapter, in order to achieve the desired level of resiliency and scalability. Even though the management model for the network will need some adjustments to accommodate for a now-virtualized infrastructure, overall network manageability is expected to improve in a virtualized network.

Before we delve into the technical detail about how a network can best be virtualized, let's understand why enterprises are virtualizing their networks. Chapter 3, "A Basic Virtualized Enterprise" explores some of the business drivers behind the virtualization of enterprise networks and discusses many of the benefits that enterprises perceive from virtualizing their networks. The challenge when virtualizing the campus is much different than that posed by the different variations of logical overlays used in the WAN. The added complexity in the WAN is largely due to the necessary interaction with Service Providers and the additional security requirements imposed by the use of shared networks.

In the same way that we propose basic principles of scalability and resiliency, that can be applied throughout the networks (LAN or WAN), we can also propose basic principles for the virtualization of networks. The architecture describing these principles is covered in our next chatper "A Basic Virtualized Enterprise."

CHAPTER 3

A Basic Virtualized Enterprise

In this chapter, we define the technical requirements posed by the need to virtualize the network. Based on these requirements, we propose and architectural framework comprised of the functional areas necessary to successfully support concurrent *virtual networks* (VNs) over a shared enterprise physical network.

Networks enable users to access services and resources distributed throughout the enterprise. Some of these services and resources are public: those accessed over the Internet, and others that are private and internal to the enterprise. Every enterprise has unique security and service level policies that govern the connectivity to the different services, whether these are public or private.

One of the basic building blocks behind the virtualized network and, in fact, a key driver is security. An important element of an enterprise's security policy is the definition of a network perimeter. In general, the level of trust inside and outside of the network perimeter differs, with end stations inside the perimeter being generally trusted and any access from outside the perimeter being untrusted by default. Communications between the inside and the outside of the perimeter must happen through a checkpoint. At the checkpoint, firewalls and other security devices ensure that all traffic that enters or leaves the enterprise is tightly controlled. Therefore, we refer to the point of entry/exit to/from the enterprise network as the network perimeter.

NOTE The network perimeter defines one layer of security and must be complemented with other security mechanisms. It is critical to incorporate mechanisms to protect the network from attacks initiated inside the perimeter. This functionality is generally provided at the network access/edge and is not impacted by the virtualization of the network.

To provide the required connectivity, create a secure perimeter and enforce the necessary policies, it is recommended that an enterprise network be based on certain functional blocks. Figure 3-1 depicts a modular enterprise network and its perimeter. The recommended functional blocks are as follows:

- The LAN/MAN transport (core and distribution)
- The LAN edge or access layer

- The Internet access module
- The data center access module
- The WAN aggregation module
- The WAN transport
- The branch

Figure 3-1 *The Modular Enterprise Network and Its Perimeter*

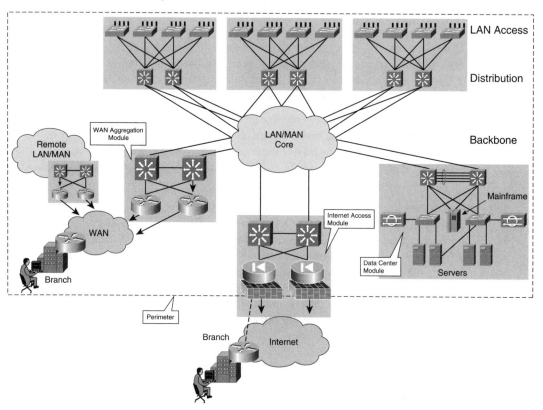

When a single enterprise network must service many different groups, it is often necessary to create virtual networks (VNs) so that each group can enjoy

- Private connectivity over a shared infrastructure.
- A dedicated perimeter in which independent policies can be enforced per group.
- User mobility (ubiquitous access to the appropriate virtual network regardless of the user's location).

At the risk of oversimplifying, a VN can be seen as a security zone. All devices within the security zone trust each other and communicate freely with each other. Meanwhile, any communication with other security zones, or other networks, must happen in a controlled manner over a highly secured perimeter or checkpoint. Thus, a virtualized enterprise network will simultaneously host many security zones, and their dedicated perimeters, over a shared infrastructure.

The Virtual Enterprise

A virtual enterprise network must provide each group with the same services as a traditional dedicated enterprise network would. The experience from an end-user perspective should be that of being connected to a dedicated network that provides connectivity to all the resources the user requires. The experience from the perspective of the network administrator is that they can easily create and modify virtual work environments for the different groups of users and adapt to changing business requirements in a much easier way. The latter derives from the ability to create security zones that are governed by policies enforced centrally. Because policies are centrally enforced, adding or removing users and services to or from a VN does not require any policy reconfiguration. Meanwhile, new policies affecting an entire group can be deployed centrally at the VN perimeter. To virtualize an enterprise network, the basic functional blocks of the modular enterprise must be enhanced to provide the following functionality:

- Dynamically authenticate and authorize users into groups
- Isolate connectivity to guarantee privacy between groups
- Create well-defined and controllable ingress/egress points at the perimeter of each VN
- Enforce independent security policies for each group at the perimeter
- Centralize the enforcement of the perimeter security policies for the different VNs by
  - Allowing secure collaboration mechanisms among groups
  - Allowing secure sharing of common resources
- Provide basic networking services for the different groups, either shared or dedicated
- Provide independent routing domains and address spaces to each group

You could use many different technologies to solve the listed challenges. The technologies available and how these can be used to meet the above requirements are the topic of the remaining chapters in the book.

From an architectural perspective, the previous requirements can be addressed by segmenting the network pervasively into VNs and centralizing the application of network policies at the perimeter of each VN. These are, of course, the policies for ingress and egress to the VN or security zone. The formation of a trusted security zone relies on traffic-isolation mechanisms rather than a distributed policy. Because traffic internal to a zone is trusted, policies are required only at the perimeter to control the access to external resources that could in many cases be shared. Figure 3-2 illustrates this concept.

Figure 3-2   *Virtual Networks with Centralized Policies at the Perimeter*

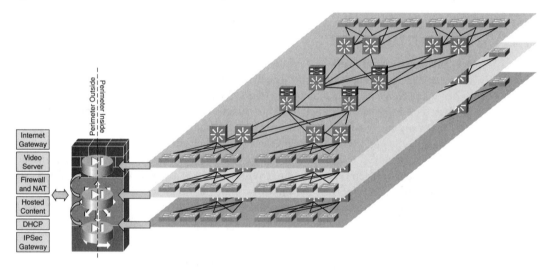

Regardless of where a user is connected, its traffic should always use the same VN and be directed through a central site of policy enforcement (VN perimeter), should it need to exit the VN. This makes users mobile and ensures that regardless of their location they will always be subject to the same policies. To ensure that users are always connected to the right VN, dynamic authentication and authorization mechanisms are required. These allow the identification of devices, users, or even applications so that these can be authorized onto the correct virtual segment and thus inherit the segment's policies.

The virtualization architecture described so far can be organized into functional areas. These functional areas provide a framework for the virtualization of networks:

- Transport virtualization
- Edge authorization
- Central services access (VN perimeter)

As you will see throughout the book, this modular framework gives the network architect a wide choice of technologies for each functional area. A key element in achieving this degree of flexibility is the definition of clear communication interfaces between the different areas.

VLANs provide an example of a communication interface between functional areas. The edge authorization module assigns a user to a VLAN, and the transport module maps that VLAN to a VN. At the destination, the transport module maps the VPN back to a VLAN. If the destination is outside the VN perimeter, the transport module hands off a VLAN to the central services access module, which maps the VLAN to the necessary virtual services. As you progress through the book, you learn that the interface between modules could very well be a label or a policy.

NOTE   There are, of course, pros and cons to using different types of communication interfaces. These are analyzed as the different technologies are discussed in detail, so read on.

Figure 3-3 shows the functional areas of the virtualized enterprise. As shown, you can use a variety of technologies for each different area.

Figure 3-3   *Virtualized Enterprise Network Functional Areas*

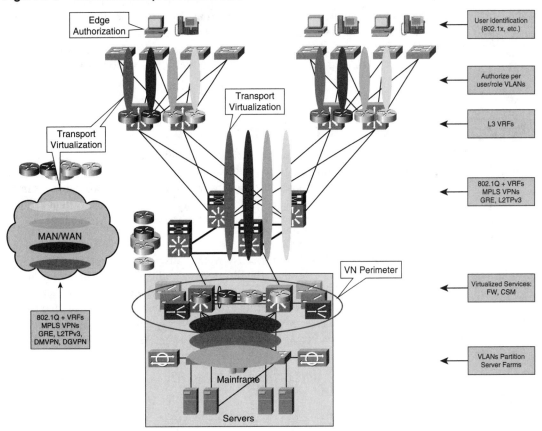

A useful way to look at Figure 3-3 and understand the role of the different functional areas is to look at it from the top down. Starting at the top, the endpoints connected to the network are authenticated and as a result of the authentication are authorized onto a specific VLAN (edge authorization). Each VLAN maintains its traffic separate from other VLANs and is mapped to a *virtual routing and forwarding instance* (VRF).

NOTE	VRFs are logical routing and forwarding tables with associated interfaces and routing processes, what could be thought of as a virtual routing instance. The section on "Control-Plane-Based Segmentation" and Chapter 4 examine the concept of a VRF in more detail.

Each VRF is connected to other VRFs in its VN and keeps its traffic separate from VRFs that belong to other VNs (transport virtualization). When traffic is destined to a resource outside the VN (for example, the data center), it is routed to the VN perimeter, where virtual services, such as firewalling and load balancers, are applied to each group (central services access—VN perimeter). Traffic destined to a subnet over the WAN is kept separate from traffic in other VNs through the virtualization of the WAN transport (transport virtualizaton).

Transport Virtualization—VNs

When segmenting the network pervasively, all the scalability, resiliency, and security functionality present in a nonsegmented network must be preserved and in many cases improved. As the number of groups sharing a network increases, the network devices must handle a much higher number of routes. Any technologies used to achieve virtualization must therefore provide the necessary mechanisms to preserve resiliency, enhance scalability, and improve security.

Chapter 2, "Designing Scalable Enterprise Networks," discussed network design recommendations that provide high availability and scalability through a hierarchical and modular design. Much of the hierarchy and modularity discussed relies on the use of a routed core. Nevertheless, some areas of the network continue to benefit from the use of Layer 2 technologies, such as VLANs, ATM, or Frame Relay circuits. Thus, a hierarchical IP network is a combination of Layer 3 (routed) and Layer 2 (switched) domains. Both the Layer 2 and the Layer 3 domains must be virtualized, and the virtualized domains must be mapped to each other to create VNs.

NOTE	The term *virtual private network* is broadly used and might have different connotations to different people. To avoid confusion, we use the term *virtual network* as an implementation-independent concept. In many implementations, a VN is actually a VPN; but as you read, you might want to avoid creating a direct association between your favorite type of VPN implementation (IPsec, *Secure Sockets Layer* [SSL], IP-VPN) and the concept of a VN, which we are here introducing.

One key principle in the virtualization of the transport is that it must address the virtualization of the network devices and their interconnection. Thus, the virtualization of the transport involves two areas of focus:

- **Data-path virtualization**—Refers to the virtualization of the interconnection between devices. This could be a single-hop or multiple-hop interconnection. For example, an Ethernet link between two switches provides a single-hop interconnection that can be virtualized by means of 802.1q VLAN tags; for Frame Relay or ATM transports, separate virtual circuits provide data-path virtualization. An example of a multiple-hop interconnection would be that provided by an IP cloud between two devices. This interconnection can be virtualized through the use of multiple tunnels (*generic routing encapsulation* [GRE] for example) between the two devices.

- **Device virtualization**—Refers to the virtualization of a networking device or the creation of logical devices within the physical device. This includes the virtualization of all processes, databases, tables, and interfaces within a device.

In turn, within each networking device, there are at least two planes to virtualize:

- **Control plane**—Refers to all the protocols, databases, and tables necessary to make forwarding decisions and maintain a functional network topology free of loops or unintended blackholes. This plane could be said to draw a clear picture of the topology for the network device. A virtualized device must posses a unique picture of each VN it is to handle, hence the requirement to virtualize the control-plane components.

- **Forwarding plane**—Refers to all the processes and tables used to actually forward traffic. The forwarding plane builds forwarding tables based on the information provided by the control plane. Similar to the control plane, each VN will have a unique forwarding table that needs to be virtualized.

Furthermore, the control and forwarding planes can be virtualized at different levels, which map directly to different layers of the OSI model. For instance, a device can be VLAN aware and therefore virtualized at Layer 2, but yet have a single routing table, *Routing Information Base* (RIB), and *Forwarding Information Base* (FIB), which means it is not virtualized at Layer 3. The different levels of virtualization come in handy, depending on the technical requirements of the deployment. Sometimes Layer 2 virtualization is enough (a wiring closet, for instance). In other cases, virtualization of other layers might be necessary.

For example, providing virtual firewall services requires Layers 2, 3, and 4 virtualization, plus the ability to define independent services and management on each virtual firewall, which some may argue is Layer 7 virtualization. We delve into firewall virtualization in Chapter 4. For now, we focus on the virtualization of the transport at Layers 2 and 3.

VLANs and Scalability

Time and experience have proven the scalability benefits of limiting the size of Layer 2 domains in a network. A large amount of this experience comes from campus networks, where highly resilient topologies with redundant links are possible. This link redundancy intrinsically creates network loops that must be controlled by mechanisms such as spanning tree. The broadcast nature of a Layer 2 domain is the main reason these redundant links behave as loops rather than redundant active paths capable of load balancing. Hence, the lack of load balancing and the complexity involved in managing large and highly resilient spanning-tree domains makes a routed infrastructure much more appropriate for large-scale highly available networks. Thus, experience has taught us that meshed Layer 2 domains have their role in the network, but they must be kept small in scale. Keep in mind that we are referring to highly meshed resilient Layer 2 domains such as those you would find in a campus. This type of problem is faced less in the WAN, where point-to-point connections tend to be at the base of the architecture and are for the most part routed. Nevertheless, the introduction of technologies that extend Layer 2 domains over an IP infrastructure has brought many of the spanning-tree concerns to the table in the *metro-area network* (MAN) and WAN.

When you are virtualizing a network, it is tempting to revisit ideas such as end-to-end VLANs. After all, mapping a group of users to a specific VLAN to create an isolated workgroup was one of the original thoughts behind the creation of VLANs. Should the VLAN traverse the entire enterprise, we could say the transport has been virtualized. This type of solution will have all the scalability problems associated with large Layer 2 domains and is therefore not desirable.

Nevertheless, the use of VLANs has its place as a way of segmenting the Layer 2 portion of the network. In an enterprise campus, this is generally the mesh of links between the access and the distribution. Remember, the recommendation is to reduce the size of the broadcast domains to something manageable, not necessarily to eliminate the broadcast domains, because too much IP subnet granularity would also represent a management challenge. So, to segment the access portion of the network, VLANs are of much use.

NOTE   Later on, in the section "Policy-Based Segmentation," you will see that there are mechanisms to achieve traffic differentiation by using code points. These techniques do not create separate broadcast domains and are effective only after entering the routed core. The use of code points will not provide separation between groups that share a broadcast domain. VLANs are required to provide Layer 2 separation at the access.

The network must preserve its hierarchy and therefore its routed core. As the periphery (access/distribution) continues to be switched (as opposed to routed), VLANs must be used for segmentation purposes. Thus, a VLAN in a wiring closet would represent the point of entry into a VN.

Because these VLANs are terminated as they reach the routed core, it is necessary to map them to segments created in the routed core. The next section looks into what is necessary in the core. From the access perspective, the VLANs must map to the corresponding segments created in the core to achieve an end-to-end VPN that spans both the switched and routed portions of the network.

We focus our analysis on a network with a routed core and a switched access. This model is widely adopted because it has been proven, optimized, and recommended by Cisco for many years.

Virtualizing the Routed Core

You can achieve the virtualization of the routed portion of the network in many ways. At the device level, the available traffic separation mechanisms can be broadly classified as follows:

- Policy-based segmentation
- Control-plane-based virtualization

Policy-Based Segmentation

Policy-based segmentation restricts the forwarding of traffic to specific destinations, based on a policy and independently of the information provided by the control plane. The policies are applied onto a single IP routing space. A classic example of this uses an *access control list* (ACL) to restrict the valid destination addresses to subnets in the VN.

Policy-based segmentation is limited by two main factors:

- Policies must be configured pervasively.
- Locally significant code points are currently used for policy selection.

The configuration of distributed policies can be a significant administrative burden, is error prone, and causes any update in the policy to have widespread impact.

The code point used for policy selection has traditionally been an IP address and therefore locally significant. Because of the diverse nature of IP addresses, and because policies must be configured pervasively, building policies based on IP addresses does not scale well. Thus, policy-based segmentation using IP addresses as code points has limited applicability. However, other code points could potentially be used. If the code point is independent of the IP addressing and globally significant (uniformly maintained throughout the network), all policies would look alike throughout the network, making their deployment and maintenance much simpler.

NOTE   An example of globally significant code points are the *differentiated services code points* (DSCPs) used for the selection of *per-hop behaviors* (PHBs) in a DiffServ *quality of service* (QoS) architecture. Different PHB policies are selected and enforced at each hop based on the traffic's DSCP label. The DSCP labels identify types of traffic through the network, regardless of source/destination subnets. DSCP is just one example of a globally significant code point; in general, any label could serve the purpose. The use of a label (code point) to identify types of traffic is a powerful concept and could be leveraged to identify traffic for policy application. Thus, if traffic is labeled appropriately, ACLs based on code points rather than IP addresses could provide a scalable alternative to policy-based segmentation.

Policy-based segmentation with the tools available today (ACLs) can address the creation of VNs with many-to-one connectivity requirements; it would be hard to provide any-to-any connectivity with such technology. This is the case for segments providing guest access to the Internet, in which many guests access a single resource in the network. This is manageable because the policies are identical everywhere in the network (allow Internet access, deny all internal access). The policies are usually applied at the edge of the Layer 3 domain. Figure 3-4 shows ACL policies applied at the distribution layer to segment a campus network.

Figure 3-4   *Hub-and-Spoke Policy-Based Segmentation*

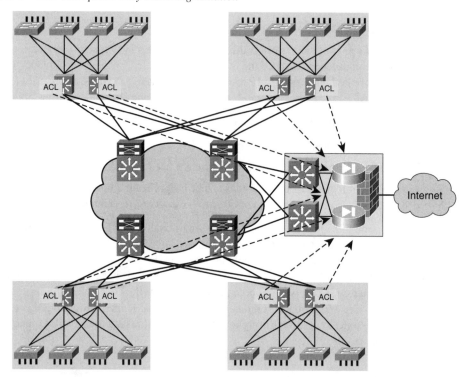

As a creativity exercise, you could attempt to design an IP-based policy to provide any-to-any connectivity between guests, while keeping them separate from the rest of the users!

Control-Plane-Based Virtualization

Control-plane-based virtualization restricts the propagation of routing information so that only subnets that belong to a VN are included in any VN-specific routing tables and updates. Thus, this type of solution actually creates a separate IP routing space for each VN. To achieve control-plane virtualization, a device must have many control/forwarding instances, one for each VN. An example of control-plane-based device segmentation is a VRF.

A VRF could be looked at as a "virtual routing instance." Each VRF will have its own RIB, FIB, interfaces, and routing processes. Figure 3-5 illustrates VRFs.

NOTE   A VRF is not strictly a virtual router because it does not have dedicated memory, processing, or I/O resources. In Chapter 4, we discuss other levels of device virtualization, such as logical routers, and proper virtual routers. For now, we use the analogy just to help you understand what a VRF is.

Figure 3-5   *Virtual Routing and Forwarding*

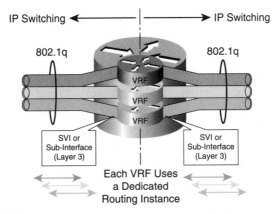

The VRF achieves the virtualization of the networking device at Layer 3. After the devices have been virtualized, the virtual instances in the different devices must be interconnected to form a VN. Thus, a VN is a group of interconnected VRFs. In theory, this interconnection could be achieved by using dedicated physical links for each VN (group of interconnected VRFs). In practice, this would be inefficient and costly. Hence, it is necessary to virtualize the data path between the VRFs to provide logical interconnectivity between the VRFs that participate in a VN. The type of data-path virtualization will vary depending on how far the VRFs are from each other. If the virtualized devices are directly connected to each other (single hop), link or circuit virtualization is necessary. If the virtualized devices are connected multiple hops apart over an IP network, a tunneling mechanism is necessary. Figure 3-6 illustrates single-hop and multiple-hop data-path virtualization.

Figure 3-6 *Single- and Multiple-Hop Data-Path Virtualization*

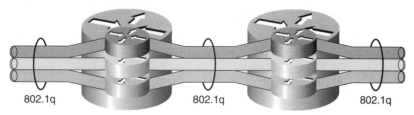

L2-based labeling allows single hop data-path virtualization

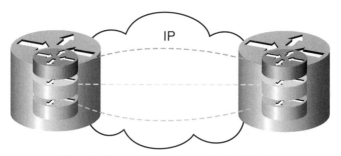

Tunnels allow multi-hop data-path virtualization

The many technologies that virtualize the data path and interconnect VRFs are discussed in Chapters 4 and 5. The different technologies have different benefits and limitations depending on the type of connectivity and services required. For instance, some technologies are good at providing hub-and-spoke connectivity, whereas others provide any-to-any connectivity. The support for encryption, multicast, and other services will also determine the choice of technologies to be used for the virtualization of the transport.

NOTE   Some technologies leverage the use of labels to "color" routing updates and/or data traffic. In theory, "coloring" allows the interconnection of virtual devices without the need for a dedicated virtual data path for each VN. For example, *multiprotocol interior Border Gateway Protocol* (MP-iBGP) uses a "coloring" mechanism to differentiate routing updates for different RFC 2547 VPNs, but the RFC 2547 forwarding plane relies on dedicated logical data paths to forward traffic (tunnels based on *label switched paths* [LSPs] or *Layer 2 Tunnel Protocol Version 3* [L2TPv3]). Other technologies such as *Multi-Topology Routing* (MTR) rely on "coloring" for both control-plane updates and forwarding, the latter implemented in a mechanism known as "class-based forwarding." Control-plane coloring for MTR is done natively in the *interior gateway protocols* (IGPs) by labeling the routing updates, much like MP-iBGP does. Chapter 4 provides more detail about the different technologies available to virtualize devices and the data path and about "coloring" for MTR.

The VRFs must also be mapped to the appropriate VLANs at the edge of the network. This mapping provides continuous virtualization across the Layer 2 and Layer 3 portions of the network. The mapping of VLANs to VRFs is as simple as placing the corresponding VLAN interface at the distribution switch into the appropriate VRF. The same type of mapping mechanism applies to Layer 2 virtual circuits (ATM, Frame Relay) or IP tunnels, which are handled by the router as a logical interface. The mapping of VLAN logical interfaces (*switch virtual interface* [SVI]) to VRFs is illustrated in Figure 3-7.

Figure 3-7   *VLAN-to-VRF Mapping*

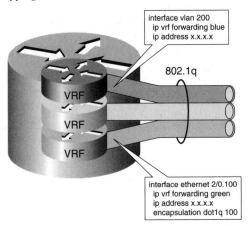

So far, we have created a virtualized transport that can keep the traffic from different groups separate from each other. The next section introduces the functionality required at the edge to place or authorize endpoints into the appropriate groups.

The LAN Edge: Authentication and Authorization

At the edge of the network, it is necessary to identify the users or devices logging on to the network so that they can be assigned to the right groups.

The process of identifying the users or devices is known as *authentication*. Two parameters affect the assignment of a user or devices: the identity of the user or device and the posture of the device. The posture of the device refers to the health of the device, measured by the level of software installed, especially operating system patches and antivirus.

When identified, the endpoints must be authorized onto the network. To this effect, the port on which an endpoint connects is activated and configured with certain characteristics and policies. This process is known as *authorization*. One example of authorization is the configuration of a port's VLAN membership based on the results of an authentication process. Another example is the dynamic configuration of port ACLs based on the authentication.

For wireless access, the concept of a "port" is replaced by an "association" between client and access point. When authorizing a wireless device, the association is customized to reflect the policy for the user or device. This customization can take the form of the selection of a different wireless LANs, VLANs, or mobility groups depending on the wireless technology used.

In this two-phased process, authorization is the most relevant to virtualization. When an endpoint is authorized on the network, it can be associated to a specific VN. Thus, it is the authorization method that will ultimately determine the mapping of the end station to a VN. For example, when a VLAN is part of a VN, a user authorized onto that VLAN will therefore be authorized onto the VN.

The main authentication scenarios for the enterprise could be summarized as follows:

- Client-based authentication, for endpoints with client software
  - 802.1x
  - NAC
- Clientless authentication, for endpoints without any client software
  - Web-based authentication
  - MAC-based machine authentication

Regardless of the authentication method, the authorization could be done in one of the following ways:

- Assigning a port to a specific VLAN
- Uploading a policy to a port, in the form of ACLs, policy maps, or even the *modular QoS command-line interface* (MQC)

VLANs map into VRFs seamlessly and are the authorization method of choice when using a VRF-based transport virtualization approach. ACL authorization could be used to achieve policy-based transport virtualization. For a transport virtualization approach based on class-based forwarding, the ability to dynamically load a QoS policy onto the access device could prove useful.

The current state of the technology provides broad support for VLAN assignment as an authorization alternative. In the cases where policy changes based on authentication are required and there is only VLAN assignment authorization available, a static assignment of a policy to a VLAN will provide the required linkage between the user authorization and the necessary policy. The policy will in effect be applied to the VLAN; as users are authorized onto different VLANs, they are subject to different policies.

Central Services Access: Virtual Network Perimeter

The default state of a VN is to be totally isolated from other VNs. In this respect, VNs could be seen as physically separate networks. However, because VNs actually belong to a common physical network, it is desirable for these VNs to share certain services such as Internet access, management stations, DHCP services, *Domain Name System* (DNS) services, or server farms. These services will usually be located outside of the different VNs or in a VN of their own. So, it is necessary for these VNs to have a gateway to connect to the "outside world." The outside world is basically any network outside the VN such as the Internet or other VNs. Because this is the perimeter of the VN, it is also desirable for this perimeter to be protected by security devices such as firewalls and *intrusion detection systems* (IDSs). Typically, the perimeter is deployed at a common physical location for most VNs. Hence, this location is known as the central services site, and the security devices here deployed can be shared by many VNs.

The creation of VNs could be seen as the creation of security zones, each of which has a unique and controlled entry/exit point at the VN perimeter. Routing within the VNs should be configured so that traffic is steered to the common services site as required. Figure 3-8 illustrates a typical perimeter deployment for multiple VNs accessing common services. Because the services accessed through the VN perimeter are protected by firewalls, we refer to these as "protected services."

Figure 3-8 *Central Site Providing VN Perimeter Security*

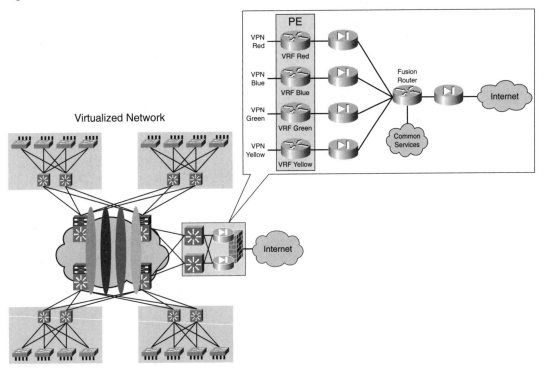

As shown in Figure 3-8, each VN is head ended by a dedicated firewall. This allows the creation of security policies specific to each VN and independent from each other. To access the shared services, all firewalls are connected to a "fusion" router. The fusion router can provide the VNs with connectivity to the common services, the Internet, or even inter-VN connectivity. The presence of this fusion router should raise two main concerns:

- The potential for traffic leaking between VNs
- The risk of routes from one VN being announced to another VN

The presence of dedicated per-VN firewalls prevents the leaking of traffic between VNs through the fusion router by only allowing established connections (connections initiated from "inside" the firewall) to return through the VN perimeter. It is key to configure the routing on the fusion device so that routes from one VN are not advertised to another through the fusion router. The details of the routing configuration at the central site are discussed in Chapter 8, "Traffic Steering and Service Centralization."

Figure 3-8 shows an additional firewall separating the fusion area from the Internet. This firewall is optional. Whether to use it or not depends on the need to keep common services or transit traffic in the fusion area protected from the Internet.

As mentioned, the common services could exist in a central location or in their own VN and therefore distributed throughout the enterprise. Depending on where the common services are located, the VN perimeter topology will vary. Figure 3-9 illustrates the different scenarios for common services positioning and the Internet firewall.

When the common services are not present, or are placed in their own VN (and therefore front-ended by a dedicated firewall context) the additional Internet firewall can be removed, as shown in scenario B.2 of Figure 3-9. If concern exists about transit traffic (between VNs or between a VN and the shared services area) being on the Internet, the firewall can be kept (see diagram A.2). The common services could be separated from the rest of the network by having their own firewall, yet not be included in a VN; this is shown in scenario B.1 in Figure 3-9.

For scenarios B.1 and B.2 in Figure 3-9, it is important to note that the fusion router is actually part of the Internet; therefore the *Network Address Translation (*NAT) pool used at the firewalls must use valid Internet addresses. The deployment of the optional Internet firewall should follow standard Internet edge design guidance, which has been extensively documented across networking literature. The reference designs proposed by Cisco and published at http://www.cisco.com/go/srnd are good sources of information. The "Data Center: Internet Edge Design" document contains a comprehensive discussion on the topic. We use scenario A.1 from Figure 3-9 to illustrate the relevant design and deployment considerations, but these considerations are applicable to other scenarios.

Figure 3-9 *Common Services Positioning*

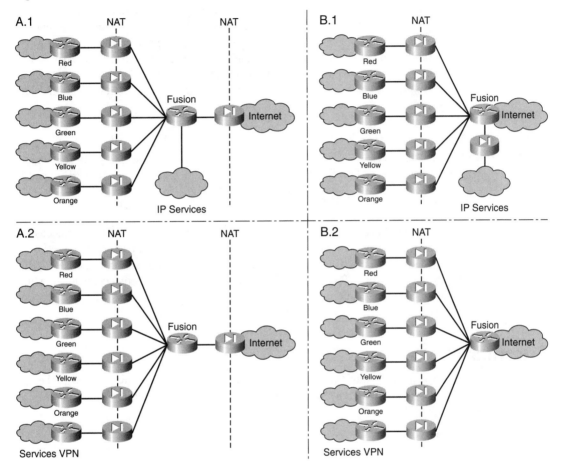

Unprotected Services

In contrast with circuit-based technologies such as ATM or Frame Relay, most Layer 3 VPN technologies allow enough flexibility for traffic to be leaked between VNs in a controlled manner by importing and exporting routes between VNs to provide IP connectivity between the VNs. Thus, the exchange of traffic between the VNs may happen within the IP core and not have to pass through the VN perimeter firewalls at the central site. This type of inter-VN connectivity can be used to provide services, such as DHCP or DNS, that do not need to be protected by the central site firewall, or that would represent an unnecessary burden to the VN perimeter firewalls. Because of the any-to-any nature of an IP cloud, there is little chance of controlling inter-VN traffic after the routes have been exchanged. We refer to these as "unprotected services." This type of connectivity must be deployed carefully because it can potentially create unwanted back doors between VNs and break the concept of the VN as a "security zone" protected by a robust VN perimeter front end. Another consideration that must be made is the fact that importing and exporting routes between VNs precludes the use of overlapping address spaces between the VNs. We discuss the use of route-importing mechanisms for the creation of common services extranet VNs in detail in Chapter 8.

NOTE   Although, these services are not protected by the VN perimeter firewalls, the IP segment to which they belong could potentially be head-ended by a firewall and therefore "protected."

The deployment of protected services does not preclude the deployment of unprotected services and vice versa. In a virtualized network, a combination of protected and unprotected services is usually provided for the different VNs. For example, the DHCP and DNS services for several VNs may be shared and accessed in an unprotected manner, while all server farms and the Internet are also shared among the different VNs, but their access must be controlled by firewall policies and an IDS.

Summary

You can use many technologies to virtualize the enterprise network. Regardless of the technologies of choice, they must provide the functionality required in the three areas discussed:

- Transport virtualization
- Edge authorization
- Central services access (VN perimeter)

The network architect should be well aware of how these functional blocks interface with each other and always keep in mind that virtualizing the network must not come at the expense of important resiliency and performance characteristics in the network. However, because of the new technologies put in place, there will be an impact in the operations and processes for the maintenance of the network. In the long term, this impact is likely to be a positive one as new operational efficiencies are gained and operational costs tend to diminish.

It is also important to remember that when virtualizing a network, not everything must be migrated onto the VNs created. VN technologies are overlaid onto the existing operational network infrastructure. Therefore, the network continues to function as it did before the virtualization, but now has VNs overlaid on top of it. The endpoints using the network could belong to the original network or to a VN. This provides a clear path to a phased migration and support for groups that do not require a dedicated VN.

CHAPTER 4

A Virtualization Technologies Primer: Theory

This chapter covers the technology used to build *virtualized networks* (VNs). As discussed previously, virtualization is not just about IPsec tunnels in the WAN—it covers a wide range of technology options on routers and switches. There are virtual partitions on routers and switches and protocol extensions that combine to maintain the end-to-end coherency of VNs across a shared infrastructure. We consider virtualization in three main sections:

- **Devices**—How is traffic separation maintained internally to a device? What are the primitives used for Layer 2, Layer 3, or Layer 4 traffic?

- **Data path**—How is traffic separation enforced across a network path? What tools are available to maintain the separation across a network?

- **Control plane**—Because data-path virtualization essentially builds an overlay topology, what changes are needed for routing protocols to function correctly?

This chapter does not cover architectures, topologies, or designs. The purpose of this chapter is to make sure you understand the technology before using it. (The world would be a better place if this principle were universally applied).

The general format for each section of this chapter is to start with a discussion of the protocol technology, highlighting any important details, with some limited configuration examples.

Network Device Virtualization

One of the characteristics of a VN is that it provides what are essentially private communication paths between members of a group over a shared infrastructure. This creates two requirements for the network infrastructure:

- **Traffic from one group is never mixed with another**—For sending and receiving traffic over shared links, tunnels (many borrowed from existing *virtual private network* [VPN] solutions) can guarantee data separation. Network devices need to enforce group separation in their internal memory (for example, during routing table lookups, access lists processing, or NetFlow statistics gathering).

- **Each VN has a separate address space**—This requirement is derived from the fact that VNs offer the same characteristics as a physical network. Address space and forwarding within it are two of the most basic aspects of any network.

NOTE	In this section, we start with a narrow definition of device virtualization as creating a separate address space within a network device. However, you can think of this as a special case of a more general definition of a virtualized device, which is the ability for an administrator to allocate device resources to different uses. The first device resource we consider is address space, but as we proceed through both the chapter and book, we include different layers of device policy control mechanisms, such as *quality of service* (QoS) and security rules. Therefore, the final picture of a virtualized device will be much closer to the general definition.

The first problem to solve is how to virtualize the forwarding plane in a way that meets the requirements for address and traffic flow separation. Depending on the type of device, the virtual separation can go by the following names:

- Virtual LAN (VLAN)
- Virtual routing and forwarding (VRF)
- Virtual forwarding instance (VFI)
- Virtual firewall context

Layer 2: VLANs

VLANs are a good example of a piece of the virtualization puzzle that has been around for quite some time. A VLAN is a logical grouping of ports on a switch that form a single broadcast domain. Ports in a VLAN can communicate only with other ports in the same VLAN. How a given switch does this is implementation dependent, but a common solution is for the switch to tag each frame with a VLAN number as it arrives on a port. When a frame is sent to other ports, the output hardware copies the packet only if it is configured with the VLAN number carried in the frame.

On an Ethernet switch, there is typically a single MAC table, which maps ports to MAC addresses. To support VLANs (and simple Layer 2 virtualization), the MAC table has a field for the VLAN number on which the station was discovered, as demonstrated in Example 4-1.

Example 4-1 *Switch MAC Table*

```
Switch# show mac-address-table
...
Non-static Address Table:
Destination Address  Address Type  VLAN  Destination Port
------------------   ------------  ----  --------------------
0010.0de0.e289       Dynamic         1   FastEthernet0/1
0010.7b00.1540       Dynamic         2   FastEthernet0/5
0010.7b00.1545       Dynamic         2   FastEthernet0/5
0060.5cf4.0076       Dynamic         1   FastEthernet0/1
```

Example 4-1 *Switch MAC Table (Continued)*

```
0060.5cf4.0077      Dynamic         1   FastEthernet0/1
0060.5cf4.1315      Dynamic         1   FastEthernet0/1
0060.70cb.f301      Dynamic         1   FastEthernet0/1
00e0.1e42.9978      Dynamic         1   FastEthernet0/1
00e0.1e9f.3900      Dynamic         1   FastEthernet0/1
```

NOTE   Note that the output in Example 4-1 was taken from
http://www.cisco.com/en/US/products/sw/iosswrel/ps5207/
products_command_reference_chapter09186a0080417db7.html#wp1021274.

The summary effect of the VLANs is to partition the switch into logical Layer 2 domains.
Each domain has its own address space and packets from one domain are kept separate from
those of another.

Layer 3: VRF Instances

VRFs are to Layer 3 as VLANs are to Layer 2 and delimit the domain of an IP network
within a router. The Cisco website has a more formal definition:

> VRF—A VPN Routing/Forwarding instance. A VRF consists of an IP routing table,
> a derived forwarding table, a set of interfaces that use the forwarding table, and a set
> of rules and routing protocols that determine what goes into the forwarding table.

Unlike the VLAN scenario, where an extra column in the MAC table is adequate, a VRF
partitions a router by creating multiple routing tables and multiple forwarding instances.
Dedicated interfaces are bound to each VRF.

Figure 4-1 shows a simple logical representation of a router with two VRFs: RED and
GREEN. The RED table can forward packets between interfaces E1/0, E1/2, and S2/0.102.
The GREEN table, on the other hand, forwards between interfaces E4/2, S2/0.103, and
S2/1.103. An interface cannot be in multiple VRFs at the same time.

Figure 4-1 *Multiple VRFs on a Router*

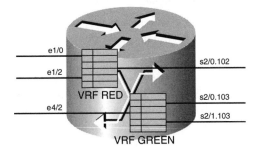

You can see in Figure 4-1 how a VRFs provide separate layer paths between routed interfaces. RED packets can never end up on a GREEN interface.

NOTE   There is a way to share routes between VRFs, but that is beyond the scope of this introduction. Interested readers should consult the references in the appendix for specialized texts on *Multiprotocol Label Switching VPNs* (MPLS VPNs).

It is easy to see VRFs on a router. Example 4-2 shows the RED and GREEN VRFs, with their interfaces. Example 4-2 shows overlapping IP addresses on the Serial interfaces. Example 4-3 gives an interface-centric view of the same data.

Example 4-2 *Displaying VRFs*

```
Router# show ip vrf
   Name                 Default RD           Interfaces
   RED                  100:1                Ethernet1/0, Ethernet1/2, Serial2/0.102
   GREEN                100:2                Serial2/0.103, Serial2/1.103, Ethernet4/2
Example 4-3 Displaying interface to VRF mapping
Router# show ip vrf interfaces
Interface       IP-Address      VRF                 Protocol
Ethernet1/0     130.22.0.33     RED                 up
Ethernet1/2     130.77.0.33     RED                 up
Serial2/0.102   130.77.0.33     RED                 up
Serial2/0.103   130.77.0.33     GREEN               up
Serial2/1.102   130.77.0.33     GREEN               up
Ethernet4/2     130.22.0.33     GREEN               up
router#
```

FIBs and RIBs

Before looking at the routing information for a VRF, we need to introduce the routing table's two main data structures, which are used to find the egress interface for a given packet: the *Forwarding Information Base* (FIB) and the *Routing Information Base* (RIB). Long gone are the days when a router maintained a single routing table on which it did linear, longest-prefix searches against destination IP addresses.

The FIB is a database of information used to forward packets. When a packet is received on a routed interface, the router looks up the destination address in the FIB to find the next hop for the packet.

The FIB structure is particularly efficient for resolving longest-prefix matches, and Cisco IOS resolves all route redirections so that a single lookup can yield the entry for the next hop of a packet. Cisco literature often mentions an adjacency concept when presenting the FIB. An *adjacency* is any node in the network that is reachable with a single Layer 2 hop. It so happens that Cisco IOS also maintains a data structure of adjacencies, which contains, among other things, interface and MAC layer rewrite information for all possible next hops. FIB entries point to the adjacency table, and in the remainder of this chapter, we group the two together and refer simply to the FIB. Hardware-based forwarding paths use the FIB concept, as does *Cisco Express Forwarding* (CEF).

Because it contains both Layer 2 and Layer 3 information, the FIB can be updated by several sources, such as routing protocol and *Address Resolution Protocol* (ARP) updates.

The RIB is the memory structure that contains classic routing data. The RIB can contain recursive routes. If a packet destination is not in the FIB, the router "punts" the packet to a slow processing path and resolves the destination next hop using the RIB.

When you enable VRFs, there are multiple instances of information in the FIB and RIB. You can see routing information with **show ip route vrf** *name* command, as shown in Example 4-3. Except for the first line, which identifies the VRF, there is no difference from the regular **show ip route** output.

Example 4-3 *VRF Routing Table Information*

```
R104#show ip route vrf RED
Routing Table: RED
Codes: C - connected, S - static, R - RIP, M - mobile, B - BGP
       D - EIGRP, EX - EIGRP external, O - OSPF, IA - OSPF inter area
       N1 - OSPF NSSA external type 1, N2 - OSPF NSSA external type 2
       E1 - OSPF external type 1, E2 - OSPF external type 2
       i - IS-IS, su - IS-IS summary, L1 - IS-IS level-1, L2 - IS-IS level-2
       ia - IS-IS inter area, * - candidate default, U - per-user static route
       o - ODR, P - periodic downloaded static route
Gateway of last resort is not set
     20.0.0.0/24 is subnetted, 1 subnets
O       20.0.0.0 [110/11121] via 40.0.0.1, 00:00:02, Tunnel0
     40.0.0.0/24 is subnetted, 1 subnets
C       40.0.0.0 is directly connected, Tunnel0
     30.0.0.0/24 is subnetted, 1 subnets
C       30.0.0.0 is directly connected, Ethernet0/0
```

The adjacencies for any routing entry in the VRF must resolve to different interfaces, even if the IP addresses on the interface are identical. Example 4-4 has a FIB entry for 40.0.0.2 from the global routing table, and Example 4-5 has the same information for the RED VRF. These examples are deliberately simple, but you can use the **show ip cef forwarding vrf** *name* **detail** command to peruse the FIB in all its glory.

Example 4-4 *FIB Output for Global Routing Table*

```
R104#show ip cef
Prefix            Next Hop        Interface
0.0.0.0/0         drop            Null0 (default route handler entry)
0.0.0.0/32        receive
40.0.0.0/24       attached        Loopback1
40.0.0.0/32       receive
40.0.0.2/32       receive
40.0.0.255/32     receive
```

Example 4-5   *FIB Output for VRF RED*

```
R104#show ip cef vrf RED
Prefix            Next Hop          Interface
0.0.0.0/0         drop              Null0 (default route handler entry)
0.0.0.0/32        receive
40.0.0.0/24       attached          Tunnel0
40.0.0.0/32       receive
40.0.0.2/32       receive
```

The term *global* is used to refer to the routing instances and tables that are not in a VRF, as in "global routing table" or "global address space."

When discussing VRFs, it is common to hear questions about resource allocation, such as "how are router resources allocated between VRFs?" This is a natural question, even if it is not logical! There are no special rules to prioritize data from one VRF to be processed quicker than data from other VRFs. A VRF exists in the memory plane of a device, not in the scheduling plane, which is what per-VRF traffic prioritization would require.

NOTE   Creating a VRF does not automatically consume a significant amount of memory. However, the expectation is that you will add routes to the VRFs and in this case be careful that the sum of entries in the virtual routing tables does not exceed the capacity of the device. In truth, this is not much different from standard best practices governing route table size.

Traffic processing happens according to the same rules as on a device with no VRFs:

1   Traffic enters the router.

2   The ingress policy is applied.

3   Routing and forwarding lookup occurs.

4   The egress policy is applied.

5   Traffic is forwarded.

Obviously, the ingress and egress policies can include QoS statements that prioritize traffic to or from a particular interface or address, but the fact that a packet belongs to a particular VRF has no impact on those policies. It simply alters what happens in Step 3 of the preceding list.

It is far more common to want to bind an interface or packet flow to a particular VRF based on policy criteria. For example, all interfaces from a certain user domain are bound to a single company VRF, or packets with a 10.0.0.0/8 source address are bound to a guest VRF. We look at this in great detail in some of the design chapters.

Virtual and Logical Routers

A VRF is not the same thing as a completely virtualized device, even if they are sometimes confused as such (it is true that some marketing literature encourages such confusion). They simply allow routers to support multiple address spaces. This is some distance from a fully virtualized device, where resources can be more or less arbitrarily allocated to tasks.

Virtualized devices do exist, however, and, to cut through the fog of confusion, it is helpful to have a taxonomy of terms to start with:

- A *logical router* (LR) uses hardware partitioning to create multiple routing entities on a single device. An LR can run across different processors on different cards of a router. All the underlying hardware and software resources are dedicated to an LR. This includes network processors, interfaces, and routing and forwarding tables. LRs provide excellent fault isolation but do require abundant hardware to implement.

- A *virtual router* (VR) uses software emulation to create multiple routing entities. The underlying hardware is shared between different router processes (note that we mean an entire instance of something like the nonkernel parts of IOS, not a single router process). In a well-implemented virtual router, users can see and change only the configuration and statistics for "their" router.

| NOTE | The previous definitions and Figure 4-2 were derived from RST-4314 2004 Networkers "Advances in Router Architecture: The CRS-1 and IOS-XR," by David Tsiang and David Ward. |

From the preceding list and Figure 4-2, which gives a pictorial idea of the difference between VRs and LRs, you can see that only the LR is completely virtualized. Because of the cost involved of having all that extra hardware and device management, LRs tend to be high-end systems. A VR is a software-based virtualization solution, where all the tasks share the same hardware resources.

In both cases, the granularity of what is virtualized can differ. Some implementations allow multiple router processes (for instance, one VR per customer domain), others allow you to allocate resources to tasks (an LR can have *Border Gateway Protocol* [BGP] running on one hardware subsystem and *Intermediate System-to-Intermediate System* [IS-IS] on another, for example).

Figure 4-2 *Logical and Virtual Routers*

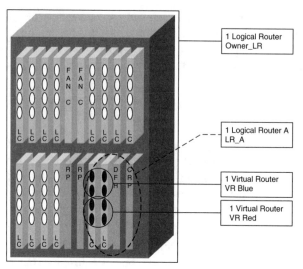

VRF Awareness

Now that there are multiple routing and forwarding instances on a router, many of the router subsystems that use the information in these tables (which is a long list) need to become "VRF aware." A VRF-aware feature can be configured to refer to routing and forwarding information from a specific VRF and understand that only certain subinterfaces can be used with certain VRFs. Without this information, the feature uses the global table. For example, to assign an interface to a VRF, the basic **interface** *ip address* command was modified to take a VRF name parameter and become **ip address vrf** *NAME* **forwarding**.

NOTE   VRF awareness is an important implementation detail. Unfortunately, no canonical list exists of VRF-aware features (the list keeps growing), so the best approach is to check the latest online documentation or pester your Cisco representative.

If all features required for a particular application are VRF aware, you can use VRFs to emulate a VR and hence provide virtualized device functionality. This is the approach you will see used in the design sections of this book.

Layer 2 Again: VFIs

VFI is a service-specific partition on a switch that associates attachment circuits in the form of VLANs with *virtual switched interfaces* (VSIs).

If that did not make much sense, it is useful to have some background on the service itself, namely *Virtual Private LAN Services* (VPLS), to understand VFIs.

VPLS is a Layer 2 LAN service offered by *service providers* (SPs) to connect Ethernet devices over a WAN. The customer devices (call them *customer edges* [CEs] for now; we review this in more detail in Chapter 5, "Infrastructure Segmentation Architectures") are all Ethernet switches. However, the SP uses a Layer 3 network running *Multiprotocol Label Switching* (MPLS) to provide this service. The device on the edge of the SP network is called a *provider edge* (PE). Its role is to map Ethernet traffic from the customer LAN to MPLS tunnels that connect to all the other PEs that are part of the same service instance. The PEs are connected with a full mesh of tunnels and behave as a logical switch, called a VSI. Another way to think about this is to see the VPLS service as a collection of Ethernet ports connected across a WAN. A VSI is a set of ports that forms a single broadcast domain.

In many ways, a VSI behaves just as you would expect a regular switch to. When a PE receives an Ethernet frame from a customer device, it first learns the source address, as would any switch, before looking at the destination MAC address and forwarding the frame. If the port mapping for the destination MAC address is unknown, or is a broadcast, the frame is sent to all PEs that are part of the VSI. The PEs use split horizon to avoid creating loops, which in turn means that no spanning tree is needed across the SP network.

Obviously, the previous explanation hides a fair amount of detail, but it should be enough to give a high-level view of what is going on.

Once again, there is a need to define and manage groups of isolated ports and tunnels on a switch. The VLAN construct is too limited, and a VRF is strictly a Layer 3 affair, so it is necessary to come up with a new virtual device structure for VPLS, called a VFI.

The VFI lists addresses of all the PEs that form a VSI. Recall that VPLS uses a full mesh of point-to-point tunnels for inter-PE connectivity, so there will be connections to each PE listed. The customer-facing ports map VLANs to a VFI name. Example 4-6 shows a short configuration extract that will make this clearer. Figure 4-3 shows the corresponding network topology. The thick line represents the VLAN that runs across the MPLS backbone and connects the VSIs on the PE devices. The CE switches "think" they are connected by a 802.1q trunk on VLAN100. The thin lines between each PE are the actual pseudowires defined in the **l2 vfi** statement of Example 4-6.

NOTE   A pseudowire is a tunnel. The term is often used in the context of a Layer 2 service.

Figure 4-3 *VPLS Topology*

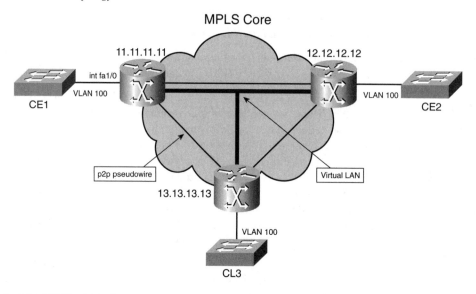

Example 4-6 *VFI Configuration*

```
l2 vfi VPLSA manual
 vpn id 100
 neighbor 13.13.13.13. encapsulation mpls
 neighbor 12.12.12.12 encapsulation mpls

interface loopback 1
 ip address 11.11.11.11 255.255.255.255
interface fastethernet1/0
 switchport
 switchport mode dot1qtunnel
 switchport access vlan 100

interface vlan 100
 no ip address
 xconnect vfi VPLSA
```

VPLS configuration has two components. The first, which we have already referred to, defines the mesh of pseudowires that together act as a virtual switch. The second maps the VLAN trunk port to a VSI using the **xconnect** command. This appears at the end of Example 4-6.

Virtual Firewall Contexts

Device virtualization is not limited to switches and routers. As a final example, consider a firewall device. For essentially economic reasons, you might want to share a single firewall between multiple different customers or network segments. Each logical firewall needs to have a complete set of policies, dedicated interfaces for incoming and outgoing traffic, and users authorized to manage the firewall.

Many vendors provide this capability today and undoubtedly have their own, well-chosen name for it, but on Cisco firewalls the term *context* is used to refer to a virtual firewall. Unlike VRFs, VFIs, or VLANs, a context is an emulation of a device (so an example of the VR concept discussed earlier in this chapter).

Firewall contexts are a little unusual in the way they assign a packet to a context. All the partitions we have seen up to now have static assignment of interfaces (you can assign IP packets to a VRF dynamically. We cover that later). A firewall module looks at an incoming packet's destination IP address or Ethernet VLAN tag to decide which context a packet belongs to. All the firewall needs is for one of the two fields to be unique. So, either each context has a unique IP address space on its interfaces or the address space is shared, but each context is in a different VLAN.

Figure 4-4 shows a simple setup with an Ethernet switch connected to a firewall context using two VLANs. The switch binds the VLANs to VRF BLUE (at the top) and VRF RED. The firewall has two different contexts. The blue one receives all frames on VLAN 101 and the red one gets VLAN 102. In this way, packets from the outside (on the right side of the figure) that belong to VLAN 101 go through a different set of firewall rules than those belong to VLAN 102.

Figure 4-4   *VRF on Switch Connected to Firewall Contexts Across VLANs*

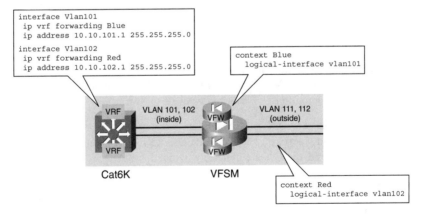

Network Device Virtualization Summary

True device virtualization allows resources to be allocated to tasks, or applications. We looked at four different primitives that virtualize the forwarding paths on switches or routers: VLAN and VFI for Layer 2, VRF for Layer 3, and contexts for firewalls. Each of these functions slightly differently. VRFs have the most extensive tie-ins with other features, which we use extensively in the design sections. Before covering data-path virtualization, one word about data center designs. We are focusing on network devices exclusively in this book and do not address the details of server and storage virtualization, which are two important topics in their own right.

Data-Path Virtualization

Connecting devices with private paths over a shared infrastructure is a well-known problem. SPs have solved this with different iterations of VPN solutions over the years. Not surprisingly, we can use and adapt many of these same protocols in enterprise networks to create virtualized Layer 2 and Layer 3 connections using a common switched infrastructure. The focus in this section is on the more relevant of the rather overwhelming menu of protocols to build a VPN. Some of this section is a review for many readers, especially the material on 802.1q, *generic routing encapsulation* (GRE), and IPsec, and we do not devote much space to these topics. However, we also include label switching (a.k.a. MPLS) and *Layer 2 Tunnel Protocol Version 3* (L2TPv3), which are probably less familiar and which consequently are covered in more detail.

NOTE   In addition to the references listed at the end of the book, we refer interested readers to Appendix A, "L2TPv3 Expanded Coverage," for more detail about L2TPv3.

Layer 2: 802.1q Trunking

You probably do not think of 802.1q as a data-path virtualization protocol. But, the 802.1q protocol, which inserts a VLAN tag on Ethernet links, has the vital attribute of guaranteeing address space separation on network interfaces.

Obviously, this is a Layer 2 solution, and each hop must be configured separately to allow 802.1q connectivity across a network. Because a VLAN is synonymous with a broadcast domain, end-to-end VLANs are generally avoided.

Generic Routing Encapsulation

GRE provides a method of encapsulating arbitrary packets of one protocol type in packets of another type (the RFC uses the expression *X over Y*, which is an accurate portrayal of the problem being solved). The data from the top layer is referred to as the payload. The bottom layer is called the delivery protocol. GRE allows private network data to be transported across shared, possibly public infrastructure, usually using point-to-point tunnels.

Although GRE is a generic X over Y solution, it is mostly used to transport IP over IP (a lightly modified version was used in the Microsoft *Point-to-Point Tunneling Protocol* [PPTP] and, recently, we are seeing GRE used to transport MPLS). GRE is also used to transport legacy protocols, such as *Internetwork Packet Exchange* (IPX) and AppleTalk, over an IP network and Layer 2 frames.

GRE, defined in RFC 2784, has a simple header, as you can see in Figure 4-5.

Figure 4-5 *GRE Header*

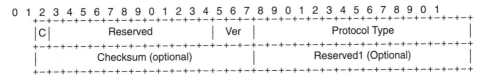

The second 2 octets of the header contain the payload protocol type, encoded using *Internet Assigned Numbers Authority* (IANA) Ethernet numbers (you can find the most recent version on http://www.iana.org/assignments/ethernet-numbers). IP is encoded as 0x800.

The simplest possible expression of a GRE header is a Protocol Type field. All the preceding fields are typically 0, and the subsequent ones can be omitted. You can find freeware implementations that work only with the first 2 octets, but all 4 should be supported.

GRE is purely an encapsulation mechanism. How packets arrive at tunnel endpoints is left entirely up to the user. There is no control protocol, no session state to maintain, no accounting records, and so forth; and this conciseness and simplicity allows GRE to be easily implemented in hardware on high-end systems. The concomitant disadvantage is that GRE endpoints have no knowledge of what is happening at the other end of the tunnel, or even whether it is reachable.

The time-honored mechanism for detecting tunnel reachability problems is to run a dynamic routing protocol across the tunnel. *Routing Protocol* (RP) keepalives are dropped if the tunnel is down, and the RP itself will declare the neighbor as unreachable and attempt to route around it. You can lose a lot of data waiting for an RP to detect a problem in this way and reconverge. Cisco added a keepalive option to its GRE implementation. This option sends a packet through the tunnel at a configurable period. After a certain number of missed keepalives (the number is configurable), the router declares the tunnel interface as down. A routing protocol would detect the interface down event and react accordingly.

GRE's lack of control protocol also means that there is essentially no cost to maintaining a quiescent tunnel active. The peers exchange no state information and must simply encapsulate packets as they arrive. Furthermore, like all the data-path virtualization mechanisms we discuss, the core network is oblivious of the number of tunnels traversing it. All the work is done on the edge.

We do not want to suggest that GRE is the VPN equivalent of a universal solvent. There is a cost to processing GRE—encapsulation/decapsulation, route lookup, and so forth—but it's in the data path.

GRE IOS Configuration

On Cisco devices, GRE endpoints are regular interfaces. This seemingly innocuous statement is replete with meaning, because anything in Cisco IOS that needs to see an interface (routing protocols, access lists, and many more) will work automatically on a GRE tunnel.

Example 4-7 shows a GRE endpoint configuration, corresponding to the R103 router of Figure 4-6.

Figure 4-6   *GRE Topology*

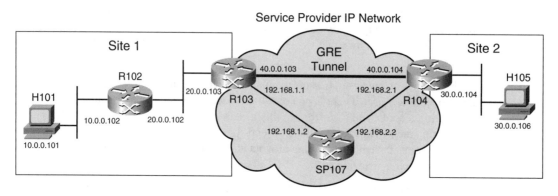

Example 4-7   *R103 GRE Configuration*

```
interface Tunnel0
 ip address 40.0.0.1 255.255.255.0
 tunnel source Serial1/0
 tunnel destination 192.168.2.1
```

The tunnel source and tunnel destination addresses are part of the transport network address space. They need to match on both endpoints so that a source address on one router is the destination address on the remote device. The router must also have a path in its routing table to the tunnel destination address. The next hop to the tunnel destination must point to a real interface and not the tunnel interface.

In this case, the router has a tunnel interface with tunnel destination of 192.168.2.1 on the public network. The 40.0.0.0/24 network used for the tunnel IP's address, however, is part of the private address space used on Sites 1 and 2.

IPsec

IPsec provides a comprehensive suite of security services for IP networks. IPsec was originally conceived to provide secure transport over IP networks. The security services include strong *authentication* (*Authentication Header* [AH]) and *Encryption* (*Header* [EH]) protocols and ciphers and key-exchange mechanisms. IPsec provides a way for peers to interoperate by negotiating capabilities and keys and security algorithms.

IPsec peers maintain a database of security associations. A *security association* (SA) is a contract between peers, which defines the following:

- The specific encryption and authentication algorithms used, such as Triple DES (*Triple Data Encryption Standard*)
- The IPsec protocol service (*Encapsulating Security Payload* [ESP] or AH)
- Key material needed to communicate with the peer

The SA is negotiated when an IPsec session is initiated. Each IPsec header contains a unique reference to the SA for this packet in a *Security Parameter Index* (SPI) field, which is 32-bit numeric reference to the SA needed to process the packet. Peers maintain a list of SAs for inbound and outbound processing. The value of the SPI is shared between peers. It is one of the things exchanged during IPsec session negotiation.

At the protocol level, there are two IPsec headers:

- **AH**—Offers nonrepudiatable authentication between two parties. The authentication service also provides for message integrity and certain instances of (identity) spoofing.
- **ESP**—Offers encrypted communication between two parties. The encryption service allows message confidentiality, integrity, nonrepudiation, and protection against spoofing and replay attacks.

It is possible to use authentication and encryption services separately or together. If used in combination, the AH header precedes the ESP header.

There are two ways to encapsulate IPsec packets. The first, called tunnel mode, encrypts an entire IP packet, including the header, in the IPsec payload. A new IP header is generated for the encrypted packet, as shown in Figure 4-7.

Figure 4-7   *IPsec Tunnel Mode Stack*

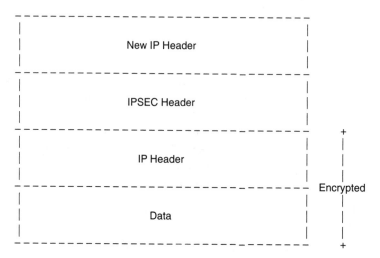

Tunnel mode adds a 20-octet overload with the new IP header. To reduce issues with packet size and fragmentation, a second mode was defined, called transport mode. Transport mode just protects the TCP/UDP layer and is shown in Figure 4-8. Tunnel mode is better than transport mode at traversing *Network Address Translation* (NAT) devices.

Figure 4-8   *IPsec Transport Mode Stack*

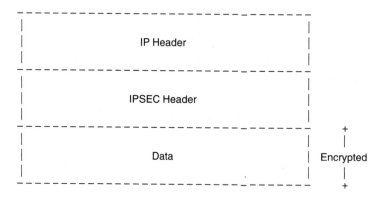

IPsec requires a lot of negotiation to bring up a session. So much so that there is a separate control channel protocol, called *Internet Key Exchange* (IKE), used to negotiate the SA between peers and exchange keys material. Note that IKE is not mandatory; you can statically configure the SAs.

IKE is not only used during tunnel setup. During confidential data exchange, the session keys used to protect unidirectional traffic may need to be changed regularly, and IKE is used to negotiate new keys.

IKE traffic itself is encrypted, and, in fact, it has its own SA. Most of the parameters are fixed as follows:

- 56-bit DES for encryption
- *Message digest 5* (MD5) algorithm or *secure hash algorithm* (SHA) hashing
- *Rivest, Shamir, Adleman* (RSA) (public key) signatures or preshared keys

IKE runs on UDP/500. IPsec uses IP protocol values of 50 and 51.

Cisco IOS IPsec Configuration

There is a lot more to IPsec than you will see here, but there are three basic parts to the configuration, which correspond to setting up SAs first for IKE, and then for the session itself, and defining which traffic to encrypt. The steps of the configuration are as follows:

1 The first basic part is the IKE policy. IKE will negotiate its own SA with the remote peer, so it too needs a policy. The **crypto isakamp policy** command defines the type of authentication, and the IP address of the remote peer and the shared secret used to protect the IKE exchanges, as indicated in Example 4-8.

Example 4-8 *IKE Policy Settings*

```
crypto isakmp policy 1
 authentication pre-share
crypto isakmp key secret address 10.0.3.11
```

2 In the second basic part is a crypto map, the role of the crypto map is to define the remote peer, the encryption and authentication algorithms (called transforms) that this router will accept to set up a SA, and the interesting traffic to be encrypted. As in so much of Cisco IOS, interesting traffic is defined using standard access lists. If a packet matches an access list entry, whatever IPsec policy is defined in the crypto map is applied to the packet. Example 4-9 has a crypto map that configures any traffic to address 10.0.3.11 that matches access list 101 to be encrypted using the IPsec service called ONE.

Example 4-9 *IPsec Crypto Map*

```
crypto map VPN 1 IPsec-isakmp
 set peer 10.0.3.11
 set security-association lifetime seconds 180
 set transform-set ONE
 match address 101
```

The authentication and encryption algorithms for this SA are defined in a transform set (so they can be shared between multiple SA definitions). The transform set is given in Example 4-10. It specifies AH and ESP services, with MD5 for authentication and DES for encryption.

Example 4-10 *IPsec Transform Set*

```
crypto ipsec transform-set ONE ah-md5-hmac esp-des
```

   3 The third step is to apply the crypto map on an outgoing interface, as in Example 4-11. This completes the puzzle. Now when packets enter or leave the Serial0 interface on this router, they are compared against access list 101 (refer back to the crypto map in Example 4-9), and if there is a match, encrypted according to the service defined in Example 4-10.

Example 4-11 *Interface with Crypto Map*

```
interface Serial0
 ip address 10.0.2.11 255.255.255.0
 no ip mroute-cache
 no fair-queue
 crypto map VPN
```

L2TPv3

NOTE Appendix A contains an expanded version of this section that discusses the L2TPv3 protocol in more detail.

The L2TPv3 protocol consists of components to bring up, maintain, and tear down sessions, and the capability to multiplex different Layer 2 streams into a tunnel.

The L2TP protocol has a both a control and data plane. The control channel is reliable. There are 15 different control message types. The major ones are for the setup and teardown of the control channel itself (see Appendix A for more detail). L2TPv3 peers can exchange capability information for the session during the setup phase. The most important of these are the session ID and cookie.

The session ID is analogous to the control channel identifier and it is a "shortcut" value that the receiver associates with the negotiated context for a particular session (for instance, payload type, cookie size, and so forth).

The cookie is an optional, variable-length field of up to 64 bits. The cookie is a cryptographically random number that extends the session identifier space so as to ensure there is little chance that a packet is misdirected because of corrupt session ID. 2^{64} is a large number and, as long as it is random, the cookie makes L2TPv3 impervious to brute-force spoofing attacks, where the attacker tries to inject packets into an active session.

After a session is established through the control session, the L2TP endpoint is ready to send and receive data traffic. Although the data header has a Sequence Number field, the data channel is not reliable. The protocol can detect missing, duplicate, or out-of-order packets, but does not retransmit. That is left to higher-layer protocols.

The RFC allows for the data channel to be set up either using the native control protocol, or statically, or using another control mechanism.

In the design sections after Chapter 5, "Infrastructure Segmentation Architectures: Theory," you will see occasions when, frankly, GRE could solve a problem just as well as L2TPv3. What then are the differences between these two protocols? Following is a list of them:

- **Ubiquity**—GRE can be found just about everywhere. It is an old (in Internet terms anyway), well-established protocol, and implementations should, by now, be robust. L2TPv3, more recent, is less prevalent.

- **Performance**—On high-speed links, especially on enterprise networks, encapsulation tax (header length and so forth) is much less of an issue than a couple of decades ago, when trying to wring every last ounce of baud rate from 1200 bps links was an important issue for network administrators the world over. At Gigabit, or 10 Gigabit speeds, the number of bytes used by a well-designed protocol is not really an issue, as long as the implementation runs in hardware. Concerning this last point, it is probably easier to find hardware implementations of GRE than L2TPv3.

- **Payload protocols**—RFC 3931 specifically states that L2TPv3 is designed to carry Layer 2 protocols. GRE is a multipurpose solution that can carry any other protocol. However, the devil is in the details, and GRE "implementations" may be limited to specific protocols (such as just Ethernet or IP). Furthermore, L2TPv3 has been extended to carry IP traffic.

- **Cookie**—This is the most fundamental difference between the two protocols. GRE has no equivalent of the Cookie field. If this is not important to you—and recall that the main advantage is to provide guarantees against spoofing—implementation issues may dictate your choice more than any difference between the protocols themselves.

L2TPv3 IOS Configuration

There are three things to configure for the L2TPv3 IOS configuration:

- Control channel parameters
- Data channel parameters
- Connection circuit parameters

To configure the first of these parameters, use the **l2tp-class** command for control channel setup. Here, you can change sequence number settings and so on, but the minimum required is the shared password known to both peers. Example 4-12 demonstrates the use of this command.

Example 4-12 l2tp-class *Command*

```
l2tp-class L2WAN
  password 7 00071A150754
```

As in classic L2TP setup, if you do not give a *hostname* parameter, the device name is used.

The second part of the configuration is for the data channel. Cisco IOS uses the **pseudowire** command, which is a generic template also used for Layer 2 over MPLS (called AToM) setup. The **pseudowire-class** specifies the encapsulation and refers to the control channel setup with the **protocol l2tpv3** *name* command (if you omit this, default control channel settings are used). The **pseudowire-class** also contains the name of the interface used as the source address of the L2TPv3 packets.

Example 4-13 *L2TP* **pseudowire-class** *Command*

```
pseudowire-class R103R104
  encapsulation l2tpv3
  protocol l2tpv3 L2WAN
  ip local interface Serial1/0
```

Figure 4-9 *L2TPv3 Topology*

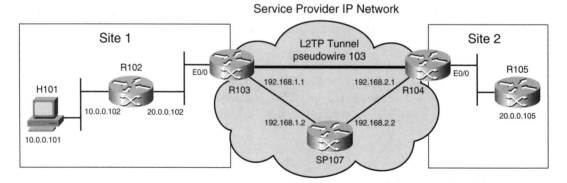

The final part of the configuration (see Example 14-14) binds the client-facing attachment circuit to the trunk port using the **xconnect** command (already introduced in the discussion on VPLS earlier in this section). The **xconnect** command defines the remote peer IP address and a unique *virtual circuit* (VC) identifier used on each peer to map the L2TPv3 payload to the correct attachment circuit. The L2TPv3 endpoints negotiate unique session and cookie ID values for each VC ID, as shown in Figure 4-9. You must configure a different

VC ID for each VLAN, port, or *data-link connection identifier* (DLCI) transported across an L2TPv3 tunnel (currently, Cisco L2TPv3 supports Ethernet, 802.1q [VLAN], Frame Relay, *High-Level Data Link Control* [HDLC], and PPP).

Example 4-14 xconnect *Command*

```
interface Ethernet0/0
 description Client Facing Port
 no ip address
 no cdp enable
 xconnect 192.168.2.1 103 encapsulation l2tpv3 pw-class R103R104
```

It's interesting that although the second and third versions of protocol differ in relatively small ways, the *command-line interface* (CLI) configuration differs significantly from the standard *L2TP access concentrator / L2TP network server* (LAC/LNS) configuration that you might have used for dialup or *digital subscriber line* (DSL) networks. However, there are obvious, and deliberate, similarities with other pseudowire solutions such as *Ethernet over MPLS* (EoMPLS).

Label Switched Paths

Label switched paths (LSPs) are an interesting hybrid of all the preceding data-path solutions: a Layer 2 data path with Layer 3 control plane. Of course, LSPs are found in MPLS networks, which is a topic that has generated entire library shelves of books and other documents. In this chapter, we present a short review of how packets traverse an MPLS network. We do not cover label distribution or any of the major MPLS applications, such as VPN or traffic engineering (MPLS VPNs are discussed in depth in Chapter 5, however).

What we are going to cover may be summarized as follows:

- An LSP is a tunnel across an MPLS network made up of individual hop-to-hop segments.
- MPLS networks uses the IP control plane.
- LSPs are set up for all known IP prefixes in the IP routing table.
- LSPs are multiplexed across physical links.
- Each node in an MPLS network forwards based on fixed-length labels instead of variable-length prefixes.
- Labels are carried in a shim header, between the Layer 2 and Layer 3 headers.
- Nodes distribute labels to adjacent nodes using a label distribution protocol.
- Basic label switching is easy to configure
- Label switching must be configured on all hops.

In a normal routing scenario, when a router needs to forward a packet, it finds the outgoing interface by looking for a matching IP address prefix in the routing table. The actual interface used for forwarding corresponds to the shortest path to the IP destination, as defined by the routing policy. Other administrative policies, such as QoS and security, may affect the choice of interface. This collection of criteria used for forwarding decisions is more generally referred to as a *Forward Equivalency Class* (FEC). The classification of a packet to FEC is done on each router along the IP path and happens independently of the other routers in the network.

MPLS decouples packet forwarding from the information in the IP header. An MPLS router forwards packets based on fixed-length labels instead of matching on a variable-length IP address prefix. The label is a sort of shortcut for an FEC classification that has already happened. Where the label comes from is discussed later in this section, but for now, it is enough to say that the labels are calculated based on the topology information in the IP routing table. RFC 3031 puts it like this:

> In MPLS, the assignment of a particular packet to a particular FEC is done just once, as the packet enters the network. The FEC to which the packet is assigned is encoded as a short fixed length value known as a "label." When a packet is forwarded to its next hop, the label is sent along with it; that is, the packets are "labeled" before they are forwarded.

> In the MPLS forwarding paradigm, once a packet is assigned to a FEC, no further header analysis is done by subsequent routers; all forwarding is driven by the labels.

Before looking at this in more detail, we need to introduce some definitions:

- **Label switching router (LSR)**—A router that switches based on labels. An LSR swaps labels. Unlike a traditional router, an LSR does not have to calculate where to forward a packet based on the IP packet header (which is a simplified way of saying it does not do FEC classification when it receives a packet). An LSR uses the incoming label to find the outgoing interface (and label). LSRs are also called *provider* (P) routers.

- **Edge LSR**—A router that is on the edge of an MPLS network. The edge LSR adds and removes labels from packets. This process is more formally called imposition and disposition (and also pushing and popping, because labels are said to go on a stack). Edge LSRs are often referred to as *provider edge* (PE) routers.

- **Customer edge (CE)**—An IP router that connects to the PE device. The CE performs IP forwarding. The PE and CE form routing protocol adjacencies.

Figure 4-10 illustrates MPLS-based forwarding, showing each of the different types of router from the preceding list.

Figure 4-10 *MPLS Forwarding*

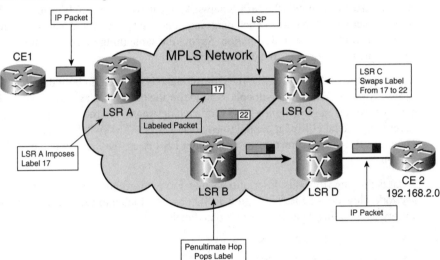

As a packet flows across the network shown in Figure 4-10, it is processed by each hop as follows:

1 At the edge of the network, as shown in Figure 4-10, edge LSR A classifies a packet to its FEC and assigns (or imposes) label 17 to the packet. A label is of local significance on that interface just like an ATM VPI/VCI or a Frame Relay DLCI.

2 In the core, LSRs, such as LSR C and LSR B, swap label values. LSR C removes the old label, 17 in the example shown in Figure 4-10, and imposes the new one, 22. The values of the ingress label and interface are used to find the values of the egress label and interface.

Note Not all MPLS forwarding modes use incoming interface. Frame mode, used in certain L2VPN services, just uses the incoming label as the same label value is advertised to all peers

---

3 LSR B, as the second-last hop in the MPLS network, removes the outermost label from the label stack, which is called *penultimate hop popping* (PHP). So, packets arrive at edge LSR D without any label, and standard IP routing is used to forward the packet. The process of removing a label is also called disposition. PHP avoids recursive lookups on edge LSR D.

4 After the label is removed, the packet is forwarded using standard IP routing.

Now the difference with standard IP forwarding should be clearer. FEC classification is done when a packet enters the MPLS network, not at every hop. An LSR needs to look only at the packet's label to know which outgoing interface to use. There can be different labels on an LSR for the same IP destination. Saying the same thing in a different way, there can be multiple LSPs for the same destination.

A key point to understand is that the control plane is identical in both the IP and MPLS cases. LSRs use IP routing protocols to build routing tables, just as routers do. An LSR then goes the extra step of assigning labels for each destination in the routing table and advertising the label/FEC mapping to adjacent LSRs. ATM switches can also be LSRs. They run IP routing protocols, just as a router LSR does, but label switch cells rather than packets.

What is missing from this description is how label information is propagated around the network. How does LSR A in Figure 4-10 know what label to use? MPLS networks use a variety of signaling protocols to distribute labels:

- **LDP**—Used in all MPLS networks
- **iBGP**—Used for L3 VPN service
- **RSVP**—Used for Traffic Engineering
- **Directed LDP**—Used for L2VPN service, such as VPLS

Label Distribution Protocol (LDP), which runs over tcp/646, is used in all MPLS networks to distribute labels for all prefixes in the nodes routing table. Referring again to Figure 4-10, LSR D and LSR B would bring up a LDP session (LSR B would have another session with LSR C and so forth). LSR D is connected to the customer 192.168.2.0/24 network and advertises this prefix to all its routing peers. LSR D also sends a label to LSR B for the 192.168.2.0 network. When LSR B's routing protocol converges and it sees 192.168.2.0 as reachable, it sends label 22 to LSR C. This process continues until LSR A receives a label from LSR C.

The complete end-to-end set of labels from LSR A to LSR D form an LSP. An LSP is unidirectional. There is another LSP, identified by a different set of labels, for return traffic from LSR D to LSR A.

Understand that two operations must complete for the LSP from LSR A to 192.168.2.0 to be functional:

- The backbone routing protocol must converge so that LSR A has a route to 192.168.2.0.
- LDP must converge so that labels are propagated across the network.

Figure 4-10 does not show a numeric value for the label between LSR B and LSR D. In fact, as already discussed, the packet on this link has no label at all, because of PHP. Nevertheless, LSR D does still advertise a special value in LDP, called an implicit null (which has a reserved value of 3), so that LSR B performs PHP.

NOTE   In fact, LSR D might use several special label values for the 192.168.2.0 prefix, such as the aggregate or explicit null.

After LSR A has all the information it needs to forward data across the MPLS network, it encapsulates outgoing packets in a shim header, shown in Figure 4-11 and defined in RFC 3032, which is inserted between the Layer 2 and Layer 3 headers. Encapsulation stacks are defined in different RFCs for Ethernet, ATM, PPP, and other media.

Figure 4-11 *MPLS Shim Header*

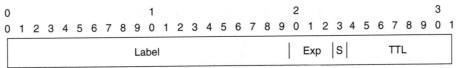

Label = 20 Bits
Exp = Experimental, 3 Bits
S = Bottom of Stack, 1 Bit
TTL = Time to Live, 8 Bits

The MPLS header is simple, as you can see in Figure 4-11. The label itself defines a flat, 20-bit address space. The EXP bits are defined as *Experimental*, but are in fact used for QoS. MPLS QoS is explained in more detail in the MPLS QoS section of this chapter. The S bit is set on the lowest label when there is more than one label on a packet, which is called a stack. The *Time-To-Live* (TTL) is analogous to the IP TTL.

Many MPLS applications, such as *virtual private networking* (VPN) and *fast reroute* (FRR), involve multiple layers, or stacks, of labels. However, an LSR forwards on the basis of the top, or outer, label values only and never looks at the inner ones.

The FIB Revisited

Label switching adds a forwarding path on a router. The FIB and RIB discussed previously in this chapter contain only IP prefixes. LDP stores labels in a *Label Information Base* (LIB), and the label values are added to the existing forwarding information in a *Label Forwarding Information Base* (LFIB). The LDP should have an entry for every non-BGP route in the routing table and all the labels advertised by LDP neighbors. The LFIB is built using a combination of the FIB and LIB. For a given prefix, if there is label in the LIB that is received from the LDP peer address as determined by the FIB, that label is installed in the LFIB and is used for forwarding.

It is important to understand that the LFIB does not replace the FIB. MPLS creates an alternative path through the router. However, IP packets continue to be forwarded using the FIB, and certain special label values can make a router do an FIB lookup.

Cisco IOS LSP Example

Figure 4-12 shows a simple MPLS topology. All routers are running MPLS on their interfaces, with LDP advertising labels to adjacent devices. The core routing protocol is *Open Shortest Path First* (OSPF), used on all interfaces. The configuration of each device is virtually identical, with the only MPLS-specific commands being activation of LDP (instead of TDP, an earlier alternative) and label switching on each interface, using the **mpls ip** command (which, for historical reasons, shows up in the output as **tag-switching ip**). Example 4-15 shows the configuration for R103 in case you want to try this at home.

Figure 4-12 *MPLS Network Topology*

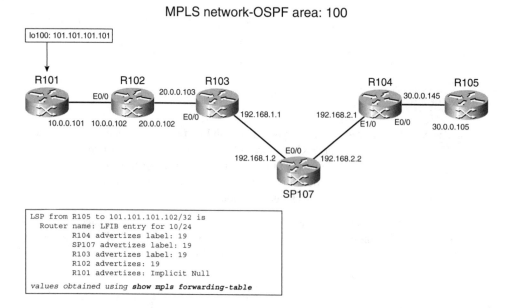

Example 4-15 *R103 Configuration*

```
mpls label protocol ldp
!
interface Ethernet0/0
 ip address 20.0.0.103 255.255.255.0
 tag-switching ip
!
interface Ethernet1/0
 ip address 192.168.1.1 255.255.255.252
 tag-switching ip
```

Three **show** commands enable you to see the mapping of routes from LIB to LFIB. Examples 4-16 through 4-18 give the output of each one in turn and trace labels used to reach R101's loopback address, 101.101.101.101, from R105. To avoid repetitive output command, we focus on R103 and R102.

Example 4-16 *R103* **show ip route** *output*

```
R103#show ip route
Codes: C - connected, S - static, R - RIP, M - mobile, B - BGP
       D - EIGRP, EX - EIGRP external, O - OSPF, IA - OSPF inter area
       N1 - OSPF NSSA external type 1, N2 - OSPF NSSA external type 2
       E1 - OSPF external type 1, E2 - OSPF external type 2
       i - IS-IS, su - IS-IS summary, L1 - IS-IS level-1, L2 - IS-IS level-2
       ia - IS-IS inter area, * - candidate default, U - per-user static route
       o - ODR, P - periodic downloaded static route
Gateway of last resort is not set
     101.0.0.0/32 is subnetted, 1 subnets
O       101.101.101.101 [110/21] via 20.0.0.102, 00:12:25, Ethernet0/0
     20.0.0.0/24 is subnetted, 1 subnets
C       20.0.0.0 is directly connected, Ethernet0/0
     10.0.0.0/24 is subnetted, 1 subnets
O       10.0.0.0 [110/20] via 20.0.0.102, 00:12:25, Ethernet0/0
     192.168.1.0/30 is subnetted, 1 subnets
C       192.168.1.0 is directly connected, Ethernet1/0
     192.168.2.0/30 is subnetted, 1 subnets
O       192.168.2.0 [110/20] via 192.168.1.2, 00:12:25, Ethernet1/0
     30.0.0.0/24 is subnetted, 1 subnets
O       30.0.0.0 [110/30] via 192.168.1.2, 00:12:25, Ethernet1/0
```

There is a one-to-one mapping between the content of the routing table in Example 4-16 and the LIB of Example 4-17. The LFIB, shown in Example 4-18, only contains labels for LSPs that cross the device. If an MPLS packet arrives with an unknown label, it is dropped.

Example 4-17 *R103 Label Information Base*

```
R103#show mpls ldp bindings
  tib entry: 10.0.0.0/24, rev 10
      local binding:  tag: 17
      remote binding: tsr: 192.168.1.2:0, tag: 17
      remote binding: tsr: 20.0.0.102:0, tag: imp-null
  tib entry: 20.0.0.0/24, rev 8
      local binding:  tag: imp-null
      remote binding: tsr: 192.168.1.2:0, tag: 16
      remote binding: tsr: 20.0.0.102:0, tag: imp-null
  tib entry: 30.0.0.0/24, rev 12
      local binding:  tag: 18
      remote binding: tsr: 192.168.1.2:0, tag: 18
      remote binding: tsr: 20.0.0.102:0, tag: 18
  tib entry: 101.101.101.101/32, rev 14
      local binding:  tag: 19
```

continues

Example 4-17 *R103 Label Information Base (Continued)*

```
             remote binding: tsr: 20.0.0.102:0, tag: 19
             remote binding: tsr: 192.168.1.2:0, tag: 19
      tib entry: 192.168.1.0/30, rev 5
             local binding:  tag: imp-null
             remote binding: tsr: 192.168.1.2:0, tag: imp-null
             remote binding: tsr: 20.0.0.102:0, tag: 16
      tib entry: 192.168.2.0/30, rev 6
             local binding:  tag: 16
             remote binding: tsr: 192.168.1.2:0, tag: imp-null
             remote binding: tsr: 20.0.0.102:0, tag: 17
```

Example 4-18 *R103 Label Forwarding Information Base*

```
R103#show mpls forwarding-table
Local  Outgoing    Prefix          Bytes tag  Outgoing    Next Hop
tag    tag or VC   or Tunnel Id     switched   interface
16     Pop tag     192.168.2.0/30   0          Et1/0       192.168.1.2
17     Pop tag     10.0.0.0/24      0          Et0/0       20.0.0.102
18     18          30.0.0.0/24      0          Et1/0       192.168.1.2
19     19          101.101.101.101/32   \
                                    0          Et0/0       20.0.0.102
```

Figure 4-12 shows the label values advertised by each LSR for prefix 101.101.101.101.
Example 4-18 shows how this label information appears in R103's LIB. There are three
entries for 101.101.101.101:

- **local binding**—The router's own, called local, which is advertised to downstream
  neighbors

- **20.0.0.102:0, tag: 19**—The label advertised by the upstream router R102

- **192.168.1.2:0, tag: 19**—The label advertised by the downstream router
  SP107

In the LFIB in Example 4-18, there is a single entry for 101.101.101.101/32. It means that
R103 will forward a packet received with value 19 onto interface Ethernet0/0. R103 also
swaps the label value. It is just a coincidence that the same values are used for the same IP
prefix on different routers. Labels have local significance.

Figure 4-12 shows that router R102 receives an implicit null label from R101 and
so performs PHP with label value 19 and forwards an IP packet on interface
Ethernet0/0.

Data-Path Virtualization Summary

We presented several different protocols that can be used for data-path virtualization. Two of them are suitable for Layer 2 traffic only: 802.1q, which is configured on each hop, and L2TPv3 which is configured end to end. IPsec is suitable for IP transport. Finally, GRE and MPLS LSPs can be used for either Layer 2 or Layer 3. GRE is another IP tunnel protocol, configured only on endpoints. MPLS creates a new forwarding path and is configured on all hops in a network.

Control-Plane Virtualization—Routing Protocols

Data-path virtualization essentially creates multiple separate logical networks over a single, shared physical topology. To move packets across these VNs, you need to need a routing protocol.

The most familiar virtualized control plane is probably *Per VLAN Spanning Tree* (PVST), which has a separate spanning-tree instance for each VLAN running on a switch. Even through PVST has been around longer than the term *virtualization*, it illustrates the central point we are making here very crisply. Different logical networks have different topologies and, therefore, different optimal paths. Switches have to run different spanning-tree calculations for each such network.

The remainder of this section deals with extensions to routing protocols to allow them to run with multiple routing instances. However, we will return to the topic of control-plane virtualization, because many different router and switch functions, such as NetFlow, DHCP, RADIUS, and so on, need to receive the same treatment and become VRF aware.

NOTE   The need for VRF awareness was introduced in the section on device virtualization earlier in the chapter. This is particular to Cisco platforms. In more general terms, features applied or related to the data path, such as NetFlow, RADIUS, and so on, need to support virtualization also—it's not as simple as creating multiple routing tables.

VRF-Aware Routing

Cisco's major *interior gateway protocol* (IGP) routing protocol implementations are VRF aware. This means that they understand that certain routes may be placed only in certain routing tables. The routing protocols manage this by peering within a constrained topology, where a routing protocol instance in a VRF peers with other instances in the same VN. No special information is added to the route advertisements to identify VRF names, so routing instances must communicate over private links.

With some protocols (for example, BGP), a single routing instance can manage multiple VRF tables; with others (for example, OSPF), a different routing process runs for every VRF. Remember that in both cases, every VRF requires a route optimization calculation, so increasing the number of VRFs does have a computational impact on a network device.

Chapter 5 has more information on the end-to-end setup. This section just covers the main concepts.

VRF per Process: OSPF

OSPF has a different routing process for each VRF. The first implementation was rather strict, with a maximum of 32 processes. Furthermore, two processes are reserved for static and connected routes. Recent software enhancements lift this limitation. You are now limited to 32 VRFs per process, but the number of processes is now fixed by the network devices' CPU and memory limitations (300 to 10,000 depending on the platform).

Example 4-19 shows how an OSPF process is associated with the RED VRF. The networks advertised by this process should be in the same VRF.

Example 4-19 *Per-VRF OSPF Configuration*

```
router ospf 2000 vrf RED
 log-adjacency-changes

 network 20.0.0.0 0.0.0.255 area 0
 network 40.0.0.0 0.0.0.255 area 0
```

VRF Address Families: EIGRP, RIP, and BGP

For the other routing protocols, a single process can manage all the VRFs, and the Cisco IOS **address-family** command is used to configure per-VRF route policy. Example 4-20 shows how to configure RIP for two VRFs, RED and GREEN. Each VRF has overlapping entries for network 13.0.0.0.

Example 4-20 *Per-VRF RIP Configuration*

```
router rip
 version 2
 !
 address-family ipv4 vrf RED
 version 2
 network 11.0.0.0
 network 13.0.0.0
 no auto-summary
 exit-address-family
 !
```

Example 4-20 *Per-VRF RIP Configuration (Continued)*

```
 address-family ipv4 vrf GREEN
 version 2
 network 12.0.0.0
 network 13.0.0.0
 no auto-summary
 exit-address-family
!
```

Example 4-21 shows an iBGP per-VRF Configuration.

Example 4-21 *Per-VRF iBGP Configuration*

```
router bgp 100
 no synchronization
 bgp log-neighbor-changes
 no auto-summary
 !
 address-family ipv4 vrf RED
 redistribute connected
 neighbor 14.0.0.1 remote-as 100
 neighbor 14.0.0.1 update-source loopback100
 neighbor 14.0.0.1 activate
 no auto-summary
 no synchronization
 exit-address-family
 !
 address-family ipv4 vrf GREEN
 redistribute connected
 neighbor 15.0.0.1 remote-as 100
 neighbor 15.0.0.1 update-source loopback200
 neighbor 15.0.0.1 activate
 no auto-summary
 no synchronization
 exit-address-family
 !
```

Multi-Topology Routing

Multi-Topology Routing (MTR) is a recent innovation at Cisco. As the name suggests, it creates multiple routing topologies across a shared, common infrastructure. However, MTR does not try to be yet another VPN solution. Instead, it creates paths through a network that you can map to different applications or classes of applications, with the understanding that, by separating traffic in this way, you can provide better performance characteristics to certain critical applications.

MTR bases its operation on the creation of separate RIBs and FIBs for each topology. The separate RIBs and FIBs are created within a common address space. Thus, MTR creates smaller topologies that are a subset of the full topology (also known as the base topology). The main difference between MTR and a VPN technology is that, with MTR, a single address space is tailored into many topologies that could overlap; whereas VPNs create totally separate and independent address spaces.

Thus, MTR must carry out two distinct functions:

- **At the control plane**—Color the routing updates, so that the different topology RIBs are populated accordingly. Based on these RIBs, the corresponding FIBs are to be written.

- **At the forwarding plane**—Identify the topology to which each packet belongs and use the correct FIB to forward the packet.

At each hop, there will be a set of prefixes and routes in the RIB for each topology. The contents of these RIBs are dynamically updated by routing protocol colored updates. Based on this RIB information, a separate FIB is built for each topology.

To forward traffic over different topologies, the router looks for a code point in each packet and chooses an FIB based on this code point. A first implementation of MTR uses *differentiated services* (DiffServ) *code point* (DSCP) as such a code point, but other code points could be used by future implementations. The DSCP value is used as a pointer to the correct forwarding table, and the packet's destination address is used to make a forwarding decision based on the information in the topology's FIB. MTR uses the terminology of color to refer to separate topologies. So, a RED value in a packet's DSCP field is recognized by the router, which will forward the packet using the RED forwarding table (FIB).

MTR must run contiguously across a network, and the color mappings must be consistent (that is, you cannot use DSCP X as Green on one hop but as Red on the next). MTR does not allow you to double dip: If the destination route is not in the routing table of the color a packet is using, the packet can either be dropped or forwarded over the base topology—there are no lookups in "backup topologies" other than the base topology (which is equivalent to regular routing).

MTR does not change how routing works; it just runs across multiple topologies (using a single process with colored updates).

Control-Plane Virtualization Summary

Control-plane virtualization refers to adaptations made to routing protocols to be able to operate on virtualized devices. We concentrated on per-VRF routing because that is the main tool we use for design. However, VRs and LRs also run separate routing instances in a similar manner to the one shown here. In all cases, there are no changes to the protocol "on the wire." MTR is an interesting new development that can also be categorized in the virtualized control-plane bucket.

Summary

This chapter covered a lot of ground. The basic idea is that there are different levels of virtualization: device, data path, and control path. There are different constructs and protocols to implement for each of these, and, depending on the problem you need to solve, you can combine these to arrive at an overall network design.

This chapter avoided all discussion of architecture, the better to focus on protocol and implementation details. The next chapter covers hub-and-spoke and RFC 2547 architectures.

Infrastructure Segmentation Architectures: Theory

This chapter brings together the technologies introduced in Chapter 4, "A Virtualization Technologies Primer: Theory," in several architectures to deliver *virtual private network* (VPN) functionality. This chapter examines how you can use alternative protocols for the different architectures and explains the ratio of scalability and complexity of the different solutions. In other words, if Chapter 4 is about ingredients, this chapter lists recipes. We are still in the realm of theory because we are not ready to look at how different architectures best fit real-world scenarios. We do that starting in Chapter 6, "Infrastructure Segmentation Architectures: Practice." This section is a necessary preparation to understand the design trade-offs we make in the practice sections.

The chapter starts with simple hop-by-hop architectures. It then covers how you can overlay tunnels to build Layer 2 and Layer 3 VPNs, with the different solutions for pure *point-to-point* (p2p) and, where they exist, *point-to-multipoint* (p2mp), or *multipoint-multipoint* (mp2mp) setups. The chapter introduces the RFC 2547 model as an alternative to overlay topologies and again iterates through several different implementations, using *Multiprotocol Label Switching* (MPLS), obviously, but also *Layer 2 Tunnel Protocol Version 3* (L2TPv3) and *generic routing encapsulation* (GRE). We conclude with a look at architectures and solutions, some of which are fairly recent, to build hierarchies of VPNs.

One final introductory word about scale. Here, we define *scale* as the property that allows an infrastructure to efficiently support large numbers of virtual networks. Specifically, an increase in the number of virtual networks should not produce a related (linear or worse) load on the underlying infrastructure, whether that load be in terms of CPU used by the control plane, throughput used by the data plane, or time spent by the operations staff.

NOTE   This chapter discusses technology commonly used to provide VPN services. The next chapter shows how to assemble these technologies into what we refer to as Virtual Networks (VN). A VN is an end-to-end virtualized network which may rely on a combination of the technologies discusses here.

Hop to Hop

Hop to hop (h2h) is a naive VPN architecture in which every node is a member of all virtualized networks. Consider the example of VLANs. To have complete networkwide reachability, whereby any end station can be part of any VLAN, all switches on the network must be part of all the VLANs. In terms of topology, h2h is a form of p2p network with no overlay capability.

Consider the classic example of a switched enterprise network with three departments: marketing, engineering, and sales. End-user populations are physically interspersed, so, horrifying though this would be in practice for both parties, an engineer and marketing expert might sit next to each other. Site policy dictates that users are allowed to send traffic only to other members of their group. In practical terms, this means that every access switch must be able to place any of its ports into the marketing, engineering, or sales VLANs (assume VLAN membership is statically configured). In an h2h architecture, the VLANS would span across the network, and every switch would be a simple Layer 2 device running *Spanning Tree Protocol* (STP), as shown in Figure 5-1.

Figure 5-1 *Layer 2 H2H Design*

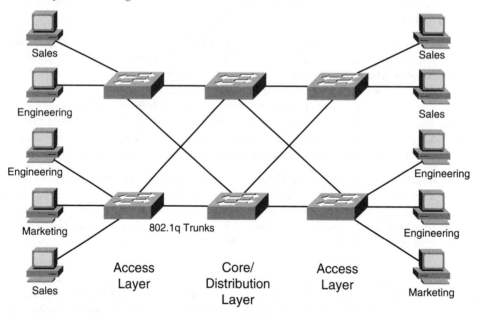

The complexity of this scenario relates to two factors, one of which is implementation dependent; the other is inherent to the architecture. The implementation limitation is running STP across a network. Unless the network is small, STP has well-known convergence limitations that make it a suboptimal protocol to calculate paths across large networks. It will work, but there is a better way!

You could argue that STP can be enhanced (and it can be: *Per VLAN Spanning Tree Plus* [PVST+], *Rapid Spanning Tree Protocol* [RSTP, 802.1w], and so forth prove this fact). With enhancement, the architecture itself is viable. There is some truth to this argument, but this sort of design does have limitations.

In our design, we are building a VPN, with a core network, which is switched Ethernet based, and customer sites, each of which has just one user. The location of sites is unpredictable and impermanent: Users are told where to sit and can be told to move (not by the networking department).

The automatic response for most readers is, probably, that naive h2h designs "do not scale." Why not? In our VPN scenario, the core network is correlated to the customer groups and sites. Each switch must run three instances of STP, one for every group. If the number of groups increases, so does the load on every switch. Note that this load is on both the control and data planes. Breaking this link is one of the keys to creating scalable VPN designs.

NOTE   The term *core* here refers to the set of network devices that make up the shared, virtualized infrastructure over which you run private networks.

Provisioning complexity is another fundamental component of scale. We can break this down into three simple questions:

- How hard is it to add a new group?
- How hard is it to add a new customer site?
- How hard is it to add a new core device?

The VLAN-based h2h design does well on some of these and badly on others. Most obviously, in the absence of protocol support (eg. VTP), adding a new group is painful because you must configure every device in the core network (remember, user location is unpredictable, so this means every device, not just devices that currently connect members of the new group).

Adding a new site, however, is simple. A single, simple command sets the port in a new VLAN. The new user can send traffic almost instantly (if the switch uses the Cisco PortFast feature).

Adding a new core switch is operationally easy, but computationally expensive because of the nature of the control-plane protocol we are using. To add a new device, just create the appropriate VLANs on the appropriate ports (or trunks) and connect them, whereupon every switch will rerun its spanning-tree calculation to compute the optimum layer path for the new topology.

In real networks, VPNs are often not so private. Groups do need to communicate, either directly or to the same destination (e-mail servers, the Internet). An issue with Layer 2 h2h design is that users are locked into their VPN, so marketing, engineering, and sales cannot communicate. Although you might think this is the ultimate productivity enhancer, it would probably have detrimental long-term effects for the company in question. There are practical answers, of course, such as running applications on multihosted servers and using *Network Address Translation* (NAT) to access the Internet, but the network solution itself is rigid.

Layer 3 H2H

The next scenario is to replace the control-plane protocol in our design and use a Layer 3 h2h solution. This time, each core node runs IP and some form of routing protocol and maintains address space virtualization using *VPN routing and forwarding instances* (VRFs).

NOTE   A hybrid solution is possible, with a Layer 2 access and Layer 3 distribution mapping VLANs to VRFs. The point of interest for us is how the introduction of Layer 3 addresses the scalability concerns mentioned in the previous section.

As Figure 5-2 shows, the data path still uses VLANs. We are just removing end-to-end spanning tree from the network. The choice of routing protocol is determined by the usual trade-offs; in practice, the network would probably run the *Open Shortest Path First* (OSPF) Protocol or *Enhanced Interior Gateway Routing Protocol* (EIGRP). Note that per-VRF support for the routing protocol implementation is a requirement for this solution.

Figure 5-2   *Layer 3 H2H Design*

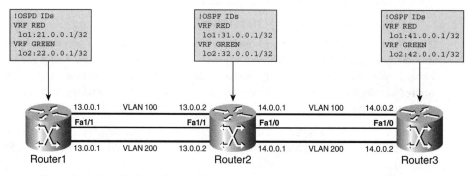

From the point of view of scale, this is the same architecture as the Layer 2 h2h design. The difference is that the control protocol is known to be robust and to work exceptionally well in large networks.

What we gain in control protocol performance, we pay for in operational complexity, however. Adding a new site is still straightforward, even if there are a couple of extra instructions to put the interface into a VRF (rather than a VLAN). Each VRF needs its own dedicated path to reach neighbors. Figure 5-2 uses VLANs to connect VRFs, but any type of tunnel would work (GRE is another simple-to-use choice).

However, configuring a new routed node is more involved than adding a new Ethernet switch. You must correctly configure the routing protocol, advertise the right networks in the right way, make sure you have routes for the *router processor* (RP) adjacencies to form, and so forth. If your network is big enough (and that does not have to be large), the added provisioning complexity is compensated for by the greater scaling characteristics of IP's control plane.

No law states that you must configure a routing protocol. Static routing brings a certain set of benefits all by itself (no STP, for example) and, in a real-world design, you can constrain the provisioning complexity with an outer layer of static routing (on the access switches, for example—which we recommend) and routing protocols running on a set of nodes that change little (distribution and core).

Adding a new user group is equally as painful for the Layer 2 scenario. Every node must be configured with the new VRF. The routing protocol must be updated with a new address family for the VRF, as discussed in Chapter 4.

Despite all these limitations, consider the advantage of the h2h design:

- From a data-plane perspective, both the h2h designs are efficient. A set of links exists for every VPN, and traffic from one site to another can use the shortest path to get there.

- The shortest path is calculated automatically.

- You can load balance traffic across equal-cost links or use policy-based routing to create paths manually.

- You have automatic recovery in case of a link failure (if there is another path, the control plane will find it) and, as of recently, you can achieve some pretty impressive reconvergence times (subsecond in the case of OSPF and EIGRP) that make the overall solution robust.

The Layer 3 h2h design also supports hierarchy well. Therefore, you do not have to build a full mesh of physical or logical links between all the CE devices (which is another way to describe the access layer). The control plane calculates the best paths no matter what topology it has to work with. This is true of the Layer 2 design, but it is just more scalable to run OSPF, for example, across a large, complex topology than it is to use STP.

Finally, our Layer 3 h2h also has correlated core/user space. Increasing the number of groups increases the load on all the core devices. One suspects that there must be a better alternative.

Single Address Space Alternatives

At this point, you might be somewhat frustrated by our intransigent obsession with overlapping address spaces. Although support for overlapping address spaces is a fundamental characteristic of a VPN and a generic requirement of virtualized infrastructure, it is not true that all enterprise networks have addresses that overlap across user groups. If we lift this mandate temporarily, what, if any, are the design alternatives that emerge?

Within a single address space, the role of the virtualized network is simply to stop user traffic from going where it should not go. The mechanisms to do this are well known, as follows:

- **Access control lists (ACLs)**—Figure 5-3 shows how to use ACLs to build a VPN. The network must establish a logical perimeter where packets are checked against group membership policy to see whether they are intended for an allowed destination. If not, the packets are dropped. The security perimeter is logical because it does not have to be implemented on the physical edge of the network. You can use VLAN separation at the access layer and implement ACLs at the distribution layer (or centralized in the data center). The ACLs must identify and permit all legitimate flows, which, in many cases, results in impractically long and complex rules. The simpler the network addressing plan and the simpler the traffic patterns, the more realistic this approach becomes.

- **Policy-based routing (PBR)**—PBR enables you to statically route packets based on criteria such as incoming interface. You could apply different PBR rules to ingress interfaces to forward only to the egress interfaces that belong to the same group. This is essentially global static routing, where the network administrator is responsible for coming up with an efficient and coherent set of rules that allow complete intra-group reachability but that forbid inter-group exchanges. Much like for ACLs, with all but the simplest topology, PBR-based VPNs can become overly complex to use in practice. In real-world scenarios, PBR is often combined with ACLs to provide a complete virtual network solution.

Figure 5-3   *ACL-Based Solution*

```
Int vlan Blue                              ...Continued for any other applicable services
ip address BlueIP                          permit tcp 10.1.250.0 0.0.0.255 10.1.6.1 eq ftp-data
!Helper in DMZ for DHCP                     permit tcp 10.1.250.0 0.0.0.255 host 10.1.7.1 eq 443
Ip address 192.168.1.1                      permit tcp 10.1.250.0 0.0.0.255 host 10.1.8.1 eq 22
Ip access-group BlueACL in                  permit tcp 10.1.250.0 0.0.0.255 host 10.1.9.1 eq 80
! Permit DHCP                               deny icmp any any log
deny tcp any any eq domain                  deny tcp any any eq ident
permit tcp any any established              deny tcp any any eq bgp
permit igmp any any                         ! Permit source address of Blue VLAN for DMZ subnet
deny ip 127.0.0.0 0.255.255.255 any log     permit ip 10.1.250.0 0.0.0.255 192.168.1.0 0.0.0.255
permit icmp 10.1.250..0 0.0.0.255 192.168.3.0   deny ip any any log
0.0.0.255
permit udp host 192.168.5.1 10.1.250.0 0.0.0.255
eq isakmp
permit esp host 10.1.250.0 0.0.0.255 host 192.168.5.1
permit tcp 10.1.250.0 0.0.0.255 host 10.1.6.1 eq ftp
```

Subnet Blue

Subnet Red

- **Constrained routing**—It is common to run some form of path selection on WAN interfaces, either because there are multiple paths to a remote destination or because a site is multihomed with several *Internet service providers* (ISPs) for its Internet access. Both *Border Gateway Protocol* (BGP) and *Optimized Exit Routing* (OER) are two technologies that enable path selection. BGP has the added benefit of allowing a router to decide whether to install a path based on a flexible set of policies.

- **Multi Topology Routing (MTR)**—Although not designed as a VPN solution, you can use MTR to create user groups and enforce traffic separation. Either the access layer or the distribution layer must set an appropriate *differentiated services code* point (DSCP) value for IP packets, based on source port or VLAN interface. Then the core would have different Layer 3 topologies for each group, and packets from group A would not be routed to an end station in group B. As a reminder, Chapter 4 briefly introduced MTR.

With the exception of MTR, neither of the two other solutions have pleasing characteristics of scale or operational simplicity. However, centralizing policy enforcement is hugely useful and is one of the major drivers for virtualizing networks. The ACL solution shown here is just insufficient, except in cases of extremely simple group membership and group topology.

H2H Summary

Although there are definite scalability limitations, with the right design requirements and with the right control plane, h2h architectures do solve legitimate problems. They are a good fit for simple and small networks where their provisioning complexity is tolerable enough for the benefits of the design to be realized.

H2h design, in the form of combined Layer 2 access and Layer 3 access distribution and core design (which we reviewed in Chapter 3) has worked extremely well in enterprise networks. Unfortunately, virtualization creates design requirements and scaling limitations that are often better solved using alternative architectures.

Tunnel Overlay for L3VPN

The tunnel overlay architecture has been in use in WANs for quite some time. Typically, GRE or IPsec is used to connect private networks together over a public infrastructure.

Tunnel-based solutions sometimes get bad press for being unscalable, or operationally complex, but this is unfair. With a correctly defined problem, tunnels often represent an excellent answer. Scalability issues can arise if you use p2p links—which is what a tunnel is—to build multipoint connectivity, which is what a LAN offers. With that caveat firmly in mind, we look first at p2p and then p2mp alternatives for Layer 3 connectivity. The next section uses the same approach to look at Layer 2 connectivity (for data center-to-data center clustering, for example).

L3VPN Using GRE and IPsec Overlay

The basic topology for a tunnel-based Layer 3 VPN is to use a hub-and-spoke architecture. In its most simple expression, such a network has a single, central site, called a *hub,* to which are connected all the other sites in the network, called spokes. The name comes from an analogy with a wheel: a single point that connects all the others.

The advantage of hub-and-spoke architecture is that the operation of the spoke routers is simple. All their traffic is forwarded to the hub router, and they use a straightforward default route. The hub must route traffic back to the correct site and announce the site addresses to the rest of the network. As long as there is some degree of flexibility in the network address plan, the hub router can aggregate the prefixes used on the site networks.

Provisioning is equally simple. The configuration is almost identical on each spoke router, with IP addresses and passwords (possibly) differing from one site to the next. It is easy to automate the setup and bulk provision many such devices quickly.

The GRE and IPsec solution uses GRE p2p tunnels between *customer premises equipment* (CPE) devices and encrypts the GRE packet with IPsec. This combination enables you to use GRE over public networks. The GRE implementation enables you to run multicast, routing protocols, or even carry non-IP traffic between sites, but by itself offers no security whatsoever. Adding IPsec to the hub-and-spoke architecture solves the security issue but adds a little more complexity to the overall picture:

- An IPsec control channel sits (*Internet Key Exchange* [IKE], which was discussed in Chapter 4) between the hub and every spoke.

- The configuration needs all the commands for security associations that encrypt the GRE packet flow (recent Cisco IOS Software improvements have made this much simpler to configure than before).

The combination of GRE and IPsec is so common that Cisco IOS configurations use a special command to enable encryption directly on the GRE tunnel interface itself. Example 5-1 shows such a configuration, in which the HUB-VPN crypto map is applied to the tunnel interface. You do not need to define an ACL that matches the local and remote addresses and IPsec protocol type (or ports); the router does this automatically, which is convenient.

Example 5-1 *GRE and IPsec Tunnel Configuration*

```
crypto dynamic-map VPN 1
set transform-set ONE
!
!
crypto map HUB-VPN 1 ipsec-isakmp dynamic VPN
!
interface Tunnel0
description VPN to Spoke1
ip address 192.168.1.1 255.255.255.252
tunnel source Serial0/0
tunnel destination 10.0.2.11
crypto map HUB-VPN
```

Note how the Comment field in Example 5-1 refers to Spoke1. This touches on one of the major drawbacks of simple hub-and-spoke networks, at least with GRE+IPsec. The hub must have a different tunnel interface for every spoke. Add a new spoke and you must also configure the hub router. Not only does this add a provisioning step, but the hub configuration file can grow to be large, which has never been known to improve the troubleshooting experience.

The gravity of the other main limitation of this architecture depends on the network traffic patterns. If spoke traffic naturally flows to the hub, which provides Internet access for an enterprise, for example, or houses the main data center, such a centralized network makes perfect sense. If there is traffic between the spokes, the topology is inefficient because inter-spoke traffic still goes through the hub router, creating an obvious bottleneck.

In fact, high-throughput networks, even one where the traffic does flow to a main site, can also pose problems because the overall network throughput is limited by either the performance of the hub router (which is not usually an absolute limitation—you can buy fast routers) or by the interface speeds on the hub, either on the ingress or egress sides. If you do have a bottleneck, the workaround is obvious: Use multiple hub routers and load balance sites between them. The simple network in Figure 5-4 has two branch sites connected to a main site, with two hub routers. The main site provides Internet connectivity for the branch sites.

Figure 5-4   *GRE+IPsec Topology with Redundant Hub Routers*

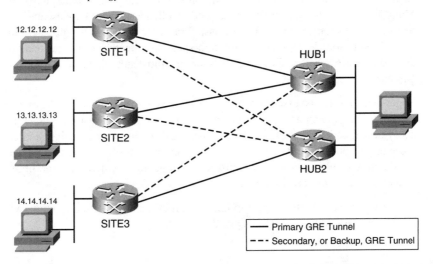

The topology of Figure 5-4 also introduces a degree of resiliency to the design that was missing in the single-hub scenario. If Hub-1 experiences a problem, traffic from Spoke-1 can be diverted to Hub-2. If the problematic device liberates itself of whatever issue was preventing it from forwarding traffic and comes back on line, the original path from Spoke-1 to Hub-2 can be restored.

Now we have introduced both robustness and complexity to the network. The most common way to fail over between GRE tunnels is to use routing protocols to detect when a tunnel goes down and use an alternative path, if there is one. Because of the way GRE tunnels are implemented in Cisco routers, you must statically configure tunnels to both hubs to do this and then make the backup path have a higher routing cost than the main one. Convergence times will not be subsecond, but the advantages of a backup path are clear.

You might wonder whether it is possible to use IKE to manage remote endpoint availability. It is true that if Hub-1 were to fail, the IKE session on Spoke-1 would go down, probably well before the routing protocol between the two devices decides, after timeouts and retransmissions, that the path is unavailable. If the router implementation supports it, this is a viable alternative method to manage tunnel redundancy and failover.

Referring back to Figure 5-4, because GRE tunnels never go down, another alternative is to use per-flow load balancing between, for example, Spoke-1 and both hubs. The economics of your network service would determine whether this is cost-effective. If you can use the second tunnel with no additional cost (because it goes over a public network for example), all is well. If it is a managed service with per-tunnel usage pricing, this might not be such a reasonable idea.

The routing in the hub site is also that much more involved because the core network must deliver the right packets to the right hub router, so there is less opportunity to aggregate prefixes.

However, the difficulty of deploying a hub-and-spoke topology should not be exaggerated. Many WANs use this sort of design perfectly well, and it should not escape your attention that the architecture is identical to a classic Frame Relay VPN, using p2p circuits between sites. The question is whether the hub-and-spoke architecture is the most suitable architecture and whether GRE and IPsec are the most suitable protocols for other connection scenarios.

Some of the issues discussed here are linked to the choice of protocols: the extra complexity of using IPsec, the reliance on routing protocols for GRE resiliency, separate interfaces for every tunnel on hub routers, and so on. Using a different protocol might address some of these issues, but it would certainly introduce another set of problems. In all cases, the architecture would remain a hub-and-spoke architecture, which is a good fit in some scenarios and a poor one in others.

The next section discusses a multipoint version of the GRE+IPsec solution, which addresses many of the limitations just discussed.

Putting It All Together: DMVPN

Dynamic multipoint VPN (DMVPN) is a solution that combines *multipoint GRE* (mGRE) and IPsec. Recall from Chapter 4 that mGRE is a p2mp implementation, in which every spoke router has a tunnel interface to reach the hub. The hub has a single interface for all the GRE tunnels. Example 5-2 shows the hub mGRE configuration, which you should compare to the standard configuration of Example 5-1.

Example 5-2 *mGRE Hub Router Configuration*

```
interface Tunnel0
 description VPN to Sites
 ip address 192.168.1.1 255.255.255.0
 no ip redirects
 ip nhrp map multicast dynamic
 ip nhrp network-id 1007
 ip nhrp holdtime 600
 ip nhrp server-only
 no ip split-horizon eigrp 302
 tunnel source Serial0/0
 tunnel mode gre multipoint
tunnel key 1007
```

The first advantage of mGRE is already clear from the example. The hub configuration has become extremely simple, with only a single static tunnel interface to worry about.

The second advantage comes from mGRE's capability to dynamically provision tunnels. If two spoke sites need to communicate, the first packet is sent to the hub along with a *Next Hop Routing Protocol* (NHRP) request for the site's IP address. When the site CPE receives the NHRP reply, it builds a tunnel directly to the destination router. Figure 5-5 shows an mGRE network with two dynamic tunnels between the spoke routers and the permanent GRE tunnels to the hub router.

Figure 5-5 *mGRE Operation*

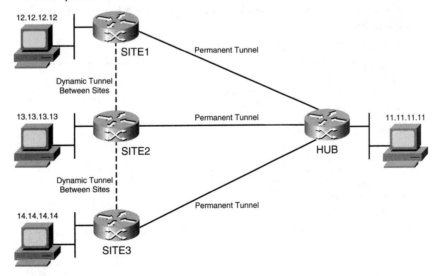

The mGRE solution still uses the same protocol stack as "simple" GRE—so the data plane does not change. Inter-site tunnels exist now, where there were none before, and you can now use NHRP to manage tunnel setup.

If your network requirements do not require strong security protection, you can deploy a DMVPN just using mGRE. Otherwise, the next layer in the DMVPN cake is IPsec. Example 5-3 shows the hub configuration with IPsec enabled. Just as for GRE+IPsec, a single command is all that is required to encrypt all the GRE tunnels that are created from this mGRE interface.

Example 5-3 *Hub DMVPN Interface Configuration*

```
interface Tunnel0
  description VPN to all Sites
  ip address 192.168.1.1 255.255.255.0
  no ip redirects
  ip nhrp map multicast dynamic
  ip nhrp network-id 1007
  ip nhrp holdtime 600
  ip nhrp server-only
  no ip split-horizon eigrp 302
  no ip split-horizon
  tunnel source Ethernet0/0
  tunnel mode gre multipoint
  tunnel key 200
 tunnel protection ipsec profile MVPN
```

The "MVPN profile" in the example refers to an IPsec crypto map, which, in this case, has the exact same instructions as the VPN crypto map of Example 5-1. The spoke routers use the same **tunnel profile** command. Example 5-4 has a typical site router configuration.

Example 5-4 *Spoke Router DMVPN Configuration*

```
interface Tunnel0
  description VPN to HUB
  ip address 192.168.1.2 255.255.255.0
  no ip redirects
  ip nhrp map 192.168.1.1 10.0.1.11
  ip nhrp map multicast 10.0.1.11
  ip nhrp network-id 1007
  ip nhrp nhs 192.168.1.1
  no ip split-horizon
  tunnel source Ethernet0/0
  tunnel mode gre multipoint
  tunnel key 200
 tunnel protection ipsec profile MVPN
```

Creating encrypted tunnels dynamically has an interesting implication for the security of this architecture. Obviously, the cryptographic credentials used by hubs and spokes must match. For example, Examples 5-3 and 5-4 must both use the same tunnel key value. However, all the IPsec security associations shown so far require the peer IP address to be configured in a router's crypto map. With DMVPN, it is not possible to know in advance which router will create a tunnel to a particular spoke or hub. The alternative is either to statically list every possible IP address, which is cumbersome, or to allow any IP address to begin an incoming IPsec session. DMVPN uses the second alternative, which removes a layer of protection in that you cannot limit who connects to a router. However, an IPsec session is established only if the peer device has the correct security credentials. Example 5-5 shows the spoke router IPsec configuration. Note the wildcard addressing in the IKE security association. The hub has something similar.

Example 5-5   *Spoke DMVPN IPsec Configuration*

```
!
crypto isakmp policy 1
 authentication pre-share
crypto isakmp key secret address 0.0.0.0 0.0.0.0
!
!
crypto ipsec transform-set ONE ah-md5-hmac esp-des
!
crypto ipsec profile MVPN
set transform-set ONE
```

Layer 3 Tunnel Summary

A network built using Layer 3 tunnels to connect IP networks has the same architectural characteristics as a network built using traditional Layer 2 circuits. The IPsec and GRE combination are widely used as a WAN solution. Resiliency and load balancing are possible using a routing protocol control plane.

DMVPN is a multipoint variation of standard hub-and-spoke architecture. The biggest advantage of using mGRE is that inter-spoke traffic does not have to go through a hub router. In addition, the configuration files are short and simple, excellent qualities in any router. You might argue that DMVPN slightly lowers the security threshold that one usually gains with IPsec because you must allow any remote router to try to begin a session, but DMVPN supports strong encryption and authentication—either certificates or shared secrets can be used to authenticate peers. DMVPN has essentially the same resiliency characteristics as standard hub-and-spoke architectures because a predefined hub router must be available for the design to function and because you need to use an additional control plane to manage primary hub selection.

Tunnel Overlay for Layer 2 VPNs

A Layer 3 VPN might not be an adequate solution for an enterprise network for several reasons, including the following:

- An enterprise might use legacy applications that rely on protocols that cannot be natively transported at Layer 3. A Layer 2 VPN is a good way of letting the rest of the network move to IP by isolating the legacy components.

- A second example is the desire to avoid deploying routers at sites where there had been none before. A Layer 2 VPN avoids this extra cost.

- Some applications are not tolerant of the latency characteristics of a Layer 3 network and need Layer 2 transport (for example, for cluster computation message exchange or data center replication).

Layer 2 VPNs offer an alternative approach. Their defining characteristic is that they transport Layer 2 (typically Ethernet but also ATM and Frame Relay) frames between sites. This is both a good and bad thing. The benefit comes from the fact that a Layer 2 VPN is agnostic about the higher-layer protocols used on the network and is less demanding of the devices placed at the edge of the LANs. The disadvantage is the absence of a Layer 3 control plane to manage reachability and segment broadcast domains across the VPN.

In many enterprise scenarios, the CPE are Ethernet switches and, obviously, any broadcasts generated on one site network must be transported to all other sites. Just like with any other VPN, a forward-looking network administrator would want redundant paths between sites. In a Layer 3 VPN, we can use sophisticated routing protocols to manage multiple paths. In an Ethernet Layer 2 VPN, we have . . . STP.

You can build Layer 2 VPNs using p2p and multipoint topologies. Because of the scalability characteristics outlined previously, it is much simpler to build p2p topologies than to create a multi-access network across a wide-area infrastructure.

The next two sections look at alternative p2p implementations, first using L2TPv3 and then using MPLS. Then we look at a multipoint solution for Ethernet, called *Virtual Private LAN Services* (VPLS). In both cases, the Layer 2 service is delivered over a Layer 3 core network.

Layer 2 P2P Overlay Using L2TPv3

An L2TPv3-based Layer 2 VPN uses p2p pseudowires between *customer located equipment* (CLE) to transport Layer 2 frames between switches. The Layer 2 frames can be 802.1q, Frame Relay, ATM, or *High-Level Data Link Control* (HDLC). The *customer edge* (CE) router is a switch, and the *provider edge* (PE) router is an L2TPv3 device.

Figure 5-6 shows L2TPv3 tunnels used to build a hub-and-spoke network. Site 3 is the hub. Sites 1, 2, and 4 are spokes. An L2TPv3 control channel sits between every hub-spoke pair, which peer routers use to negotiate unique session and cookie IDs for each VLAN or port bound to the L2TPv3 tunnel. Very advantageously, the VPN and its topology is totally transparent to the CLE, which has exactly the same configuration on a LAN with a direct physical link to its Layer 2 next hop.

Figure 5-6   *L2TPv3 Overlay Network*

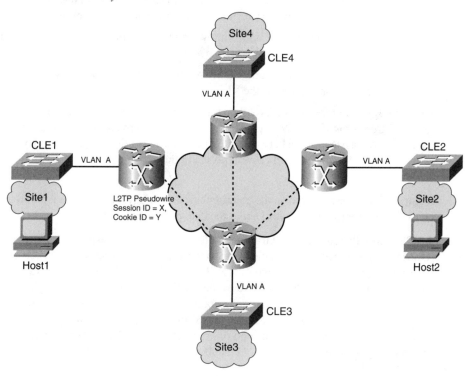

The CLE in the network in Figure 5-6 runs a spanning tree across the VPN. Note that some commercial Layer 2 VPN services are not *bridge protocol data unit* (BPDU) transparent, so a spanning tree cannot run across the WAN links.

The L2TPv3 core network, which runs IP, provides path redundancy between sites. If the core can reconverge quickly enough, a tunnel could even change its path without dropping sessions. In any event, the customer STP does not need to calculate alternative paths across the VPN—the L2TPv3 transport handles this.

The Layer 3 overlays presented previously in this chapter used the IP control plane to create a hub-and-spoke topology. Spokes have default routes to the hub, which has routes for each prefix used at the different spoke sites. Most Layer 2 protocols do not work like that. Ethernet, for example, expects to be able to flood packets to all peers. No mechanism at either the Ethernet layer (nor in L2TPv3) enables the creation of a hierarchy without using address learning (and flooding) between switches.

Consider again Figure 5-6 and suppose that Host1 on Site 1 needs to reach Host2 on Site 2. These sites are connected through Site 3. Both hosts are in VLAN A, which is also configured on Site 4.

- When Host1 sends its *Address Resolution Protocol* (ARP) request, this is broadcast to all sites on the VLAN, and so all the switches create an entry in their mac-address table to map the respective MAC addresses to the correct port (pseudowire).

- Host 2 sends a unicast reply, which allows the Site 1 switch to update its mac-address table with that information, too.

- When another host on the same VLAN sends data, the same process happens, with flooding and learning across the VLAN.

The topology in Figure 5-6 has no loops for STP to contend with, and you could disable spanning tree across the VPN links. However, if there were redundant links between CLE devices—a pseudowire between Sites 1 and 2, for example—STP would be required to disable one of the trunk ports (trunk ports are those that connect the CLE to the WAN).

So far, we have concentrated on the control plane across Layer 2 VPNs, but, before moving on to the next topic, a quick word about the data plane is in order.

A VPN is usually required to be transparent to the protocol it transports. *Quality of service* (QoS) settings, signaling information, and so forth should be preserved as packets or frames go from one place to the next. The L2TPv3 RFCs, discussed in Chapter 4, define encapsulation rules that allow peers to exchange Ethernet frames. For example, the *cyclic redundancy check* (CRC) field is removed before the frame enters the pseudowire and is recalculated at egress. *Type of Service* (TOS) bit settings are not changed. Other encapsulation rules enable the transport of Frame Relay (or ATM and so on) and define how to carry congestion notification and *Local Management Interface* (LMI) signaling.

Layer 2 P2P Overlay Using MPLS

MPLS offers an alternative way to build up Layer 2 VPNs.

MPLS *link switched paths* (LSPs) are also p2p tunnels where labels rather than session IDs are used to multiplex user traffic on trunk interfaces. In a way, that is analogous to the L2TPv3 scenario, an MPLS-based Layer 2 VPN, which is shown in Figure 5-7, uses a control-plane protocol to exchange label values for user VLANs or ports that are bound to pseudowires (yes, it is the same term as L2TPv3, which borrowed it from MPLS) on PE routers.

Figure 5-7   *MPLS-Based Layer 2 VPN*

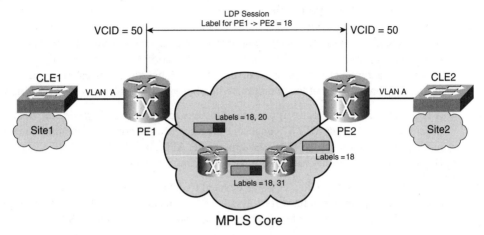

MPLS Core

To understand how MPLS Layer 2 VPNs work, there are two questions to answer here:

- How are labels exchanged between PE routers?
- How are packets forwarded across the core?

Label exchange is implementation dependent. Most vendors use directed *Label Distribution Protocol* (LDP), but at least one uses BGP. Chapter 4 explained that labels have link local (or device local) significance, and different label values are used by each *link switching router* (LSR) along an LSP. The LDP runs between each LSR to announce prefix-to-label mappings. In a Layer 2 VPN, a LDP session runs directly between PE routers. LDP was chosen over other signaling protocols used in MPLS networks (BGP, *Resource Reservation Protocol* [RSVP]) because it is well suited to p2p setup and the majority of Layer 2 VPN deployments use a p2p topology.

When an interface is bound to a pseudowire, the PE creates a label value for that port (or VLAN) and sends it to the remote PE. On Cisco devices, the remote PE address is configured with the xconnect statement introduced in Chapter 4.

LSPs are unidirectional, so there can be different label values at either end of a pseudowire for a particular VLAN. Compare this to L2TPv3, which negotiates a common session and cookie ID.

NOTE   Without wanting to start a "my protocol is best" debate, there are other differences between the two protocols. For example, the session+cookie address space is much bigger than the 20-bit label space, which makes spoofing that much harder. L2TP has its own control plane, which it can use to set up and tear down sessions according to traffic needs, and which can list failover destinations for tunnels. MPLS uses the IP control plane, and the cost of maintaining a LSP is essentially nothing, so there is not much need to remove labels until and unless the prefix (or Layer 2 port) is no longer reachable.

When a frame is received on a PE, it is encapsulated in MPLS, and the label value that identifies the VLAN or port on the remote PE is imposed on the label stack. But this is not enough. The next-hop LSR expects a label that identifies the *Forwarding Equivalence Class* (FEC) classification for this packet, and that lets it find the outgoing label in its *LSP forwarding information base* (LFIB). Therefore, a second label, corresponding to the IP address of the remote PE, is pushed onto the packet's label stack. This label will be swapped at each hop and popped at the penultimate hop before the packet exits the MPLS network.

A large set of RFCs, collectively and affectionately referred to as *draft-martini*, defines the different "Layer x over MPLS" encapsulation rules and the control-plane functionality required to transport Frame Relay, Ethernet, PPP, ATM, or HDLC over MPLS networks. However, interoperability issues still exist between vendors.

A significant portion of Chapter 4 was devoted to device virtualization, so it is natural to ask how devices are virtualized for Layer 2 VPNs. The answer (for Ethernet) is simple: VLANs. The LSPs or L2TP tunnels behave like interfaces bound to an 802.1q VLAN.

NOTE   The hub-and-spoke scenarios had no device virtualization when using a single address space. If each site has multiple virtual networks, however, each tunnel can be bound to VRFs.

Ethernet Layer 2 VPN services are commercialized using service definitions based on definitions made by the Metro Ethernet Forum. These include variations on p2p, such as Ethernet Relay and Ethernet Wire services. One has full Layer 2 transparency (and therefore carries BPDUs, for example), whereas the other only transports data frames. Some service descriptions are intended for router CPE, others for bridges. Interested readers are directed to the Metro Ethernet Forum website for more information (http://www.metroethernetforum.org/).

Layer 2 VPN MP2MP Using MPLS (VPLS)

We already touched on VPLS to introduce the concept of *VPN forwarding instances* (VFIs) in Chapter 4. From an architecture perspective, VPLS uses a full mesh of p2p MPLS pseudowires to emulate an Ethernet switch.

Service providers have long wanted a value-added service to connect the countless Ethernet segments on customer networks. The ideal solution allows a customer to plug any Ethernet device into a WAN port and the service provider network then transparently forwards frames to their destination. Commercial offerings based on ATM exist, often called something like Transparent LAN service. Managed multipoint Layer 2 VPN services have not succeeded in becoming universal.

Some inherent properties of Ethernet are a real challenge to duplicate using a p2p infrastructure. VPLS—which is a mp2mp service built on top of p2p pseudowires—tries to mitigate these in the following way:

- **Auto-provisioning**—Devices can be added to an Ethernet network without any prior configuration. VPLS implements auto-provisioning much like an Ethernet switch does. Every new MAC address is flooded on all pseudowires in a *virtual switch interface* (VSI). The ARP reply information is used to create an entry on the PE to map a MAC address to a pseudowire.

- **Auto-discovery**—In the context of a VPN, the problem is to provide a mechanism for every PE to discover its VLAN "peers." The standard proposals for VPLS have not yet addressed auto-discovery. One vendor's implementation uses BGP (draft-kompella) to announce VLAN membership between PEs. Other ideas include doing a lookup in a central repository using RADIUS or *Domain Name System* (DNS) protocols.

- **Multicast support**—Multicast and broadcast are treated in the same way: Frames are flooded across all pseudowires.

Some of the other issues that arise with VPLS relate to scale. A full mesh of connections is expensive, of course, but many WAN traffic patterns are still client/server in nature, for which hub-and-spoke topologies can be a better fit.

In addition, Ethernet addresses cannot be aggregated. Every address on the LAN must be stored in a VFI table, which can place an obvious strain on PE memory. Using a router as the CPE can help mitigate this problem because only the router addresses need to be advertised across the VPLS network—but this approach invites the question of why not use a Layer 3 VPN service in the first place.

Layer 2 VPN Summary

This section showed how you can use L2TPv3 and MPLS to build p2p Layer 2 VPNs across a Layer 3 network. Regardless of the protocol, the architecture is the same. Managing loops and redundant paths is more challenging than in an equivalent p2p Layer 3 VPN because of well-understood characteristics of the Layer 2 control plane. Both protocol- and implementation-related details affect how Layer 2 protocols are carried across the Layer 3 cloud (these are often arcane, but exist nevertheless).

VPLS is a Layer 2 mp2mp architecture that emulates an Ethernet switch, using a full mesh of Layer 2 pseudowires, all which run over an MPLS network (with its IP control plane). VPLS, like *LAN Emulation* (LANE) before it, often *appears* compelling because of the attractiveness of any-to-any reachability offered by the service.

However, VPLS is a complex beast and, in our opinion, Layer 3 VPNs offer a much more scalable and robust solution that similarly moves the burden of routing from the CE into the provider network. When true Layer 2 connectivity is required, a sparse mesh of p2p circuits is often enough for most designs.

Peer-Based Model for Layer 3 VPNs

Almost all the VPN architectures that we have looked at so far have a trait in common: They all use an overlay model. CPE devices peer each other, oblivious to the fact that all their control- and data-plane traffic is tunneled across a network.

The architecture used by the VPNs that we examine in this section differs. It was first proposed in RFC 2547 and is often referred to with this moniker. The major difference is that CE and PE routers form a peer relationship. PE routers use *Multiprotocol BGP* (MP-BGP) to exchange customer route information.

In a Layer 3 scenario, this greatly reduces the routing complexity on the CE routers (which is the value of such a service to a customer). Now, the PE is the next hop for every CE. Figure 5-8 shows the peer relationship at the edge of the network. Compared to pure overlay solutions, the PE has more work to do. The details will become clearer as you proceed through this section.

Figure 5-8 *RFC 2547 Control-Plane Interaction*

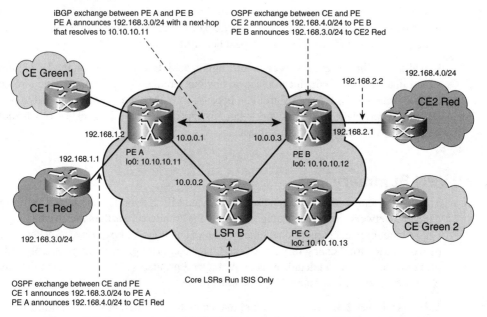

Figure 5-8 shows a simple RFC 2547 network with two VPNs connected over a core network. The RED network has two sites, which use 192.168.3.0/24 and 192.168.4.0/24. The VPN must connect these together.

PE A and PE B peer with CE1 and CE2, respectively, and use OSPF to exchange routes. CE1 advertises 192.168.3.0/24, and CE2 advertises 192.168.4.0/24 over the dedicated link that connects to the PE router. When the routing protocols over the VPN connection converge, a **show ip route** command on CE2 will show 192.168.3.0/24 with a next hop of 192.168.2.1, which is an address on PE B.

Note that the CE-PE links are part of the customer address space.

When PE A receives an OSPF update from CE 1, it first stores the route in the RED VRF table. PE A has MP-BGP sessions open with PE B and PE C (only the first of these is shown in Figure 5-8). To provide Layer 3 reachability across the network core, the PEs must advertise customer routes to each other. Thus, for the RED VPN, PE A announces reachability information for prefix 192.168.3.0/24 to PE B, but in a modified form called a VPNv4 address. PE A also received route updates from its peers. In this case, it will learn that 192.168.4.0 is reachable through 10.10.10.12 (PE B's loopback address).

The BGP *Network Layer Reachability Information* (NLRI) exchange has important additional attributes, too, most notably the following:

- VPNv4 address (8 + 4 bytes): 1:1:192.168.3.0/24 with next hop of 10.10.10.11
- Route target (RT, 7 bytes)
- VPN label (3 bytes)

Now we will review each of the items announced with MP-BGP.

RFC 2547 provides address separation between VPNs by using VRFs on PE routers, dedicated interfaces between CE and PE, and by creating an extended VPNv4 address space across the core network. VPNv4 addresses are created by concatenating a *route distinguisher* (RD) with the customer route prefixes. Every VPN must have different RDs (note that there can be more than one RD). PEs store customer IPv4 routes in VRF tables and exchange corresponding VPNv4 routers with other PEs. A traffic analyzer would see only VPNv4 data in the *internal BGP* (iBGP) packets. Each PE is configured so as to map an RD to every VRF. The iBGP session uses this value when it exchanges the prefixes in the VRF with other PEs. VPNv4 prefixes are used only in the control plane. Actual packets (at least with all current implementations) maintain their IP address format for source and destination. In addition, no change occurs to routing exchanges between CE and PE, which use standard IPv4.

PEs rewrite the next-hop address information (which would be CE address) and replace it with one of their own addresses—that is part of the core network address space. In this way, a PE can send traffic destined for another part of a customer VPN over the core network using standard routing lookups.

When the time comes to forward traffic to CE2, PE A will do a lookup to find the route to 192.168.4.0, which will resolve to 10.10.10.12, and PE A must do another *forwarding information base* (FIB) lookup to find the route to this address. This time the next hop will be 10.0.0.2, which is an LSR. The core routing protocol of Figure 5-8 announces the 10.0.0.0 prefixes, which includes the addresses used by the PE routers as their BGP identifier.

The next two sections discuss two forwarding-plane alternatives to carry the intra-VPN traffic, first with MPLS and then with L2TPv3.

Note the presence of the VPN label in the preceding list. Each PE generates a 20-bit label value for the VPN the address is associated with. The data plane uses this label to identify which VRF should be used to forward a packet received on a core-facing interface.

The RFC 2547 model naturally creates a full mesh between PEs, so every CE can reach any other CE in two hops. It is possible to constrain inter-CE reachability, even as far as creating a hub-and-spoke topology, using *route targets* (RTs). RTs are extended BGP communities that are announced between PEs.

A PE can be configured to export prefixes with a certain RT and import only prefixes that match a specified RT value. RTs allow arbitrary meshes to be built between sites.

Both RD and RT are encoded in a numeric format, usually based on the autonomous system of the site 100:1. Despite the common format, no link exists between the two. You can use multiple RD values within the same VPN with the restriction of one RD per VRF, but it is better to have a one-to-one mapping for operational simplicity.

Figure 5-9 shows PE1 and PE2 routers that export prefixes with a "Spoke" RT value of 100:1 and use 200:1 for import. PE3 imports the 200:1 routes into VRF_IN, which it then distributes to the CE_Hub1 router. CE_Hub2 announces these routes back to PE3, where they are placed in VRF_OUT, then exported with a 200:1 route-target value. As a result, traffic between CE1 and CE2 is routed through the Hub site.

Figure 5-9 *Hub-and-Spoke Using RTs*

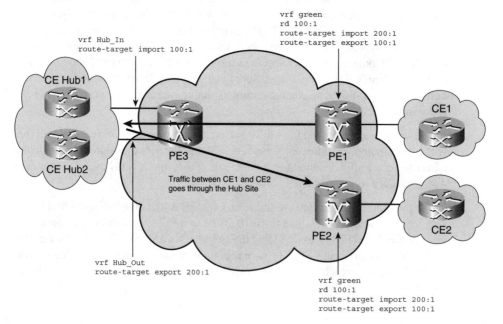

The details follow:

- PE1, PE2, and PE3 exchange prefixes using iBGP. PE1 imports only routes that have an RT equal to 200:1, so only routes from PE3 are loaded into its VRF.

- PE3 imports routes from both PE1 and PE2 because they have an RT equal to 100:1. These routes are placed in VRF_IN. PE3 exports routes received from CE_Hub2 to the two other BGP peers using RT 200:1.

- When CE1 sends a packet to CE2, it first goes to PE1.

- PE1 looks up the CE1 prefix in its VRF and finds the next hop is PE3.

- The packet is encapsulated in whatever protocol is required to traverse the VPN core and forwarded to PE3.

- PE3 looks in its VRF and finds the next hop for CE2 to be Hub_CE1. The packet is forwarded across the Hub site network to Hub_CE2, which has a next-hop to reach CE2 to be PE3. The packet is now forwarded to PE3, which does a lookup in VRF_OUT and finds the next-hop to be PE2.

- PE2 does a VRF route lookup and sends an IP packet to its destination across the dedicated interface that connects it to CE2.

In the default, full-mesh scenario, PE1 and PE2 of Figure 5-9 would install each other's routes so that packets from CE1 to CE2 would follow the most direct path across the core.

The RFC 2547 model supports auto-discovery but not auto-provisioning. If you add a new network at a site, reachability information is automatically propagated to all the other sites. With Layer 3 VPNs, you can also use route aggregation to simplify which prefixes must be advertised between sites.

Provisioning is not complicated, nor is it automatic because, as with any BGP session, you must configure the routes to announce on a PE (and, potentially, the route prefixes to import on other PEs, but this is not obligatory). If you add a new site connected to a new PE, every other PE must be configured to bring up an iBGP session with that PE. RFC 2547 allows the use of BGP *route reflectors* (RRs), which remove the N-squared connectivity between PEs, thus helping to scale to large numbers of sites, and make provisioning a one-time operation on any PE (which only peers with the RR).

The choice of BGP gives the RFC 2547 architecture well-understood properties of scale and robustness. As the protocol used to manage Internet backbone routes, BGP is known to be suitable for large networks. It also supports flexible policy statements. BGP was extended to work in RFC 2547 architectures; the result is known as MP-BGP and can announce VPNv4, VPNv6, IPv4, and IPv6 routes. Customers are free to use any routing protocol on CE-PE links. The only caveat is that the PE implementation must be able to store the routes in a VRF (and hence must be VRF-aware). Standard route redistribution allows appropriate routes to be announced to and imported from MP-BGP.

MPLS-VPN is the most common implementation of RFC 2547, and we examine it first. The RFC describes both the MP-BGP control plane and the MPLS-based forwarding plane. However, a role exists for a more generalized model that runs over IP networks, and we look at emerging proposals to run RFC 2547 over L2TPv3 and mGRE tunnels.

NOTE   The statement at the beginning of this section posited that almost all the previous VPNs were overlays. Which one wasn't? VPLS. The CLE peers with the network at Layer 2.

RFC 2547bis the MPLS Way

MPLS VPNs are built with a double layer of label. The inner VPN route label identifies the customer VRF, and the outer tunnel label identifies the next hop on the LSP to the egress PE. The easiest way to understand the operation is through an example. Figure 5-10 shows an end-to-end MPLS VPN example with routing information across the network.

Figure 5-10 *MPLS VPN Forwarding*

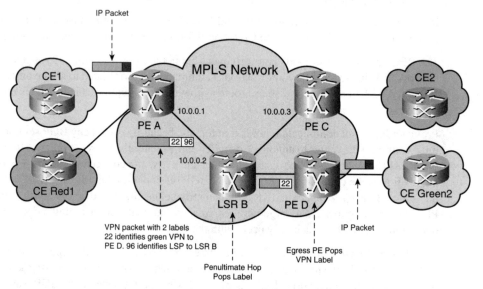

Before traffic is forwarded, PE routers must prepend labels so that the packet can reach the right VRF on the right PE. Figure 5-10 shows a packet going from CE green1 to CE green2.

1 PE A identifies the next hop (PE D) for this packet as a BGP neighbor.

2 PE A first imposes a label, 22, that will identify the VPN routing table to PE D. This label was advertised by the neighbor, PE D, during the exchange of BGP prefixes.

3 The packet must now travel across the MPLS network, so PE A imposes another label, 96, that identifies the next-hop LSR on the IGP path to PE D. This label was advertised by the downstream LSR (LSR B) using LDP.

4 Each LSR in the core swaps labels and forwards the packet as normal toward PE D. The penultimate hop pops the outer label. In Figure 5-10, there is only one hop to the egress LSR, so LSR B removes the outer label.

5 PE D uses the remaining label, 22, to identify the GREEN VPN routing table to use for the packet and then pops the label from the packet.

6 PE D next does an IP lookup in the VPN routing table to find the outgoing interface and forwards the IP packet to CE green2, which will route it to its destination.

It is important to understand that the LSRs have no view of the VPN traffic. They forward labeled traffic along LSPs established by whatever routing protocol is running in the core network. Of course, the choice of IGP can be completely different from the IGPs running on the CE-PE links—the two do not talk to each other.

Labeled packets are found only in the core network. The CE-PE links use IP. The last step of the list also describes a *penultimate hop popping* (PHP) operation (PHP was introduced in Chapter 4). When the last LSR pops the outer label, it reveals the packet's inner label. PE D can use a single LFIB lookup to find the VRF to use. It does a second lookup to find the outgoing CE interface.

An MPLS VPN uses two protocols for signaling. The underlying MPLS network uses LDP between LSRs to announce labels for the prefixes in their routing tables. The PEs use MP-BGP to announce VPN route labels. No correlation exists between the two different label spaces.

Here is a succinct summary of MPLS-VPN operation from draft-ietf-l3vpn-greip-2547-03:

> In "conventional" BGP/MPLS IP VPNs ([BGP-MPLS-VPN]), when an ingress PE router receives a packet from a CE router, it looks up the packet's destination IP address. . . .As a result of this lookup, the (ingress) PE router determines an MPLS label stack, a data link header, and an output interface. The label stack is prepended to the packet, the data link header is prepended to that, and the resulting frame is queued for the output interface. The bottom label in the MPLS label stack prepended to the packet is called the VPN route label ([BGP-MPLS-VPN]). The VPN route label will not be seen until the packet reaches the egress PE router. This label controls forwarding of the packet by the egress PE router. The upper label in the MPLS label stack is called the tunnel label ([BGP-MPLS-VPN]). The purpose of the tunnel label is to cause the packet to be delivered to the egress PE router which understands the VPN route label.

Recall that *Ethernet over MPLS* (EoMPLS) and VPLS also use double label stacks, but they have different signaling protocols (directed LDP).

MPLS VPNs have been a successful service, with many hundred operational networks worldwide. Some carriers, however, might be simultaneously attracted to the merits of the

RFC 2547 model but resistant to the need to deploy MPLS to support it. For them, there are other proposals that allow 2547 to run over an IP core, that use alternatives to labels for forwarding, but still use labels for VPN identification.

RFC 2547bis Forwarding-Plane Alternatives

The two proposals that we examine in this chapter decorrelate the RFC 2547 control and data planes. Both retain MP-BGP for customer route distribution and continue to use labels for VPN route table identification. However, the core network is no longer based on MPLS, but uses standard IP. The PE-CE reference architecture is maintained.

MPLS over mGRE

This architecture uses dynamic GRE tunnels between PEs to carry customer packets. Route distribution between CE-PE and PE-PE works just like in MPLS-VPN solution. The important difference is how a PE forwards traffic across the core.

Figure 5-11 shows a sample topology that uses the same network addresses as the MPLS VPN example in Figure 5-10. When PE A needs to route a packet from CE1 to CE2, it consults its GREEN VRF table to find the BGP next-hop address (PE D) and the VPN route label announced by PE D. It prepends the label to the packet and looks up the next-hop address, outgoing interface, and encapsulation information in the FIB. PE A then prepends a GRE header to the labeled packet, with a source and destination IP addresses corresponding to the public addresses of PE A and PE D, respectively. The GRE type field indicates an MPLS payload.

Figure 5-11 *MPLS over mGRE Example*

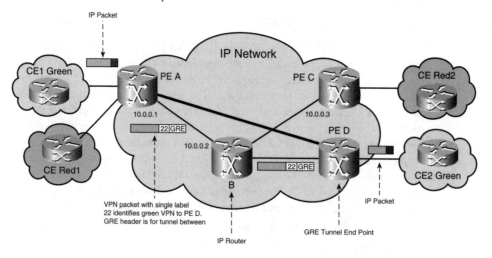

The inter-PE routes are learned using a standard IGP. No extra control-plane information is in the core network.

The *dynamic* moniker refers to the fact that the GRE tunnels are never seen as a possible path by routing protocols running on the PE, nor do routing adjacencies form across them. In fact, given the lack of protocol state, this solution really uses GRE as an encapsulation method to traverse an IP core.

One point mentioned in the draft RFC that merits discussion here is the greater susceptibility to spoofing of the core network. With MPLS, the provider can simply discard any labeled packets received at the edge of its network, so it is hard for a malicious user to introduce spoofed packets into MPLS networks. With MPLS over GRE, however, no equivalent boundary exists. The PE receives and forwards IP, so it would have to use some other filtering mechanism to enforce an antispoofing policy.

MPLS over L2TPv3

MPLS over L2TPv3 uses exactly the same principle as the GRE solution just discussed, except with an L2TPv3 data plane. Once again, BGP distributes customer routes and VPN route labels. Recall from the discussion in Chapter 4 that L2TPv3 has its own control plane, and information negotiated during session establishment is found in the data-plane header, notably session ID and cookie ID.

Session and cookie IDs are also used in this architecture. However, their roles differ from what we saw previously. The session ID was a session multiplexer: Different sessions have different identifiers within the same tunnel. Here, a label plays this role, so the session ID value is used only to indicate to the receiving L2TPv3 engine that the incoming packet belongs to a Layer 3 VPN service and that additional processing is required by another subsystem. The cookie ID is still used for antispoofing protection. The value can be generated statically or randomly and can either be global per PE or local per session.

The session and cookie identifiers are announced using MP-BGP but, just as for MPLS over GRE, different implementations could use another protocol.

The forwarding plane is similar if more complex than with the GRE solution. Consider the network in Figure 5-12. When CE1 sends data to CE2, PE A first performs a route table lookup to find the BGP next hop and VPN label identifier. It also finds the L2TPv3 session and cookie identifiers for the remote PE. PE A then does a second lookup to identify the IP address of the PE D and encapsulates the packet in an L2TPv3 frame and sends it. The core is a completely standard IP network.

On the ingress, PE D removes the outer L2TPv3 header and verifies session and cookie values. If they are valid, the packet's label is used to identify the correct VRF, and output processing continues as usual. Compared to GRE, antispoofing is somewhat enhanced because PE D can drop incoming packets that do not have a correct cookie ID.

Is there any great difference between using one of these IP-based encapsulations to create a Layer 3 VPN service compared to using MPLS? The major difference is clearly that the core network is still IP, so no migration is necessary to start offering a VPN service. The disadvantage is that you lose some useful MPLS-based tools, such as fast reconvergence (which is being developed for IP) and traffic engineering.

Figure 5-12 *MPLS over L2TPv3 Example*

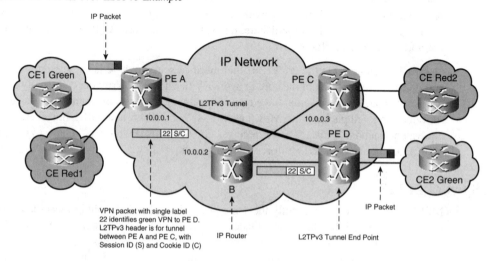

Inter-Autonomous System Connectivity: Another Application of Tunnels

Can an enterprise itself use MPLS VPN and still transit a commercial MPLS VPN service? Can a transit provider use MPLS VPN to connect ISP sites that might themselves use MPLS VPN? In other words, is it possible to have a hierarchy of VPN services?

The answer is yes, and two solutions are presented here. Each uses MPLS in the core network. We have retained their original service provider context during discussion, but the solutions can be—and have been—used in any large network that requires some form of hierarchical transport of labeled packets.

Do all transport providers have to use MPLS if their customers decide to? Obviously not. It is possible to tunnel labeled packets across an IP core using the MPLS over GRE or MPLS over L2TPv3 encapsulation discussed previously in this chapter. In fact, tunneling is probably the easiest solution, and we recommend that enterprise network administrators use that approach unless valid reasons encourage the use of one of the following solutions. Some examples will be given in Chapter 7.

Carrier Supporting Carrier

Carrier supporting carrier (CsC) is a two-layer IP VPN solution designed to allow a backbone carrier to use MPLS VPN (or L2TPv3) to carry traffic belonging to customers' carriers that use MPLS VPNs.

Before looking at the solution, it is a good idea to understand the problem being solved. An MPLS PE router holds all the routes of all the sites to which it connects. In a normal scenario, although this number can be large, the expectation is that an individual VPN would require at most hundreds or perhaps thousands of entries in a VRF. However, if the customer is itself an ISP, carrying routes belonging to their customers, the potential exists to require the backbone PE to carry an impossibly large number of routes. The CsC solution addresses this issue.

CsC is based on the observation that the label switched domain of an MPLS VPN network (that is, the backbone network) only needs routing information to reach provider (P) routers—the customer routing domain is invisible to the core.

In a CsC scenario, the ISP needs to share the global routing table with the backbone carrier only. The CsC backbone routers (labeled CSC-PE1, CSC-P, and CSC-PE2 in Figure 5-13) carry the next-hop routes for the ISP carrier networks so that an LSP exists between ISP sites. Note that the next-hop routes should not be aggregated because that would break the end-to-end LSP.

Figure 5-13 *CsC Topology*

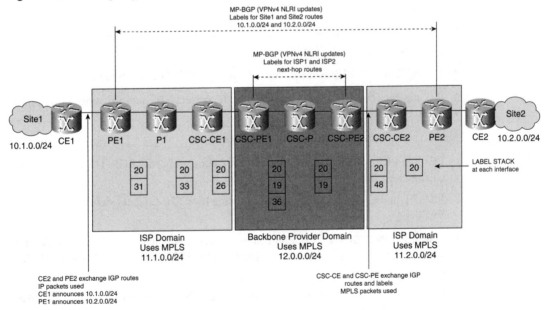

Figure 5-13 shows the CsC topology.

The major differences between CsC and a standard MPLS VPN solution are as follows:

- CE-PE interface use MPLS.

- CE-PE exchange routes and labels.

- Packets on the CsC backbone have three labels on their label stack.

Figure 5-13 shows CsC data-plane operation, specifically the label stack of a packet as it traverses the ISP and backbone carrier networks:

1 CE1 sends a packet with a destination address in the 10.2.0.0/24 network. The next hop for this address is PE1.

2 PE1 pushes two labels: the VPN identifier, 20, and the next-hop label announced by P1, 31.

3 P1 does a label swap and forwards the packet with outer label value of 33.

4 CSC-CE1 does a label swap and forwards the packet with outer label 26. This label was announced by CSC-PE1.

5 CSC-PE1 removes label 26 and pushes two labels onto the stack. Label 19 is the VPN identifier that identifies the ISP's VRF. Label 36 is the value announced by the CSC-P router, which is the next hop on the CSC backbone network.

6 CSC-P performs a PHP operation and forwards the packet with outer label value 19.

7 CSC-PE2 matches the incoming label value to the correct VRF and pushes label 48 before forwarding to CSC-CE2.

8 CSC-CE2 does a PHP and forwards the packet with outer label value of 20.

9 PE2 matches the incoming label value to the correct VRF and forwards an IP packet to the customer router, CE2.

Figure 5-13 also illustrates the control-plane operation:

1 PE1 and PE2 exchange labels and VPNv4 routes using MP-BGP. The labels identify customer VRFs.

2 PE1, P1, and CSC-CE1 exchange labels using LDP. These labels identify the next-hop FEC.

3 CSC-CE1 and CSC-PE1 exchange labels and routes. There are two ways to do this. The first uses LDP; the second, specified in RFC 3107, uses external BGP (eBGP) to exchange IPv4 and labels.

4 CSC-PE1 and CSC-PE2 exchange labels and VPNv4 routes using MP-BGP. These labels identify customer VRFs.

5 CSC-PE1, CSC-P, and CSC-PE2 exchange labels using LDP.

The rest of the label-exchange operation is the same.

CSC-CE2 and CSC-PE2 are eBGP or LDP routing peers. CSC-CE2 announces itself as the next-hop address for the 11.2.0.0/24 network to CSC-PE2, which will store them in the ISP VRF. CSC-PE2 announces the 11.2.0.0 prefixes (as VPNv4 addresses) to CSC-PE1 using iBGP. CSC-PE1 in turn announces the prefixes (and label) to CSC-CE1 for 11.2.0.0 using eBGP (or LDP). CSC-CE1 redistributes the 11.2.0.0/24 routing information into its IGP so that it can be learned by all the other P routers in the ISP1 network. After the protocols converge on the ISP network, an LSP is available from PE1 to PE2 for their iBGP session to carry 10.2.0.0 prefix information and in turn allow CE1 to send traffic to CE2.

To summarize, the CSC-CE is a LSR on the ISP network and exchanges routes and labels with other LSRs in the ISP core. CSC-CE also exchanges routes and labels with CSC-PE, which is part of to the backbone provider. Because the CSC-CE only needs routing and label information to reach other ISP core routers, the CSC-PE only has to carry this information in its VRF tables. MPLS runs on the CSC-CE and CSC-PE link.

The data-plane operation explanation above described how labels are pushed or popped on packets as they cross different parts of the ISP and backbone provider's network. Figure 5-14 shows the final label stack of the packet at is leaves CSC-PE1.

Figure 5-14 *CsC Label Stack*

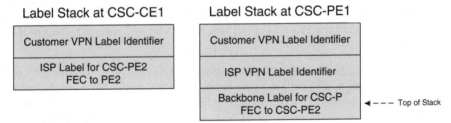

Inter-Autonomous System Routing

CsC is suitable for transport carriers but might be overkill for two providers who peer to allow reachability to each other's customers across their core networks. Inter-autonomous system routing for MPLS VPN is a solution that allows two autonomous systems to exchange routing information. There is a clear analogy with standard BGP exchanges between service providers.

Figure 5-15 shows the inter-autonomous system solution topology. In each area, an *Autonomous System Boundary Router* (ASBR) router has an eBGP relationship with a peer in the other autonomous system and an iBGP session with the PE routers in its own area. The ASBR learns VPNv4 prefixes from iBGP and exports this information in eBGP. For the next hop to be visible within an autonomous system, the ASBR announces itself as the next hop. The ASBR also generates VPN route identifier labels for all the prefixes that it learns from iBGP peers. These labels are sent using eBGP to the next ASBR. There is no LDP session between ASBR devices.

Figure 5-15 *Inter-Autonomous System Topology*

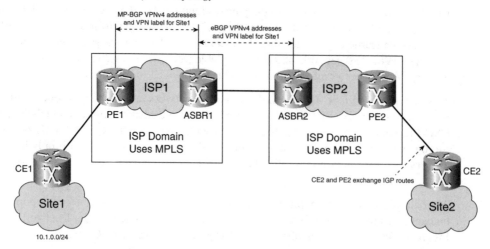

Because the ASBR is also an iBGP peer (that is, a PE), it will take routes learned through eBGP and announce them to all the PEs in its autonomous system. While doing so, it announces itself as the next-hop router—in standard MPLS VPN fashion—and creates new labels for the prefixes. PEs will install routes into VRFs by applying standard RT values matching.

The forwarding plane in each autonomous system is identical to standard MPLS VPNs. ASBR2 appears as a PE within its autonomous system, so the IGP label is removed by the penultimate hop. ASBR2 looks up the label in its LFIB and finds a new label and next hop: ASBR1. It forwards the packet to ASBR1, which performs a similar LFIB lookup and this time finds the next hop to be PE1 with yet another VPN label. ASBR1 then does a second lookup to find the IGP label needed to reach PE1 and forwards the packet.

Note that although there are new labels on each network segment, the VPNv4 addresses are global across both autonomous systems. The RD value appended at a PE in AS1 is accepted by another PE in AS2.

Inter-Autonomous System Connectivity Summary

In this section, we looked at two different solutions to connect MPLS VPNs. The first, CsC, involved a hierarchical topology with a Tier 2 service provider that uses MPLS to provide VPN service to its customers, connecting across a Tier 1 backbone provider that also uses MPLS VPN for its customers. Compared to a standard RFC 2547 network, the main differences in a CsC network is that the CsC-CE and CsC-PEs exchange labels and routes, and there are three labels on packets crossing the backbone network.

The second solution, inter-autonomous systems, is simpler and involves two ASBR routers from different ISPs establishing a peering relationship using eBGP. VPNv4 addresses and

VPN labels are exchanged from one inter-autonomous system PE to another and are used in the data plane to route packets between customer sites.

There is another, simple alternative to connect MPLS clouds using tunnels. We looked at MPLS over GRE and MPLS over L2TPv3 in another context earlier in the chapter and so do not go into additional detail here.

Summary

This chapter covered a lot of territory. It presented different architectures for network virtualization. The basic alternative is to use some form of tunnel overlay, with your choice of protocol and at your choice of OSI layer, and a peer architecture based on RFC 2547.

In the tunnel category, we reviewed 802.1q trunks; GRE-based Layer 3 VPNs; DMVPN, which combines mGRE and IPsec; and L2TPv3 and MPLS-based p2p Layer 2 circuits. VPLS is something of a hybrid because customer and PE devices have a peer relationship of sorts, but PEs maintain a full mesh of LSPs across the core network.

In the peer category, we covered the RFC 2547 architecture and the predominant implementation using MPLS. We also discussed alternative core protocols for this architecture, using GRE and L2TPv3.

Finally, we introduced hierarchical Layer 3 VPNs. CsC has a transport MPLS VPN running "beneath" customer VPNs. Inter-autonomous system allows eBGP to allow service providers to form a peer relationship between their autonomous systems. L2TPv3 or GRE can be used to transport MPLS over IP core networks using the same extensions as discussed in the RFC 2547 section.

The next chapter puts these architectures to use in design scenarios relevant to enterprise networks.

PART II

Enterprise Virtualization
Techniques and Best Practices

CHAPTER 6

Infrastructure Segmentation Architectures: Practice

This chapter analyzes how the virtualization technologies and architectures introduced in Chapter 4, "A Virtualization Technologies Primer: Theory," and Chapter 5, "Infrastructure Segmentation Architectures: Theory," can effectively be used in the enterprise, specifically in campus networks and *metropolitan-area networks* (MANs).

Chapter 5 discussed the trade-off between scalability and complexity in the different VPN architectures. Based on scalability and complexity, different architectures apply to different places in the network. Depending on where in the network a VPN architecture is used, there will be deployment subtleties and best practices to follow. This chapter delves into the implementation details and best practices for the application and combination of different VPN architectures in the enterprise campus network and MAN.

We focus mainly on the campus and the MAN in this chapter, but the *virtual networks* (VNs) created in the campus and MAN must be extended over the WAN. The extension over the WAN poses a different set of challenges, and the techniques used to tackle these challenges build upon those techniques used to virtualize the campus network and MAN. Chapter 7, "Extending the Virtualized Enterprise over the WAN," is devoted to the virtualization of the WAN.

Hop-to-Hop VLANs

The first level of segmentation found in any campus network is based on VLANs. Given the scalability limitations of large broadcast domains, the span of VLANs must be kept limited below a certain diameter. The use of VLANs for the virtualization of the network is a viable solution for small networks or portions of a large network. Chapter 2, "Designing Scalable Enterprises," discussed the reasons for not extending VLANs throughout the network and the benefits of having a routed core. However, in a small topology, you can use VLANs to provide segmentation. This is true for portions of the campus network such as the access-distribution module or the LAN portion of a small branch. In these network scenarios, the topology is small enough that the *Spanning Tree Protocol* (STP) can be used successfully and deterministically to support resilient paths. The limited diameter of the network allows for efficient and reliable spanning-tree reconvergence, limits the reach of a broadcast storm, and makes the spanning-tree domain manageable from a troubleshooting perspective.

Deployment recommendations for these domains follow the well-known rules of spanning-tree root bridge positioning and link-cost handling. We do not go into the details of Layer 2 network design, but we do insist that these domains be kept small because they do not provide any failure containment.

Figure 6-1 depicts a campus network and highlights the access-distribution block where traffic segmentation can be achieved by means of VLANs. The following are the configuration details necessary to implement VLAN segmentation in the access-distribution block. Note that these do not differ from the well-known common practices for multiple VLAN and STP creation.

Figure 6-1 *Layer 2 Access-Distribution Block*

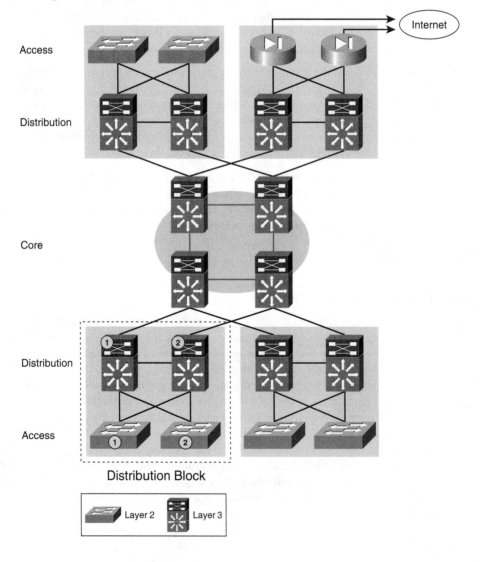

To begin, we need to create the necessary VLANs. To follow standard campus network design best practices, we must avoid spanning VLANs over different access switches. As a result, each user group will have a different VLAN ID on each access switch. The VLANs at the access must be matched at the distribution, which means the number of VLANs at the distribution equals the number of groups times the number of access switches connected to the distribution. The VLANs are the same in both switches in a distribution pair. For Cisco IOS-based switches, Example 6-1 shows the commands needed to create the necessary VLANs for groups Red and Blue on the different access and distribution switches.

NOTE   The examples show the commands used on a Catalyst 6500 running Native IOS.

Example 6-1 *VLAN Segmentation in Access and Distribution*

```
! Access-1
vlan 3 name RED
vlan 4 name BLUE
! Access-2
vlan 5 name RED
vlan 6 name BLUE
! Distribution-1 & Distribution-2
vlan 3 name RED1
vlan 4 name BLUE1
vlan 5 name RED2
vlan 6 name BLUE2
```

After the VLANs have been created, they must be interconnected throughout the network. You do this by creating 802.1q trunks to carry the VLAN traffic between the switches. Because the access switches are dual homed to the distribution, you must create two trunks to connect each access switch to the distribution pair. Each trunk will carry all VLANs between access and distribution. Example 6-2 illustrates this.

Example 6-2 *Data Path Virtualization in Access/Distribution*

```
! Access-1 & Access-2
interface gigabitethernet 4/1
   description Uplink to Distribution-1
   switchport mode trunk
   switchport trunk encapsulation dot1q
interface gigabitethernet 4/2
   description Uplink to Distribution-2
   switchport mode trunk
   switchport trunk encapsulation dot1q
! Distribution-1 & Distribution-2
interface gigabitethernet 4/1
   description Downlink from Access-1
   switchport mode trunk
   switchport trunk encapsulation dot1q
interface gigabitethernet 4/2
   description Downlink from Access-2
   switchport mode trunk
   switchport trunk encapsulation dot1q
```

Create a *switch virtual interface* (SVI) for each VLAN at the distribution switch, as shown in Example 6-3. At this point, you do not assign an IP address to these interfaces. These interfaces are used to map the traffic to the necessary *virtual routing and forwarding instances* (VRFs) later on. When you have completed the VRF assignment, you assign IP addresses to these.

NOTE   In a campus network that is not virtualized, you could have assigned IP addresses to the SVIs at this point. In a virtualized campus network, you must assign the SVIs to the necessary VRFs before you can assign IP addresses to the interfaces.

Example 6-3   *Virtual Routed Interfaces for VLANs*

```
! Distribution-1
interface vlan 3
   description SVI for RED1
  interface vlan 4
   description SVI for BLUE1
interface vlan 5
   description SVI for RED2
interface vlan 6
   description SVI for BLUE2
! Distribution-2
interface vlan 3
   description SVI for RED1
interface vlan 4
   description SVI for BLUE1
interface vlan 5
   description SVI for RED2
interface vlan 6
   description SVI for BLUE2
```

Finally, assign access ports to the VLANs. Example 6-4 shows the static configuration of access ports.

Example 6-4   *Assigning Access Ports to the Different VLANs*

```
! Access-1
interface gigabitethernet 6/1
   description Host in the RED group
   switchport mode access
   switchport access vlan 3
interface gigabitethernet 6/11
   description Host in the BLUE group
   switchport mode access
   switchport access vlan 4
! Access-2
interface gigabitethernet 6/1
   description Host in the RED group
   switchport mode access
   switchport access vlan 5
```

Example 6-4 *Assigning Access Ports to the Different VLANs (Continued)*

```
interface gigabitethernet 6/11
   description Host in the BLUE group
   switchport mode access
   switchport access vlan 6
```

Over a common infrastructure, we have created multiple virtual Layer 2 networks, each of which has its own virtual workgroup space (VLANs), virtual paths (VLANs on a trunk), and dedicated routed virtual interfaces (SVIs). The Layer 2 portion of the network is generally used to access a larger-scale routed network. The following sections discuss some of the mechanisms to virtualize the routed portions of the network. The virtual segments created at Layer 2 and those created at Layer 3 will be associated by common use of the SVIs we have created in this section.

Layer 3 Hop to Hop

This technique involves the use of VRFs at every hop and the interconnection of the VRFs by means of a Layer 2 circuit such as that identified by an 802.1q tag or a *data-link connection identifier* (DLCI). Because this technique requires VRFs to be configured and mapped to Layer 2 circuits at every hop, it is generally used to segment the routed portion of a small campus network. This is not a viable solution in an IP-based WAN, where we do not have control over every IP hop. For the IP WAN scenario, multihop techniques provide a viable alternative. Multihop techniques are described in the section "Tunnel Overlay for Layer 3 VPNs."

VRF-lite was originally introduced as "Multi-VRF CE" to extend multiple VPNs from a provider edge (PE) onto non-*Multiprotocol Label Switching* (MPLS) *customer edge* (CE) devices supporting multiple VRFs. This basically involves a single routed hop and a single link between the PE and CE (that is, no resiliency), as shown in Figure 6-2.

Figure 6-2 *Multi-VRF CE Original Application*

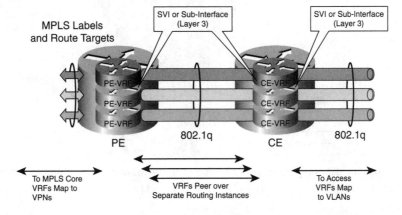

However, you can extend the principle over multiple hops to create virtual campus networks as depicted in Figure 6-3. This also brings to the table the use of multiple links to provide path resiliency.

Figure 6-3   *Layer 3 Hop-to-Hop Segmented Campus Network*

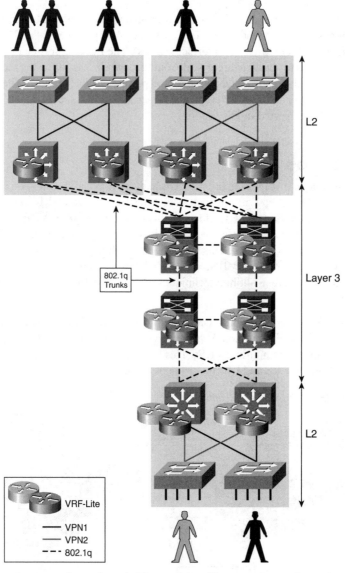

We use the network topology in Figure 6-4 to illustrate the configuration required to create Layer 3 *hop-to-hop* (h2h) virtual campus networks.

Figure 6-4   *Small Campus Network*

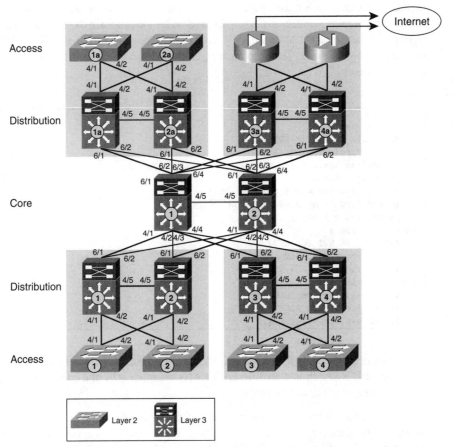

The first step is to create the necessary VRFs. For the h2h Layer 3 solution, it is necessary to create a VRF for each group at every Layer 3 hop. Unique *route distinguishers* (RDs) must be used for every VRF on a router. Although the RDs across multiple hops do not need to match, it is easier to use a single RD for each group throughout the network. Therefore, all VRFs belonging to the RED group in our example will use the same RD everywhere in the network. This RD differs from the RD used for any other group and is therefore unique. The commands in Example 6-5 create the RED and BLUE VRFs. These commands must be applied at every routed hop in the network. In our example, these are all the distribution and core switches.

Example 6-5   *Creating VRFs*

```
ip vrf red
    rd 10:10
ip vrf blue
    rd 20:20
```

After the VRFs have been created, the routed interfaces on the distribution switches (SVIs) created in Example 6-3 must be associated with the VRFs. This is achieved via the **ip vrf forwarding** <name> command, which is used under the interface to be associated with the VRF (see Example 6-6). After the SVIs have been associated with the VRFs, an IP address can be assigned to these. This step must be completed on every distribution switch in the campus network.

Example 6-6 *Adding Interfaces to VRFs*

```
! Distribution
interface vlan 3
   description SVI for RED1
   ip vrf forwarding RED
   ip address x.x.x.x x.x.x.x
   interface vlan 4
   description SVI for BLUE1
   ip vrf forwarding BLUE
   ip address x.x.x.x x.x.x.x
interface vlan 5
   description SVI for RED2
   ip vrf forwarding RED
   ip address x.x.x.x x.x.x.x
interface vlan 6
   description SVI for BLUE2
   ip vrf forwarding BLUE
   ip address x.x.x.x x.x.x.x
```

As you can see, the SVIs for RED1 and RED2 (VLANs 3 and 5) are both associated with the same RED VRF. Thus, two different VLANs are made part of a common routing space by associating them to the same VRF.

The VLANs connecting to the distribution and their routed interfaces (SVIs) are to be treated in the same manner as they would be in a nonvirtualized network. For example, first-hop resiliency features such as the *Global Load Balancing Protocol* (GLBP) or *Hot-Standby Redundancy Protocol* (HSRP) can be enabled on the SVIs you just included in the VRFs in the same way they would be enabled in a nonvirtualized network.

So far, you have created VLANs and associated these to different VRFs at the distribution. The steps followed so far are common to most campus network virtualization approaches; how the VRFs, at the different distribution switches, are interconnected varies depending on the technologies and VPN architectures used.

For the specific case of the Layer 3 h2h VPN, we need to associate the VRFs at the distribution with those in the core. The first step is to convert the links in the routed core to dot1q trunks. If consistent interface numbers are used, the template configurations in Example 6-7 would apply to all distribution switches and to all core switches.

NOTE   Converting the core links to dot1q trunks is not equivalent to extending Layer 2 domains over the core. These links remain routed; therefore, the VLANs carried on each link differ.

Example 6-7   *Converting Core Links to Trunks*

```
! Distribution switches
interface gigabitethernet 6/1
   description To Core-1
  switchport mode trunk
  switchport trunk encapsulation dot1q
interface gigabitethernet 6/2
   description To Core-2
  switchport mode trunk
  switchport trunk encapsulation dot1q
! Core switches
interface gigabitethernet 4/1
   description To Distribution-1
  switchport mode trunk
  switchport trunk encapsulation dot1q
interface gigabitethernet 4/2
   description To Distribution-2
  switchport mode trunk
  switchport trunk encapsulation dot1q
interface gigabitethernet 4/3
   description To Distribution-3
  switchport mode trunk
  switchport trunk encapsulation dot1q
interface gigabitethernet 4/4
   description To Distribution-4
  switchport mode trunk
  switchport trunk encapsulation dot1q
interface gigabitethernet 6/1
   description To Distribution-5
  switchport mode trunk
  switchport trunk encapsulation dot1q
interface gigabitethernet 6/2
   description To Distribution-6
  switchport mode trunk
  switchport trunk encapsulation dot1q
interface gigabitethernet 6/3
   description To Distribution-7
  switchport mode trunk
  switchport trunk encapsulation dot1q
interface gigabitethernet 6/4
   description To Distribution-8
  switchport mode trunk
  switchport trunk encapsulation dot1q
```

Because these trunks are meant to be multiple virtual *point-to-point* (p2p) routed links rather than VLAN extensions, you need to create routed interfaces for the VLANs on each core link. These could be SVIs or subinterfaces. We create SVIs for our example. We need to create one SVI per link for each VRF. In our example, a core switch has nine links and therefore requires the creation of nine SVIs for every VRF supported. Each subinterface will be automatically associated to a VLAN, and therefore a core router in our example will require nine dedicated VLAN IDs per VRF. Furthermore, care must be taken for those VLAN IDs to match the IDs used in any adjacent switches.

A numbering convention can prove useful in this scenario. We use four digits, as outlined in Table 6-1.

Table 6-1 *Numbering Convention Used for Trunk ID Assignment*

Digit	Significance
1st Most Significant Digit (leftmost)	1 = Uplink; 2 = Link between peers
2nd	VRF: 1-RED, 2-BLUE
3rd	Core end of the link
4th LS Digit (rightmost)	Distribution end of the link

For instance, VLAN 1214 is used to transport BLUE traffic between Core1 and Distribution 4. VLAN 1124 transports RED traffic over the link between Core2 and Distribution 4. And VLAN 2112 is used to transport RED traffic between Core1 and Core2 and is reused to transport traffic between Distribution 1 and 2, too.

Example 6-8 illustrates the creation of the different VLAN IDs required to interconnect the different RED VRFs and the BLUE VRFs.

Example 6-8 *Creating VLAN IDs for Core Data Path Virtualization*

```
! Core1
vlan 1111 name C1toD1 RED
vlan 1112 name C1toD2 RED
vlan 1113 name C1toD3 RED
vlan 1114 name C1toD4 RED
vlan 1115 name C1toD5 RED
vlan 1116 name C1toD6 RED
vlan 1117 name C1toD7 RED
vlan 1118 name C1toD8 RED
vlan 2112 name C1toC2 RED

vlan 1211 name C1toD1 BLUE
vlan 1212 name C1toD2 BLUE
vlan 1213 name C1toD3 BLUE
vlan 1214 name C1toD4 BLUE
vlan 1215 name C1toD5 BLUE
vlan 1216 name C1toD6 BLUE
vlan 1217 name C1toD7 BLUE
```

Example 6-8 *Creating VLAN IDs for Core Data Path Virtualization (Continued)*

```
vlan 1218 name C1toD8 BLUE
vlan 2212 name C1toC2 BLUE
! Core2
vlan 1121 name C1toD1 RED
vlan 1122 name C1toD2 RED
...
vlan 2112 name C1toC2 RED

vlan 1221 name C1toD1 BLUE
vlan 1222 name C1toD2 BLUE
...
vlan 2212 name C1toC2 BLUE
! Distribution 1
vlan 1111 name C1toD1 RED
vlan 1211 name C1toD1 BLUE
vlan 1121 name C2toD1 RED
vlan 1221 name C2toD1 BLUE
vlan 2112 name D1toD2 RED
vlan 2212 name D1toD2 BLUE
! Distribution 2
vlan 1112 name C1toD2 RED
vlan 1212 name C1toD2 BLUE
vlan 1122 name C2toD2 RED
vlan 1222 name C2toD2 BLUE
vlan 2112 name D1toD2 RED
vlan 2212 name D1toD2 BLUE
```

Finally, you must use the ip vrf forwarding name command to associate the routed interfaces (SVIs) with the VRFs, as shown in Example 6-9

Example 6-9 *Assigning SVIs to the Appropriate VRFs*

```
! Distribution 1
interface vlan 1111
   description C1-D1 RED
   ip vrf forwarding RED
   ip address x.x.x.x x.x.x.x
interface vlan 1211
   description C1-D1 BLUE
   ip vrf forwarding BLUE
   ip address x.x.x.x x.x.x.x
interface vlan 1121
   description C2-D1 RED
   ip vrf forwarding RED
   ip address x.x.x.x x.x.x.x
interface vlan 1221
   description C2-D1 BLUE
   ip vrf forwarding BLUE
   ip address x.x.x.x x.x.x.x
interface vlan 2112
   description D1-D2 RED
```

continues

Example 6-9 *Assigning SVIs to the Appropriate VRFs (Continued)*

```
    ip vrf forwarding RED
    ip address x.x.x.x x.x.x.x
interface vlan 2212
    description D1-D2 BLUE
    ip vrf forwarding BLUE
    ip address x.x.x.x x.x.x.x
! Core1
interface vlan 1111
    description C1-D1 RED
    ip vrf forwarding RED
    ip address x.x.x.x x.x.x.x
interface vlan 1211
    description C1-D1 BLUE
    ip vrf forwarding BLUE
    ip address x.x.x.x x.x.x.x
interface vlan 1112
    description C1-D2 RED
    ip vrf forwarding RED
    ip address x.x.x.x x.x.x.x
interface vlan 1212
    description C1-D2 BLUE
    ip vrf forwarding BLUE
    ip address x.x.x.x x.x.x.x
interface vlan 2112
    description D1-D2 RED
    ip vrf forwarding RED
    ip address x.x.x.x x.x.x.x
interface vlan 2212
    description D1-D2 BLUE
    ip vrf forwarding BLUE
    ip address x.x.x.x x.x.x.x
! Core2
interface vlan 1121
    description C2-D1 RED
    ip vrf forwarding RED
    ip address x.x.x.x x.x.x.x
interface vlan 1221
    description C2-D1 BLUE
    ip vrf forwarding BLUE
    ip address x.x.x.x x.x.x.x
interface vlan 1122
    description C1-D2 RED
    ip vrf forwarding RED
    ip address x.x.x.x x.x.x.x
interface vlan 1222
    description C1-D2 BLUE
    ip vrf forwarding BLUE
    ip address x.x.x.x x.x.x.x
interface vlan 2112
    description D1-D2 RED
    ip vrf forwarding RED
    ip address x.x.x.x x.x.x.x
```

Example 6-9 *Assigning SVIs to the Appropriate VRFs (Continued)*

```
interface vlan 2212
   description D1-D2 BLUE
   ip vrf forwarding BLUE
   ip address x.x.x.x x.x.x.x
```

At this point, a logical topology overlay of VRFs and virtual routed links has been created. The next step is to enable the control plane (that is, turn on the necessary routing protocols).

A separate *interior gateway protocol* (IGP) process is required for the population of routes in each VN. In our example, we have two VNs: RED and BLUE.

When using the *Enhanced Interior Gateway Routing Protocol* (EIGRP), each process is represented by an address family. The configuration of each address family is identical to that of the traditional nonvirtualized EIGRP. Any EIGRP configuration that needs to be done at the interface level must be done on the routed interfaces associated with the VRFs (subinterfaces or SVIs). The configuration in Example 6-10 illustrates EIGRP address families.

Example 6-10 *EIGRP Address Families*

```
router eigrp 200
  address-family ipv4 vrf RED
    network 1.0.0.0
    network 10.0.0.0
    no auto-summary
    exit-address-family
  address-family ipv4 vrf BLUE
    network 2.0.0.0
    network 20.0.0.0
    no auto-summary
    exit-address-family
```

When using *Open Shortest Path First* (OSPF), multiple instances of the routing protocol are required. The configuration of each instance is identical to that of the traditional nonvirtualized OSPF. Any OSPF configuration that needs to be done at the interface level must be done on the routed interfaces associated with the VRFs (subinterfaces or SVIs). The configuration in Example 6-11 illustrates how different OSPF instances are associated with different VRFs.

Example 6-11 *Multiple Instances of OSPF*

```
router ospf 1 vrf RED
 network 1.0.0.0 0.255.255.255 area 0
 network 10.0.0.0 0.255.255.255 area 0
 !
router ospf 2 vrf BLUE
 network 2.0.0.0 0.255.255.255 area 0
 network 20.0.0.0 0.255.255.255 area 0
```

A proven best practice in IGP design and deployment is that of making the IGP hierarchical. Doing so improves scalability, minimizes convergence times, and prevents events or problems from propagating throughout the entire routed network and causing a global reconvergence of the protocol. In an EIGRP network, you achieve hierarchy by summarizing portions of the network; and in an OSPF network, the concept of areas allows the structuring of the hierarchy. These concepts are discussed in some detail in Chapter 1, but there are books specifically dedicated to routing protocol design. The same best practices for IGP design that have been perfected over the years apply to each of the IGP instances that are created when using a routed h2h virtualization approach. If you use the principles of hierarchy and modularity, all address families will benefit from the scalability and resiliency that characterize a traditional nonvirtualized network.

Because each address family is deployed in a hierarchical and symmetrical way, all the mechanisms of resiliency, failover, and scalability will work in the same way as they did for a nonvirtualized network. In addition, the access-distribution block will interact with the core to provide resiliency and failover functionality in the same way as it would for a nonvirtualized enterprise. Therefore, the distribution model in which spanning tree is combined with first-hop redundancy protocols such as HSRP and GLBP continues to operate identically, only that the model is now replicated for each VPN. Similar considerations apply when using a routed access model.

Single Address Space Solutions

When segmenting the Layer 3 portion of the network, several levels of separation can be achieved. The most basic one is simply restricting the prefixes that can be reached by a group of hosts. You can achieve this over a single address space with *access control lists* (ACLs). As you may already be thinking, the scenarios in which this is viable are few because of the limited flexibility of ACL rules (which are defined based on IP addresses). In general, you can use ACLs for scenarios requiring connectivity of many hosts to a centralized resource. Guests who should be restricted to only access the Internet are an example of a group that could be isolated by means of ACLs. Creating ACLs for groups that have a need for peer-to-peer traffic is impractical because of the endless number of combinations and permutations that must be taken into account to write these ACLs.

NOTE   Future technologies such as role-based ACLs may allow the creation of ACLs based on user role rather than IP address. This will simplify ACL rules dramatically, allowing the scalable use of ACLs for control of peer-to-peer traffic. For the time being, we limit our discussion to the currently available technologies. Remember, however, that with the right enhancements, a single address space solution based on ACLs could prove powerful. The main advantage of continuing to use a single address space is that the routing and switching environment in the enterprise remains unaltered.

By distributing ACLs around the Layer 3 edge of the network (usually the distribution switches), it is possible to restrict the list of prefixes that can be reached by certain hosts. This is a rudimentary mechanism for creating separate user groups and is illustrated in Figure 6-5.

Figure 6-5   *Distributed ACL-Based Reachability Control*

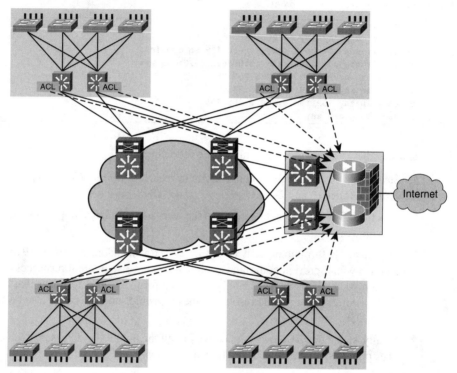

The use of ACLs can restrict access to a resource, but it cannot determine which route will be followed to access this resource. *Policy-based routing* (PBR) enables you to steer traffic over a specific route. This capability is of interest when different groups accessing the same services must be subject to different types of control before accessing the shared services. For instance, in an environment where guests are provided with Internet access, both visitors and employees use the same Internet gateway, but guest traffic must traverse accounting and monitoring devices before reaching the Internet gateway. PBR could be used to divert the guest traffic to the control devices, while employee traffic continues to flow freely to the Internet access gateway.

A combination of ACLs and PBR might allow the creation of different user groups. However, these mechanisms require intensive configuration and are extremely static (and therefore hard to scale and maintain).

In Example 6-12, we provide the ACL and PBR configuration necessary to provide guest Internet access as described previously. Instead of assigning the SVIs at the distribution to VRFs, ACLs are applied to these interfaces, thus acting on any traffic entering the Layer 3 portion of the network and enforcing any reachability restrictions or privileges that the user group may have.

Example 6-12 *Guest Internet Access Based on ACLs*

```
ip access-list extended GUEST-RACL
 10 permit udp any any eq bootps
 20 permit udp any host <DNS-Server-IP> eq domain
 30 permit tcp any host <web-auth-device-IP> eq www
 40 deny ip any 10.0.0.0 0.255.255.255
 50 deny ip any 172.16.0.0 0.15.255.255
 60 deny ip any 192.168.0.0 0.0.255.255
 70 permit ip any any
```

The access list in Example 6-12 achieves the following:

- Statements 10 and 20 allow connectivity to receive *Dynamic Host Configuration Protocol* (DHCP) and *Domain Name System* (DNS) services.

- Statement 30 provides connectivity to the web-auth appliance to perform the authentication process.

- Statements 40 through 60 deny connectivity to private addresses (RFC 1918). Notice that this would prevent communication to the enterprise internal resources only when private addresses are the only ones used for that. For enterprises that leverage public addresses for private resources, these specific subnets should also be added in the ACL.

- Finally, statement 70 allows connectivity to all the public IP addresses (excluding the ones previously specified, as mentioned previously).

NOTE   The ACL in Example 6-12 is generic enough to be seamlessly applied to all distribution routers. Note that this is possible only because of the simplicity of the guest Internet access requirement.

The ACL must be applied to the first-hop SVI in every guest VLAN at the distribution. The use of routed ACLs is preferred over VLAN ACLs because they are applied unidirectionally and we are not concerned about restricting return traffic. The configuration in Example 6-13 applies the ACL to the corresponding SVI.

Example 6-13 *Applying ACLs to a Group*

```
interface Vlan50
  description Wired-guest-floor1
  ip address 10.124.50.2 255.255.255.0
  ip access-group GUEST-RACL in
```

As discussed previously, should guest traffic need to be subject to special controls before going to the Internet, ACLs are not enough. PBR can complement the solution by rerouting guest traffic to the control devices right before it goes to the Internet gateway. The policy defined in Example 6-14, when applied inbound at the penultimate hop before reaching the Internet gateway, will allow guest traffic to use a different path to reach the Internet.

Example 6-14 *Path Differentiation with PBR*

```
ip access-list extended TO-BBSM
  permit ip 10.121.150.0 0.0.0.255 any
  permit ip 10.121.160.0 0.0.0.255 any
  permit ip 10.122.150.0 0.0.0.255 any
.................................................
  permit ip 10.128.160.0 0.0.0.255 any
!
route-map guest-to-BBSM permit 10
  match ip address TO-BBSM
  set ip next-hop 172.18.3.30
```

These statements simply match any traffic coming from one of the guest subnets (TO-BBSM ACL) and set the next hop for this traffic to the address of the policy-enforcement device. It is important to keep in mind that the PBR policy is applied only to inbound traffic (from the perspective of the device).

Tunnel Overlay for Layer 3 VPNs

One significant limitation of h2h solutions is their scalability. A tunnel overlay can potentially enhance the scalability of the VPN solution and even simplify its configuration by removing any VPN state from the core. Nevertheless, the tunneling mechanisms might have their own scaling and complexity challenges. In the following sections, we examine some of the deployment scenarios in which tunnels may be a viable virtualization technique.

GRE Tunnels

As discussed in Chapter 5 unicast *generic routing encapsulation* (GRE) tunnels are p2p links, whereas LANs and MANs are multipoint IP clouds providing any-to-any connectivity. An overlay of tunnels onto a MAN or LAN will therefore restrict the connectivity that these networks can provide. In general, an overlay of p2p tunnels is well suited for the formation of a hub-and-spoke logical topology. Such a topology may be useful in scenarios where many users must be isolated in a segment that only provides access to a limited set of centrally located resources. For example, when you are providing guests with Internet access, visitors only require connectivity to the Internet gateway, which would be placed at the hub of the hub-and-spoke topology. Another case in which a hub-and-spoke topology may prove useful is that of providing access to a remediation server for hosts that have been quarantined by a *network access control* (NAC) mechanism. When implementing NAC, an agent on the host analyses the status of patches, operating system revisions, viruses, and other parameters defined as part of an enterprise's policy. If the host is compliant with the policy (that is, all parameters match the required profile), the host is allowed on to the network. If the host is not compliant, it is forced into a quarantine network where it is prevented from connecting to the production network and can only access a remediation server and download any required patches or fixes. This quarantine network presents clear many-to-one connectivity requirements and may be deployed by a hub-and-spoke tunnel overlay.

In an enterprise campus network, the deployment of the logical hub-and-spoke overlay is done at the distribution layer. This means that the tunnel endpoints will be present in the distribution layer switches. Hence, the distribution layer switches require a mechanism to associate the VLANs in the access-distribution with the appropriate mesh of tunnels. This can be achieved by means of PBR or more efficiently by mapping both the VLANs and the tunnels to VRFs. We explore these associations later in the section "Mapping Traffic to Tunnels."

Figure 6-6 illustrates a campus network scenario in which a mesh of GRE tunnels is overlaid to form a *virtual private network* (VPN).

Figure 6-6   *GRE Tunnel Overlay*

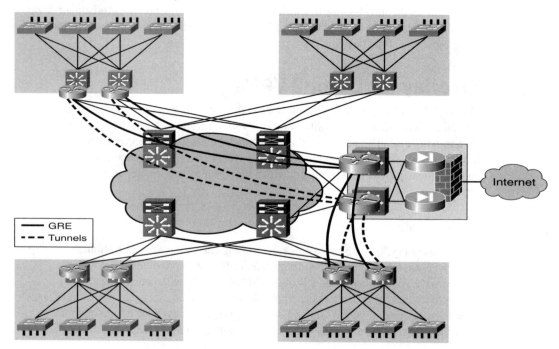

The configuration for Hub-1 in Example 6-15 includes a tunnel for each spoke router.

Example 6-15 *GRE Overlay Hub Configuration*

```
interface Loopback0
 description src GRE p2p tunnel
 ip address 10.126.101.1 255.255.255.255
!
interface Tunnel0
 description GRE p2p tunnel
 ip vrf forwarding guest
 ip address 172.16.101.1 255.255.255.252
 ip mtu 1400
 tunnel source Loopback0
 tunnel destination 10.125.100.253
```

The configuration at the spoke includes a tunnel for each hub router. In this example, there are two hub routers, and therefore each spoke will have two tunnels, one pointing to each hub router. The tunnel interfaces have been assigned to a VRF to steer the appropriate traffic into the tunnels. We explore this further in the section "Mapping Traffic to Tunnels." Example 6-16 shows the two tunnels configured on one of the spoke routers.

Example 6-16 *GRE Overlay Spoke Configuration*

```
interface Loopback0
 description src GRE tunnel to hub-1
 ip address 10.125.100.253 255.255.255.255
!
interface Loopback1
 description src GRE tunnel to hub-2
 ip address 10.125.200.253 255.255.255.25
!
interface Tunnel0
 description GRE tunnel to hub-1
 ip vrf forwarding guest
 ip address 172.16.101.2 255.255.255.252
 ip mtu 1400
 tunnel source Loopback0
 tunnel destination 10.126.101.1
!
interface Tunnel1
 description GRE tunnel to hub-2
 ip vrf forwarding guest
 ip address 172.16.201.2 255.255.255.252
 ip mtu 1400
 tunnel source Loopback1
 tunnel destination 10.126.201.1
```

As shown in the examples, two levels of address space are involved in this setup. One is the global address space, which contains the loopback interfaces used as endpoints to create the tunnels. The other level of address space contains the addresses in the VRFs, which include the tunnel interfaces. Therefore, the 10.x.x.x network in the example is in the global table and is used to create the tunnels; the 172.16.x.x networks exist on the VRF and tunnel overlay.

NOTE	Each of these address spaces will require its own control plane. We will discuss this in the upcoming section "Resiliency and Routing Considerations."

Multipoint GRE Tunnels

Multipoint GRE (mGRE) tunnels provide a more scalable way of handling the aggregation of multiple GRE tunnels at a hub site. The configuration of many tunnel interfaces at the hub is replaced by a single multipoint tunnel interface. When using multiple p2p tunnels, each spoke site is associated to a tunnel, and therefore routing traffic onto the correct site is done based on tunnel interface. This is the same routing paradigm followed by a router with many physical interfaces. When you are using mGRE at the hub, the router has a single interface onto which all spoke sites are mapped. In this scenario, the routing table at the hub maps all spoke prefixes to the same interface (the multipoint tunnel). A mechanism is necessary at the hub to determine which spoke of the multipoint tunnel traffic is destined for. This mechanism could be *Tunnel Endpoint Discovery* (TED), *Border Gateway Protocol* (BGP), or the *Next Hop Resolution Protocol* (NHRP).

NOTE	NHRP, defined in RFC 2332, is a Layer 2 address-resolution protocol and cache, similar to *Address Resolution Protocol* (ARP) and Frame Relay inverse-ARP. When a tunnel interface is an mGRE, NHRP tells the mGRE process where to tunnel a packet to reach a certain address. NHRP is a client/server protocol where the hub is the server and the spokes are the clients. The hub maintains an NHRP database where it registers, for each spoke, the mapping between the physical address (used as GRE tunnel destination) and the logical address assigned to the spoke tunnel interface. Each spoke provides this information to the hub, sending an NHRP registration message at boot time.

The use of an mGRE hub and NHRP is a subset of the *dynamic multipoint VPN* (DMVPN) architecture described in Chapter 5. A complete DMVPN implementation would also include an encryption component. However, encryption is usually not of relevance in the campus or the private MAN. This discussion does not include the encryption component of DMVPN; if required, it could be easily overlaid onto the proposed solution.

The configuration steps required to create the hub-and-spoke overlay network using mGRE interfaces on the hub devices are detailed below; the configuration samples refer to the devices highlighted with a circle in the network diagram in Figure 6-7.

Figure 6-7   *Hub-and-Spoke Using mGRE Technology*

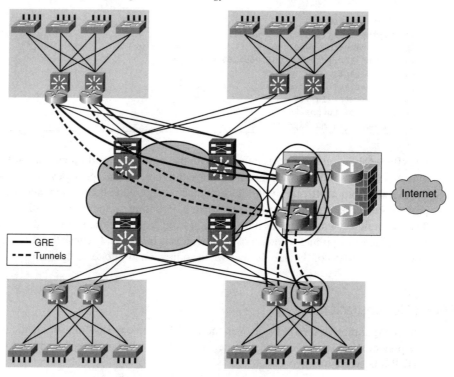

The topology, shown in Figure 6-7, consists of two headend Catalyst 6500 switches, each with an mGRE tunnel interface that connects to all the spoke routers. Every spoke is configured with two p2p GRE tunnel interfaces, each going to the respective headend.

Hub mGRE Configuration

The main advantage of using the mGRE technology for the hub devices is the fact that only one tunnel interface (with corresponding loopback) needs to be defined. In addition, a single subnet (in this example, 172.16.100.0/24) is required to connect the hub to all the spokes eventually defined at the edge of the enterprise network.

Example 6-17 shows the configuration required to create an mGRE interface on the hub and to enable the NHRP functionality.

Example 6-17 *mGRE hub Configuration*

```
interface Loopback0
 description src mGRE tunnel for Guest
 ip address 10.126.100.254 255.255.255.255
 !
```

continues

Example 6-17 *mGRE hub Configuration (Continued)*

```
interface Tunnel0
 description mGRE tunnel for Guest
 ip vrf forwarding guest
 ip address 172.16.100.1 255.255.255.0
 no ip redirects
 ip nhrp map multicast dynamic
 ip nhrp network-id 100
 tunnel source Loopback0
 tunnel mode gre multipoint
```

NHRP is enabled on the mGRE interface with the command **ip nhrp network-id** *value*, where the value specified must match the one configured on the spoke devices. In addition, the **ip nhrp map multicast dynamic** command is required to enable dynamic routing protocols to work over the mGRE tunnel when IGP routing protocols use multicast packets. The **dynamic** keyword prevents the hub router from requiring a separate configuration line for a multicast mapping for each spoke router; this is important because the goal is to avoid any reconfiguration of the hub devices when adding a new spoke component.

Spoke GRE Configuration

The configuration of the spoke devices shown in Example 6-18 is almost identical to the one previously described for the p2p scenario; the only difference is the addition of the NHRP-related commands.

Example 6-18 *mGRE Spoke Configuration*

```
interface Loopback0
 description src GRE tunnel for Guest to hub-1
 ip address 10.124.100.253 255.255.255.255
 !
interface Loopback1
 description src GRE tunnel for Guest to hub-2
 ip address 10.124.200.253 255.255.255.255
 !
interface Tunnel0
 description GRE tunnel for Guest to hub-1
 ip vrf forwarding guest
 ip address 172.16.100.2 255.255.255.0
 ip nhrp network-id 100
 ip nhrp nhs 172.16.100.1
 ip nhrp registration timeout 60
 tunnel source Loopback0
 tunnel destination 10.126.100.254
 !
interface Tunnel1
 description GRE tunnel for Guest to hub-2
 ip vrf forwarding guest
 ip address 172.16.200.2 255.255.255.0
```

Example 6-18 *mGRE Spoke Configuration (Continued)*

```
ip nhrp network-id 200
ip nhrp nhs 172.16.200.1
ip nhrp registration timeout 60
tunnel source Loopback1
tunnel destination 10.126.200.254
```

Similarly to the hub case, the command **ip nhrp network-id** *value* is used to enable the NHRP process on the tunnel interfaces (the values specified must match the values configured on the two hubs). In addition to that, **ip nhrp nhs** needs to be added to specify the address of the NHRP server (hub). Finally, **ip nhrp registration timeout** *seconds* is required to tune the frequency (in seconds) at which the spokes send the NHRP registration messages to the hubs. This command is required to allow a spoke to reregister in case the connectivity with the hub is interrupted and restored; by default, that would happen every 2400 seconds.

NOTE   The command **ip nhrp map multicast** is not required on the spoke devices; the reason for this is that the tunnel interface is p2p, so all multicast packets will be automatically sent to the hub.

As already discussed in the GRE p2p scenario, a mapping from the logical VLAN interface (SVI) defining the guest subnet and the guest VRF is also required. Example 6-19 shows the mapping between VRFs and SVIs.

Example 6-19 *Mapping Subnets to VRFs*

```
interface Vlan11
 description Wired Guest subnet
 ip vrf forwarding guest
 ip address 172.16.31.2 255.255.255.0
 standby 11 ip 172.16.31.1
 standby 11 priority 105
 standby 11 preempt
```

Mapping Traffic to Tunnels

To create an end-to-end group, traffic from the access VLANs must be mapped to the different logical tunnel overlays. This mapping can be achieved based on IP policies with PBR or based on the traffic source with VRFs. The next sections describe how to achieve this mapping.

PBR

You can use PBR to force traffic over a specific interface or toward a specific next hop. When using PBR to steer traffic into a GRE tunnel, you can take one of two approaches:

- Statically route traffic onto the local tunnel interface:

```
Router(config)# access-list 1 permit ip 1.1.1.1
Router(config)# access-list 2 permit ip 2.2.2.2
Router(config)# !
Router(config)# interface GigabitEthernet 4/1
Router(config-if)# ip policy route-map equal-access
Router(config-if)# exit
Router(config)# route-map equal-access permit 10
Router(config-route-map)# match ip address 1
Router(config-route-map)# set ip interface tunnel 0
Router(config-route-map)# exit
```

- Steer traffic to a next hop that is at the remote end of the tunnel:

```
Router(config)# route-map equal-access permit 10
Router(config-route-map)# match ip address 1
Router(config-route-map)# set ip default next-hop remote_address
Router(config-route-map)# exit
```

In either case, the decision to act upon traffic will be based on an IP policy. Therefore, the challenges involved with using PBR to steer traffic into a mesh of tunnels are similar to the scaling challenges faced when using distributed ACLs in a campus network or MAN. A more flexible and scalable solution is provided by VRFs.

VRFs

VRFs allow the creation of independent routing spaces. The tunnel interfaces in the overlay can be made part of the separate routing space created by a VRF. When the tunnel interfaces are part of a VRF routing space, they are also included in the routing table as a valid path to reach certain prefixes. Therefore, if the tunnel interfaces are the preferred route to reach subnets in the remote VRFs, steering traffic into the tunnels is a matter of simple IP forwarding.

It is important to clarify that only traffic that has been assigned to a VRF will eventually make it into the tunnels. The steering of traffic into the tunnels starts with the assignment of traffic to a VLAN or interface that is bound to a VRF. This traffic will eventually use the tunnels because these should be the preferred interfaces for reaching the remote VRFs and their associated subnets. Figure 6-8 illustrates the associations between VLANs, ports, VRFs, and finally tunnels that achieve the mapping of traffic to a tunnel mesh.

Figure 6-8   *Traffic Mapping Between VLANs, VRFs, and Tunnels*

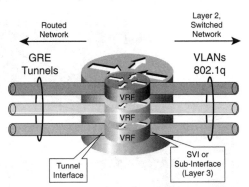

Resiliency and Routing Considerations

The enterprise campus network is characterized by an abundance of resilient high bandwidth links. The same can be said about certain portions of the MAN. The possibility of deploying multiple links drives a highly resilient network design that involves having multiple devices (usually two) connecting each subnet to the routed core. This resilient connection of a subnet to the core is often referred to as *multihoming.* When overlaying a logical tunnel mesh to such an environment, it will be necessary to deploy multiple tunnels per site to preserve the resiliency provided by the multihomed array. For the purposes of this discussion, we examine the scenario in which there are dual distribution switches per site (or distribution block) and, therefore, there are dual tunnels connecting each distribution router to the headend at the hub distribution block. Figure 6-9 illustrates the tunnel mesh required to support a resilient distribution.

Equal-cost routes to the destination network via the redundant tunnels will help load balance traffic over the two tunnels. These routes could either be learned dynamically from a routing protocol or statically configured.

NOTE	The GRE header hides the flow information in all packets. Even if a network is enabled with equal-cost paths for load balancing, traffic sent over a single GRE tunnel will always follow the same path and therefore not be load balanced. Traffic is best load balanced per flow and not per packet to avoid out of sequence packet reception. As the GRE header encapsulates (hides) the flow information, the routers cannot properly determine which packets belong to which flow to load balance the flows. Nevertheless, the flows can be identified before entering any tunnel, and load balancing can happen over multiple tunnels.

Figure 6-9 *Resilient GRE Tunnel Overlay*

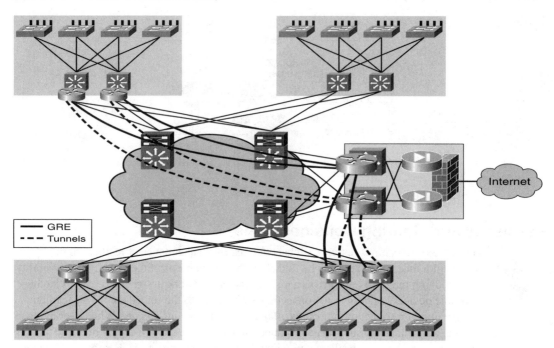

In principle, the core of the network should be able to recuperate from a failure in the core without a need for multiple tunnels. The IP network should reconverge and provide an alternate path for the original tunnel to continue forwarding traffic. This is true for failures that occur inside the core. However, this is not the case when the failure occurs at the tunnel endpoints (campus network distribution) or beyond the endpoints (access-distribution uplinks).

If a distribution switch fails, or if any of the uplinks from the access switches fail, the redundant distribution switch should take over and continue to forward traffic upstream and downstream.

The failover is straightforward for traffic originated at the failed site. Regular spanning-tree and first-hop resiliency mechanisms such as HSRP will ensure that traffic is diverted around a local failure. The multiple tunnels will be active at all times, providing a path for the traffic being sent regardless of the failover state of the distribution block.

Failover of traffic received at a failed distribution block is slightly more involved. For this scenario, the local "healthy" distribution block would need to send traffic only over the tunnels that terminate on the remaining "healthy" switch at the remote failed distribution block. Figure 6-10 illustrates local and remote failure scenarios.

Figure 6-10 *Local and Remote Failures*

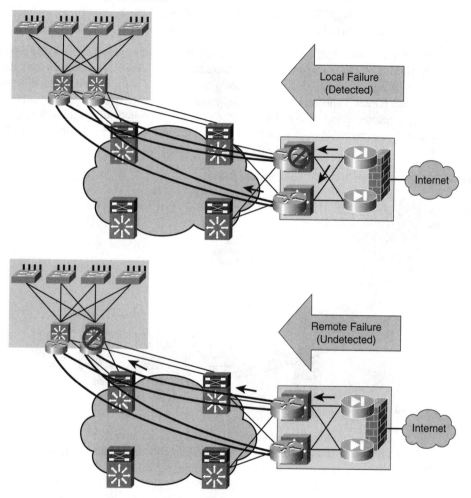

One important consideration to make when working with GRE tunnels is that these do not have a keepalive mechanism. This means that if one end of the tunnel goes down, the other end will not be informed of this failure and will continue to forward traffic over the failed tunnel, which will result in "blackholed" traffic. This is exactly the situation encountered in the remote failure scenario described earlier and illustrated in Figure 6-10. Deploying a dynamic routing protocol that peers over the tunnels is one way of providing a mechanism for dynamic tunnel failure detection (other mechanisms such as GRE tunnel keepalives are available in specific platforms). The routing entry for a prefix reachable over a failed tunnel should age out as the advertising neighbor is lost. Traffic should no longer be forwarded over the failed tunnel interface, forcing all traffic over the remaining healthy tunnel. Thus, a dynamic routing protocol provides both load-balancing information and remote failure signaling. It is therefore critical to enable a routing protocol over the GRE tunnel mesh.

This is easily done when using VRFs to map traffic to tunnels. It becomes a bit more involved when using PBR to steer traffic into the tunnel mesh, requiring tracking mechanisms and detailed route filtering. We will now analyze these two scenarios.

Figure 6-11 shows VRFs mapped to a redundant mesh of tunnels between two redundant distribution blocks. To provide remote failure detection, an IGP is enabled on the VRFs, and IGP peering is established over the tunnels. When traffic is forwarded by the distribution switch, a tunnel is chosen based on the information in the VRF (routing table). Because the VRF is updated dynamically by the IGP, it will only contain healthy routes. Therefore, if a prefix is not reachable over a specific tunnel, this route will not be listed in the VRF as a valid alternative and no traffic will be forwarded over this tunnel.

Figure 6-11 *IGP on VRFs for Dynamic Tunnel Failure Detection*

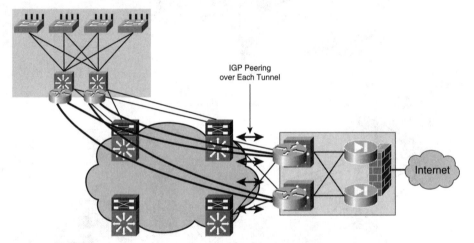

When no VRFs are present and traffic is steered into the tunnels by means of PBR, a dynamic routing protocol will be of little help in choosing a healthy tunnel to forward traffic. PBR will steer traffic into the failed tunnel regardless of the state of the routing protocol; in this respect, it is equivalent to having static routes that override any dynamically learned routes. Therefore, it is necessary to provide conditional PBR functionality, which means the static PBR routes will only be enforced if the routes are feasible (that is, if the tunnel is healthy and the routes are learned over the tunnel). Therefore, to achieve resiliency when using PBR to steer traffic into the tunnels, two components are necessary:

- A dynamic routing protocol over the tunnels
- Conditional PBR functionality

Without the dynamic routing protocol, the conditional PBR functionality has no way of determining whether the tunnel is healthy. Hence, both elements are required.

NOTE	It is important to highlight that we have proposed using either PBR or VRFs to steer traffic into the tunnel mesh, but not a combination of them. In the current implementation, PBR and VRFs do not interoperate.

Regardless of the technique used to steer traffic into the tunnels, a routing protocol must be overlaid to the tunnel mesh. Certain considerations must be made for the deployment of an IGP over GRE tunnels, including the following:

- **NHRP registration delay**—When the connection of the spoke to the network comes up, it is ready to begin sending routing protocol information because the tunnel interface is configured as p2p. At the other end, the hub router cannot begin sending routing protocol information until NHRP registrations arrive from each spoke device and the NHRP cache gets populated.

- **GRE tunnel bandwidth**—Cisco recommends statically configuring the bandwidth parameter on GRE tunnel interfaces to the actual bandwidth available on the link. The default bandwidth of a GRE tunnel is 9 kbps. This might cause a couple of issues. First, any routing protocol using bandwidth as a metric receives misleading information. Second, Cisco EIGRP assigns half of this bandwidth for the use of the routing protocol, which most likely would be insufficient.

- **IP maximum transmission unit (MTU)**—It is important, especially when using OSPF, to check that the IP MTU settings match on the tunnel interfaces on both sides of the link. The recommended MTU value is 1400 bytes, which leaves room for GRE and IPsec overhead (if needed) and avoids packet fragmentation.

- **OSPF interface types and priority**—In the hub-and-spoke topology described previously, the mGRE tunnel interface is considered p2p from an OSPF standpoint. Because the same interface will start receiving hellos and OSPF packets from different spokes, that would prevent the establishment of adjacencies. To fix the problem, the OSPF network type should be configured in a "point-to-multipoint" architecture on both the hubs and all the spokes.

Based on these considerations, the configuration of the generic hub-and-spoke GRE interfaces would need to be changed as shown in Example 6-20 (configuration excerpt valid for OSPF).

Example 6-20 *Enabling OSPF on a Hub-and-Spoke mGRE Overlay*

```
! Hub
interface Tunnel0
 description mGRE tunnel
 bandwidth 1000
 ip vrf forwarding guest
 ip address 172.16.100.1 255.255.255.0
 no ip redirects
 ip mtu 1400
```

continues

Example 6-20 *Enabling OSPF on a Hub-and-Spoke mGRE Overlay (Continued)*

```
 ip nhrp map multicast dynamic
 ip nhrp network-id 100
 ip ospf network point-to-multipoint
 tunnel source Loopback0
 tunnel mode gre multipoint
! Spoke
interface Tunnel0
 description GRE tunnel to hub-1
 bandwidth 1000
 ip vrf forwarding guest
 ip address 172.16.100.2 255.255.255.0
 ip mtu 1400
 ip nhrp network-id 100
 ip nhrp nhs 172.16.100.1
 ip nhrp registration timeout 60
 ip ospf network point-to-multipoint
 ip ospf priority 0
 tunnel source Loopback0
 tunnel destination 10.126.100.254
```

The hub devices will learn all the routes for the spoke subnets out of the same mGRE interface. The additional information contained in the NHRP cache allows the hubs to be able to route back the traffic to the proper spokes. Example 6-21 shows *command-line interface* (CLI) output valid for an EIGRP example.

NOTE   Notice how every prefix is reachable over the same tunnel 0 interface, but via different next-hop routers.

Example 6-21 *Hub Routes in a Hub-and-Spoke mGRE Overlay*

```
! Hub
6500-Int-1#sh ip route vrf guest
Routing Table: guest
Codes: C - connected, S - static, R - RIP, M - mobile, B - BGP
       D - EIGRP, EX - EIGRP external, O - OSPF, IA - OSPF inter area
       N1 - OSPF NSSA external type 1, N2 - OSPF NSSA external type 2
       E1 - OSPF external type 1, E2 - OSPF external type 2, E - EGP
       i - IS-IS, su - IS-IS summary, L1 - IS-IS level-1, L2 - IS-IS level-2
       ia - IS-IS inter area, * - candidate default, U - per-user static route
       o - ODR, P - periodic downloaded static route
Gateway of last resort is 172.18.1.30 to network 0.0.0.0
     172.16.0.0/16 is variably subnetted, 4 subnets, 2 masks
D       172.16.11.0/24 [90/297244672] via 172.16.100.2, 00:00:05, Tunnel0
                       [90/297244672] via 172.16.100.3, 00:00:05, Tunnel0
D       172.16.21.0/24 [90/297244672] via 172.16.100.4, 00:00:05, Tunnel0
                       [90/297244672] via 172.16.100.5, 00:00:05, Tunnel0
D       172.16.31.0/24 [90/297244672] via 172.16.100.6, 00:00:05, Tunnel0
                       [90/297244672] via 172.16.100.7, 00:00:05, Tunnel0
```

Example 6-21 *Hub Routes in a Hub-and-Spoke mGRE Overlay (Continued)*

```
C       172.16.100.0/24 is directly connected, Tunnel0
        172.18.0.0/24 is subnetted, 1 subnets
C       172.18.1.0 is directly connected, Vlan181
S*    0.0.0.0/0 /0] via 172.18.1.30
```

Encryption Considerations

Encryption of the tunnel overlay is rarely a requirement in a campus or MAN environment. Chapter 5 "Infrastructure Segmentation Architectures: Theory" discussed how to enable encryption over a GRE tunnel. Should there be an encryption requirement, the same principles would apply to the logical overlays described in this section. We study encryption in much more detail in Chapter 7 "Extending the Virtualized Enterprise over the WAN."

Layer 3 VPNs

Chapter 5 discussed the subtleties of RFC 2547bis. We now delve into some recommendations about how to deploy this architecture in the campus network and MAN. The main motivation for an enterprise to adopt this architecture is scalability. So far, all the techniques we have presented have scalability restrictions at different levels.

RFC 2547bis the MPLS Way

Although RFC 2547bis VPNs are scalable, they require sophisticated software and hardware that may not be readily available throughout the enterprise. Therefore, MPLS VPNs are likely to be adopted in large campus network deployments that actually resemble a MAN.

Campus Network / MAN Deployment

When you are deploying RFC 2547bis, the recommendation is to position the PEs at the edge of the routed domain. Thus, the first Layer 3 hop that traffic from a host encounters (usually the distribution switches) would ideally be a PE router. When using MPLS to deploy RFC 2547bis, pushing the PE role to the distribution switches implies that all devices in the routed domain must support label switching (a.k.a. MPLS), and all distribution switches must support PE functionality, which is basically the capability of supporting multiple VRFs, *multiprotocol iBGP* (MP-iBGP), and MPLS.

In this scenario, there are no CE routers because the PE routers (distribution switches in this case) are directly connected to the user subnets or VLANs. User VLANs are terminated at the distribution switches (PE), where the VLANs belonging to a group are mapped onto the VRF for the corresponding group, as described previously.

The deployment of RFC 2547bis requires a core IGP for the interconnection of the PEs. This IGP is the same as the IGP used in a nonvirtualized campus network or MAN and should be designed according to standard hierarchical best practices for campus network and MAN design. The core IGP serves a dual purpose: It allows the establishment of

MP-iBGP sessions between the PEs, and it provides the global IP information for the establishment of *label switched paths* (LSPs) between PEs. When all traffic is assigned to VPNs, the core IGP should not carry information on user prefixes. However, the fact that the core IGP can carry user prefixes if necessary is a powerful migration tool that we exploit in a later section.

Label switching and a *Label Distribution Protocol* (LDP) must be enabled on all platforms. On the P routers, this must be enabled on all interfaces. On the PE routers, label switching is only to be enabled on the core-facing interfaces (those facing the P routers). Example 6-22 shows the commands to enable MPLS at the global and interface level.

Example 6-22 *Enabling MPLS*

```
mpls label protocol ldp
tag-switching tdp router-id Loopback0 force
...
interface GigabitEthernet1/1
 description To P1 - intf G3/0/0
 ip address 125.1.100.50 255.255.255.252
 tag-switching ip
 !
```

RFC 2547bis also requires a full mesh of MP-iBGP neighbor relationships between all PEs. This full mesh is used to populate the VRFs with VPN routes. The reason for a full mesh is that iBGP is nontransitive, and therefore any prefix that is to be announced by a PE over iBGP must be a directly connected prefix. The scalable alternative to full mesh of BGP sessions is the use of *route reflectors* (RRs), which we discuss in more detail in the section "BGP Best Practices: Route Reflectors."

The general configuration for MP-iBGP on a PE follows. In this particular example, the PE is peering with a pair of RRs (125.1.125.15 and 125.1.125.16), and there are two VRFs, which include directly connected subnets into their BGP advertisements through the command **redistribute connected**. Let's look at it step by step. As illustrated in Example 6-23, you must create the BGP process and the iBGP neighbor sessions with the RRs. This is no different from any regular BGP deployment, and there is no multiprotocol element to this step.

Example 6-23 *Enabling BGP Neighbor Sessions*

```
router bgp 1
 no synchronization
 bgp log-neighbor-changes
 neighbor 125.1.125.15 remote-as 1
 neighbor 125.1.125.15 update-source Loopback0
 neighbor 125.1.125.16 remote-as 1
 neighbor 125.1.125.16 update-source Loopback0
 no auto-summary
 !
```

After the neighbor sessions have been created, these sessions must be activated within the VPNv4 address family and the extended **community** attribute must be enabled for each neighbor, as illustrated in Example 6-24. At this point, we are enabling the multiprotocol portion of BGP. As discussed in previous chapters, the extended **community** attribute will carry important VPN information such as the *route targets* (RTs). Simultaneously, the VPNv4 *Network Layer Reachability Information* (NLRI) updates will carry other important VPN information such as the *route distinguishers* (RDs).

Example 6-24 *Enabling VPNv4 Updates and the Extended Community*

```
address-family vpnv4
neighbor 125.1.125.15 activate
neighbor 125.1.125.15 send-community extended
neighbor 125.1.125.16 activate
neighbor 125.1.125.16 send-community extended
exit-address-family
!
```

Finally, the BGP characteristics for each VRF must be configured. This is done under the VRF address family and for each VRF. Any BGP configuration and tailoring is to be done under the VRF address families. This can include route redistribution directives, addition and alteration of attributes, route-map policy enforcement, and so on. This is illustrated in Example 6-25, where we use the **redistribute connected** command to include the directly connected VLANs in the BGP updates. This, of course, assumes that VLAN interfaces have been previously assigned to the VRFs.

Example 6-25 *Configuring BGP per Address Family*

```
address-family ipv4 vrf red-voice
redistribute connected
no auto-summary
no synchronization
exit-address-family
!
address-family ipv4 vrf red-data
redistribute connected
  no auto-summary
no synchronization
exit-address-family
!
```

Multi-VRF CE Deployments

Many enterprise platforms do not support MPLS PE functionality. However, it is necessary to extend the VPN separation achieved in the MPLS cloud to non-MPLS routed platforms located in the periphery of the MPLS domain.

Most Cisco enterprise platforms support VRF-lite functionality, which is also known as multi-VRF CE functionality. Multi-VRF CE refers to the capability of CE platforms to host multiple VRFs. By connecting the VRFs at a CE with those at the PEs of a network, it is possible to extend the separation achieved by an MPLS VPN to non-MPLS hops in the periphery of the MPLS cloud. An MPLS VPN network surrounded by multi-VRF CE devices is illustrated in Figure 6-12.

Figure 6-12 *MPLS VPNs with Multi-VRF CE*

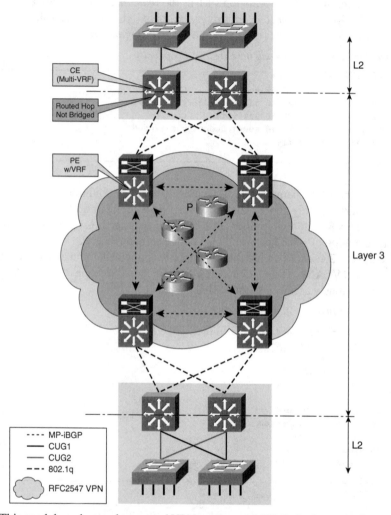

This model can be used to extend VPNs onto non-MPLS platforms in the campus network and MAN, especially in the WAN. We explore WANs in more detail in the next few chapters. To deploy the multi-VRF CEs, it is necessary to complete the following steps. We outline only the necessary steps here because the configuration detail has been discussed previously in the section "Layer 3 Hop to Hop."

Step 1   Create VRFs on the non-MPLS platforms.

Step 2   Create 802.1q trunks on the PE-CE links.

Step 3   Associate each pair of VRFs to be interconnected with a VLAN on the 802.1q trunk. By assigning SVIs to VRFs.

Step 4   Configure dynamic routing between the PE and CE for each pair of VRFs

Step 5   Redistribute the PE-CE IGP routes in each VRF into the corresponding MP-iBGP address family at the PE.

Step 6   Redistribute the MP-iBGP routes in each VRF into the corresponding PE-CE IGP instance.

RFC 2547bis over L2TPv3

We highlighted the fact that for a network to support RFC 2547bis VPNs over MPLS, every Layer 3 hop in the network must be MPLS capable. More precisely, every PE and P router must be a *label switched router* (LSR; that is, MPLS enabled).

As discussed in Chapters 4 and 5, the reason for requiring MPLS is that the VPN traffic is tunneled between PEs to preserve its separation. These tunnels are dynamic and are known as *label switched paths* (LSPs).

It is not uncommon for an enterprise to have a core that contains non-MPLS devices. In this case, running RFC 2547bis over *Layer 2 Tunnel Protocol Version 3* (L2TPv3) provides an alternative in which only IP forwarding capabilities are required in the core. L2TPv3 tunnels can be established dynamically between PEs and substitute for the role of the LSPs in an MPLS VPN network.

Another scenario in which a non-MPLS solution is of value is that in which an enterprise wants to deploy RFC 2547bis VPNs over a core composed of multiple autonomous systems. An MPLS-based VPN solution requires the deployment of a separate VPN domain for each autonomous system. This fragments the VPN network and requires sophisticated inter-autonomous system routing mechanisms to be able to join the VPNs in the different autonomous systems. Because L2TPv3 tunnels require only IP connectivity to be established, these can traverse multiple autonomous systems without any special consideration. Therefore, an L2TPv3-based solution is ideal for the deployment of RFC 2547bis VPNs over a multi-autonomous-system core.

NOTE   When you are using L2TPv3 to traverse several autonomous systems, the MP-BGP sessions used to carry VPNv4 updates are still internal BGP sessions. The multiple autonomous systems simply provide IP connectivity and do not influence the autonomous system characteristics of the MP-iBGP overlay. Thus, a single BGP autonomous system is overlaid onto a multi-autonomous-system IGP cloud.

It is important to highlight that this solution continues to use all the components of RFC 2547bis except for the LDP and the LSPs. Therefore, all the considerations and best practice recommendations for core IGP, MP-iBGP, resiliency, and scalability are valid for any implementation of RFC 2547bis and are therefore discussed in a separate section.

RFC 2547bis over GRE

The scenario for GRE as a replacement for LSPs brings similar benefits as L2TPv3. Differences are inherent to the way the tunneling technologies work, but these are beyond the scope of relevance for virtualization and are more of an implementation debate.

Similar to L2TPv3-based RFC 2547bis, the GRE option continues to leverage MP-iBGP and a core IGP, and therefore all the best practices that are discussed in the following sections are applicable to all implementations of RFC 2547bis, including MPLS, GRE, and L2TPv3-based solutions.

IGP Best Practices

As explained in Chapter 2, the core IGP must be deployed in a hierarchical manner; and, where possible, redundant paths must be exploited to provide *equal-cost multipath* (ECMP) routing. A design with equal-cost paths will largely simplify the overlaying BGP and MPLS design and allow the campus network and MAN to continue benefiting from the fast convergence and load-balancing characteristics it has traditionally enjoyed.

The guidelines for IGP deployment can be summarized as follows:

- Provide a hierarchical topology onto which the routing protocol can be laid.
- Provide a routing protocol hierarchy by creating zones or summarizing.
- Create symmetric topologies leading to equal-cost path formation.
- Enable ECMP routing to exploit the use of equal-cost paths for load balancing and improved failover.
- Optimize routing protocol convergence.

If all this is done optimally, the benefits of load sharing, rapid reconvergence, and containment of failures will be inherited by the overlaying VPN architecture. Therefore, providing rapid failover or load sharing in an enterprise VPN network might not be a matter of implementing complex MPLS-based traffic engineering, but this functionality may be available due to the design of our core IGP. The next few sections explore many guidelines that help our VPN overlay benefit from the resilient characteristics of our core IGP.

BGP Best Practices: Route Reflectors

As discussed, for each VPN to have a complete routing table, there must be a full mesh of iBGP sessions between all PEs. This will become hard to scale quickly and would require the reconfiguration of all PEs every time a PE is added or removed from the network. It is therefore recommended that *route reflectors* (RRs) be used and that all PEs peer with these RRs.

In general, it is recommended that the RRs be kept out of the data path. This limits the load on the RRs, protects them from attackers by limiting their reachability, and allows a choice of platforms optimized for memory-intensive tasks and control-plane functionality vs.

platforms engineered to forward large amounts of traffic at high speed. It is also advisable that the RRs not be PE routers (for similar reasons).

RRs should be deployed in a resilient array to avoid creating a single point of failure in the network. Because this resiliency is based on TCP connections (or BGP sessions), it is possible to distribute the resilient RRs anywhere in the network to increase their availability.

BGP Best Practices: Route Distinguishers and ECMP Routing

When we are discussing VRFs and BGP, one concept that may be confusing is that of route distinguishers (RDs), their function and how they differ from *route targets* (RTs).

RDs are 64-bit labels that locally identify a prefix as part of a VRF. These 64-bit RDs are prepended to the IPv4 prefixes in the routing table to form VPNv4 prefixes. MP-iBGP updates carry these RDs as part of the VPNv4 NLRIs. However, the RDs will not determine whether a received NLRI is included in a particular VRF or not; therefore, some other coloring is required to decide which VRF the received routes are to be placed into.

RTs have more of a global role and are used to "color" the MP-iBGP routing updates between the PEs and determine which VRFs will or will not accept the routing updates. Thus, the RTs determine the formation of VPNs and also allow inter- VN route updates necessary for the creation of extranets.

Because the updates carry both an RT and RD value, it is possible to receive multiple updates for a single prefix and be able to differentiate the updates based on the RD value.

In a network that uses dual PEs to connect each prefix into the core, it is important to preserve the routing updates from both PEs for resiliency reasons. Campus networks and MANs are examples of networks that use dual PEs to provide resilient connectivity paths for the networks at each site.

We have recommended the use of RRs for the establishment of the required iBGP sessions. When an RR receives many updates to the same prefix, its default behavior is to choose one of the routes (the best route from its perspective) and discard the rest. Therefore, when dual PEs advertise the same prefixes twice, the RR "reflects" only its preferred routes and discards the redundant routes (and with them the information on the resilient paths we put so much effort into creating). If the updates are not identical, however, the RR "reflects" both routes. One way of making the updates unique is by assigning different RDs to each PE. In the example illustrated in Figure 6-13, the RR receives two updates for subnet 111.111.111.0: one from PE-1 and another from PE-2. Subnet 111.111.111.0 is in VRF red-data.

If VRF red-data is configured with the same RD on both PEs, the RR will advertise subnet 111.111.111.0 as reachable only via PE-1 or PE-2 but not both. Example 6-26 shows the BGP tables for the RR and the remote PEs. As seen in the example, the redundant route information is lost at the RR. We focus on the red-data VRF for this illustration.

Figure 6-13 *Multipath Routing and RRs*

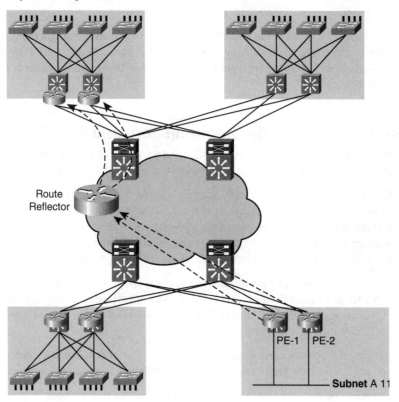

Example 6-26 *Equal-Cost Routes Lost During Route Reflection*

```
! PE-1
ip vrf red-data
 rd 10:1031
 route-target export 10:103
 route-target import 10:103
!
```

```
! PE-2
ip vrf red-data
 rd 10:1031
 route-target export 10:103
 route-target import 10:103
!
```

```
! Route reflector
7200-DC2-RR1#show ip bgp vpnv4 rd 10:1031
BGP table version is 7344946, local router ID is 125.1.125.15
Status codes: s suppressed, d damped, h history, * valid, > best, i—internal,
              r RIB-failure, S Stale
Origin codes: i—IGP, e—EGP, ?—incomplete
```

Example 6-26 *Equal-Cost Routes Lost During Route Reflection (Continued)*

```
    Network             Next Hop           Metric LocPrf Weight Path
    Route Distinguisher: 10:1031
    *>i1.1.1.1/32        125.1.125.5             2    100     0 ?
    *>i3.3.3.11/32       125.1.125.5             2    100     0 ?
    *>i3.3.3.13/32       125.1.125.5             2    100     0 ?
    *>i111.111.111.0/24 125.1.125.5             0    100     0 ?
    * i                  125.1.125.6             0    100     0 ?
    *>i125.1.101.0/30    125.1.125.5             0    100     0 ?
    ! PE-3
    7600-DC2-PE3#show ip route vrf red-data
    Routing Table: red-data
    Gateway of last resort is 125.1.125.17 to network 0.0.0.0
    ...
         111.0.0.0/24 is subnetted, 1 subnets
    B        111.111.111.0 [200/0] via 125.1.125.5, 00:00:09
```

When VRF red-data is configured with a different RD value on each PE, the RR will
advertise subnet 111.111.111.0 as reachable via PE-1 and PE-2. Example 6-27 displays the
corresponding configuration and BGP tables.

Example 6-27 *Equal-Cost Routes Preserved by Using Distinct RDs*

```
! PE-1
ip vrf red-data
 rd 10:1031
 route-target export 10:103
 route-target import 10:103
!
```

```
! PE-2
ip vrf red-data
 rd 10:1032
 route-target export 10:103
 route-target import 10:103
!
```

```
! Route reflector
7200-DC2-RR1#show ip bgp vpnv4 rd 10:1031
BGP table version is 7344894, local router ID is 125.1.125.15
    Network                   Next Hop            Metric LocPrf Weight Path
Route Distinguisher: 10:1031
    *>i1.1.1.1/32                125.1.125.5            2    100     0 ?
    *>i3.3.3.11/32       125.1.125.5             2    100     0 ?
    *>i3.3.3.13/32       125.1.125.5             2    100     0 ?
    *>i111.111.111.0/24  125.1.125.5             0    100     0 ?
    *>i125.1.101.0/30    125.1.125.5             0    100     0 ?
7200-DC2-RR1#show ip bgp vpnv4 rd 10:1032
BGP table version is 7344894, local router ID is 125.1.125.15
    Network                   Next Hop            Metric LocPrf Weight Path
Route Distinguisher: 10:1032
    *>i111.111.111.0/24  125.1.125.6             0    100     0 ?
```

continues

Example 6-27 *Equal-Cost Routes Preserved by Using Distinct RDs (Continued)*

```
! PE-3
7600-DC2-PE3#show ip route vrf red-data
Routing Table: red-data
Gateway of last resort is 125.1.125.17 to network 0.0.0.0
     1.0.0.0/32 is subnetted, 2 subnets
...
B      111.111.111.0        [200/0] via 125.1.125.6, 00:04:20
                            [200/0] via 125.1.125.5, 00:01:50
```

We have managed to populate the control plane with the necessary redundant routes. For the PEs to use the redundant routes for load-sharing purposes, it is necessary to enable the "iBGP multipath" capability on the PE routers. Doing so ensures that all available paths are used and traffic is balanced over these. The iBGP multipath command is used under the VRF address family configuration, as shown in Example 6-28.

Example 6-28 *iBGP Multipath*

```
address-family ipv4 vrf red-data
redistribute connected metric 1
redistribute ospf 1 vrf red-data match internal external 1 external 2
maximum-paths ibgp unequal-cost 8
no auto-summary
no synchronization
exit-address-family
```

Migration Recommendations

The introduction of MPLS and *multiprotocol BGP* (MBGP) in the enterprise represents a large technological leap from traditional campus network and MAN architectures. One of the main concerns for enterprises adopting these advanced technologies is having a nondisruptive migration strategy.

At a high level, the strategy should be based on creating all the necessary VN components before migrating any users from the original global routing space. In this manner, users continue to operate in their original environment while the new virtual environments are created. In the context of the MAN and LAN, we assume the enterprise is in control of all routed hops and if there are any leased circuits these are Layer 2 circuits. The scenario in which the enterprise deploys MPLS over its own Layer 3 infrastructure is also referred to as a self-deployed MPLS scenario.

You can complete the following control-plane changes without causing any disruption of the production traffic (notice that the core IGP remains untouched):

- Creation of VRFs at the PEs
- MP-iBGP configuration of the PEs

When ready to migrate the forwarding-plane to MPLS, the following guidelines will minimize downtime:

- Enable label switching one link at a time.

- Alter one link at a time to ensure that a redundant path always exists to forward production traffic. Try to migrate backup links first.

- Enable label switching at both ends of each link before moving to the next link.

- Migrate the least-critical portion of the network first and verify that traffic in the global table continues to be forwarded before migrating any other parts of the network.

At this point, all core links are migrated to tag switching, several VRFs are configured, and active MP-iBGP sessions exist between these VRFs. However, none of the user subnets have been included in any of the VRFs. Therefore, all user traffic continues to be routed as usual, although an MPLS label is used to forward the traffic. At this stage, it is advisable to verify that the VPNs are fully functional by using dummy prefixes and verifying that these are populated on the correct VRFs.

When users are ready to be migrated, you have two options:

- Use a maintenance window to migrate the users to the VRFs.

- Temporarily replicate the global table onto the VPN being populated. Doing so allows devices in the VPN and devices in the global table to continue to communicate with each other during the migration. After all required devices have been migrated to the VPN, the global routes can be eliminated from the VPN because they are no longer necessary. Although this approach reduces the perceived downtime, it does not fully eliminate it because ports go down momentarily when moved from one VLAN to another.

Layer 2 VPNs

As enterprises virtualize their networks, some might require the support of non-IP or nonroutable traffic in these virtualized environments. To support this type of traffic, it is necessary to extend Layer 2 domains across the enterprise network. In general, the extension of Layer 2 domains is discouraged because of all the scalability issues discussed in Chapter 2. Therefore, when pervasive any-to-any connectivity is required, it is highly advisable that a routed alternative be evaluated before considering any sort of Layer 2 extension. The requirement for Layer 2 extensibility is usually limited to the interconnection of a few sites to support legacy protocols or the interconnection of server farms. It is important to maintain the scale of this requirement as small as possible. As we study the different alternatives for extending Layer 2 connectivity, it will become evident that these are practical in solving a limited connectivity requirement and will cease to scale rapidly.

Instead of attempting to extend VLANs throughout the enterprise, the creation of VPNs for nonroutable traffic calls for the use of Layer 2 VPN or tunneling technologies that will provide the desired Layer 2 connectivity over the enterprise's routed core. In brief, the requirements for this type of Layer 2 connectivity are as follows:

- **Mainly p2p connectivity**—In many cases, the requirement for Layer 2 connectivity will be restricted to interconnecting a couple of sites only. For example, enterprises consolidating disperse server clusters will require, in general, the interconnection of two data centers.

- **Some multipoint connectivity**—For many reasons, enterprises might require the support of legacy (non-IP) protocols in their network. The hosts using these legacy protocols will require peer-to-peer connectivity. As the support for legacy protocols is gradually phased out across the industry, the support for these is maintained by transparently tunneling the information to interconnect the hosts.

- **Resiliency**—No single point of failure must be allowed when interconnecting the sites at Layer 2. This has interesting implications in the combination and use of different technologies.

Ethernet over MPLS

The following sections explore two of the most common MPLS-based Layer 2 VPN technologies: *Ethernet over MPLS* (EoMPLS) and *Virtual Private LAN Services* (VPLS).

Providing Point-to-Point Connectivity

EoMPLS pseudowires are by definition p2p Layer 2 connections. The basic operating principle of a pseudowire is that of being able to take any traffic received on an ingress port and transparently send it over to the egress port at the other end of the pseudowire (as shown in Figure 6-14).

Figure 6-14 *EoMPLS Pseudowires*

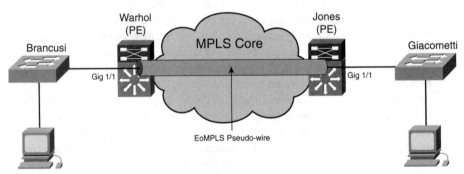

Two types of ports can be mapped to EoMPLS tunnels:

- **Routed physical ports**—This mode of operation is known as port mode.

- **Logical subinterfaces on a routed port**—This mode of operation is referred to as VLAN mode.

The creation of the pseudowire is achieved by encapsulating the traffic received on the "cross-connected" ingress port and switching it to the remote end based on the encapsulation header. The use of the encapsulation header allows the traffic to remain untouched as it traverses the routed cloud. When traffic arrives at the remote end, the encapsulation headers are removed, and traffic is forwarded out the egress port without any alterations. Because all traffic received on a cross-connected port is forwarded transparently, the PEs do not learn any MAC addresses on the cross-connected ports. Thus, the pseudowires effectively behave as a link extension or a virtual wire, which is commonly referred to as a pseudowire. Therefore, in the figure above, switches Giacometti and Brancusi appear as if directly connected by an Ethernet link.

An EoMPLS virtual circuit can be created between a pair of PE devices on opposite sides of the MPLS-enabled campus network or MAN to transparently carry the traffic between the two cross-connected ports. The cross-connected ports on each PE device receive and tunnel all the Ethernet frames from the Layer 2 switches at the edge. The configuration required for enabling this functionality on the PE interfaces is simple, as demonstrated in Example 6-29.

Example 6-29 *EoMPLS Pseudowire Configuration*

```
interface GigabitEthernet1/1
 description EoMPLS vc to Brancusi
 no ip address
 no cdp enable
 xconnect 3.3.3.1 1 encapsulation mpls
```

The **xconnect** command is basically the only command required, and it is used to specify the remote PE loopback address (for example, on Brancusi it is 3.3.3.1).

One restriction to be aware of is the size of the packets that can be sent over the pseudowire. Because there is no check done on the packets by the routers at the endpoints of the pseudowire, it is possible to exceed the valid MTU in the routed core by sending large packets. If the packet size is close to the MTU limit supported by the routed core, the addition of headers could generate packets of an MTU greater than what the network can support. In this case, jumbo frame support might be required in the network core.

Providing Multipoint Connectivity

As discussed, EoMPLS is a p2p technology. Any attempt to provide multi-site connectivity has to involve a combination of multiple p2p connections.

When you are combining multiple Layer 2 p2p connections, a hub-and-spoke logical topology can provide multipoint connectivity by aggregating and switching all traffic at the hub. Because a hub-and-spoke topology is loop free, there is no strict requirement on the use of STP.

EoMPLS circuits take all traffic on an interface and tunnel it over the MPLS core. Unfortunately, a single interface cannot be mapped to multiple EoMPLS pseudowires.

Therefore, you must use a distinct physical interface at the hub site for each remote site that needs to be connected. In other words, each pseudowire requires a dedicated physical interface at each end. To switch traffic between the different sites, you must aggregate these different interfaces onto a Layer 2 bridge at the hub site; this functionality can be provided by a separate switch, as shown in the figure. If this seems awkward, it is because EoMPLS was designed with p2p wire emulation in mind, not for multipoint switched-connectivity purposes.

In Figure 6-15, three physical links would be required on the hub PE to connect to the three different sites; the configuration for each of these interfaces is similar to the one displayed before, with an **xconnect** command on each interface to establish the EoMPLS virtual circuit with the remote PEs.

Figure 6-15 *Multipoint Connectivity Emulation with EoMPLS*

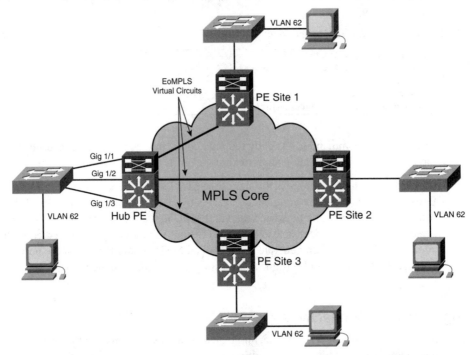

Resilient Pseudowire Topologies

Traffic entering an EoMPLS tunnel is not checked for integrity or validity. Therefore, any type of traffic can be forwarded over an EoMPLS pseudowire. This allows the transparent forwarding of Layer 2 control traffic such as STP *bridge protocol data units* (BPDUs), *Cisco Discovery Protocol* (CDP), *VLAN Trunking Protocol* (VTP), 802.3ad *Link Aggregation Control Protocol* (LACP), and so on. This allows the use of some traditional Ethernet protocols over the pseudowires to provide failure detection and failover mechanisms that enable resiliency.

Multiple Tunnels and CE STP

Because the EoMPLS pseudowires transparently forward all traffic they receive, the logical topology illustrated in Figure 6-16 is equivalent to directly connecting the edge switches (Brancusi and Giacometti) with two Ethernet links. This clearly forms a Layer 2 loop. Because the pseudowires forward all traffic transparently, including STP BPDUs, it is possible to run spanning tree between Brancusi and Giacometti to block the loop and to provide a resilient path in case of failures.

Figure 6-16 *Resilient Pseudowires*

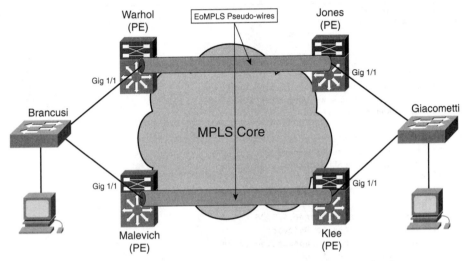

The use of the *Rapid Spanning Tree Protocol* (RSTP) allows optimal reconvergence and subsecond failover times in this array. However, this model does not provide any load balancing between the two pseudowires, and as a matter of fact, only half of the capacity in the network is used. The following section looks at alternatives that can provide load balancing and resiliency. However, the failover times for these alternatives are significantly slower.

Multiple Tunnels and CE Link Aggregation

To deploy resilient pseudowires between a pair of sites without creating a Layer 2 loop, you can bundle the two pseudowires to create a port channel. You should use a dynamic negotiation protocol to ensure that if a local link connecting to the PE fails, the remote site can detect the failure. The dynamic negotiation options include the following:

- PAgP (port aggregation protocol, a Cisco proprietary EtherChannel negotiation protocol)
- LACP (IEEE 802.3ad standard link aggregation protocol)

However, the timers on both these protocols provide relatively slow failure detection, in the order of 90 seconds.

Using *UniDirectional Link Detection* (UDLD) to provide failure detection can help lower the failover time between redundant circuits. The expected failover times with UDLD in aggressive mode vary between 20 and 40 seconds depending on the hardware used and the possibility of tuning the UDLD timers.

The configuration in Example 6-30 would be required on each of the switches establishing the bundle. Notice that these are not the PEs with the cross-connects, but the edge switches feeding traffic into the PEs.

Example 6-30 *Establishing an EtherChannel over EoMPLS Across Sites*

```
udld aggressive
udld message time 7

...

interface Port-channel1
 switchport trunk encapsulation dot1q
 switchport trunk allowed vlan 62
 switchport mode trunk
!
interface GigabitEthernet1/0/25
 description link to Warhol
 switchport trunk encapsulation dot1q
 switchport mode trunk
 channel-group 1 mode desirable
!
interface GigabitEthernet1/0/26
 description link to Malevich
 switchport trunk encapsulation dot1q
  switchport mode trunk
 channel-group 1 mode desirable
```

The connections between the Layer 2 switch and the PEs are trunk links; therefore, various Layer 2 domains (VLANs) can be transparently extended using the same EoMPLS virtual circuits.

VPLS

As described in Chapter 5, VPLS provides a mechanism to provide multipoint Layer 2 connectivity over an MPLS switched infrastructure. At first, this may sound like a scalable alternative to extending VLANs across the enterprise. However, it is important to keep in mind that VPLS has its own scalability limitations:

- Virtual circuit proliferation. Each VFI is in reality a full mesh of p2p pseudowires. As the number of sites increases, the mesh of pseudowires becomes more complex.

- The lack of intelligent broadcast and multicast handling can cause large-scale traffic replication and flooding throughout the network.

- Every PE must learn all the MAC addresses associated to a VFI. If this is intended to replace end-to-end VLANs, the number of MAC addresses to be learned may well be close to the full capacity of most high-end switching platforms.

- By deploying VPLS, we are effectively converting a Layer 3 core back to Layer 2. With this conversion, all the scalability and resiliency limitations of a plain Layer 2 network come back into play.

VPLS is by no means an alternative to Layer 3-based segmentation. Although it can provide any-to-any connectivity, it can only do it effectively for a limited number of hosts and sites.

NOTE   When used in a service provider setting, VPLS has different requirements than when used in an enterprise. The scalability concerns for VPLS in a service provider setting are much different. For instance, the enterprise might intend to use VPLS for Layer 2 extensibility, whereas the service provider might require a routed hop to access the VPLS cloud and therefore not extend the customer's Layer 2 domains.

Because VPLS has been designed to cover a specific need in the service provider space, its availability on enterprise platforms is limited and its cost is high (when available).

VPLS could provide a valid alternative for small-scale multipoint Layer 2 connectivity. However, the cost-benefit ratio may not be justifiable (and hence our focus on multipoint solutions based on EoMPLS) .

Summary

You can combine many available technologies to allow the virtualization of an enterprise network. The resulting architectures have diverse levels of scalability and allow different types of connectivity. As the requirements of the enterprise grow, the sophistication of the technology required will also expand, potentially taking an enterprise from the deployment of simple ACLs to the implementation of an MPLS core.

Regardless of the technology chosen, you must preserve the resiliency and scalability of the network. This chapter explored the applicability of the different technologies and how you should approach these to maintain the desired level of resiliency and scalability.

Extending the Virtualized Enterprise over the WAN

Because of the variety of technology alternatives available from service providers, the WAN is an interesting part of the enterprise network. Depending on the services offered by the provider, the enterprise will have different levels of control over the WAN. In many cases, the enterprise will require the use of overlay logical networks to fulfill its WAN connectivity requirements. These logical overlays become more sophisticated when they must support multiple *virtual networks* (VNs). This chapter analyzes the different WAN scenarios the enterprise faces and discusses the technology alternatives and best practices for maintaining multiple VNs over the different WAN offerings.

WAN Services

The most common WAN services currently offered by providers are as follows:

- **IP services**—Layer 3 *virtual private networks* (VPNs) or the Internet
- **Layer 2 circuits**—Traditional Frame Relay, ATM, or Ethernet Layer 2 circuits

In addition, it is common for an enterprise to deploy overlay networks on top of these services. Some of the most widely used overlays are as follows:

- *Point-to-point generic routing encapsulation* (p2p GRE)
- Hub-and-spoke *multipoint GRE* (mGRE)
- *Dynamic multipoint VPN* (DMVPN)

The following sections describe these services and overlays in more detail.

IP Services

IP services are among the most common types of WAN services available from providers. These can be public services such as the Internet or private IP VPNs. In either case, IP services provide any-to-any site connectivity to the enterprise. Such connectivity makes the service particularly attractive to the enterprise because it can integrate the WAN IP cloud into its own Layer 3 routing.

Figure 7-1 shows a *Multiprotocol Label Switching* (MPLS)-based provider cloud with separate IP VPNs for customers X and Y. The figure displays shared services offered by the provider and the capability of creating extranet connectivity for partners to customers X/Y.

Figure 7-1 *WAN IP Services*

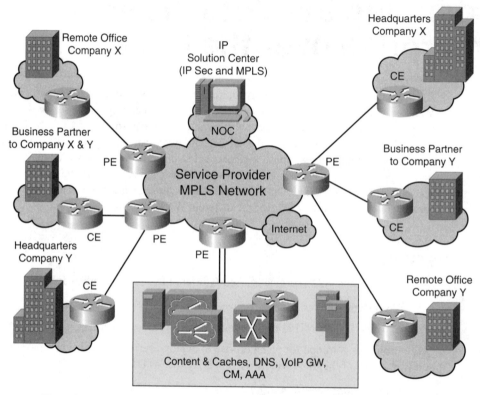

To optimize their operations and minimize their costs, service providers use different technologies to provide IP connectivity for enterprises. One widely used technology is MPLS; other alternatives to create IP VPNs are based on *Layer 2 Tunnel Protocol Version 3* (L2TPv3) or even GRE. However, the technology used by the service provider should not matter to the enterprise. All an enterprise should be concerned about is the fact that it is getting IP services. This service implies routed hops in the WAN that the enterprise does not control.

The lack of control over the Layer 3 hops in the IP WAN affects the capability of the enterprise to maintain multiple VNs per customer across the WAN cloud. It is important to note at this point that the scenario we face is the need to create multiple VNs inside each customer VPN present in the provider network. For instance, customer X might have two internal groups: contractors and employees. In this case, Customer X requires a single service provider VPN and two VNs, one for contractors and one for employees, to be transported separately inside the service provider VPN.

To maintain the separation between VNs across the IP WAN, an overlay of logical circuits is usually required. For example, a full mesh of GRE tunnels between the *customer edge* (CE) routers provides a logical topology in which the enterprise controls all routed hops. For the purposes of IP control and forwarding, the tunnels create a direct logical connection between the enterprise routers, thus bypassing the provider's routers. This overlay allows the enterprise to use h*op-to-hop* (h2h) virtualization techniques in an IP WAN.

Other alternatives include the use of separate IP VPN services per group and the use of *carrier supporting carrier* (CsC) services from the WAN provider. We discuss all these options in detail later in this chapter.

Layer 2 Circuits

Layer 2 circuits such as Frame Relay and ATM circuits are the traditional way in which service providers have offered WAN connectivity. More recent technologies have extended these offerings to include Ethernet services, allowing the enterprise to connect to the WAN over a familiar Ethernet interface. Whichever the case, these p2p Layer 2 circuits can be deployed in a hub-and-spoke topology or in a full mesh, as depicted in Figure 7-2. Over these topologies, enterprises can deploy and manage their own IP routing. This gives the enterprise complete control over the IP forwarding and control planes, which enables it to implement different IP-based technologies to provide the desired segmentation in the WAN.

Figure 7-2   *WAN Layer 2 Circuits*

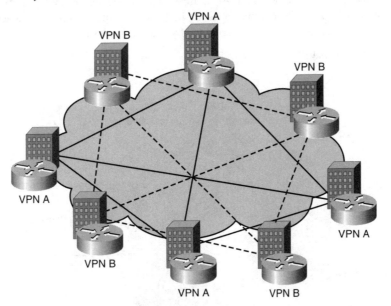

P2P GRE

Point-to-point GRE tunnels can be overlaid onto a private IP VPN or a public IP service such as the Internet. As discussed previously, this tunnel overlay creates a logical topology for the enterprise to deploy its own IP routing independently of the IP routing provided by the service provider. Thus, there are two independent IP control planes in operation:

- **The service provider control plane**—Used to provide connectivity between the GRE endpoints and enable the overlay logical topology. Only the IP prefixes for the GRE endpoints in the CE devices need to be included in the service provider control plane.

- **The enterprise control plane**—Uses the logical overlay topology to create adjacencies and define routes to enterprise prefixes.

The enterprise routing process sees the mesh of GRE tunnels as the set of interfaces it can use to forward traffic and reach the different destinations. The enterprise prefixes need to be included only in the enterprise routing process, which also includes the GRE tunnel interfaces, as described in Chapter 6, "Infrastructure Segmentation Architectures: Practice." Therefore, the enterprise will use a separate interior gateway protocol (IGP) that peers over the mesh of GRE tunnels.

Figure 7-3 shows how the address spaces for the provider cloud and the enterprise are kept separate as the service provider peers over the physical topology and the enterprise peers over the logical tunnel overlay. In the diagram, the 192.168.x.0/24 and the 10.0.0.0/24 networks are part of the enterprise address space inside the logical topology established by the tunnels. The physical interfaces are in the service provider address space, illustrated with the 172.x.x.x IP addresses on the physical interfaces in Figure 7-3.

Figure 7-3 *P2P GRE Tunnel Overlay on an IP WAN*

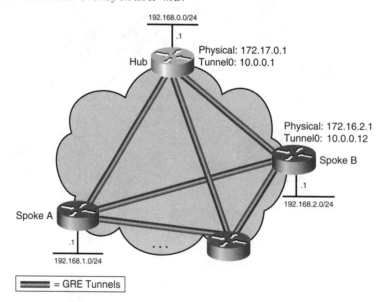

The mesh of GRE tunnels can be seen as a form of VPN in itself, a view further enhanced by the association of the GRE tunnel mesh to independent routing tables or *virtual routing and forwarding* (VRF) instances. Another important element that enhances this type of deployment is the ability to encrypt the GRE connections with IPsec. The combination of GRE and IPsec is instrumental in providing concurrent support for encryption and multicast traffic. The multicast support provided through the GRE encapsulation is necessary for the deployment of the enterprise IGP over the mesh of tunnels. Encryption is critical whenever the IP service is shared with other users.

Multipoint GRE

The GRE tunnel overlay solution can be improved by consolidating the multiple tunnel interfaces used at a hub site into single multipoint tunnel interfaces. However, this approach is restricted to providing a hub-and-spoke logical topology in which the hub hosts a *multipoint GRE* (mGRE) tunnel interface and each spoke has a single p2p GRE tunnel going back to the hub. Even though we use the same any-to-any Layer 3 adjacency mesh that is used for the p2p GRE overlay, traffic between spokes will always transit the hub site as shown in Figure 7-4. DMVPN, described in the next section, provides a means to achieve a more efficient spoke-to-spoke traffic path.

Figure 7-4   *mGRE Tunnel Overlay on an IP WAN*

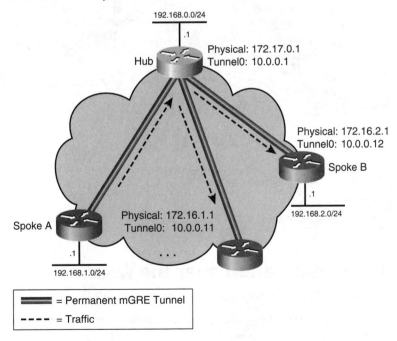

Dynamic Multipoint VPN

Dynamic multipoint VPN, better known as DMVPN, provides a mechanism to build an efficient and manageable GRE tunnel overlay with encryption. DMVPN relies on the use of multipoint GRE interfaces at the hub-and-spoke sites while dynamically building tunnels between spokes to allow direct spoke-to-spoke connectivity.

The solution relies on the *Next Hop Resolution Protocol* (NHRP). Each spoke registers its address with the NHRP database at the hub when it first connects. This information is then used to provide tunnel selection at the hub site. At the spokes, the NHRP database is queried by the spokes to resolve the real addresses of destination spokes and build direct tunnels between spokes, as shown in Figure 7-5. DWVPN is analyzed in more detail in Chapter 5.

Figure 7-5   *DMVPN Overlaid to an IP WAN*

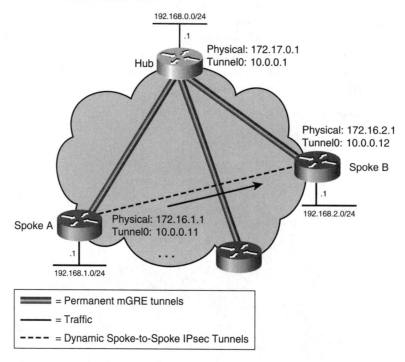

Extending Segmentation over the WAN

Two main types of connectivity can be provided over a WAN:

- Interconnectivity of segmented metropolitan-area networks (MANs) and campuses networks
- Aggregation of branches requiring segmentation

Subtle differences exist between supporting the interconnection of segmented MANs/campus networks and the aggregation of segmented branches. However, you can apply the available techniques to either scenario. The techniques for extending VNs over the WAN include the following:

- MPLS over Layer 2 circuits
- Multiple VPNs from the service provider
- CsC
- MPLS over GRE tunnels
- RFC 2547 VPNs over L2TPv3 IP tunnels
- Multi-VRF interconnected with mGRE/DMVPN overlays
- RFC 2547 VPNs over mGRE/DMVPN

In this section, we analyze the different techniques from both perspectives (site interconnection and branch aggregation). Each of the options can address the scenario in which segmentation is required at some branches and not required at others, as depicted in Figure 7-6. Branches that do not require segmentation might have to be placed in their own VRF, the default common VRF, or the global table at the headend depending on the enterprise requirements.

Figure 7-6 *Segmented and Nonsegmented Branches*

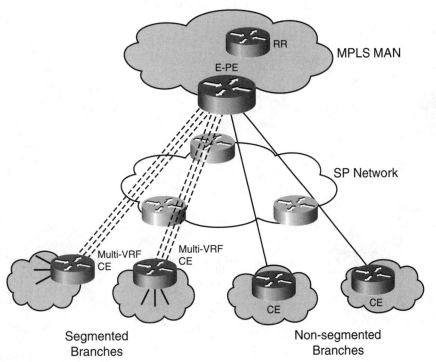

NOTE   As we analyze the different options, it is important to understand that all traffic is originally
forwarded using the global routing table. As VNs are created, traffic that does not require
segmentation can continue to use the global routing table, whereas segmented traffic can be
assigned to VNs as needed.

MPLS over Layer 2 Circuits

The simplest deployment model for connecting MANs and campus networks that have
been segmented by means of RFC 2547/MPLS VPNs is to use MPLS over Layer 2 circuits.
You can also use this method for branch aggregation, however, the use of Layer 2 circuits
for branch aggregation is becoming less and less common. The goal is basically to build
one large MPLS network in which the WAN simply provides Layer 2 connectivity but does
not participate in the IP routing of the enterprise.

This model requires the enterprise to have Layer 2 connectivity between the different sites
either via a legacy WAN (Frame Relay/ATM) or via a Layer 2 VPN service from a provider.
The solution involves converting the edge devices into *provider* (P) or *provider edge* (PE)
devices and making the WAN part of the MPLS MAN/campus network. Figure 7-7 shows
a legacy Layer 2 WAN service and a Layer2 VPN service. The router roles have been
labeled with the prefixes E and P for enterprise and provider, respectively. For example,
E-PE is enterprise PE; whereas P-PE is provider PE.

Figure 7-7   *Layer 2 WAN Offerings: Legacy and L2VPN*

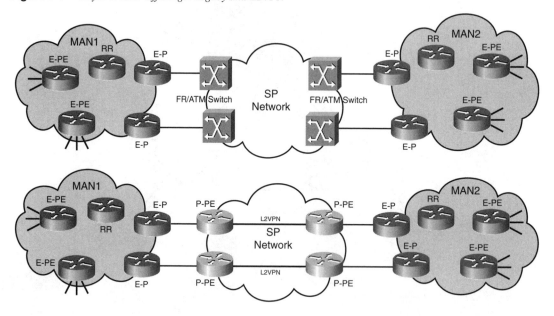

The LANs and MANs to be interconnected are already MPLS enabled and configured with enterprise-deployed RFC 2547 VPNs. As shown in Figure 7-7, the WAN edge router used for interconnecting MANs/LANs plays the role of an E-P device. That is, it is a P router in the enterprise MPLS network.

From a control-plane perspective, the following protocols run over the Layer 2 links:

- An IGP such as *Enhanced Interior Gateway Routing Protocol* (EIGRP) or *Open Shortest Path First* (OSPF) Protocol for MPLS device reachability. This enables the E-PE, E-P, and *route reflectors (*RRs) to reach each other.

- *Label Distribution Protocol* (LDP)

- *Multiprotocol internal Border Gateway Protocol* (MP-iBGP) for VPN route and label distribution among the E-PE devices (preferably through an RR).

Configuring this solution simply involves expanding the enterprise core to include the WAN. From the RFC 2547 VPN perspective, the following must be configured on the E-P routers:

- The IGP must be extended to have the E-P routers peer over the WAN interfaces. This is standard routing protocol configuration.

- A label distribution protocol must be enabled on each WAN edge (E-P) router. The global configuration must include the following commands:

```
ip cef
mpls label protocol ldp
```

- The E-P WAN interfaces and the interfaces facing the MPLS MAN or campus must be label switched. One of the following commands must be present under the interfaces:

```
mpls ip
tag-switching ip
```

From a forwarding perspective, irrespective of the Layer 2 service (legacy or Layer 2 VPN), the enterprise-edge device label switches packets like a normal P router, and the service provider should transparently forward the labeled packets across its network.

When the different MANs or LANs are in different autonomous systems, the extension of MPLS over the WAN is not as straightforward as discussed so far. When faced with multiple autonomous systems, it is necessary to interconnect these autonomous systems appropriately. Generally, you can interconnect separate autonomous systems to support end-to-end VPNs in three ways. The different options are defined in RFC 2547bis and discussed in detail in the MPLS-specific literature; therefore, this text is limited to briefly introducing the different inter-autonomous system models.

VRF-to-VRF Connections at the Autonomous System Border Routers

This model, which is also known as back-to-back VRFs, is equivalent to connecting two totally separate MPLS clouds back to back on a pair of PE routers. This procedure involves two PEs (one from each autonomous system) connected back to back through several subinterfaces (one subinterface per VPN). In this model, the PEs see each other as multi-VRF CEs. *External Border Gateway Protocol* (eBGP) is used to exchange routing information between one autonomous system and another.

MP-eBGP Exchange of Labeled VPN-IPv4 Routes Between Adjacent ASBRs

In this model, the PE routers use *multiprotocol internal BGP* (MP-iBGP) to redistribute labeled VPN-IPv4 routes to an *Autonomous System Border Router* (ASBR) either directly or through an RR. The ASBR then uses *multiprotocol external BGP* (MP-eBGP) to redistribute those labeled VPN-IPv4 routes to an ASBR in a neighboring autonomous system, which in turn distributes them via MP-iBGP to the PE routers in that autonomous system.

Multihop MP-eBGP Between Remote Autonomous Systems

This model enables the direct multihop MP-eBGP peering of PEs in one autonomous system with PEs in another. Thus, no VPN routes in the ASBRs interconnect the two autonomous systems. The ASBRs still have to exchange labeled VPN-IPv4 routes to provide reachability and label information to the PEs in either autonomous system; however, these updates do not contain VPN-specific routes.

Using MPLS over Layer 2 Circuits for Segmented Branch Aggregation

This model assumes that the enterprise has existing Layer 2 services for connecting branches. MPLS must be enabled over these Layer 2 links to provide segmentation through MPLS VPNs. Because such Layer 2 connectivity is typically hub and spoke or partial mesh, the MPLS overlay also inherits the same connectivity characteristics. Spoke-to-spoke communication then happens through the hub site.

The branch aggregation router becomes an E-P router, as shown in Figure 7-8. The branch routers become E-PE routers with VRF interfaces facing the branch and MPLS-enabled interfaces facing the headend. The E-P router at the headend label switches all interbranch traffic and all traffic between the branches and the MPLS-enabled MAN or campus network.

Figure 7-8   *Branch MPLS Segmentation over Layer 2 Circuits*

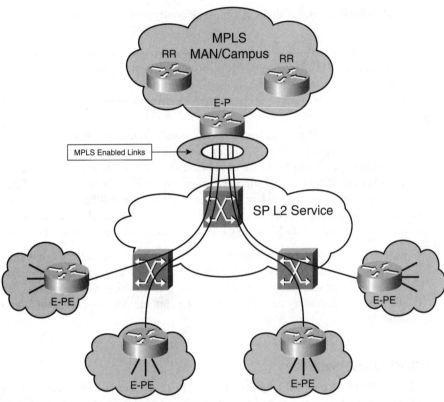

Because the branch routers are converted into E-PE devices, they extend the reach of
the campus network/MAN MPLS cloud. As with any PE router, each remote-branch PE
router maintains an LDP session and an IGP session with its neighboring P routers (in this
case, the headend aggregator). The PEs also maintain MP-iBGP sessions with the RRs
(or other PEs), which typically reside behind the headend aggregating device.

The configuration of the headend is identical to that discussed earlier in this section for an
E-P router. Because the branch router is an E-PE router, it is configured as follows:

- The IGP must be extended to have the E-PE routers peer over the WAN interfaces with
  the E-P at the headend.

- A label distribution protocol must be enabled on each E-PE access router. The global
  configuration must include the following commands:

```
ip cef
mpls label protocol ldp
```

- The E-PE WAN interfaces must be label switched. Use the **mpls ip** command under
  the WAN interfaces.

- The necessary VRFs must be configured on the E-PE.
- MP-iBGP peering with the RR must be configured.

NOTE	See the section "RFC 2547bis the MPLS way" in Chapter 6 for further information about the last two configuration items.

When segmentation is not required at certain branches, those branch routers do not need to have their WAN connection MPLS enabled. At the headend, this is not a problem when using separate p2p connections for each branch because each interface can be configured independently. When using multipoint connections, it is recommended that different multipoint connections be used for MPLS-enabled and non-MPLS-enabled branches. Note that when non-MPLS enabled branches are present, the headend device must also act as a PE device to terminate the VPNs to which the non-MPLS branches will be connected.

In general, these Layer 2 circuit meshes can be considered private enough to not require encryption. However, if encryption is required, one option is to create an overlay of encrypted GRE tunnels and deploy MPLS on top of these encrypted tunnels. This configuration is necessary because encryption is not natively supported on *label switched paths* (LSPs) .

Benefits and Drawbacks

The decision to deploy MPLS over a Layer 2 infrastructure is largely based on the type of WAN service agreements and circuits the enterprise has in place. The enterprise's relationship with the service providers could determine the enterprise's ability to select a Layer 2 or an IP service. When a choice can be made, it is important to understand the benefits and drawbacks of the different approaches. Benefits of deploying MPLS over a Layer 2 infrastructure include the following:

- The enterprise has complete control over the IP infrastructure.
- There is virtually no dependency on provider services for the extension of enterprise VNs or even the enterprise's choice of technology.

Drawbacks include the following:

- Encryption poses a challenge because it can require a tunnel overlay.
- Traffic patterns are only as good as the Layer 2 circuit mesh. True any-to-any connectivity requires a full mesh, which tends to be expensive.
- Service providers are steering away from the Layer 2 type of service and offering more cost-effective services such as IP VPNs. Therefore, it may be hard for the enterprise to benefit from an end-to-end Layer 2 circuit-based WAN.

Contracting Multiple IP VPNs

When an enterprise wants to extend segmentation to the branches, or even interconnect segmented campus networks/MANs, a simple solution is to obtain multiple Layer 3 VPN services from a provider and map each internal VN to a separate service provider Layer 3 VPN. In such a scenario, the branch routers become multi-VRF CEs, and the headend can be either a multi-VRF CE or an E-PE, depending on the segmentation approach used at the headend site.

To implement this solution, the enterprise VNs must be terminated at the WAN edge. The interconnection between enterprise VNs and provider VPNs is achieved by connecting VRFs back to back at the enterprise-provider edge. These back-to-back connections involve the use of a subinterface on each pair of VRFs to connect back-to-back logical links between the enterprise VRFs and their corresponding provider VRFs. Routing information must be exchanged over each logical link associated to the subinterfaces. This exchange can be achieved either by a separate instance of an IGP on each subinterface or by a separate eBGP address family peering over the logical link.

Table 7-1 outlines the configuration details for an E-PE, P-PE pair. Note that this is similar to a multi-VRF CE-to-PE configuration as described in Chapter 6.

Table 7-1   *E-PE to P-PE Configuration for Back-to-Back VRFs*

E-PE	P-PE
```ip vrf red rd 10:10 ip vrf blue rd 20:20 interface gigabitethernet 6/1.1111 description RED to Provider encapsulation dot1q 1111 ip vrf forwarding RED ip address 10.10.10.1 255.255.255.252 interface gigabitethernet 6/1.1211 description BLUE to Provider encapsulation dot1q 1211 ip address 10.10.10.5 255.255.255.252 router bgp 100 no bgp default ipv4-unicast bgp log-neighbor-changes ! address-family ipv4 vrf RED neighbor 10.10.10.2 remote-as 200 neighbor 10.10.10.2 activate no auto-summary no synchronization exit-address-family ! address-family ipv4 vrf BLUE neighbor 10.10.10.6 remote-as 200 neighbor 10.10.10.6 activate no auto-summary no synchronization exit-address-family !```	```ip vrf red rd 10:10 ip vrf blue rd 20:20 interface gigabitethernet 6/1.1111 description RED to enterprise encapsulation dot1q 1111 ip vrf forwarding RED ip address 10.10.10.2 255.255.255.252 interface gigabitethernet 6/1.1211 description BLUE to enterprise encapsulation dot1q 1211 ip address 10.10.10.6 255.255.255.252 router bgp 200 no bgp default ipv4-unicast bgp log-neighbor-changes ! address-family ipv4 vrf RED neighbor 10.10.10.1 remote-as 100 neighbor 10.10.10.1 activate no auto-summary no synchronization exit-address-family ! address-family ipv4 vrf BLUE neighbor 10.10.10.5 remote-as 100 neighbor 10.10.10.5 activate no auto-summary no synchronization exit-address-family !```

NOTE   In this table, we included only the details pertaining to the back-to-back connection
            between devices to avoid confusion. Redistribution of the VPN routes in each of the address
            families is done automatically into eBGP.

Figure 7-9 shows three user groups extended to many branch sites. Each user group is
mapped to a separate IP VPN service in the provider cloud. Different subinterfaces connect
the different VRFs in the E-CE devices with the multiple VRFs in the P-PE devices. These
connections provide the mapping between the enterprise VRFs and the service provider
VPNs.

Figure 7-9   *Branch Segmentation Using Multiple Service Provider VPNs*

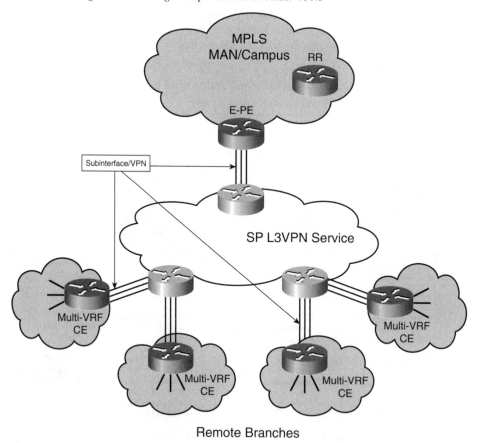

Each CE runs a routing protocol such as OSPF, EIGRP, or BGP with the P-PE on a per-
VRF basis. All design recommendations and best practices that are applicable to a single

VPN service (in terms of routing, *quality of service* (QoS), multicast, and so on) apply to each of these VPN instances, too.

Benefits and Drawbacks

Because of the potential high cost of this approach, it is unlikely to be frequently encountered. Nevertheless, some of the benefits and drawbacks are listed here.

The benefits of this approach include the following:

- Simple from a technical perspective
- Simplified management through outsourcing of the WAN

The drawbacks of this approach include the following:

- Requires a separate PE-CE routing process for each VPN at each site
- Increased service provider dependence
- Can become cost prohibitive based on number of VRFs and sites

This solution is generally limited to a small number of branches that require segmentation with a low number of VRFs. It can also be implemented among a few campus networks that host only a small number of VNs. The limitation is not necessarily in its scalability, but in its cost. If the service provider bills for each VPN offered, the cost of this service will quickly become unmanageable. Nevertheless, if the service provider offers VPN bundles, this can be a viable solution to support a small number of VNs.

Another consideration is the cost of connecting a site to a VPN. If the VPN is also billed by number of connected sites, the use of multiple VPNs might not be suitable for the segmentation of many branches.

Carrier Supporting Carrier (CsC)

Carrier supporting carrier (CsC) was originally developed for MPLS VPN-enabled service providers to support other MPLS/VPN providers (hence its name). With the adoption of MPLS VPNs in large enterprises, CsC is a service that service providers could provide to large enterprises, too. Therefore, you can think about it as a "carrier supporting enterprise service."

The enterprise must obtain a label transport service from a provider. In other words, the labels and label exchange for the enterprise should be transported somewhat transparently between enterprise sites by the service provider. Therefore, the enterprise WAN edge devices should act as though they are directly connected E-P devices. CsC allows such a transparent label transport without requiring the creation of tunnels. WAN extensibility techniques, other than CsC, require the overlay of a logical topology that is usually based on IP tunnels to provide logical direct connectivity between E-P or E-PE routers.

A label transport service is an elegant solution because it does not require a static IP tunnel overlay and the labels can be "tunneled" natively by the service provider MPLS network label stacking mechanisms. Thus, the service provider can continue to provide the any-to-any connectivity from the IP VPN without added complexity. The service provider network ensures that the packet is forwarded to the correct enterprise network location based on the incoming label. The best part is that this process is relatively transparent to the enterprise.

For the carrier to be able to carry the enterprise VNs, certain control-plane information must be exchanged between the enterprise and the provider and between the enterprise sites. As shown in Figure 7-10, the control plane has two added relationships:

- An IPv4 route and label exchange between the E-P facing the provider and the P-PE. The only routes that must be exchanged are the E-PE and E-RR loopback addresses in the enterprise global table. This can be achieved in one of two ways:

  — Run an IGP with the P-PE to advertise the loopback addresses and an LDP to advertise the labels associated with those loopback addresses.

  — The service provider can run MP-eBGP to advertise the loopback addresses along with their associated labels.

- The enterprise must also run MP-iBGP between its RRs to exchange VPNv4 routes and label information for its own VPNs.

Figure 7-10 *CsC*

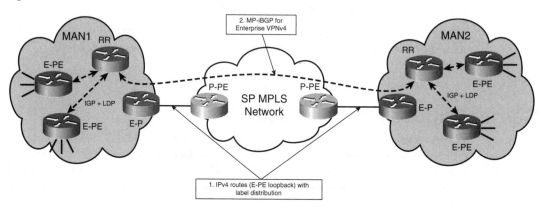

In terms of the configuration, the E-P routers facing the provider must be configured to label switch on the WAN interfaces. This configuration involves enabling MPLS globally (**ip cef**, **mpls label protocol ldp**) and enabling MPLS under the WAN interfaces (**mpls ip**). No VRFs have to be configured on the E-P routers.

NOTE   Alternatively, you could use eBGP to carry the necessary label information instead of having the label carried by LDP. This is alternative represents a different way of achieving CsC, one that does not require the WAN interfaces to participate in the LDP. For the purposes of our discussion, we focus on the LDP-based model.

In addition, you must configure a routing protocol for the global routing table to learn and advertise the addresses of the different PEs and RRs. If you are using the same IGP as the enterprise uses internally, the configuration is as simple as including the subnet for the WAN interface in the IGP. For OSPF, this would be something along the lines of Example 7-1.

Example 7-1   *Using OSPF to Advertise E-PE and E-RR Addresses into the Provider*

```
router ospf 1
 network 1.0.0.0 0.255.255.255 area 0
 network 10.0.0.0 0.255.255.255 area 0
 network x.x.x.x y.y.y.y area 0 ß this is the network for the WAN interface
   connecting to the provider
```

If using eBGP, you must configure eBGP peering between the E-P at the edge and P-PE routers and redistribute the enterprise IGP into the eBGP process and vice versa, as shown in Example 7-2.

Example 7-2   *Using eBGP to Advertise E-PE and E-RR Addresses into the Provider*

```
router ospf 1
 network 1.0.0.0 0.255.255.255 area 0
 network 10.0.0.0 0.255.255.255 area 0
 redistribute bgp 100 subnets
!
router bgp 100
 no synchronization
 bgp log-neighbor-changes
 neighbor 172.1.12.15 remote-as 65023
 neighbor 172.1.12.15 update-source Loopback0
 redistribute ospf 1 match internal external 1 external 2
 no auto-summary
!
```

Finally, the RRs on the different enterprise MPLS networks must MP-iBGP peer with each other. The peering must convey VPNv4 routes, and therefore the peering RRs must be activated under the VPNv4 address families so that the updates can carry the route targets, distinguishers, and label information as shown in Table 7-2.

Table 7-2 *Establishing an MP-iBGP Session Between RRs on Different Sites*

RR for Site 1	RR for Site 2

`router bgp 100`
` no synchronization`
` bgp log-neighbor-changes`
` neighbor 125.1.125.15 remote-as 100`
` neighbor 125.1.125.15 route-reflector`
`  client`
` neighbor 125.1.125.15 update-source`
`  Loopback0`
`no auto-summary`
` !`
`address-family vpnv4`
` neighbor 125.1.125.15 activate`
` neighbor 125.1.125.15 route-reflector`
`  client`
` neighbor 125.1.125.15 send-community`
`  extended`
`exit-address-family`
`!`
	`router bgp 100`
	` no synchronization`
	` bgp log-neighbor-changes`
	` neighbor 172.1.125.16 remote-as 100`
	` neighbor 125.1.125.16 route-reflector`
	`  client`
	` neighbor 172.1.125.16 update-source`
	`  Loopback0`
	`no auto-summary`
	` !`
	`address-family vpnv4`
	` neighbor 172.1.125.16 activate`
	` neighbor 125.1.125.16 route-reflector`
	`  client`
	` neighbor 172.1.125.16 send-community`
	`  extended`
	`exit-address-family`
	`!`

NOTE We have shown a separate RR for each site. In theory, multiple sites could share a single RR, and therefore the two RRs in the example could be consolidated onto a single platform and thus simplify the configuration. However, this is discouraged because the reachability of the RR, and therefore the integrity of the VPN control plane, would be subject to the availability of the WAN links. In the event of loss of WAN connectivity, all VPN routes (local and remote) would be lost, precluding remote and local connectivity within the RFC 2547 VPNs. By using an RR at each site, you preserve local connectivity during a WAN failure.

After the necessary control-plane information is in place (IPv4 routes and labels for PEs and RRs, VPNv4 routes and labels for enterprise VPN prefixes), packets are forwarded by the formation of an extended LSP. This extended LSP provides an end-to-end path between the ingress E-PE and the egress E-PE. The process is transparent to the enterprise because all enterprise devices continue just to switch based on an outer LSP label and do not manage additional labels.

For the extended LSP to traverse the provider cloud, the enterprise LDP labels are swapped with the provider VPN label through the following process (refer to Figure 7-11):

- The P router at the enterprise edge (E-P1) receives a labeled packet from the MAN1 and label switches it based on the label learned via the provider for E-P2 (LDP2).

- The provider PE (P-PE1) swaps the incoming top label (LDP2) with the VPN label advertised by P-PE2 (service provider-SP-VPN). The SP-VPN label is treated as the VPN label within the provider network.

- P-PE1 prepends the top label (service provider LDP) to switch traffic over the LSP from P-PE1 to P-PE2.

- P-PE2 receives the packet with the service provider LDP label popped (because of *penultimate hop popping* [PHP]). It swaps the exposed label (service provider VPN) with the label advertised by E-P2 (LDP3).

- E-P2 swaps the top label (LDP3) and sends it across the MAN2 network to the appropriate PE.

The VPN label remains untouched through the provider cloud as the provider switches traffic between its P-PEs based on the additional SP-LDP label, which achieves the desired tunneling of the extended LSP. Thus, the provider VPN label participates in the formation of the enterprise-extended LSP as it is "tunneled" through the provider network. The result is that it acts as a single hop in the extended enterprise LSP, as shown in Figure 7-11.

Figure 7-11 *CsC Forwarding*

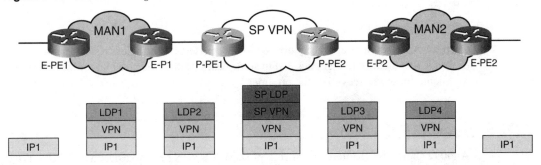

Although technically optimal, this solution is rare to find because few providers offer CsC as a service to enterprises. The reasons are many, most of them business related. Only time will tell how these business models evolve and whether CsC will become a standard part of the service provider VPN offering. One thing is certain, the pressure from enterprises to obtain such services is constantly growing as more enterprises deploy MPLS and seek to extend VNs over the WAN.

Using CsC for Segmented Branch Aggregation

You can also use CsC to extend the segmentation between a campus network and the enterprise's branches. The branches are aggregated over an IP VPN; therefore, they enjoy any-to-any connectivity. By using CsC to support the branch segmentation, you preserve the any-to-any connectivity.

In this scenario, the branch access router acts as a PE. This is just a degenerate case of the CsC scenario discussed in the previous section. The sole difference between the scenarios is that in the previous case, the exchange of IPv4 routes and labels was performed by an E-P router. In this scenario, the E-PE at the branch is directly connected to the backbone carrier and must now exchange IPv4 routes and labels with the P-PE.

Benefits and Drawbacks

CsC is a clean, technical alternative to extending MPLS VPNs across an MPLS-based provider network. Some of the benefits and drawbacks of using a CsC service are listed here.

The benefits include the following:

- Preserves the underlying any-to-any connectivity delivered by the provider VPN
- Requires minimal additions to the control plane
- Seamlessly extends the MPLS LSPs (complex inter-autonomous system consolidation models are not required)

The main drawbacks include the following:

- Scarce provider offering
- Encryption requires a tunnel overlay
- Complex to troubleshoot

Currently CsC services are rarely offered to enterprises. Nevertheless, CsC has some desirable technical characteristics and in some cases it might be possible for the enterprise to procure these services from the provider.

MPLS over GRE

Another alternative to interconnect enterprise MPLS VPN networks over a WAN IP service is to create a mesh of GRE tunnels over the WAN IP cloud and enable label switching on the GRE interfaces. This setup achieves two benefits:

- Bypasses the provider P and PE nodes that we have no control over and on which we cannot enable MPLS or other segmentation techniques
- Provides a logical topology that can be MPLS enabled and therefore become part of the enterprise's MPLS VPN core

As shown in Figure 7-12, in this scenario, the WAN edge router plays the role of an E-P device.

Figure 7-12 *MPLS over GRE*

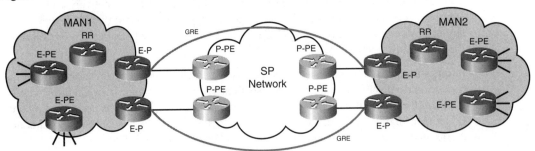

A p2p GRE tunnel is set up between each edge router pair if a full mesh is desired. From a control-plane perspective, the following protocols are expected to be run within the GRE tunnels:

- An IGP such as EIGRP or OSPF for MPLS device reachability (this makes the E-PE, E-P, and RRs reachable to each other)
- LDP, to allow the formation of LSPs over which traffic is forwarded
- MP-iBGP for VPN route and label distribution between the E-PE devices

After the GRE tunnels have been established, the configuration of this solution exactly matches that used to deploy MPLS over Layer 2 circuits. The only difference is that instead of enabling label switching on the WAN interfaces, it is enabled on the tunnel interfaces. Therefore, the *command-line interface* (CLI) should look like this:

```
interface Tunnel0
  description GRE tunnel to E-P2
  bandwidth 1000
  ip address 172.16.100.2 255.255.255.0
  ip mtu 1400
  tag-switching ip
  ip ospf network broadcast
  ip ospf priority 0
  tunnel source Loopback0
  tunnel destination 10.126.100.254
```

After the route/label distribution has been completed in the control plane, the enterprise edge device acts like a *label switching router* (LSR/P) where it treats the GRE interfaces as normal access interfaces. Figure 7-13 shows end-to-end packet flow between campus networks/MANs.

Figure 7-13 *MPLS over GRE Packet Flow*

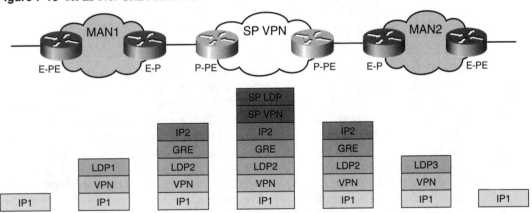

The figure shows how the MPLS label (LDP2) is maintained constant between the E-P routers. The LDP2 label remains constant because the GRE tunnel overlay makes the two E-P routers appear as directly connected. The figure also shows the encapsulating GRE header used as the packet traverses the service provider cloud. Note that the header is imposed by the E-P routers and that the tunnels are established based on the IP reachability in the provider cloud. The latter is represented by the IP2 portion of the header.

The traffic inside the service provider cloud may or may not be MPLS switched, thus the service provider LDP and service provider VPN labels are present only if the service is an MPLS VPN. However, this should be of no concern to the enterprise and is mentioned here only for completeness.

Figure 7-14 shows an interesting variation of the use of VPNs over GRE tunnels. In this scenario, the WAN edge devices are also acting as E-PE devices. Note that this is equivalent to having the PE routers connected back to back. Because of PHP, no LDP label or even an LSP is formed between the E-PEs. In other words, no label swapping occurs, and there is no need for a LDP. The only use for labels in this scenario is to identify the VRF for which the traffic in the tunnel is destined. The VPN labels are used for multiplexing and demultiplexing traffic between the tunnel and the appropriate VRFs.

Figure 7-14 *RFC 2547 VPNs over GRE Packet Flow*

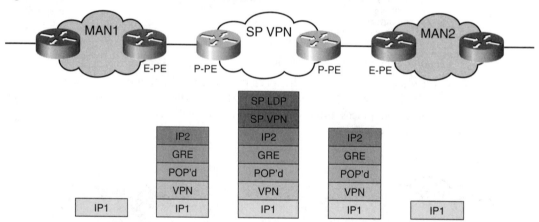

Clearly, this network is not using label switching, nor does it need label switching functionality. However, support for RFC 2547 VPNs is still required. Therefore, this type of overlay model is usually referred to as *2547 over X*. In this particular scenario, it would be 2547 over GRE. Note that this differs from MPLS over GRE because no support exists in the solution for label switching. Therefore, if the edge devices support 2547 over GRE but not MPLS over GRE, these cannot be used as label switching P routers. It is not uncommon to find enterprise-grade platforms that can support 2547 over GRE but not support full MPLS over GRE. The difference in functionality, although apparently subtle, is critical to the design of the network. The network architect must clearly understand the type of VPN role required at the WAN edge to make the right choice of hardware.

NOTE   At of the time this writing, support for 2547 over X is more common than support for MPLS over X.

2547 over GRE has been superseded by 2547 over mGRE, which incorporates all the flexibility of dynamic multipoint tunnel interfaces. The technical details and configuration of this approach are identical to those of the 2547 over L2TPv3 implementation. The sole difference is the encapsulation being used; all other architectural and configuration details are comparable. Therefore, we defer this discussion to the next section as we discuss 2547 over L2TPv3.

Benefits and Drawbacks

Deploying MPLS (or RFC 2547) over a mesh of GRE tunnels allows the enterprise to extend their MPLS network over almost any IP network. As always, there are both challenges and benefits with this type of WAN extension.

The benefits of deploying MPLS over GRE tunnels include the following:

- The solution is independent from the provider.
- GRE tunnels can be easily encrypted with IPsec.
- The edge routers can perform as P or PE routers, potentially allowing a single MPLS network to be deployed across the MAN/campus/WAN frontier.

The drawbacks include the following:

- Maintaining the GRE tunnel mesh can be cumbersome.
- Any-to-any connectivity requires a full mesh of tunnels.
- *Maximum transmission unit* (MTU) considerations must be made in the WAN core, especially as more MPLS services are added. The WAN core is not controlled by the enterprise, so MTU size must be limited at the edges.

The extension of MPLS VPNs over GRE tunnels is useful in scenarios that require the aggregation of a limited number of sites in a hub-and-spoke logical topology. Any-to-any connectivity for many sites is better addressed by dynamic mechanisms, such as CsC or RFC 2547 over DMVPN. DMVPN-based mechanisms are discussed in some of the following sections.

RFC 2547 VPNs over L2TPv3 Tunnels

L2TPv3 tunnels provide a transport alternative to GRE. You can use them to create a Layer 3 tunnel overlay similar to that created with GRE tunnels in the previous section. An L2TPv3 mesh supports 2547 over L2TPv3; however, MPLS over L2TPv3 is not an option to date because, as discussed in the previous section, 2547 over L2TPv3 and MPLS over L2TPv3 offer two different types of functionality.

To aggregate segmented branches, L2TPv3 must be implemented on the hub router and every branch router having segmentation requirements. The extension of the segmentation into the campus network at the headend can be achieved by h2h VRFs or even by pushing the PE and L2TPv3 tunnel termination functionality all the way into the distribution layer of the campus.

In this case, the solution is simple: It is basically a tunnel overlay using VPN labels to mux/demux traffic in and out of the tunnels for the different VPNs, which is similar to the 2547 over GRE solution described in the previous section. Figure 7-15 illustrates the forwarding of packets in an L2TPv3-based 2547 VPN deployment.

Figure 7-15 *RFC 2547 VPNs over L2TPv3 Packet Flow*

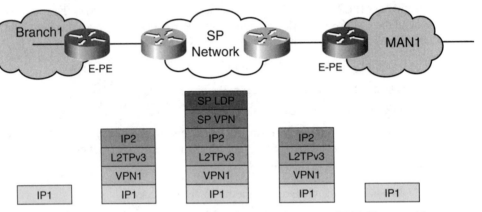

The packet flow is similar to that discussed for 2547 over GRE. There are, however, two differences in the solution:

- It uses an L2TPv3 header rather than a GRE header.

- L2TPv3 uses dynamically established multipoint tunnels, which are comparable to mGRE tunnels.

The use of dynamic multipoint tunnels requires some configuration subtleties. However, these details are the same whether we use mGRE tunnels or L2TPv3 tunnels. The following discussion focuses on L2TPv3 tunnels, but keep in mind that the exact same considerations, and even the same configuration, apply to an mGRE-based approach.

The main consideration when configuring dynamic multipoint tunnels is that they need to reside in their own address space. To this effect, you must configure a dedicated VRF for the resolution of next-hop addresses (for example, tunnel endpoints). For this reason, this VRF is known as the *resolve in VRF VRF*, or RiV VRF. The RiV VRF is straightforward:

```
ip vrf my_riv
  rd 1:1
```

The multipoint tunnel interfaces must be included in the RiV VRF. The following table details the commands to create the tunnel for both the mGRE and the L2TPv3 configurations. As you can see, there is only one configuration difference between the two types of encapsulation.

mGRE	Multipoint L2TPv3
| ```
interface Tunnel1
 ip vrf forwarding my_riv
 ip address 123.1.1.3 255.255.255.255
 tunnel source Loopback0
 tunnel mode gre multipoint l3vpn
 tunnel key 123
end
``` | ```
interface Tunnel1
 ip vrf forwarding my_riv
 ip address 123.1.1.3 255.255.255.255
 tunnel source Loopback0
 tunnel mode l3vpn l2tpv3 multipoint
end
``` |

You must configure a route map to ensure that the next hop is resolved within the RiV VRF:

```
route-map SELECT_UPDATES_FOR_L3VPN_OVER_TUNNEL permit 10
 set ip next-hop in-vrf my_riv
```

A static route within the VRF ensures that all traffic is sent over the tunnel interface:

```
ip route vrf my_riv 0.0.0.0 0.0.0.0 Tunnel1
```

You must configure MP-iBGP to peer between the PE and the RRs. To ensure that the next hop for these updates is resolved in the RiV VRF, you now apply the previously created route map to incoming updates:

```
router bgp 100
 network 200.0.0.3
 neighbor 123.1.1.2 remote-as 100
 neighbor 123.1.1.2 update-source Loopback0
 !
 address-family vpnv4
 neighbor 123.1.1.2 activate
 neighbor 123.1.1.2 route-map SELECT_UPDATES_FOR_L3VPN_OVER_TUNNEL in
 !
```

One significant benefit of using a tunnel overlay and extending it end to end (pushing the PE routers all the way to the edges of the IP cloud) is that the entire IP network (including campuses, branches, MANs, and the WAN) can potentially be segmented by a single RFC 2547 VPN domain. This is possible even across autonomous system boundaries in the global table. In other words, the enterprise can have multiple autonomous systems across its IP network. As illustrated in Figure 7-16, regardless of the autonomous system structure of the IP network, an end-to-end mesh of tunnels can be overlaid onto it, and a single autonomous system MP-iBGP process can span the entire network to provide 2547 VPN functionality without any of the inter-autonomous system complexities encountered when using MPLS.

In the figure, the enterprise provides IP connectivity through many autonomous systems. L2TPv3 leverages this connectivity to establish an end-to-end overlay topology. An independent (single Autonomous System) MP-iBGP process rides on top of this logical overlay to provide a single unified RFC 2547 VPN environment that bypasses the inter-autonomous system boundaries. Because no LDP exchange takes place in this solution, the fact that the connections are traversing multiple autonomous systems does not affect the connectivity; hence, the inter-autonomous system label distribution hassles can be avoided.

Figure 7-16 *RFC 2547 VPNs over L2TPv3 Across Autonomous System Boundaries*

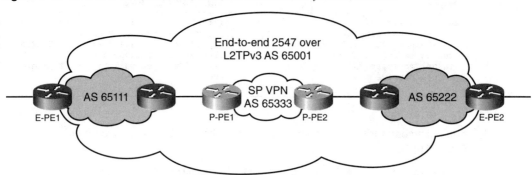

This is true for 2547 over L2TPv3 and 2547 over mGRE deployments. Because no LDP or LSP formation occurs between the PEs, you can actually distribute them across different autonomous systems without breaking the RFC 2547 VPN. However, the same is not true for a service such as MPLS over GRE. In this case, it is not possible to circumvent the inter-autonomous system communication requirements posed by the LDP-based LSP establishment required in an MPLS over X solution.

On the other hand, if the campus network or MAN is already segmented with MPLS VPNs and this MPLS deployment is to be preserved, the enterprise is faced with managing an inter-autonomous system exchange point to integrate the MPLS campus/MAN networks with the non-MPLS L2TPv3 WAN network.

The most straightforward solution to this problem is to provide CsC services over the L2TPv3-based VPN cloud. The L2TPv3 portion of the network will be the backbone carrier, whereas the MPLS portion of the network will be the customer carrier. Figure 7-17 shows the packet flow for this CsC scenario.

This CsC solution has the same control-plane requirements discussed previously for standard CsC (IPv4 routes and labels for PEs and RRs, VPNv4 routes and labels for enterprise VPN prefixes). In the same way that traditional CsC forms an "extended" LSP by swapping the LDP label in the MPLS packet for a VPN label in the backbone carrier area, this particular CsC implementation swaps labels LDP1 and LDP2 for a VPN label in the L2TPv3 backbone (called "IP VPN" in this example).

NOTE	In this case, the enterprise owns and controls both the backbone carrier and the customer carrier portions of the network. Therefore, the limitation on service offerings is no longer present.

Figure 7-17 *RFC 2547 VPNs over L2TPv3 as CsC Backbone Carrier*

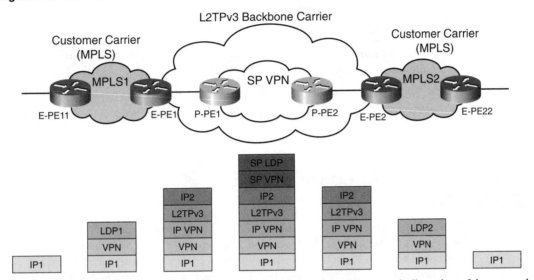

To configure this CsC solution, you configure the "backbone carrier" portion of the network for 2547 over L2TPv3 as described previously and enable MPLS on the "customer"-facing interfaces of the 2547 over L2TPv3 PEs. The rest of the CsC configuration is identical to that described previously in the "Carrier Supporting Carrier (CsC)" section of this chapter.

Inter-autonomous system communication models provide alternative approaches to solving this problem. We introduced the different inter-autonomous system models in the section "MPLS over Layer 2 Circuits." These are fairly complex approaches; therefore, we limit ourselves just to mentioning them rather than providing a detailed description:

- Back-to-back VRFs at the ASBRs
- ASBR-to-ASBR with MP-eBGP (MP-eBGP exchange of labeled VPN-IPv4 routes between adjacent ASBRs)
- ASBR-to-ASBR with multihop eBGP using RR (multihop MP-eBGP between remote autonomous systems)

Benefits and Drawbacks

Deploying RFC 2547 VPNs over IP tunnels does eliminate the need for label switching in the core. However, there are other important benefits to this approach, and some challenges.

The benefits of this solution include the following:

- Can traverse multiple autonomous systems seamlessly if L2TPv3 is spanned end to end.
- An end-to-end deployment can remove the need for the enterprise to have MPLS support end to end.

- Can provide CsC services to MPLS portions of the network, totally independent of the provider service offerings.

The drawbacks include the following:

- Encryption is not natively supported and can require the utilization of bulk encryption solutions such as *dynamic group VPN* (DGVPN).
- MPLS-based services are not available because the solution does not use MPLS.
- RFC 2547 over L2TPv3 is available in a limited subset of the enterprise product line.

VRFs Interconnected by a GRE or DMVPN Overlay

This model simply leverages a mesh of GRE tunnels to create dedicated back-to-back connections between VRFs. In this manner, a group of VRFs on different sites are interconnected by a logical tunnel overlay to form a VN. Of course, each VN has a dedicated tunnel overlay and dedicated VRFs at each site, thus forming totally separate logical networks for each group.

You can use this model over a Layer 2 or Layer 3 service from a provider. If you do so, the enterprise needs to purchase only a single VPN or a single set of Layer 2 circuits from the provider. The enterprise then uses a combination of multi-VRF and GRE tunnels to overlay its own VNs onto the purchased service.

In this model, the headend has one mGRE tunnel per VRF. The branches have either a GRE or mGRE tunnel for each VRF. P2p GRE is used if no spoke-to-spoke communication is required. mGRE is required when spoke-to-spoke communication between branches is necessary.

DMVPN provides for dynamic spoke-to-spoke communication and encryption. If you configure mGRE on certain spokes, they have the ability to create dynamic tunnels to other spokes (which should also be configured with mGRE). This subset of the DMVPN functionality is discussed in detail in Chapter 5, "Infrastructure Segmentation Architectures: Theory."

Most enterprises have only a partial-mesh requirement. In other words, large sites might need to be meshed together, but the smaller sites typically connect only to the headend and form a hub-and-spoke topology. Therefore, the deployment is generally a combination of GRE and mGRE at the spokes, as illustrated in Figure 7-18.

The hub device, while aggregating the branches, also hosts all the different VRFs. It can be either a PE if the headend site is RFC 2547 enabled or a multi-VRF hop if h2h segmentation is used at the headend site.

Figure 7-18 *Multi-VRF Interconnected with mGRE/DMVPN*

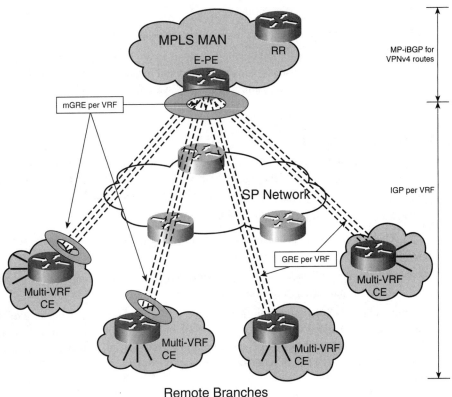

An IGP instance runs within each VPN between the hub and each of the spokes. If the hub site is RFC 2547 enabled, the IPv4 addresses learned from the spokes are converted to VPNv4 addresses before being advertised into the 2547 cloud using MP-iBGP. As discussed in Chapter 6, the IGP serves a dual purpose:

- Dynamic exchange of routing information
- Remote failure detection on GRE tunnels

This type of deployment is suitable for branch aggregation in enterprises with a small number of branches and a small number of user groups or segments. The scalability of this solution is limited not only by the capacity of the headend devices but also by the manageability of an increased number of groups and sites.

Similar considerations apply to a DMVPN-based solution. A separate DMVPN is required to interconnect each group of VRFs and form a VPN. This involves the following components:

- mGRE tunnels per VRF at each site (the hub and all participating spokes)

- An NHRP server at the hub site
- NHRP client capabilities at the spokes
- Dynamic encryption security associations between sites

How this all works together is described in detail throughout Chapter 5. How this can be deployed in a campus is discussed in thorough detail in Chapter 6. Similar guidelines apply to the WAN, so rather than repeating those here, we refer back to Chapter 6.

Benefits and Drawbacks

DMVPN is a branch aggregation technology familiar to many enterprises. For a limited number of groups, you can leverage DMVPN to interconnect VRFs and form VPNs over the WAN. Benefits of using this approach include the following:

- Encryption is built in to this solution.

- This solution uses technologies that might be familiar to the enterprise operations personnel.

- The simpler hardware capabilities required by this solution might allow for a broader choice of platforms in the enterprise.

The main drawback with this solution is that it has limited scalability because of the proliferation of DMVPN or mGRE tunnel mesh instances. Therefore, this solution is ideal for an enterprise extending a small number of groups to several branches; as the number of groups increases, you should consider other approaches.

RFC 2547 VPNs over DMVPN

Instead of deploying a separate DMVPN overlay for each customer VN, you can use a single DMVPN overlay and multiplex the different user segments (VNs) over this single DMVPN. The VNs are multiplexed into the tunnel by using VPN labels in the same way it is done for 2547 over GRE deployments. This model, illustrated in Figure 7-19, is recommended mainly for branch aggregation where most communication is between the hub and the branches, but not between branches. Because DMVPN is a widely deployed solution for branch aggregation, enterprises that currently use the technology will find the capability to multiplex segments into their existing DMVPN extremely useful.

This model provides the flexibility of dynamic tunnel creation along with enhanced scalability without some of the scalability limitations of the multi-VRF-based solutions described in the previous section. The scalability is improved because no one-to-one mapping occurs between the tunnel overlay and the VRFs. Instead, a single tunnel overlay can be shared for transporting many VNs.

Figure 7-19 *RFC 2547 over mGRE/DMVPN*

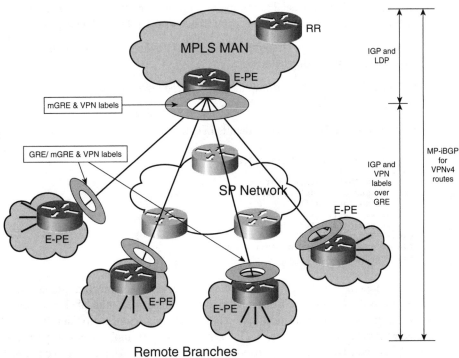

Remote Branches

The control plane for an RFC 2547 VPN environment running over DMVPN must include the following:

- The tunnel source addresses (physical interface addresses) for the branches and headend must be advertised into the provider network. These can be advertised dynamically or statically.

- A static GRE tunnel must be configured between the branch PE and the headend. The headend acts as a PE router.

- An IGP running in the enterprise global space over the GRE overlay is necessary to provide connectivity between PEs and between PEs and the RRs.

- MP-iBGP sessions are required with RR from PEs, where the branch router's BGP source address is the tunnel interface address. This forces the BGP next-hop lookup for the VPN route to be associated with the tunnel interface.

- NHRP must be configured between the hub and the spokes.

The spokes can use a p2p GRE tunnel only if spoke-to-spoke communication is not required; otherwise, they need to use mGRE. In addition, you can use IPsec to encrypt the GRE/mGRE tunnels because the encryption occurs after the GRE encapsulation.

The configuration is fairly straightforward. The following sample configuration for a hub PE shows a few interesting details:

- The GRE mode differs from that used for 2547 over mGRE.

- Tunnel interface is label switched (**tag-switching ip**).

- The hub is an NHRP server (details in Chapter 6).

```
interface Tunnel1
ip address 10.1.1.1 255.255.255.0
 no ip redirects
 ip nhrp authentication test
 ip nhrp map multicast dynamic
 ip nhrp network-id 100
 tunnel source 7.7.7.2
 tunnel mode gre multipoint
 tunnel key 123
 tunnel protection ipsec profile mpls
 tag-switching ip
!
```

As illustrated in Figure 7-20, when forwarding packets, the branch router attaches the appropriate VPN label for the destination. It then encapsulates the labeled packet in a GRE tunnel with the hub P as the destination before sending it to the provider. Because the service provider provides Layer 3 VPN service in this example, it further prepends its own VPN and LDP labels for transport within its network. The hub PE receives a GRE-encapsulated labeled packet. It decapsulates the tunnel headers and selects the appropriate VRF to do an IP lookup and forward the packet.

Figure 7-20   *RFC 2547 over mGRE/DMVPN—Forwarding Plane*

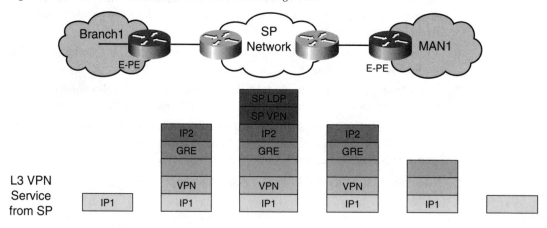

Benefits and Drawbacks

One of the most attractive features of an RFC 2547 over DMVPN deployment is the possibility of leveraging an existing DMVPN overlay and simply enabling VPN labeling over the existing DMVPN. The VNs traveling over the DMVPN inherit all the benefits of the DMVPN but also the shortcomings.

The benefits of this method include the following:

- Enterprises can leverage their existing DMVPN infrastructure to aggregate branches.
- Dynamic spoke-to-spoke tunnels provide direct communication between branches.
- Built-in encryption provides privacy for traffic in transit over the WAN.

The drawbacks include the following:

- This method is best suited for hub-and-spoke connectivity requirements. Any-to-any connectivity is better addressed by other techniques such as CsC.
- Scaling limits are much lower than those encountered in any-to-any connectivity solutions.

Summary

You have many alternatives when extending a virtualized enterprise over a WAN. The choice of which alternative to use ultimately depends on the available provider WAN service, the technology the enterprise devices can support, and the network operator's preferences based on an analysis such as that carried out throughout this chapter.

In general, the extension of the virtualization requires one of three conditions:

- Control of all IP hops in the WAN
- Creation of a logical overlay capable of bypassing uncontrollable IP hops in the WAN
- A service from the provider capable of carrying the VN information for the customer

This chapter discussed the implications, pros, and cons of these different scenarios. Ultimately, it is up to the network operator to decide which of the scenarios is the most adequate for their network.

CHAPTER 8

Traffic Steering and Service Centralization

One main advantage of a virtualized enterprise network is the ability to create tightly controlled and flexible communication interfaces between the different *virtual networks* (VNs). This capability also allows the deployment of services that are centrally accessible and common to many VNs. An example of such a service is access to the Internet. The centralization of the access to these services provides a common point of policy enforcement and control for all VNs.

This chapter focuses on the different alternatives that you can use to provide shared services in a virtual enterprise network. Both the central site access alternatives and the routing adjustments necessary to steer traffic to these policy enforcement points are discussed in detail.

Shared Services: Protected vs. Unprotected

We begin our discussion by broadly categorizing services that are shared by many VNs. As discussed in Chapter 3 "A Basic Virtualized Enterprise," these services can be grouped into protected or unprotected categories, depending on how they are accessed.

Unprotected Services

A service that can be accessed openly without subjecting the traffic to any sort of security check is considered an unprotected service. An unprotected service is reachable from one or more VNs without having a policy enforcement point between the service and the requesting host. The best-path routes to reach an unprotected service may be present in the different VNs that can access the service. In general, this type of access is used to provide shared *Dynamic Host Configuration Protocol* (DHCP) or *Domain Name System* (DNS) services to the different VNs without adding unnecessary load to the firewalls that are used to control access to other shared services that must be protected.

Protected Services

Some services must be accessible from the VNs only after certain security policies are enforced. We will see these as protected services. To be able to enforce the necessary security policies in a manageable way, access to these services must happen through a common policy enforcement point. At this policy enforcement point, traffic from the VNs could be subject to dedicated per-VN policies or to a shared policy. When the policies are dedicated, each VN has its own perimeter, and all VN perimeters are collocated. When the policies are shared, all VNs use the same perimeter. The perimeter could be defined by the presence of a firewall or a series of security devices. Firewalls and other security devices can be virtualized to create multiple logical devices, allowing a single physical device to host multiple perimeters for multiple VNs. Clearly, when the VN perimeters are implemented with logical devices, the perimeters for the different VNs will be collocated in a common point of policy enforcement.

Because all traffic reaching the services must be routed through a common point of policy enforcement, the routing between a requesting host and a service could potentially be suboptimal. However, significant inefficiencies occur only in specific scenarios, such as when the shared services themselves are part of a VN and therefore physically remote to the common point of policy enforcement. This leads to the potential "tromboning" of traffic that must travel to the central point of policy enforcement and back just to hop between VNs. In general, because shared services that are to be protected are centrally located, they will most likely be accessed optimally.

NOTE	We use the analogy of the trombone shape to see traffic patterns that travel a long distance to hit a policy enforcement point and return over roughly the same path. These traffic patterns resemble the physical characteristics of the tubes in a trombone.

Examples of protected services include server farms and Internet access. When regulating access to the Internet, it becomes evident that not only is it necessary to control access to the service from the VNs, but it is also critical to control access initiated from the service area toward the VNs. In general, it is not desirable for any VN to be accessed from the Internet; thus, access into the VNs from the services area is generally prohibited.

When VNs must communicate with each other in a controlled manner, you can change the policies at each VN perimeter to provide such access. In this particular inter-VN connectivity application, the policies must be open enough to allow externally initiated communication into the VNs.

Unprotected Services Access

The use of *VPN routing and forwarding instances* (VRFs) and *multiprotocol Border Gateway Protocol* (MP-BGP) allows enough flexibility for traffic to be leaked between VPNs. This is achieved by importing and exporting routes between VRFs to provide IP connectivity among different VNs. You can use this type of inter-VN connectivity to provide services that do not need to be protected by the central site firewalls or that would represent an unnecessary burden to the VN perimeter firewalls. Because of the any-to-any nature of an IP cloud, little chance exists of controlling inter-VN traffic after the routes have been exchanged.

NOTE   Although these services are not protected by the VN perimeter firewalls, the IP segment to which they belong can potentially be headended by a firewall and thus be "protected."

Because it is unsecured, you must deploy this type of connectivity carefully; it can potentially create unwanted back doors between VNs and break the concept of the VN as a "security zone" protected by a robust VN perimeter front end. In general, the deployment should be targeted at the creation of extranet VNs. Extranet VNs can communicate with many VNs; however, they do not provide a transit zone between the VNs that communicate with it. In routing terms, this means that the extranet VN contains routes to the client VNs, and the client VNs contains routes to the extranet VN; however, the routes from one client are not leaked to another client through the extranet VN.

Importing and exporting routes between VNs precludes the use of overlapping address spaces between the VNs. If address reuse is necessary, you must deploy a routed VN perimeter with *Network Address Translation* (NAT) capabilities. The guidelines for such deployment are discussed later in this chapter. When routes are imported between VRFs, the exchange of traffic between VNs follows the shortest path within the IP core. This prevents inter-VN traffic from traversing the VN perimeter firewalls at the central site. If the shared resources are physically close to the requesters, it is desirable to avoid an inefficient "trombone" traffic pattern that travels all the way to the central services site and back.

It may be tempting to consider this approach as a means to provide peer-to-peer connectivity across VNs. To provide peer-to-peer connectivity, however, all prefixes in one VRF must be leaked to another VRF and vice versa. After this is done, the separation between the VRFs is lost and the original purpose of having the VRFs is defeated. Therefore, the use of route imports and exports is devoted mainly to the creation of extranet VNs rather than enabling controlled communication between VNs.

The extranet capability by means of imports and exports is versatile and has found many applications within enterprises, especially in shared data centers. The following sections cover several useful scenarios that arise when importing and exporting routes between VRFs. This is by no means exhaustive, but the intention here is to provide the necessary fundamentals for creative individuals to adapt the technology to their particular needs.

Basic Import/Export Mechanism

Importing and exporting routes between different VRFs is a function of *multiprotocol interior Border Gateway Protocol* (MP-iBGP). An MP-iBGP update carries the extended community attribute, which contains both the *route distinguisher* (RD) and the export *route targets* (RTs) for the prefixes being announced. The RTs contain the information that allows the importing and exporting of prefixes to happen.

When a router receives an MP-iBGP update, the RTs in the import statements for each VRF are compared to the RTs received with the update (which correspond to the export statements on the VRF sending the update). Thus, a prefix is installed in a VRF when the RT in the MP-iBGP update matches an RT in an import statement for the receiving VRF.

A single VRF can have many import and export statements, each with a different RT value. Thus, a single prefix might be announced with many different RT values, which can be selectively imported into specific VRFs on specific routers.

It is important to keep in mind that when a VRF learns a prefix by means of MP-iBGP, it does not advertise this prefix to its other neighbors. In other words, MP-iBGP is not transitive and does not reflect routing updates. Hence, prefixes are imported and exported between VRFs and not between VNs. When a prefix is imported/exported between two VRFs, it is not automatically advertised to other VRFs in the destination VN.

You can use route maps to filter which prefixes received in an MP-iBGP update are to be imported into a VRF. Their use allows a finer level of granularity in selecting which routes are leaked between VRFs. This level of granularity can prove useful when only certain hosts or segments should be reached from outside the VN they belong to.

Multiplatform Deployment

In general, you can use BGP to transport routing information between different physical routers. To allow this communication, it is necessary to establish BGP sessions (which are TCP connections) between the routers. These sessions are defined by the **neighbor** statements in the BGP configuration.

In the scenario shown in Figure 8-1, the updates travel over the BGP connections and are imported into the VRFs that match the RTs in the extended community, as explained earlier.

In the example, we used an RT of 3:3 for the RED VN. Notice that this RT value is imported and exported by all VRFs. Also, note that BGP has been configured with the necessary **neighbor** statements and that each neighbor has been activated under the VPN version 4 (vpnv4) address family to handle the extended community attribute.

Figure 8-1   *RT Imports and Exports Across Platforms*

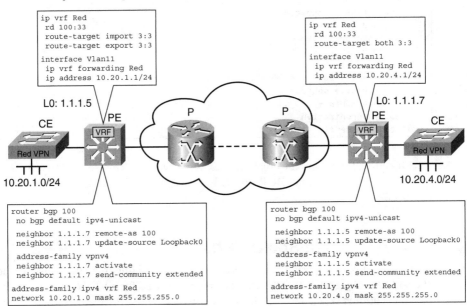

```
ip vrf Red
  rd 100:33
  route-target import 3:3
  route-target export 3:3
interface Vlan11
  ip vrf forwarding Red
  ip address 10.20.1.1/24
```

```
ip vrf Red
  rd 100:33
  route-target both 3:3
interface Vlan11
  ip vrf forwarding Red
  ip address 10.20.4.1/24
```

LO: 1.1.1.5

LO: 1.1.1.7

CE   PE

P   P

PE   CE

VRF

VRF

Red VPN

Red VPN

10.20.1.0/24

10.20.4.0/24

```
router bgp 100
  no bgp default ipv4-unicast

  neighbor 1.1.1.7 remote-as 100
  neighbor 1.1.1.7 update-source Loopback0

  address-family vpnv4
  neighbor 1.1.1.7 activate
  neighbor 1.1.1.7 send-community extended

  address-family ipv4 vrf Red
  network 10.20.1.0 mask 255.255.255.0
```

```
router bgp 100
  no bgp default ipv4-unicast

  neighbor 1.1.1.5 remote-as 100
  neighbor 1.1.1.5 update-source Loopback0

  address-family vpnv4
  neighbor 1.1.1.5 activate
  neighbor 1.1.1.5 send-community extended

  address-family ipv4 vrf Red
  network 10.20.4.0 mask 255.255.255.0
```

Single-Platform Deployment

It is possible to import and export routes between different VRFs within a single physical router. In this case, no BGP sessions are established between routers because, obviously, there is a single router. However, it is still necessary to enable an MP-BGP process within the router to enable the exchange of routes between VRFs based on the RTs and the **import/export** statements. The commands in Example 8-1 illustrate the BGP configuration required to enable local importing/exporting of routes. Notice that there are no **neighbor** statements, and therefore there are no statements under the vpnv4 address family either.

Example 8-1   *Local Importing and Exporting of Routes*

```
router bgp 100
  bgp log-neighbor-changes
  !
  address-family ipv4 vrf BLUE
    redistribute connected
    no auto-summary
    no synchronization
  exit-address-family
  !
  address-family ipv4 vrf RED
```

continues

Example 8-1   *Local Importing and Exporting of Routes (Continued)*

```
    redistribute connected
    no auto-summary
    no synchronization
 exit-address-family
 !
 address-family ipv4 vrf SERVICES
    redistribute connected
    no auto-summary
    no synchronization
 exit-address-family
```

This functionality allows the creation of extranets when VRFs are used to provide a level of router virtualization, but BGP/MPLS VPNs (RFC 2547) are not necessarily being deployed.

Any-to-Any and Hub-and-Spoke VPNs

To create an any-to-any VPN, it is necessary to export and import all the routes for the VPN at every site. This means that the **export** statements used for a VRF on one router must match the **import** statements used by all other VRFs in the VPN and vice versa. Figure 8-2 shows three sites and a VPN named RED, which has been created by importing and exporting RT RED in the RED VRFs on every router.

Figure 8-2   *Any-to-Any VPNs*

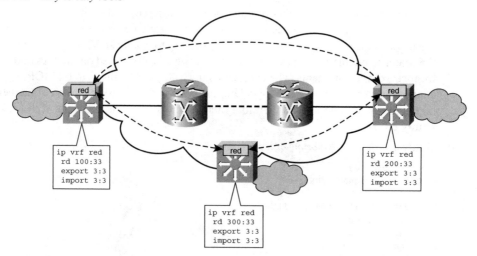

NOTE	A VPN is built by RT exchange; the RD is locally significant and does not determine any relationship between a VRF on one device and a VRF on another device. In the example, different RDs are used for the same VPN on different platforms to illustrate this.

By using asymmetric **import** and **export** statements between different BGP neighbors, it is possible to create VPNs in which spoke sites can only communicate with a hub location. Figure 8-3 again shows three sites. This time, the configuration is provided to allow communication only between the spokes and the hub site for the BLUE VPN. Note that the spokes cannot talk to each other in this configuration because the routes between spokes have not been explicitly exchanged.

Figure 8-3   *Hub-and-Spoke VPNs*

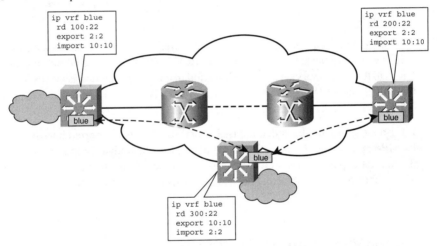

Extranet VPN

It is common to require the sharing of services in one VPN with many other VPNs. The use of asymmetric **import** and **export** statements across different VPNs allows many VPNs to communicate with a shared extranet VPN. In this scenario, the VPNs have routes for the extranet and vice versa, but the extranet does not act as a transit area between VPNs. Therefore, although the VPNs are kept separate from each other, they can connect to shared resources. Figure 8-4 illustrates how to configure this scenario.

Figure 8-4 *Extranet VPN*

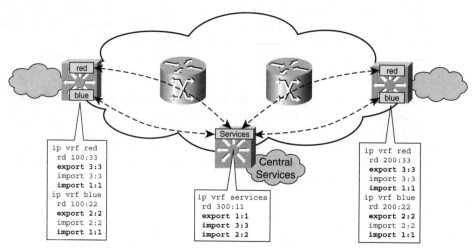

As shown in the example, the routes for the shared services VRF are exported with a RT of 1:1. These are imported into the RED and BLUE VRFs, allowing communication from the VRFs to the shared services. Communication in the other direction is achieved by importing the BLUE and RED routes into the services VRF. The latter is achieved by importing RTs 2:2 and 3:3, which correspond to BLUE and RED routes, respectively.

It is important to highlight that the BLUE and RED routes imported into the Services VRF by MP-iBGP are not re-advertised. In other words, the updates imported with RTs 2:2 and 3:3 are not exported with an RT of 1:1 (or any other RT for that matter) by the Services VRF; therefore, this configuration will not provide connectivity between the RED and BLUE VRFs.

Localized Inter-VPN Communication

As you may have noticed by now, it is necessary to explicitly import all routes that are to be present in a VPN. Furthermore, because of the nontransitivity of iBGP, you must do this at every physical router that will participate in the VPN.

Therefore, importing a route into a VRF on a single physical router does not populate this route into all VRFs in a VPN. In other words, when a route is imported onto a VRF on a single physical router, that route is not automatically advertised to other physical routers participating in the VPN. To populate the route in all VRFs participating in the VPN, it is necessary to explicitly import the prefixes into each and every VRF.

Figure 8-5 helps illustrate this concept better. In the three-site scenario in Figure 8-5, we have created RED and BLUE VPNs with full any-to-any connectivity within each VPN. Selective imports and exports are used to interconnect the RED and BLUE VPNs only at Site 1.

Figure 8-5   *Localized Communication Between RED and BLUE VPNs*

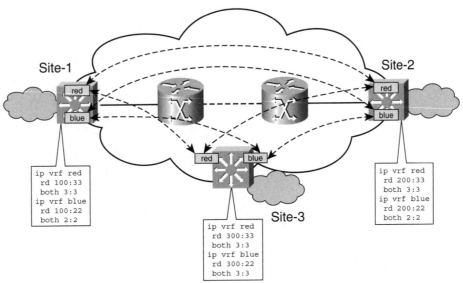

Site-1

```
ip vrf red
 rd 100:33
 both 3:3
ip vrf blue
 rd 100:22
 both 2:2
```

Site-2

```
ip vrf red
 rd 200:33
 both 3:3
ip vrf blue
 rd 200:22
 both 2:2
```

Site-3

```
ip vrf red
 rd 300:33
 both 3:3
ip vrf blue
 rd 300:22
 both 3:3
```

NOTE   The **both** command used in the configuration is equivalent to separate **import** and **export** statements for the RT specified. Thus, **both 2:2** is equivalent to typing **import 2:2** and **export 2:2** under the same VRF.

To interconnect the RED and BLUE VPNs only at Site 1, you must add a new RT to the configuration. In Figure 8-6, we use a value of 5:5 to export and import routes between the BLUE and RED VPNs. By adding the import and export statements on both VRFs (RED and BLUE), we can establish communication between the VRFs. Because this is done only on the site-1 physical router, this includes only routes that are local to Site 1; routes that have been learned from other sites via BGP will not be exchanged across VPNs.

In this manner, you can create localized inter-VPN connectivity if required. A more practical scenario is to create localized extranet VPNs (which just means creating an extranet on a single site). In the example shown in Figure 8-7, this setup implies configuring the extranet only on the routers on Site 1. Doing so provides connectivity only between prefixes and extranet resources local to Site 1.

Local extranet routes are exported with RT 5:5, and local routes are exported with RTs 52:52 and 53:53 for BLUE and RED, respectively. The use of alternate RTs for the BLUE and RED VRFs allows us to ensure that the local extranet VRF is populated only with local routes for RED and BLUE. We could have used the existing 2:2 and 3:3 RTs for BLUE and RED, but this would have installed routes from Sites 2 and 3 on the local extranet VRF for Site 1.

Figure 8-6 *Inter-VPN Local Connectivity*

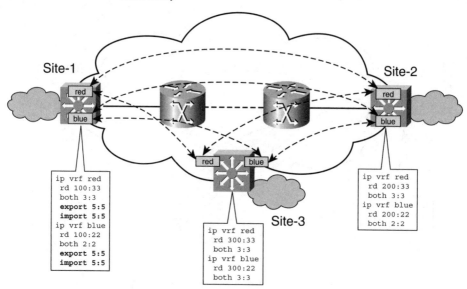

```
ip vrf red
  rd 100:33
  both 3:3
  export 5:5
  import 5:5
ip vrf blue
  rd 100:22
  both 2:2
  export 5:5
  import 5:5
```

```
ip vrf red
  rd 300:33
  both 3:3
ip vrf blue
  rd 300:22
  both 3:3
```

```
ip vrf red
  rd 200:33
  both 3:3
ip vrf blue
  rd 200:22
  both 2:2
```

Figure 8-7 *Extranet VPN Local Connectivity*

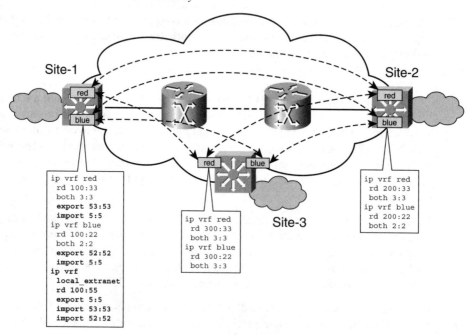

```
ip vrf red
  rd 100:33
  both 3:3
  export 53:53
  import 5:5
ip vrf blue
  rd 100:22
  both 2:2
  export 52:52
  import 5:5
ip vrf
  local_extranet
  rd 100:55
  export 5:5
  import 53:53
  import 52:52
```

```
ip vrf red
  rd 300:33
  both 3:3
ip vrf blue
  rd 300:22
  both 3:3
```

```
ip vrf red
  rd 200:33
  both 3:3
ip vrf blue
  rd 200:22
  both 2:2
```

Leaking Traffic with the Global Table

In many cases, it is necessary to reach resources in the global table from within a VRF and vice versa. One classic example of this requirement is the deployment of network management stations in a VRF. These stations need to access subnets in the global table that provide management access to *provider* (P) and *provider edge* (PE) routers.

The mechanisms to use in this case differ from those used to create communication between VRFs. Instead of using MP-BGP, you must use static routes to forward traffic between the global table and the necessary VRFs.

The topology in Figure 8-8 illustrates how to achieve this. In the example in this figure, we provide communication between subnet 10.0.2.0/30 in the BLUE VRF and subnet 10.1.2.4/30 in the global routing table.

Figure 8-8   *Traffic Leaking Between a VRF and the Global Table*

You can create static routes within a VRF that point to a prefix in the global table by using the physical interface as the next hop to the desired destination. When creating the route from the VRF to the global, a physical interface not assigned to a VRF provides a valid next hop to the global table prefix. When creating the route from the global to the VRF, the next hop is an interface that exists inside the destination VRF. The configuration in PE-4, as shown in Example 8-2, achieves the desired result.

Example 8-2   *Static Routes Between a VRF and the Global Routing Table*

```
!
ip vrf vpn2
rd 200:1
route-target export 200:1
route-target import 200:1
!
interface Serial1/0
ip address 10.1.2.5 255.255.255.252
no ip directed-broadcast
!
interface Serial2/0
ip vrf forwarding blue
ip address 10.0.2.1 255.255.255.0
no ip directed-broadcast
!
ip classless
ip route 10.0.2.0 255.255.255.252 Serial2/0
ip route vrf blue 10.1.2.4 255.255.255.252 Serial1/0
!
```

The first static route (IP route 10.0.2.0 255.255.255.252 Serial 2/0) is installed in the global table and provides connectivity in the global to VRF direction. Notice that the next hop is interface Serial 2/0, which is included in the BLUE VRF.

The second static route (IP route VRF blue 10.1.2.4 255.255.255.252 Serial 1/0) is installed in the VRF and uses Serial 1/0 as its next hop. Interface Serial 1/0 is not in a VRF and therefore provides a valid next hop to destinations in the global table.

When using Ethernet interfaces, you must add a next-hop IP address and the next-hop interface to the static route configuration. This allows the router to determine which IP to resolve through the *Address Resolution Protocol* (ARP) when using a LAN interface. In our example, the static route in the global would become this:

```
ip route 10.0.2.0 255.255.255.252 Ethernet2 10.0.2.2
```

The static route from the VRF to the global would be this:

```
ip route vrf blue 10.1.2.4 255.255.255.252 Ethernet1 10.1.2.6
```

The **show** commands in Example 8-3 illustrate the resulting routing entries.

Example 8-3 *Static Route Entries Between VRFs and the Global Routing Table*

```
PE-4# show ip route 10.0.2.0
Routing entry for 10.0.2.0/30
Known via "static", distance 1, metric 0 (connected)
Routing Descriptor Blocks:
* directly connected, via Serial2/0
Route metric is 0, traffic share count is 1
PE-4# show ip route vrf blue 10.1.2.4
Routing entry for 10.1.2.4/30
Known via "static", distance 1, metric 0 (connected)
Redistributing via bgp 1
Advertised by bgp 1
Routing Descriptor Blocks:
* directly connected, via Serial1/0
Route metric is 0, traffic share count is 1
```

You can use the **global** keyword as an alternative configuration to the static route providing connectivity from the VRF to the global table. In the preceding example, the static route in the VRF would become this:

```
ip route vrf blue 10.1.2.4 255.255.255.252 10.1.2.6 global
```

However, there isn't an equivalent keyword in the global-to-VRF direction, so the static route for the return traffic would remain the same:

```
ip route 10.0.2.0 255.255.255.252 Serial2/0
```

Protected Services Access

To allow secured communication across VNs and between VNs and shared services, you must create unique points of ingress and egress to and from each VN. You can do so easily by configuring the routing inside each VN to forward traffic destined outside the VN to a specific gateway. After traffic reaches this gateway, it can be controlled by means of *access control lists* (ACLs), firewalls, *intrusion detection systems* (IDSs), or any other in-band security mechanism that is considered necessary. This is equivalent to treating each VN as if it where a physically separate network.

When connecting separate networks to a common resource, each network must be headended by a security device to control access to the network. The device typically used is a firewall. When accessing the Internet, the place in the network where such a firewall is deployed is known as the Internet edge. When referring to other services beside the Internet, you will see this as the VN perimeter rather than the Internet edge. If you are thinking they are similar and could be one and the same, you are on the right track. Figure 8-9 illustrates a typical perimeter deployment for multiple VNs accessing common services.

Figure 8-9   *Central Site Providing VPN Perimeter Security*

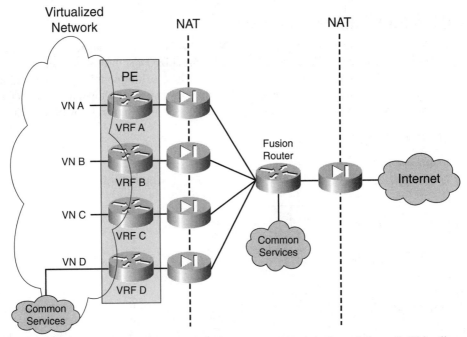

As shown in Figure 8-9, each VN is headended by a dedicated firewall. This allows the creation of security policies that are specific to each VN and independent from each other. To access the shared services, all firewalls are connected to a "fusion" router. The fusion router can provide the VNs with connectivity to the common services, the Internet, or even inter-VN connectivity.

The presence of this fusion router should raise two main concerns:

- The potential for traffic leaking between VNs
- The risk of routes from one VN being announced to another VN.

The presence of dedicated firewalls at the perimeter of each VN prevents the leaking of traffic between VNs through the fusion router by allowing only established connections to return through the VN perimeter. The key is to configure the routing on the fusion device so that routes from one VN are not advertised to another through the fusion router. The details of the routing configuration at the central site are discussed in the "Multiple Common Services/Internet Edge Sites" section.

Figure 8-9 also shows an additional firewall separating the fusion area from the Internet. This firewall is optional. Whether to use it depends on the need to keep the common services or transit traffic in the fusion area protected from the Internet.

Although the following discussion focuses mostly on providing Internet access, it can be generalized to provide access to any external resource for a VN. An external resource can also include resources in other VNs; thus, a resource in VN D is considered an external resource for VN A, and therefore that resource can be accessed through the secure VN perimeter.

Firewalling for Common Services

As VNs proliferate, headending each VN onto its own firewall can become both expensive and hard to manage. Cisco Firewalls can be virtualized and thus offer a separate context for each VN on the same physical appliance. The resulting topology is depicted in Figure 8-10. The difference between this topology and those shown in previous figures is that a single physical firewall now provides a dedicated logical firewall to each VN.

Figure 8-10 *Virtual Firewall Contexts*

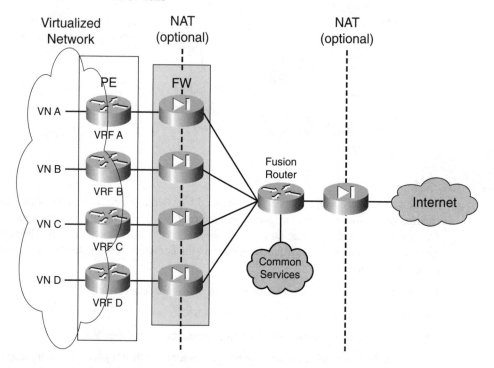

The concept of virtual firewalls or firewall contexts has been implemented on Cisco Firewall appliances and in the integrated *Firewall Service Module* (FWSM) for the Cisco Catalyst 6500.

The integration of the firewall functionality onto the PE platform allows the topology depicted in Figure 8-9 to be consolidated onto a single physical device, as shown in Figure 8-11. The logical topology remains unchanged: The firewall functionality is carried out by a FWSM within the PE, and the fusion router is implemented by the creation of a VRF inside the same PE. Note that the "fusion" VRF does not connect to the VN as a separate router.

Figure 8-11 *Single-Box Implementation of the VPN Perimeter Gateway*

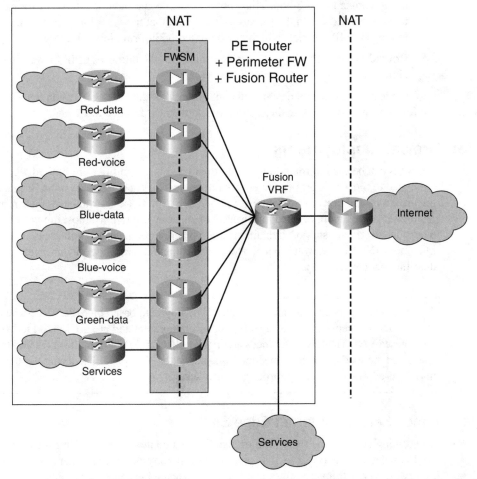

A single-box perimeter implementation is feasible when there is a single common services/ Internet site. However, when there is more than one services site and both resiliency and load distribution are desired among those sites, it is necessary to move the fusion VRF outside the PE router and use a separate physical fusion router (mostly because of the need for separate router IDs and separate BGP processes to provide the desired resiliency through appropriate external BGP [eBGP] peering). An alternative to deploying separate routers is provided by the use of Cisco IOS features that can allow eBGP relationships within a single platform. The topologies and necessary routing configuration for single-and multiple-service site support are discussed in the section on "Routed Firewall Deployments."

Routed Firewalls and Transparent Firewalls

Both firewalls and virtual firewall contexts can operate in one of two modes:

- **Transparent mode**—The firewall simply bridges the traffic it receives without introducing a Layer 3 hop. Thus, both the inside and outside interfaces for each firewall context are in the same subnet. Traffic that traverses the transparent firewall is subject to IP policies, which can be based on information at Layers 2 through 4.

- **Routed mode**—The firewall acts as a router for the purposes of IP forwarding and allows NAT.

Each mode requires careful design and configuration of the routing between the VRFs and the fusion router. We explore these subtleties in the next few sections.

Routed Firewall Deployments

Firewalls can be used in routed mode, but their routing capabilities are limited when compared to those of a proper router. Therefore, special considerations must be made to integrate a routed firewall into any network. When firewalls are virtualized, their routing feature set is even more restrictive. Because of capacity limitations, most firewalls that can be virtualized do not support dynamic routing when virtualized. We will analyze the integration of virtual firewalls in a network with a single Internet edge and in a network with dual Internet connectivity.

NOTE	To illustrate the concepts in this section, a VN deployment based on MPLS VPNs has been chosen. The concepts apply to any VN type of deployment and are not limited to MPLS VPN based VNs. The few differences are in the redistribution of default routes into the VN space and the load balancing considerations inside the VN space. The terms VN and VPN may be used interchangeably throughout this section.

Single Common Services/Internet Edge Site

The routing between the fusion router, the different contexts, and the VNs must be configured with care. Because of its place in the topology, the fusion router has the potential to mix the routes from the different VNs when exchanging routes dynamically with the different VNs. However, because a firewall in routed mode supports only static routing when configured for multiple contexts, the mixing of VN routes is not a concern.

Connectivity between VNs is achieved by the sole configuration of the fusion router; however, the firewalls are configured to allow established connections only; that is, to allow only connections initiated from the inside of the firewall. Therefore, all VNs can reach the fusion router, and the fusion router can return traffic to all the VNs, but the VNs cannot communicate with each other through the fusion router unless specific policies are set on the different firewall contexts to allow inter-VN communication through the VN perimeter gateway.

The static routing configuration for the perimeter gateway is summarized in Figure 8-12 and described in the steps that follow. The detail is provided only for one VN (VN red-data); other VNs will require similar configuration.

Figure 8-12 *Routing Considerations at the VN Perimeter*

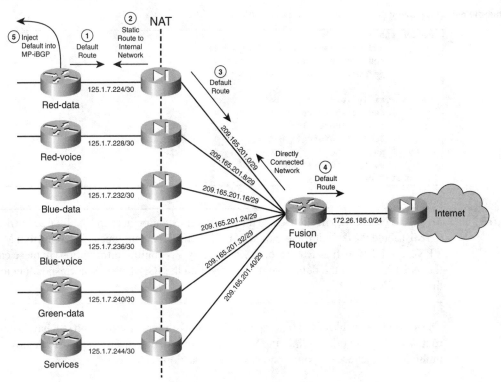

1 Create a default route for the internal VRF (red-data):

   ```
   7600-DC1-SS1(config)#ip route vrf red-data 0.0.0.0 0.0.0.0 125.1.7.226
   ```

2 Create a static route for the inside of the firewall to reach the internal network (red-data VPN):

   ```
   np-fwsm/red-data(config)#route inside 125.1.0.0 255.255.0.0 125.1.7.225 1
   ```

3 Create a static default route for the outside of the firewall to send traffic to the fusion router/VRF:

   ```
   np-fwsm/red-data(config)#route outside 0.0.0.0 0.0.0.0 209.165.201.2 1
   ```

NOTE   The fusion router is directly connected to the outside prefixes, so no special configuration is required.

   4   Create a static default route for the fusion router/VRF to communicate with the *Internet service provider* (ISP).

```
7200-IGATE-DC1(config)#ip route vrf fusion 0.0.0.0 0.0.0.0 172.26.185.1
```

   5   Inject the default route created in Step 1 into MP-iBGP, as demonstrated in Example 8-4.

Example 8-4   *Advertising a Default Route into a VN with MP-iBGP*

```
router bgp 1
        address-family ipv4 vrf red-data
        redistribute static
        default-information originate

address-family ipv4 vrf red-data
        redistribute connected
        redistribute static
        default-information originate
        no auto-summary
        no synchronization
    exit-address-family
```

NOTE   MPLS VPNs use MP-iBGP to carry the routing information in each VN. Step 5 shows how to redistribute the default route into MP-iBGP. Other VN techniques, different from MPLS VPNs, use IGPs such as EIGRP or OSPF to carry VN routing information. In these cases the redistribution of the default routes is done into the IGP instances corresponding to the different VNs.

This procedure enables us to integrate the firewall with static routing and still have a default route dynamically injected into the VPNs. The next section discusses how to deploy multiple Internet access points and have them back up each other.

Multiple Common Services/Internet Edge Sites

Multiple sites are usually deployed for access to the Internet, and therefore we focus our discussion on Internet access. However, as mentioned previously, the same principles apply for other shared services that are accessible over a common network.

When you are using multiple access points to the Internet (or the common services area), resiliency is one of the main goals, along with load balancing. The proposed solution uses two common services sites, each of which injects a default route into each virtual network (VN). As the default routes are received at the different PEs, the preferred route is chosen by the PE based on its proximity to the common services sites. This proximity is determined based on the metric of the *interior gateway protocol* (IGP) running in the core of the network (all other BGP attributes should be equal between the two advertised default routes).

In the particular case of Internet access, some sites will use the first Internet edge site and others will use the second based on their proximity to one Internet edge site or another. This achieves site-based load balancing and minimizes the use of the internal enterprise links by choosing the closest Internet gateway to send traffic to the Internet in the most efficient manner. Figure 8-13 shows a sample topology.

Figure 8-13 *Internet Edge Sites and IGP Proximity*

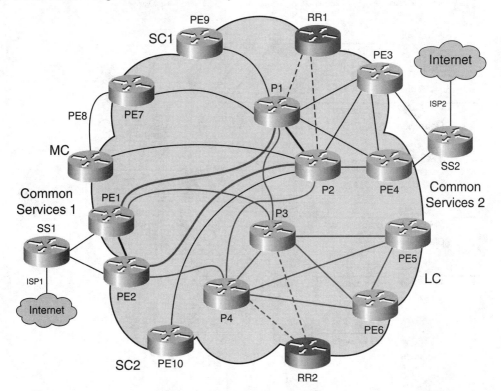

In the case where one Internet edge site dies, all Internet traffic should be rerouted to the live Internet site. For failures that occur within the enterprise network, this failover is provided by the reconvergence of the core IGP and the overlaid MP-iBGP. However, because we are injecting static default routes into the VNs, if the failure is in the ISP, this failure will remain undetected and traffic will be blackholed unless there is a dynamic mechanism to report this failure and trigger a routing reconvergence to use the second Internet edge site.

To do this, a dynamic routing protocol can be used to conditionally inject the default routes into the VNs. This means that a default route is originated and injected into a VN from the Internet edge router if, and only if, this route is valid—for example, if the route exists in the edge router table (see Step 8 below). To achieve this dynamic notification over the perimeter firewalls, eBGP can be used to establish a connection across the firewall contexts (contexts do not support dynamic routing protocols). Figure 8-14 summarizes the routing relationships. Because eBGP peering is required, and this cannot be established between VRFs in a single box, a separate physical router is required for the fusion role.

Figure 8-14 *Internet Edge Sites and IGP Proximity*

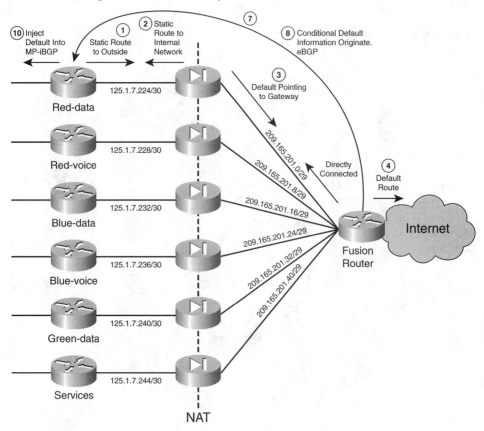

The following steps must be completed to achieve the necessary BGP peering and inject the default routes conditionally:

1 On the internal VRF, create a static route to the outside firewall subnet (209.165. 201.0 /29):

```
7200-IGATE-DC1(config)#ip route vrf red-data 209.165.201.0 255.255.255.248
125.1.7.226
```

2 On the inside firewall interface, create a static route to the internal VPN summary prefix:

```
np-fwsm/red-data(config)#route inside 125.1.0.0 255.255.0.0 125.1.7.225 1
```

3 On the outside firewall interface, create a static default route to the Internet gateway:

```
np-fwsm/red-data(config)#route outside 0.0.0.0 0.0.0.0 209.165.201.2 1
```

NOTE   The fusion router is directly connected to the outside firewall prefixes, so no special configuration is required.

---

4 On the fusion router, create a default route pointing at the Internet gateway (172.26.185.1 /32):

```
7200-IGATE-DC1(config)#ip route 0.0.0.0 0.0.0.0 172.26.185.1
```

5 Configure static NAT entries for the internal VRF BGP peering address. These are necessary to establish the bidirectional TCP sessions for BGP peering. For any type of communication to be initiated from the outside of the firewall, a static NAT entry is required by the firewall; otherwise, the connection is rejected:

```
static (inside,outside) 209.165.201.3 125.1.7.225 netmask 255.255.255.255
norandomseq
```

6 Open the necessary firewall policies to permit BGP peering over the firewall, as demonstrated in Example 8-5.

Example 8-5   *Allowing BGP Peering Through the Firewalls*

```
access-list allow_any extended permit ip any any log debugging
!Allows sessions initiated from the inside of the firewall (i.e. the VPN)
access-list allow_any extended permit tcp host 125.1.7.225 eq bgp host 209.165.201.2
  eq bgp
access-list allow_bgp extended permit tcp host 209.165.201.2 eq bgp host
209.165.201.3 eq bgp
!
access-group allow_any in interface inside
access-group allow_bgp in interface outside
```

7 Configure the internal VRFs and the fusion router as BGP neighbors, as demonstrated in Example 8-6.

Example 8-6   *BGP Neighbors at the Internet Edge*

```
!Fusion Router!!!!!!!!!!!!!!!!!!!!!!!!!!!!!!!!!!!!!
router bgp 10
 no synchronization
 bgp log-neighbor-changes
 redistribute static
 neighbor 209.165.201.3 remote-as 1
 neighbor 209.165.201.3 ebgp-multihop 255
 !
!PE router: Red-data VRF!!!!!!!!!!!!!!!!!!!!!!!!!!!!!!!
```

continues

Example 8-6 *BGP Neighbors at the Internet Edge (Continued)*

```
router bgp 1
 no synchronization
 bgp log-neighbor-changes
 neighbor 125.1.125.15 remote-as 1
 neighbor 125.1.125.15 update-source Loopback0
 neighbor 125.1.125.16 remote-as 1
 neighbor 125.1.125.16 update-source Loopback0
 neighbor 209.165.201.2 remote-as 10
 no auto-summary
 !
 address-family vpnv4
 neighbor 125.1.125.15 activate
 neighbor 125.1.125.15 send-community extended
 neighbor 125.1.125.16 activate
 neighbor 125.1.125.16 send-community extended
 exit-address-family
 !
 address-family ipv4 vrf red-data
 redistribute connected
 redistribute static
 neighbor 209.165.201.2 remote-as 10
 neighbor 209.165.201.2 ebgp-multihop 255
 neighbor 209.165.201.2 activate
 maximum-paths eibgp 2
 no auto-summary
 no synchronization
 exit-address-family
 !
```

8 Originate a default route at the fusion router and send it over BGP to the internal
   VRFs. Use conditional statements so that the default route is advertised only if it is
   present in the local routing table (for instance, if the Internet service is available), as
   demonstrated in Example 8-7.

Example 8-7 *Conditional Default Routes*

```
router bgp 10
 no synchronization
 bgp log-neighbor-changes
 redistribute static
 neighbor 209.165.201.3 remote-as 1
 neighbor 209.165.201.3 ebgp-multihop 255
 neighbor 209.165.201.3 default-originate route-map SEND_DEFAULT
 neighbor 209.165.201.3 distribute-list 3 in
 no auto-summary
 !
 ip classless
 ip route 0.0.0.0 0.0.0.0 172.26.185.1
 no ip http server
 !
 !
```

Example 8-7 *Conditional Default Routes (Continued)*

```
access-list 1 permit 0.0.0.0
access-list 2 permit 172.26.185.1
access-list 3 deny    any
!
route-map SEND_DEFAULT permit 10
 match ip address 1
 match ip next-hop 2
 set metric 0
 set local-preference 100
```

9 Prevent any BGP updates from the inside network coming onto the fusion router, as
demonstrated in Example 8-8. If the fusion router is allowed to receive VPN routes
via e-BGP, it will replicate the received routes onto its other e-BGP peers. This
basically injects routes from one VPN into another, and therefore these updates must
be prevented.

Example 8-8 *Filtering BGP Updates to Avoid Inter-VPN Route Leaking*

```
router bgp 10
 no synchronization
 bgp log-neighbor-changes
 redistribute static
 neighbor 209.165.201.3 remote-as 1
 neighbor 209.165.201.3 ebgp-multihop 255
 neighbor 209.165.201.3 default-originate route-map SEND_DEFAULT
 neighbor 209.165.201.3 distribute-list 3 in
 no auto-summary
!
ip classless
ip route 0.0.0.0 0.0.0.0 172.26.185.1
no ip http server
!
!
access-list 1 permit 0.0.0.0
access-list 2 permit 172.26.185.1
access-list 3 deny    any
!
```

10 Inject the default routes created in step 8 into the VNs. In this example this implies
injecting the defaults into the different MP-iBGP address families at the PE as
described in step 5 of the "Single Common Services Site" section. With other VN
techniques (non-MPLS) this could require injecting the defaults into an IGP.

We have discussed how to integrate routed firewalls for the single edge and redundant Internet
edge scenarios. The mechanisms and topology discussed were tested and documented using
a separate physical router to act as the fusion router. In theory, you could use a VRF to play
the role of fusion router, and thus it may be possible to collapse the entire topology into a
single device. This, however, requires special functionality.

A separate router might be required for two main reasons:

- Providing separate router IDs for BGP peering
- Providing separate BGP router processes for eBGP

With upcoming Cisco IOS versions, these requirements will be addressed by features that allow the rewrite of router IDs per VRF and the creation of multiple BGP process IDs for each VRF. The changes will allow the deployment of the logical topology discussed within a single physical router. In any case, the routing principles to use are the same.

Routing Considerations

The following two sections discuss some routing details that you need to keep in mind when deploying the Internet edge as discussed.

Advertising Multiple Routes into MP-iBGP

Advertising more than one default route or advertising multiple routes for the same prefix must be done with care. The default behavior of a *route reflector* (RR) is to make a decision based on metrics and attributes and reflect only the best one of the advertised routes. The result is that all PEs will always receive the route that is best for the RR, which is not necessarily the best route for the PE to reach the Internet.

To achieve load balancing and redundancy from injecting multiple routes for a common destination in our topology, it is important that the RR actually reflects all the routes it receives, so that the route selection can actually be done at the ingress PEs. To achieve this, the routes must be advertised with different RDs. For example, in Figure 8-13, the default route advertised by Common Services Site 1 (SS1) is sent with an RD of 10:103; the default route sent by Common Services Site 2 (SS2) is sent with an RD of 101:103. In this manner, some sites will prefer SS2; others will prefer SS1, based on proximity.

Load balancing across the enterprise core can be achieved by instructing BGP to install multiple paths in the routing table (**ibgp multipath**). It is tempting to use unequal-cost paths and load balance across all possible paths. However, doing so can affect the way traffic to the Internet is handled and can cause the use of suboptimal paths to access the Internet.

NOTE	The considerations here discussed for load balancing with iBGP do not apply when using Equal Cost Routing within IGPs in a non-MPLS VN deployment.

In the proposed scenario, the requirement is for certain portions of the network to prefer one Common Services Site over another. Therefore, the load balancing is done per site, rather than per flow. For instance, site SC1 would always try to use SS1 first because it is the closest Internet access site. On the other hand, if unequal paths are allowed to be installed in the routing table, SC1 would send some flows over SS1 and others over SS2, potentially congesting low-speed links that would not be used if only one path had been installed on the routing table.

However, the best solution is hardly to turn BGP multipath off, but to set the BGP multipath capability to install only multiple equal-cost paths. This is important because equal-cost load balancing is desirable between sites. Because only equal-cost paths can be installed in the table, the Internet will be accessed consistently via either SS1 or SS2 depending on the proximity of the site. If a failure is detected, the routing protocols must determine which sites are still available and recalculate the paths to the Common Services Sites to make a decision on where to exit to the Internet.

Asymmetric Return Paths

A classic problem faced when multihoming to the Internet is when traffic exits the enterprise out of one gateway and the return traffic is received over a different gateway. The implications are many, the main one being that the return traffic would normally not be able to get through the firewall because there would not be a session established at the return firewall because the traffic originally left the network through a different firewall.

In the proposed scenario, the asymmetry of the return path is handled by using different global NAT address pools outside the different Internet gateways. Each Internet gateway advertises a unique address pool, thus eliminating ambiguity in the return path. For example, the source address of traffic leaving SS1 is rewritten to a prefix advertised only by SS1. Therefore, the return traffic for a stream that entered the Internet through SS1 would have to come through SS1 because the Internet has routes to the SS1 address pool only through SS1.

Network Address Translation (NAT)

When operating in routed mode, a firewall establishes a connection between the inside and the outside for each flow that is to traverse the firewall. These connections are in the form of NAT entries, regardless of address translation being or not being configured on the firewall.

The default behavior of firewalls is to allow the establishment of flows that are initiated from the inside network. Provided that the ACLs allow it, upstream traffic should flow through the firewall without a problem. For the return path, however, a valid NAT entry in the connection table is required for the firewall to allow return traffic through. This NAT entry is dynamically created when the flow is initiated from the inside; connections initiated from the outside will not dynamically create an entry in the firewall.

This unidirectional mechanism prevents connections from being initiated from the outside the network. For a connection to be successfully initiated from the outside of the network, a NAT entry for the internal destination address should exist in the firewall table before the connection can be established. Therefore, if connections initiated from the outside network are required, static NAT entries must be created to make the specific prefixes available to the outside of the firewall. To allow outside initiated connections, the creation of a static NAT entry is necessary, even if the firewall is configured to not translate addresses (**nat 0**).

Benefits of NAT

Being able to translate addresses confers many benefits. The main ones can be summarized as follows:

- Internal networks are hidden from the outside world. With NAT, it is not necessary for the Internet to be aware of the internal addressing scheme of the enterprise.

- Internal networks can use private address spaces as defined in RFC 1918. This use proves particularly helpful when deploying VNs because the deployment of VNs can accelerate the depletion of the IP address space available to the enterprise. This requires restricting extra-VN communication to happen through the VN perimeter where addresses can be NATed. For instance, inter-VN route leaking would not work if there were any address overlaps between the private spaces used.

Dynamic NAT

Address translation can be done dynamically. When an inside station attempts to connect to a site outside the firewall, a dynamic mapping of the source address of the inside station to a globally (outside) significant address is made. The globally significant address to be used is defined by a configured address pool. Therefore, each connection is identified by a unique NAT entry. However, there is the potential for the number of connections to exceed the number of addresses available in the translation pool, in which case any new connection would not be successful.

An alternative to regular NAT is *Port Address Translation* (PAT). With PAT, you can use a single IP address for the global pool. Multiple connections can be associated to the same IP address and will be uniquely identified by a unique Layer 4 port number. Thus, a single global address can accommodate thousands of connections.

Static NAT

When internal resources must be made available outside the firewall, you must provide a predictable presence for the internal resource on the outside of the firewall.

By default, all addresses internal to the firewall are not visible to the outside. When addresses are not being translated, they might be visible to the outside, but they still would not be reachable, because reachability from the outside requires an entry in the firewall connection table to be present ahead of time.

Static NAT assigns a globally significant address to the internal resource and adds an entry to the firewall connection table. This address is fixed so that it can be reached from the outside in a consistent manner. The entry in the connection table makes it possible for the outside to connect to the inside resource provided that the necessary policy is in place.

NAT in the VN Perimeter

A combination of dynamic and static NAT is required at the VN perimeter. Dynamic NAT is used to allow connectivity for sessions established from the inside of the network. Static NAT is required to allow BGP peer establishment and connectivity to resources shared from inside a service VN.

Dynamic NAT can be established by using either NAT or PAT. When using NAT, you must provide the outside interface of the firewall with an IP prefix that can accommodate the entire global address pool to be used in the translation. Figure 8-15 shows the scenario for the red-data VN in our example.

Figure 8-15 *NAT for the Red VN*

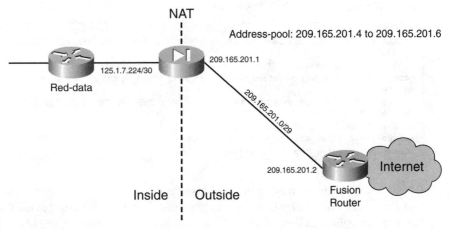

Each connection from the red-data VN to the Internet creates one NAT entry and therefore uses one of the addresses in the address pool. Thus, the number of possible concurrent connections is limited to three in this specific scenario. Notice that a 29-bit address mask (rather than 32 bits) has been used for the point-to-point connection to accommodate the NAT address pool.

The commands in Example 8-9 configure the red-data firewall context to allow this kind of connectivity.

Example 8-9 *Dynamic NAT with a Finite Global Address Pool*

```
! Create the dynamic NAT Pool
global (outside) 1 209.165.201.4-209.165.201.6 netmask 255.255.255.248
nat (inside) 1 125.1.0.0 255.255.0.0
!The following commands allow outbound connectivity
!Allow sessions initiated from the inside of the firewall (i.e. the VPN)
access-list allow_any extended permit ip any any log debugging
access-group allow_any in interface inside
```

Alternatively, PAT can provide dynamic translation without the limitation of the exhaustion of the global address pool. Configuring PAT is almost identical to configuring NAT; the difference is that instead of defining a global range, a single IP is configured, as demonstrated in Example 8-10.

Example 8-10 *Port Address Translation Allows Many-to-One Address Translations*

```
! Create the dynamic PAT Pool
np-fwsm/red-data(config)#nat (inside) 1 125.1.0.0 255.255.0.0
np-fwsm/red-data(config)#global (outside) 1 209.165.201.4
Global 209.165.201.4 will be Port Address Translated
```

A static NAT entry is required to allow BGP peering between the fusion router and the internal VRF. The necessary ACLs must be configured to allow this type of connectivity, too. Care must be taken to open the firewall exclusively to the relevant BGP traffic. The configuration shown in Example 8-11 takes care of this.

Example 8-11 *Static NAT Entries Allowing BGP Peering Through the Firewall*

```
! Create the static translation for the inside (125.1.7.225) peer
static (inside,outside) 209.165.201.3 125.1.7.225 netmask 255.255.255.255
norandomseq
! Allow bgp tcp session between the neighbors only and in both directions
access-list allow_any extended permit tcp host 125.1.7.225 eq bgp host 209.165.201.2
eq bgp
access-list allow_bgp extended permit tcp host 209.165.201.2 eq bgp host
209.165.201.3 eq bgp
! Apply policies in both directions
access-group allow_any in interface inside
access-group allow_bgp in interface outside
```

Other static NAT entries may be required if servers inside a VN will be made available outside the VN. As the number of servers to publish increases, the use of static PAT may come in handy. For detailed information on static PAT and more details on NAT in general, see the FWSM configuration guide at http://www.cisco.com/univercd/cc/td/doc/product/lan/cat6000/mod_icn/fwsm/fwsm_2_2/fwsm_cfg/index.htm.

Transparent Firewall Deployments

When NATing is not necessary, you can use the firewalls in transparent mode. This mode simplifies the routing significantly, allowing complete functionality to be achieved by means of dynamic IGPs.

Figure 8-16 summarizes the routing relationships necessary at the VN perimeter. This setup is as simple as having all VRFs peer with the fusion router/VRF. The fusion router will inject a default route into the IGP, and this will be redistributed into MP-iBGP at the PE.

Figure 8-16 *Transparent Firewalling at the VPN Perimeter*

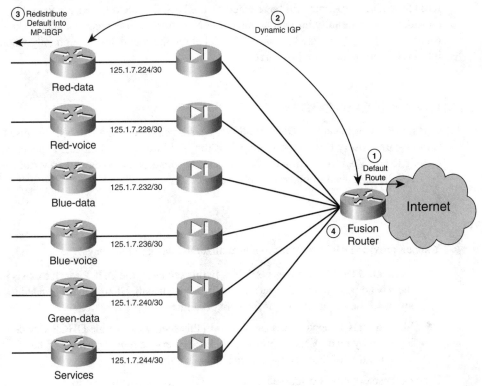

Because of the bridged nature of the firewalls, you can establish the peering between the VRFs and the fusion router directly with an IGP. On the other hand, you cannot use the firewalls for NAT, and therefore all VRFs must use valid and unique IP address spaces.

The configuration is simple and consists of the following steps. This is standard Internet edge configuration and must be done for each VN.

Step 1   Create a default route pointing to the Internet on the fusion router/VRF (for example: **ip route vrf fusion 0.0.0.0 0.0.0.0 172.26.185.1**).

Step 2   Advertise the default route in the IGP used between the fusion router and the VRFs at the PE.

Step 3   Redistribute the IGP into MP-iBGP at the PE and vice versa.

Step 4   Filter the routing updates between the VRFs at the fusion router to avoid advertising routes from one VRF into another.

The communication between VRFs is prevented by the default behavior of the firewall, which allows only internally initiated connections. Therefore, with the default firewall policies, a connection initiated from RED to BLUE will be allowed through the RED firewall context, but will be rejected by the BLUE context because it would be considered an externally initiated connection. Nevertheless it is recommended to keep the routes from being populated across VRFs and allow these updates through only when inter-VRF communication is desired.

Providing IP Services

Certain IP services such as DHCP and DNS can be shared by many VNs. Because these services are closely tied to the structure of the IP addressing scheme, it is necessary to be able to add VN information to some service requests and also be able to virtualize the services themselves and make them VN aware.

DHCP

You can provide DHCP services in a virtualized network in two ways:

*   **Dedicated DHCP services per VN**—In this scenario, the DHCP service exists inside the VN address space. The service itself is not virtualized and does not need to be aware of the virtualization of the network either.

*   **Shared DHCP services across VNs**—In this scenario, a single DHCP service is shared by many VNs. Therefore, the DHCP service must be aware of the virtualization of the network and must also be virtualized.

Each of these options is discussed in more detail in the following sections.

Dedicated DHCP Services per VN

When each VN has its own DHCP service, the only added required functionality is that any router relaying DHCP messages be able to unicast these messages using a VRF rather than the global table.

The DHCP relay functionality allows the DHCP multicast-based conversation to be relayed over a unicast UDP connection directly to a known DHCP server when the DHCP server is not in the same subnet as the client. To unicast this traffic in a VN, the DHCP relay feature must be able to look up the destination address in a VRF table rather than the global table.

This is the basic level of VRF awareness for the DHCP relay functionality.

Shared DHCP Services

To share a DHCP service among many VNs, it is necessary to virtualize the DHCP service. What this means is that the DHCP server will contain a set of scopes for each VN. For instance, the DHCP server might contain a partition for the BLUE VN with several scopes providing addresses in several subnets. Simultaneously, the DHCP server might contain a totally separate partition with the scopes and subnets for the RED VN. Each partition in the DHCP server is equivalent to a traditional nonvirtualized DHCP server and services a particular VN.

It is, of course, necessary to provide a way of differentiating DHCP messages from one VN from DHCP messages from another so that the correct partition can be used to service the different DHCP requests for the different VNs.

Thus, the infrastructure must be able to not only relay the DHCP messages over a VN, but must also be capable of tagging certain DHCP messages as originated within a specific VN.

Option 82 (a field in the DHCP messages) can be used to carry the information related to which VN the message belongs to. This information is added to the DHCP message by the DHCP relay agent. Therefore, when the message reaches the DHCP server, it will be linked to the partition that corresponds to the VN in the option 82 field.

For example, in the network in Figure 8-17, the DHCP server contains two partitions, one for the RED VN and one for the BLUE VN.

Figure 8-17 *Shared DHCP Services*

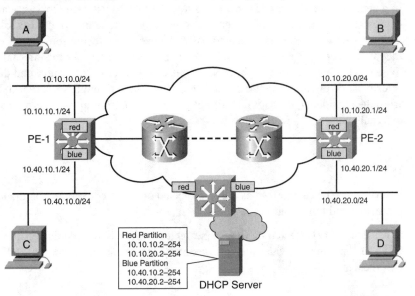

When host C (which is in the BLUE VN) makes a DHCP request, it will be seen by PE-1. PE-1 will then assign the tag corresponding to BLUE in the Option 82 field of the request, write 10.10.10.1 in the giaddr (gateway IP address) field of the request, and unicast the request to the DHCP server. When the DHCP server receives the request, it will choose the appropriate scope based on both Option 82 and the giaddr fields. Note that without option 82, the DHCP server would have two different partitions to choose from, but no criteria to decide.

Domain Name System (DNS) Services

The provisioning of *Domain Name System* (DNS) services for VNs using valid Internet addresses is straightforward and requires no special consideration. On the other hand, the provisioning of DNS for VNs using private addresses as defined in RFC 1918 can pose certain challenges depending on the level of functionality desired.

At a basic level, DNS services can be shared by all VNs if these are only used to resolve names of hosts that are outside the VNs. In this scenario, all VNs must simply be able to reach the DNS server that will be outside the VNs in a *demilitarized zone* (DMZ) or a central services site.

When the requirement is to resolve the names of internal hosts while using private IP addressing, it is necessary to deploy a DNS server inside each VN. This internal server allows the resolution of the internal names. This DNS server should be able to query external DNS servers for the resolution of Internet names.

In general it is recommended that separate internal and external DNS servers be deployed. The internal DNS server relays requests from the internal hosts to the external DNS server, which then proceeds to begin the necessary resolution queries on behalf of the internal server. To obtain the desired result, it is necessary for the internal DNS server to be reachable from outside the VN. To this effect, a static NAT entry and the necessary rules must be put in place at the firewall to allow the internal DNS server to be accessed from the outside. Note that this will not provide resolution of the internal names for external queries.

Summary

A service can be categorized as either protected or unprotected based on the level of protection and type of access required.

When deploying protected services, a perimeter model based on dedicated firewall contexts and a fusion router provides the best flexibility and a centralized point of policy enforcement.

When you are deploying unprotected services, you can use many innovative routing scenarios to create communication between VNs and extranet connectivity. The fact that the services are labeled as unprotected does not mean that these cannot be protected by firewalls and other security mechanisms; it just means that the model does not intrinsically protect the services and that they would have to be secured by other means.

Certain services such as DHCP and DNS can be shared among the different VNs as long as the appropriate functionality is in place.

CHAPTER 9

Multicast in a Virtualized Environment

This chapter discusses how to carry multicast data in a virtualized network environment. There are two main transport architectures: *point-to-point* (p2p) and *multicast virtual private network* (mVPN). We examine each in turn, with a discussion of the design trade-offs and an example to show the basic configuration steps involved.

In a virtualized network, the multicast source and recipient are not always in the same *Virtual Network (VN)*. Therefore, we discuss how you must configure these devices to support scenarios when the source is in the same *VPN routing and forwarding instance* (VRF), a different VRF, or in the global routing table.

All these discussions assume a familiarity with the basic concepts of multicast, such as *reverse path forwarding* (RPF) checking, shared trees, and the rudiments of *Protocol Independent Multicast* (PIM) operation. Therefore, we start the chapter with a short introduction to IP multicast, which you can safely skip if you are already familiar with the content.

Multicast Introduction

This section provides a quick review of IP multicast. For more information on IP multicast, you can check the authoritative references included in Appendix C and D. Multicast is a term that refers to the ability to send data to a group of receivers. Multicast is used in a wide variety of applications, such as the following:

- Stock price data in financial networks
- Network control protocols, such as *Open Shortest Path First* (OSPF)
- IETF zeroconf protocol (used in the Mac OSX Bonjour feature)
- IP/TV

In terms of everyday applications, newspaper delivery uses multicast; you get a paper only if you request (and pay for) it. Cable and broadcast television do not use multicast; all the channels in your subscription package are transmitted to your home, whether you watch them or not.

In networks, multicast provides an elegant solution to two sets of problems. First, multicast is a convenient way to discover resources and peers, such as the use of multicast to communicate between OSPF peers on a shared segment. Second, multicast allows a source to send data to a group of listeners without having to know anything about the group's members.

NOTE   In our discussion, we contrast network multicast with broadcast. However, broadcast is really a special case of multicast. The difference everyone refers to when decrying broadcast as a "bad thing" is how well network resources are used. Sending any data to all end stations is expensive and should be done only within a limited scope. Multicast routing technology aims to provide the mechanisms to efficiently send data to groups.

IP-based television is an excellent example of an application that would be impossible on a large scale without multicast. As already pointed out, (non-IP) television uses a broadcast model today. The data rates are such that it is not cost-effective to pump hundreds of channels worth of data over broadband links to homes. The last-mile connections are a bottleneck (especially in much of the United States—other parts of the world are luckier). With multicast technology, an end station can receive data for just a single channel by joining a corresponding multicast group. When the subscriber changes channel, the end station simply changes group. As a result, IP/TV providers need to send only a small subset of the total available data over last-mile links. (Our model is actually a naive implementation of IP/TV. In reality, IP/TV has a variety of deployment scenarios.)

There are a number of requirements to manage groups on a network:

- The ability to identify groups (Class D addressing)
- The ability for a host to join and leave a group (*Internet Group Management Protocol* [IGMP])
- The ability to route multicast packets (PIM)

RFC 1122 reserves a the range of IP addresses from 224.0.0.0 through 239.255.255.255 as a special category called Class D addresses that are reserved for multicast. A multicast source sends data to a group using a Class D destination address just as a unicast source sends data using an address from outside this range. Routers have forwarding tables that map multicast addresses to outgoing interfaces. These tables are built using multicast routing protocols; the most common in use today is PIM.

Any IP endpoint can join any group at any time by using IGMP. No restrictions apply as to the topology imposed by the network; however, devices may be said to be form a tree, with the source at the root, group members as the leaves, and edges as the network paths that connect them. Figure 9-1 shows how a tree is built up as hosts join a group.

Figure 9-1   *Multicast Groups Form a Tree*

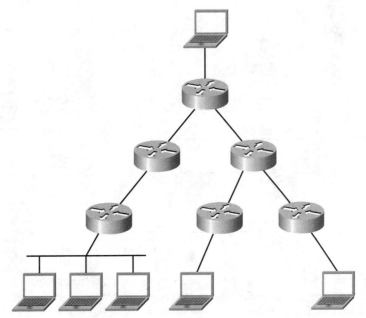

The next two sections introduce IGMP and PIM.

Internet Group Management Protocol (IGMP)

The IGMP protocol allows routers to manage group membership on their directly connected interfaces. End stations use IGMP to join and leave groups. The protocol has two basic types of messages: query and report.

The formal definition of query and report are (quoting from RFC 3376) as follows:

- **Query**—Membership queries are sent by IP multicast routers to query the multicast reception state of neighboring interfaces.

- **Report**—Version 3 membership reports are sent by IP systems to report (to neighboring routers) the current multicast reception state, or changes in the multicast reception state, of their interfaces.

In practice, a query message allows multicast routers to periodically poll for group membership. The router sends a query to ask: "Who wants data from this group?" Multicast hosts signal group membership with a report message. Routers then forward multicast packets on all interfaces on which they received an appropriate report message.

Figure 9-2 shows this interaction with the router querying for members of group 239.1.1.1. Both hosts A and B are members of this group, and host B replies with its IGMP report.

Figure 9-2 *IGMP Query/Report Interaction*

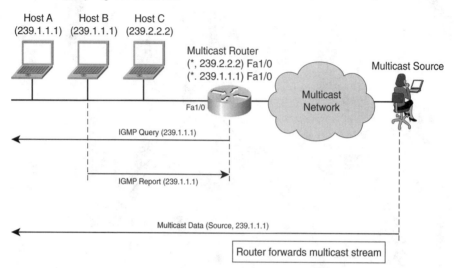

The queries sent by routers can be general or specific. General refers to all groups known on a receiving interface. Specific, as you might expect, refers to a particular group, or a group-source pair (this last feature is for *Source-Specific Multicast* [SSM], something that we do not cover here). So, the router can ask: "Who is interested in this specific group?" or "Who is interested in this specific group from this specific source?"

Report messages can be used to join a particular group in either INCLUDE or EXCLUDE mode. In INCLUDE mode, the recipient lists the groups (and, optionally, the source) in which they are interested. In EXCLUDE mode, the recipient simply tells the multicast router which groups it does not want to receive.

Starting from IGMPv2, multicast hosts can join a group without first waiting for a query by sending an unsolicited report message. If this is the first request for a particular group, the router arranges to receive the multicast stream (as discussed in the next section) and forwards the packets on the interface on which it received the report. To stop receiving a stream, a recipient sends an IGMP leave message. A router that receives a leave message must first determine—with a query—whether there are any other recipients on that interface before shutting off the flow of packets.

The IGMP protocol goes to some lengths to avoid chattiness. For example, it defines a random host-based timer mechanism to avoid multiple simultaneous reports being sent in reply to every single query. For any given group, a router needs to receive only a single report on an interface to forward data on that interface.

IGMP is lightweight in its state requirements. An end system tracks only its own group memberships. A router need only track active group memberships on an interface. Note that IGMP does not address how hosts discover multicast sources in the first place—that is the hosts' responsibility.

IGMP packets, which are never forwarded by a router (they are sent with a *Time To Live* [TTL]=1), are themselves sent to multicast addresses, either 224.0.0.1 (all systems), 224.0.0.22 (all IGMPv3-capable routers), or to a group address (in the case of reports and group-specific queries).

Multicast Routing

IGMP manages the interaction between hosts and routers. Therefore, a different mechanism is required to route traffic from the source to the last-hop router. This is where multicast routing comes in.

You must solve two problems:

* Building a distribution tree to connect members of a group to the source
* Forwarding multicast traffic along the distribution tree

Let's start with forwarding first because it is the simpler of the two. Although it uses the same packet format and runs across the same network devices, multicast forwarding differs from unicast routing in one important respect: Routers use a packet's source address to determine which outgoing interfaces to use. Forwarding traffic away from a source (or down the distribution tree, to be more exact) instead of toward a known destination is called *reverse path forwarding* (RPF). Routers also uses RPF to check that incoming packets are received on the interface closest to their source. This is called a RPF check. Packets that fail the RPF check are dropped. RPF and RPF Checking are critical concepts in multicast forwarding. Consider the network shown in Figure 9-3.

Figure 9-3   *Multicast Forwarding*

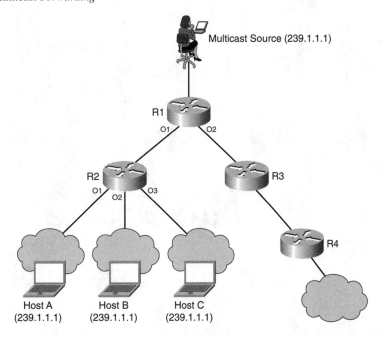

Router R1 receives traffic sent by source S to group address 239.1.1.1. Using its multicast forwarding table, R1 works out that the packets should be sent on interfaces R1-O1 and R1-O2. The next router, R2, does a similar lookup and forwards packets on interfaces R2-O1, R2-O2, and R2-O3. Forwarding—and replication—continues in this way along the distribution tree until data is delivered to all multicast receivers. Each router in the example also performs a RPF check when it receives the multicast packet.

There are two types of tree: source tree and shared tree. Before we discuss them, note the use of some new notation when discussing multicast routing: (S,G) denotes a source S in group G; (*,G) denotes any source in group G.

Source Trees

The source is the root of the distribution tree. All data is forwarded from the source to the leaves. In a naive implementation, when router R1 in Figure 9-3 receives a packet from source S to group 239.1.1.1, it uses RPF to identify which interface it would have used to reach S (in this case, R1-O1 is the egress interface for the shortest path to S).

Source trees use the shortest path to connect root and leaves. Source-tree-based protocols, such as *Distance Vector Multicast Routing Protocol* (DVMRP) and PIM dense mode, were once widely deployed. However, most networks now prefer shared-tree.

Figure 9-4 *Dense-Mode Pruning and Flooding*

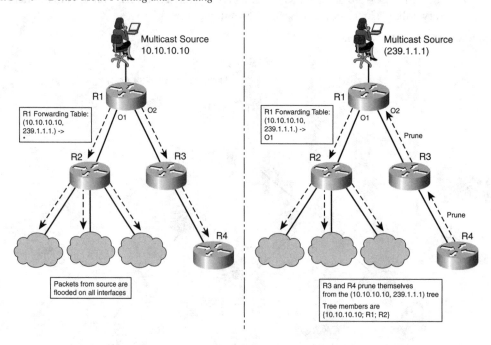

Shared Trees

Source trees build different shortest-path trees for every source in a group; in other words, for every (S,G) pairing. shared trees use a single tree for all sources in a group; that is, there is a single tree for every (*,G) combination. Figure 9-5 shows how shared-tree forwarding works. All sources in a group send data to a central *rendezvous point* (RP), R1, which is the root of the shared tree.

Like everything else in life, shared-tree-based forwarding is not perfect. First, the path between source and leaf is suboptimal compared to the shortest path in source tree. Second, the RP is a potential bottleneck through which all the group's data must flow.

Figure 9-5   *Shared-Tree Forwarding*

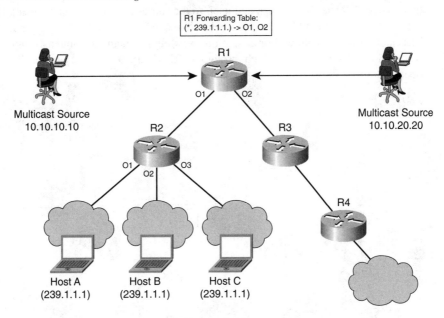

Protocol Independent Multicast (PIM)

PIM is an *Internet Engineering Task Force* (IETF) protocol designed to allow multicast forwarding independently of any unicast routing protocol (unlike, say *Multicast OSPF* [MOSPF]). PIM is a parasitic protocol. It relies on unicast routing tables—whatever their source—as the basis of its own forwarding decisions. Therefore, PIM routers do not send or receive multicast routing announcements.

PIM has two modes of operation:

- **Dense mode (PIM-DM)**—Uses a source-tree to deliver data. PIM-DM floods packets on outgoing interfaces—identified by RPF checks based on the unicast forwarding table—until it receives a prune message. When pruned, data will not be sent on an interface until either the router reverts to flooding or a graft message is received from a downstream router. Figure 9-4 illustrates the pruning and flooding operation used in PIM-DM.

- **Sparse mode (PIM-SM)**—Uses shared-tree distribution. Downstream routers use join messages to explicitly add themselves to the distribution tree (for example, after receiving an IGMP report from an end station). If a router receives a report message and it is not already part of the (*,G) tree, it also sends a PIM join message in the direction of the preconfigured RP.

We have already established how data is multicast from the RP to downstream routers. How does it get from the source to the RP in the first place? The first-hop router plays a special role in PIM. It encapsulates the multicast packet in PIM-SM-register packets and unicasts them to the RP. The RP can then add itself to the source tree for the source using PIM join messages. In fact, any PIM receiver can elect to move from shared to source tree in this way. The intention was to allow shortest-path forwarding for bandwidth-intensive applications that could not—or should not—go through an RP. Figure 9-6 shows sample PIM-SM operation for (*,239.1.1.1).

Figure 9-6   *PIM-SM*

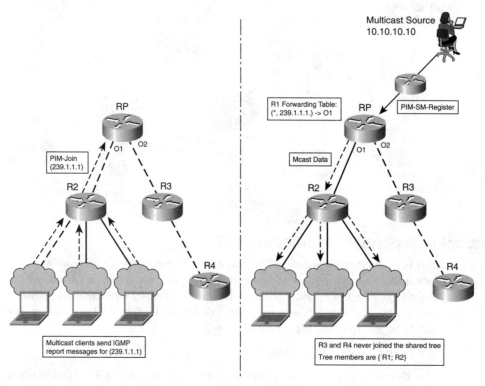

PIM trees are unidirectional. Traffic flows from the RP downward, not the other way around. Bidirectional PIM allows for traffic to flow between all members of a group by building a spanning-tree network with the RP as the root node. After a PIM shared tree is built, each member node can forward traffic upstream without going through any special registration or negotiation. The last-hop router joins the source tree and sends a prune message to the RP. In this way, a new branch of the shared tree is created, and traffic that initially flowed through the RP now bypasses it. In Cisco IOS, you can prevent the switchover of traffic from shared to source tree using the ip pim spt-threshold command.

VRFs and Multicast

This section describes how multicast operates with VRFs. A VRF, as described so far, contains only unicast routes. A key concept is that of an associated multicast table for each VRF.

With regular multicast, the global routing table uses an associated multicast table to handle multicast traffic and build the necessary distribution trees based on the information received from its PIM adjacencies. Each VRF can have its own associated multicast routing table. These multicast tables are known as *multicast VRFs* (mVRFs).

Each multicast VRF can be associated to a separate instance of PIM-SM. For each instance of PIM-SM, the router maintains a PIM adjacency with each of the PIM-capable routers (or VRFs) that are adjacent to the multicast-enabled VRF. These PIM instances, which populate the mVRFs, are referred to as VN-specific PIM instances (because they exist within a VN).

Therefore, the addition of multicast functionality to a VRF has two main components:

* mVRFs
* VN-specific PIM instances

The model used is the same as that used for traditional handling of multicast, but it is replicated for each VRF by creating a dedicated table and a dedicated PIM instance.

When deploying hop-to-hop virtual networks, each hop will have an mVRF and a VN-specific PIM instance for each virtual network. The adjacencies for the VPN-specific PIM instances are established over the interfaces associated to the multicast-enabled VRF. Figure 9-7 illustrates the support for multicast in a single-virtual network hop-to-hop VN scenario. As other virtual networks are added, this model is replicated for each virtual network.

As you can see in the figure, the Red virtual network is created by associating the Red VRFs on both R1 and R2 to a logical interface Ethernet 1.100 on each router. The Red virtual network uses the logical link between E1.100 in R1 and E1.100 in R2 to establish unicast routing adjacencies and to forward traffic. When a Red mVRF and a Red VPN-specific PIM instance are created on R1 and R2, the Red VPN-specific PIM instance uses the logical interfaces (E1.100) to form VN-specific PIM adjacencies between R1 and R2 for the Red virtual network. Therefore, the multicast distribution trees for the Red virtual network use the logical links associated with the unicast topology (E1.100) and leverage the Red unicast VRFs to complete the necessary RPF checks.

Figure 9-7 *Multicast Support for Hop-to-Hop Layer 3 VNs*

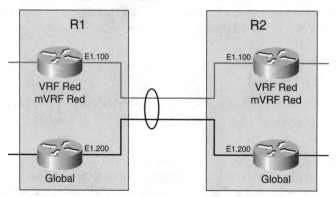

When both the source and the destination of a multicast stream exist within the same virtual network, you can rely on the VN-specific PIM instances to build the necessary multicast distribution trees within the VN space, as we have explained so far. Because the entire distribution tree exists within a single virtual network, the information in the unicast VRFs should allow the successful completion of the RPF check for the multicast source. If the source belongs to a separate VN, its prefix will not be present in the unicast VRF and, therefore, the RPF check would be unsuccessful. To get around this, extranet mVPN functionality is necessary. You can read more about this extranet functionality in the "Multicast Across VRFs" section later in this chapter.

Our discussion so far is true only for hop-to-hop VRF deployments that do not rely on *Multiprotocol interior Border Gateway Protocol* (MP-iBGP) for the formation of the unicast VNs according to the model proposed in RFC 2547. For RFC 2547 networks, mVPN provides a mechanism to distribute multicast traffic within a VN—provided that the source and destination of the multicast traffic are both inside the same VN. mVPN is largely based on the creation of overlaid IP multicast tunnels and is explained in detail later in the chapter.

Multicast Sourced from an External IP Network

In many cases, the source of the multicast stream does not belong to any VN. In other words, the source of the multicast stream exists in an address space that is outside the VN network although the destination or subscribers belong to a VN.

When we see an address space outside of the VN network, we do not mean the global table in the VN network, but a totally separate network. As discussed in "Multicast Across VRFs" section in this chapter, multicast traffic sourced from the global table must be handled differently.

Provided that all VNs have a unique (nonoverlapping) address space, a shared-services access topology can be created that allows the multicast to be sourced into the VNs. At this shared-services communications point, each mVRF establishes controlled unicast routing and PIM communication with the fusion router, which is outside the VN address space and connects to the multicast source. This shared-services topology, as depicted in Figure 9-8, is similar to that discussed in Chapter 8, "Traffic Steering and Service Centralization."

Figure 9-8   *Shared-Services Topology Sourcing Multicast Traffic*

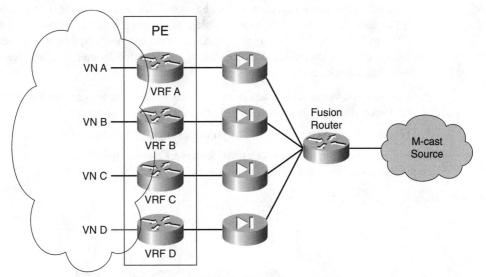

From the multicast perspective, the fusion router sees each mVRF simply as a neighboring device. The necessary unicast routing information must be injected from the fusion router into the different unicast VRFs so that the RPF check of the external source can be successful inside the VRFs.

NOTE   At the PE shown in the topology, the RPF in each VRF returns the VRF interface connecting the VRF to the fusion router and the fusion router itself as the RPF interface and RPF neighbor, respectively.

Notice that the firewalls in the topology shown in Figure 9-8 must be configured in one of two ways:

- **Firewalls in transparent (bridged) mode**—The firewall is transparent to the entire multicast process and should be configured to allow multicast traffic through.

- **Firewalls in routed mode**—The firewall is a routed hop and must therefore be able to allow and participate in the PIM, RPF, and multicast forwarding processes.

You can deploy this topology without firewalls, but you would need to implement tight *access control lists* (ACLs) to prevent the fusion router from becoming a transit router between the different VRFs. Keep in mind that in this scenario the fusion router's role is to provide access to the multicast source, not to provide communication between VNs.

Nevertheless, it is possible to use the fusion router to provide inter-VN communication. The firewall (or ACL) policies to achieve this must be crafted with much care. Some of the detail required to provide inter-VN unicast connectivity is discussed in Chapter 8.

Because we can provide unicast connectivity between VNs, we can use the shared-services topology to provide a workaround to the problem of sourcing multicast in one VN for subscribers in a different VN. From the perspective of the receiver VN, the multicast source is accessible from the shared-services area through the "fusion" router. Two achieve this, two conditions must be met:

- The unicast address for the sender must be reachable from the receiver VN through the fusion router. This allows the RPF check to complete successfully.

- The sender and receiver VRFs PIM processes must peer with the fusion router.

As shown in Figure 9-9, this approach provides a workaround equivalent to having separate IP networks all connected through the fusion router.

Figure 9-9   *Multicast Across VNs Through a Fusion Area*

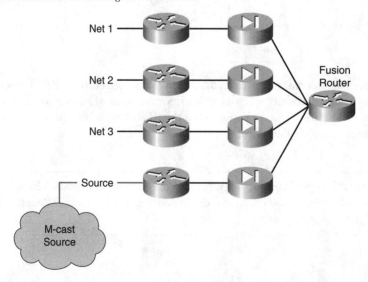

However, this method of supporting multicast presents two problems:

- Complex and hard-to-manage ACLs are necessary to provide limited inter-VN connectivity without totally merging together all the VRFs involved.

- Each VN requires its own copy of the multicast stream, even though the stream is the same and travels over the same physical topology.

A more-efficient, manageable, and secure way of supporting multicast across VNs is provided by the mVPN extranet model described in the next section. This model basically solves the two limitations by allowing the sharing of multicast streams across different VNs and the use of different VRFs for RPF checks without the need to leak unicast routes between VRFs.

Multicast Across VRFs (mVPN Extranet)

When the multicast traffic is sourced from one VN and the receivers are in other VNs, the source of the multicast is usually referred to as an extranet. We have already described the mechanisms to move unicast traffic and routing information across VPNs, but there are many challenges in doing the same for multicast traffic. mVN extranet provides the functionality to allow multicast sourced in one VN to be received in other VNs without compromising the security and scalability of the VN environment.

Certain terms are instrumental in our discussion of mVPN extranet, so we will define these before delving into the details:

- **Source mVRF**—A VRF that can reach the source directly or via a directly connected *customer edge* (CE) device

- **Source provider edge (PE)**—The PE router that has the source mVRF

- **Receiver mVRF**—A VRF in which multicast routing states are populated based on PIM/IGMP join packets received from interfaces connected to a subscriber segment or CE router with subscribers behind it

- **Receiver PE**—The PE router that has the receiver mVRF

The multicast handling options described so far assume the source mVRF and receiver mVRF are both members of the same VN. However, when the source mVRF and receiver mVRF are in different VNs (a.k.a. intranets), the following problems arise:

- Multicast traffic must be able to traverse different VNs.

- RPF check information from other VNs (sender) must be available in the receiver VN.

mVPN extranet leverages the *multicast distribution trees* (MDTs) created by mVPN in each VN and expands these MDTs to include sources and receivers from other VNs. Thus, multicast traffic travels either over the MDT for the source or the destination. The traffic is leaked or replicated between VNs either at the source PE or the receiver PE. We focus on the replication at the receiver PE. Traffic at the source PE is sent over the MDT for the source VN over to the receiver PE.

At the receiver PE, traffic is replicated to all the receiver mVRFs and finally delivered to all subscribers connected to the receiver PE. By replicating traffic at the receiver PE, it is possible to use a single MDT and send a single multicast stream to service subscribers from multiple VNs. Thus, this implementation basically uses a single MDT that is shared by all VNs participating in the extranet. This is the most efficient scenario and is the Cisco default implementation of mVPN extranet.

An alternative implementation could replicate traffic at the source PE. Traffic would then have to travel over the different MDTs for each VN, and multiple copies of the multicast stream would have to be sent over the network.

At this point, you must be wondering how the RPF check is completed. Instead of leaking unicast routes between VRFs to allow the successful completion of the RPF check, mVPN extranet allows a receiver mVPN to use the source mVRF unicast table for its RPF check. In other words, any VN with a subscriber can look into the unicast VRF where the source exists to complete its RPF check. This does not require the leaking of routes between the different unicast VRFs. Therefore, you can create a multicast extranet without necessarily creating a unicast extranet.

mVPN Transport

The previous section discussed the different multicast sources deployment options and how to partition devices to accommodate each choice. In the rest of the chapter, we look at how to transport multicast traffic between virtual devices.

We present three main options:

- Global
- Overlay
- mVPN

The following sections discuss each of these options in detail

Global

The simplest architecture—just as with unicast transport—is not to virtualize at all. In this scenario, multicast traffic from each virtual network is routed using the global address space. The core and the virtual networks are part of a single multicast domain.

Figure 9-10 shows such a network. The access layer uses VLANs. Multicast and unicast traffic to and from the wiring closet is transported first in Ethernet frames and then encapsulated in 802.1q and delivered to the distribution switches.

Figure 9-10 *Multicast in Global Space*

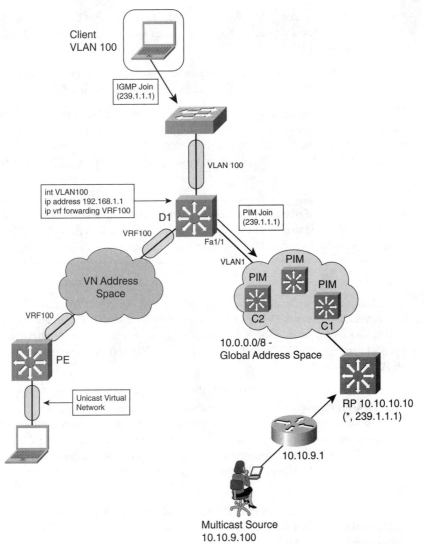

The following scenario is an example of how the global address space runs PIM-SM:

1 RP for group 239.1.1.1 is configured in the data center. The RP address, 10.10.10.10, is in the global address space.

2 Clients in VLAN100 send IGMP join requests, which are propagated to the distribution switches.

3 The distribution switch, D1, is configured to use RP 10.10.10.10.

4 A multicast source, 10.10.9.100, in the data center wants to send to the 239.1.1.1 group. The first-hop router, 10.10.9.1, unicasts the data stream in PIM-SM register packets to the RP.

5 The RP forwards the multicast stream to downstream routers in the core, C1 and C2. Multicast traffic is replicated across the core until it reaches D1.

The challenge with the scenario shown in Figure 9-10 is on the distribution switch. Assume that D1 receives a packet with a source-destination pair of (10.10.9.100, 239.1.1.1) on interface Fa1/1. When D1 first runs a RPF check, the unicast forwarding table would show that the route to 10.10.9.100 does indeed use interface Fa1/1, so RPF succeeds.

NOTE If the source is itself in a VRF, the route from the source's first hop to the RP must be leaked into the global table to allow PIM-SM register packets to reach their destination. By global table, we mean a dedicated VRF for multicast traffic.

Next, D1 needs to replicate the packet to all members of group 239.1.1.1. The client is in a different virtual network (VLAN100)—Figure 9-10 reinforces the separation visually, with oblong shapes on the interfaces that are part of a separate unicast virtual network. On D1, the SVI associated with VLAN100 is mapped to VRF100. So, how can multicast traverse VLANs at Layer 2?

The answer is to use Layer 2 VLAN leaking, such as Cisco *Multicast VLAN Registration* (MVR), to allow select Layer 3 multicast streams to be injected from one VLAN to another. MVR, which was designed for service provider IP/TV environments, allows selective forwarding across VLAN boundaries. When service providers use Layer 2 access solutions for video delivery, multicast is delivered across the network in a dedicated VLAN and must be injected into subscribers' VLANs in the access layer switch—it is a Layer 2 equivalent of VRF route leaking.

When enabled, MVR listens for IGMP join and leave messages in the unicast VLANs and modifies the multicast forwarding table to include or remove the recipient's interface. In the example in Figure 9-10, MVR runs on D1. When the clients send an IGMP join, MVR updates the global multicast forwarding table with an entry for (*,239.1.1.1) on VLAN100. This allows D1 to send a PIM join request to the RP. When receiving downstream data, MVR allows outgoing packet header information to be written such that (10.10.9.100,239.1.1.1) is encapsulated in VLAN100 and forwarded to the client.

Using the global address space to transport multicast is not as easy as it looks. MVR is a Layer 2 solution that may be deployed on a fusion switch to multiplex unicast and multicast Layer 3 data from two different VLANs onto an access layer VLAN. Configuration requires identifying source and receiver ports. In the example, Fa1/1 in VLAN1 would be the source port. Interface VLAN100 would be the one of the receiver port. You can deploy MVR using a dedicated fusion switch as a low-cost method of joining two Layer 3 domains to a last-leg Layer 2 domain. Figure 9-11 shows the fusion-switch deployment model. The fusion functionally can be deployed on the Access switch.

Figure 9-11 *MVR Fusion Switch*

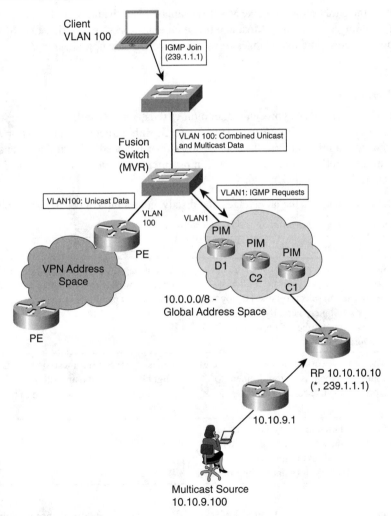

The disadvantages of MVR are as follows:

- Single multicast address space.

- Core network has (*,G) state for every group. If the number of groups is small, this might not be an issue. Also, because many core networks are already native multicast, they have state.

- Multicast traffic is not virtualized—anyone can join any group (manual MVR configuration can address this).

- MVR ports are manually configured.

Assuming that something like MVR is available, the advantage of the global address design is that migration is easy. Most enterprise core networks are multicast enabled already and need no configuration changes or software or hardware upgrades.

Tunnel Overlay

Just as with unicast, you can tunnel multicast data across an IP core. The architecture is a p2p overlay of the sort presented in Chapter 5, "Infrastructure Segmentation Architectures: Theory." In this scenario, the core network does not need to be multicast enabled. All multicast traffic is tunneled across it, most often using *multiprotocol generic routing encapsulation* (mGRE).

Table 9-1 outlines the advantages and disadvantages typical of an overlay network.

Table 9-1 *Overlay Network Advantages and Disadvantages*

Advantages	Disadvantages
Overlays offer an easy migration path by containing the VRF-aware multicast feature set on select routers. Deployment can proceed incrementally so as to increase the number of hops in the network.	Use of p2p (or *point-to-multipoint* [p2mp] with mGRE) overlay does not take advantage of multicast capabilities in the core network.
The core network does not run multicast routing, so there is no requirement to store group state for every VPN.	Unless there is a full mesh of tunnels, packets might be delivered using suboptimal routes across the core as they go from spoke to hub to spoke again.
GRE (and mGRE) is available with hardware-based forwarding, so this architecture does not involve unacceptable performance compromises.	

The network shown in Figure 9-12 uses GRE. The GRE endpoints are terminated in VRFs and OSPF (or *Enhanced Interior Gateway Routing Protocol* [EIGRP]) is used to route VN traffic across the network. GRE packets themselves are routed across the underlying core network using OSPF in a different address space (from the VNs). The global address space does not run multicast routing.

Figure 9-12 *GRE Tunnel Overlay with Multicast*

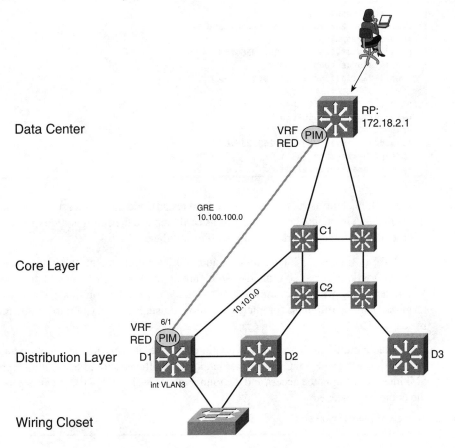

The first step is to build the GRE tunnel infrastructure between each hop and to place them in the appropriate VRFs. Example 9-1 shows the configuration on C1, one of the core switches.

NOTE It might be necessary to create a unique tunnel source-loopback interface for every tunnel. Certain hardware architectures require this to be able to hardware-switch GRE traffic.

Example 9-1 *GRE Configuration on C1*

```
ip vrf RED
 rd 200:1
interface Loopback2000
 description RED GRE tunnel 200 on C1
 ip address 10.10.10.1 255.255.255.255
```

continues

Example 9-1 *GRE Configuration on C1 (Continued)*

```
interface Tunnel 200
 description GRE tunnel between D1 and RP
 ip vrf forwarding RED
 ip address 10.100.100.1 255.255.252
 tunnel source Loopback2000
 tunnel destination 10.10.10.2

interface TenGigabitEthernet 4/5
 description core link to D1
 dampening
 ip address 10.10.2.6 255.255.255.0
 ip ospf hello-interval 1
 ip ospf dead-interval 3
```

When the tunnel infrastructure is in place (and tested), add the multicast configuration. We used GRE for simplicity, but you can just as easily replace the configuration in Example 9-1 with mGRE. Multicast works equally well over either.

Each VRF in Figure 9-12 has a unicast and multicast component, the latter configured with per-VRF multicast commands, which are applied both globally and per interface. When deploying VRFs over multiple hops, activate per-VRF multicast at every GRE termination hop. You must complete the following steps at every hop to enable multicast for each VRF.

First, enable multicast, both globally and in each VRF at every hop (but not on the core interfaces, such as the TenGigabitEthernet ports). Multicast should be running on both the SVI interfaces facing the access and the tunnel interfaces in VRF RED. Example 9-2 shows the commands needed.

Example 9-2 *Multicast Configuration on D1*

```
!
ip multicast-routing
!
ip multicast-routing vrf RED
!
! Enable multicast on all interfaces
!
! access interface requires multicast
interface vlan 3
 description SVI for RED
 ip vrf forwarding RED
 ip address 172.19.1.1 255.255.255.0
 ip pim sparse-mode
!
! interface loopback1000
! part of core address space
 description RED GRE tunnel 200 on D1
 ip address 10.10.10.2 255.255.255.255
```

Example 9-2   *Multicast Configuration on D1 (Continued)*

```
!
interface Tunnel 200
 description RED to C1
 ip vrf forwarding RED
 ip address 10.100.100.2 255.255.255.252
 tunnel source loopback1000
 tunnel destination 10.10.10.1
 ip pim sparse-mode
!
! core interface requires no multicast
interface TenGigabitEthernet 6/1
 description core link to C1
 dampening
 ip address 10.10.1.5 255.255.255.0
 ip ospf hello-interval 1
 ip ospf dead-interval 3
```

Each VN needs a PIM RP. The RP must be inside the VRF, as shown in Example 9-3. The RP device in Figure 9-12 also has a GRE tunnel to C1, which is not shown in the following example.

Example 9-3   *RP Configuration*

```
! Create a loopback to source the RP
interface Loopback111
 description loopback to source rendezvous point
 ip vrf forwarding RED
 ip address 172.18.2.1 255.255.255.0
 ip pim sparse-mode
! Make one or more routers eligible to serve as RP (global config)
ip pim vrf RED rp-address 172.18.2.1
ip pim vrf RED send-rp-announce Loopback111 scope 10
ip pim vrf RED send-rp-discovery scope 10
ip pim vrf RED rp-candidate Loopback111
```

The final step is to configure the RP address on all the multicast routers in the RED VRF. One option is to use a static configuration, as follows:

```
ip pim vrf RED rp-address 172.18.2.1
```

Alternatively, you can use the auto-rp feature, which allows PIM routers to learn RP addresses dynamically.

mVPN

mVPN was designed to allow service providers to offer multicast service to their enterprise customers. An mVPN network uses the RFC 2547 architecture and shares many of the characteristics of a *Multiprotocol Label Switching* (MPLS) VPN.

One major challenge solved by mVPN is that of core router state requirements. Recall from the discussion of global address space transport earlier in the chapter that every core router has (*,G) state for every VN on the network. In a large network, this just is not realistic. Service providers must carefully manage resource requirements in their core networks. Furthermore, in a VN environment, enterprise customers retain control over multicast group creation. Service providers want to isolate themselves from this.

Similarities exist between the problem of managing customer multicast groups and that of managing customer routes. In both cases, a core network needs to be isolated from customer route (or group creation) and, again in both cases, core routers should not store customer route (or group information) in their memory.

NOTE

Before looking at mVPN in detail, it is worth pointing out that other proposals exist to address this problem. One is to use VPN-IP PIM, which runs multicast in the core network and leaks customer group information and combines the customers (S,G) and RD to give a unique (RD:S,G) multicast route. This provides separate group spaces to each customer but involves a potentially large resource requirement in the core.

Another proposal is to connect PEs using p2mp tunnels. PEs would replicate multicast traffic from CE routers as unicast to other PEs, which would then forward the packets as multicast again. The core network resources are isolated in this scenario, but at the cost of transferring work to the PE CPU.

mVPN uses a concept of multicast domains, which is a connected set of mVRFs. Each customer has their own multicast domain, and all customer multicast groups are mapped to their domain across the service provider network. A PE router has as many multicast domains as there are customers connected to it. For any given multicast domain, all the relevant PEs are connected together in an MDT. A PE is part of MDT x if it has a connection to customer xs CE. MDT termination points are called *multicast tunnel interfaces* (MTIs). More formally, the MTI is the interface that points to the MDT from an mVRF.

mVPN requires the core network to run IP multicast to forward mVPN packets between PEs. Note that the requirement is only for native multicast—there is no need for any special features in the core. Each customer appears as a multicast group, so core routers need to store one (*,G) entry only on a per-VPN basis, with an RP for each group (and assuming bi-directional PIM). Again, this is similar to MPLS VPNs, for which P routers need to route only between PEs. mVPN *provider* (P) routers only know how to multicast between PEs.

As stated earlier, all the PEs in a multicast domain are connected in an MDT. There can be more than one MDT per domain:

- **Default MDT**—The default tree connects to all PEs in a domain. It is used for customer control-plane traffic, but can also be used for data-plane traffic. As the name implies, there is always a default MDT in a multicast domain.

- **Data MDT**—A tree for data-plane traffic. A data MDT connects PEs with active sources and PEs with active receivers on the customer network.

One early criticism with the multicast domain approach lay in the fact that all PEs are part of a default MDT, so they receive multicast traffic for all customer groups, whether they need to or not. To alleviate this, mVPN allows PEs to create data MDTs dynamically that connect only the devices that are part of a particular group. The creation of data MDTs are triggered by data rates in excess of a configured threshold. The same MTI is used to access both the default and data MDTs. Figure 9-13 shows a default and data MDT running on an mVPN network.

Figure 9-13 *Default and Data MDTs*

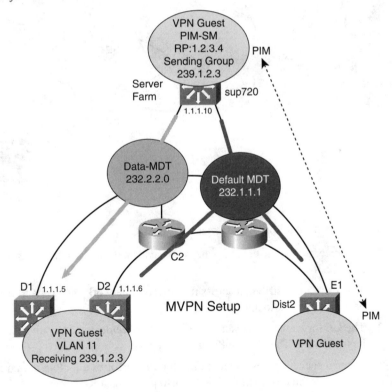

Figure 9-14 shows the two pieces of mVPN that we have not yet covered: CE-PE and PE-PE routing adjacencies.

A PE has PIM adjacencies with CEs in the same way that a PE is a unicast peer with a CE. PEs also have PIM adjacencies with each other. Depending on the implementation, the mVPN can transport sparse, dense, sparse-dense, bidirectional, and SSM, which means that enterprise networks should not have to make any changes to use an mVPN service. PIM RPs can either be on CE or PE routers (they are part of the customer address space). In either case, you can configure the other PIM routers with static RP information or use auto-rp to perform dynamic RP discovery. PIM control traffic goes over the default MDT, as does all dense-mode (S,G) and shared-tree (*,G) traffic.

Figure 9-14 *mVPN CE-PE Adjacencies*

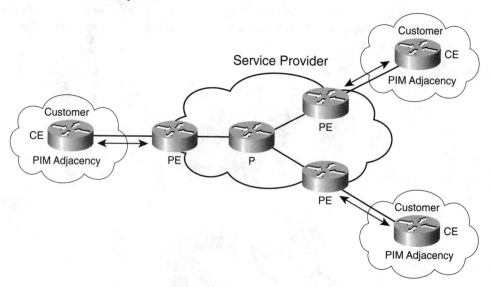

mVPN forwarding follows this scenario:

- A source, Sc, on the customer network sends a packet to a multicast group address, 232.1.2.3.

- This packet is distributed across the customer network and needs to cross the service provider network to another site.

- The CE forwards the packet with address source/destination pair (Sc,232.1.12.3) to its mVPN PE. The CE and PE are PIM peers.

- When a packet arrives on an mVRF, the PE performs a lookup to find the outgoing interface, which is an MTI. The PE also performs a RFP check.

- Customer packets forwarded across the MTI are first encapsulated in GRE.
- The source/destination of the outer IP header is (Spe,239.1.1.1), where Spe is the source address of the PE and 239.1.1.1 is the group address of the MDT (239/8 is the recommended range for group addresses).
- The GRE packets are then forwarded to their multicast destination, with normal RFP check and replication at each hop.
- The egress PE removes the GRE heading from packets received on an MTI, after first performing an RFP check. It then does a lookup in the mVRF and performs a second RFP check against Sc before replicating (if needed) and forwarding the packet to the CE router.

RPF checking is a critical component of multicast forwarding. RPF on the CE-PE and global network (PE-P and P-P) interfaces is straightforward because unicast routing entries can be used to check whether a packet is received on the right incoming interface. However, PEs also have PIM adjacencies with each other and exchange packets through the MTI. The MTI is never announced in unicast routing updates, so standard RPF checks would fail.

To provide a mechanism for RPF to succeed on MTIs, when a packet is received on an MTI, the PE router checks to see whether the source address of the outer packet matches the BGP next-hop of the source address of the inner packet. It also checks whether the source of the outer packet is a PIM peer in the mVRF. RPF succeeds if both these conditions hold. Note that this means that PIM and BGP must use the same address. A PE also uses MP-BGP to announce a new default MDT to its peers.

mVPN is another option for deploying multicast over virtualized enterprise networks. Core switches play the role of P, and the mVPN PE function is in the distribution layer.

The advantages of mVPN are that it provides a scalable way to transport multicast traffic while meeting the requirements of a VPN, such as private address space support. VPN multicast packets are themselves multicast across default or data MDTs. The core network runs native IP multicast features only. The forwarding path uses GRE, so hardware acceleration is available. Finally, mVPN is transparent to multicast running inside the virtual networks—as long as some form of PIM is used.

The disadvantages of mVPN include configuration and troubleshooting—there are a lot of protocols to set up and debug. In addition, PEs often need a software upgrade to get the mVPN feature set.

Basic mVPN configuration is not as hard as you might imagine. Consider the network in Figure 9-15, which overlays mVPN over the topology introduced in Figure 9-12.

Figure 9-15 *mVPN Network with Default MDT*

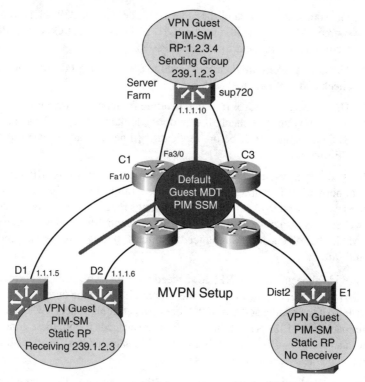

Assuming that MP-BGP and VRFs are already configured, the first step, shown in Example 9-4, is to enable native multicast routing on all the core switches. All modes of PIM are supported.

Example 9-4 *mVPN Native Multicast Configuration on C1*

```
!
ip multicast-routing
!
!
interface GigabitEthernet1/1
 ip pim sparse-mode
!
interface FastEthernet3/2
 ip pim sparse-mode
!
ip pim ssm default
```

Example 9-5 shows the configuration on D1 that creates an mVRF and assigns the 239.1.1.1 group address to the default MDT and 239.2.2.0 to the data MDT.

All other PEs that connect to the Guest VRF must use the same group address for the MDTs.

Example 9-5 *MVRF and MDT Configuration on D1*

```
ip vrf Guest
 rd 200:1
 route-target export 200:1
 route-target import 200:1
 mdt default 239.1.1.1
 mdt data 239.2.2.0 0.0.0.255 threshold 1
!
ip multicast-routing
ip multicast-routing vrf Guest
!
! interface used for PIM and MP-BGP updates
interface Loopback0
 ip address 10.100.100.1 255.255.255.255
 ip pim sparse-mode
!
! wiring-closet-facing interface
interface Vlan11
 ip vrf forwarding Guest
 ip pim query-interval 2
 ip pim sparse-mode
!
ip pim vrf RED rp-address 1.2.3.4
```

Example 9-6 gives the MP-BGP portion of D1's configuration. The loopback0 address is used as the MP-BGP source address in Example 9-6 (highlighted in Example 9-6 and 9-5). BGP sessions must exist with all the other mVPN peers.

Example 9-6 *D1 BGP Configuration*

```
router bgp 100
 no bgp default ipv4-unicast
 neighbor 1.1.1.7 remote-as 100
 neighbor 1.1.1.7 update-source Loopback0
 neighbor 1.1.1.10 remote-as 100
 neighbor 1.1.1.10 update-source Loopback0
 !
 address-family vpnv4
 neighbor 1.1.1.7 activate
 neighbor 1.1.1.7 next-hop-self
 neighbor 1.1.1.7 send-community extended
 neighbor 1.1.1.10 activate
 neighbor 1.1.1.10 next-hop-self
 neighbor 1.1.1.10 send-community extended
 exit-address-family
```

continues

Example 9-6 *D1 BGP Configuration (Continued)*

```
!
address-family ipv4 vrf guest
redistribute connected
no auto-summary
no synchronization
exit-address-family
```

Some final notes on Examples 9-4 through 9-6: The Guest RP address, 1.2.3.4, is part of the Guest VRF address space. VLAN11 is a CE-PE type interface. There must be another PIM router on this interface that peers with D1, with the standard PIM configuration, and none of the MDT statements of Example 9-5.

Connecting the WAN

We have so far concentrated on scenarios with local-area connectivity. You might wonder whether it is possible to run multicast across a public WAN? Yes, it is. The manner in which you do so depends greatly on the services offered by your local providers.

If the provider has an mVPN service, you can connect your core devices across it. Figure 9-16 shows two deployment models. The top one connects a native PIM network over a wide-area mVPN service. The bottom one runs an enterprise mVPN network over a service provider mVPN service. In the second scenario, the mVPN service connects enterprise mVPN P devices that run native PIM. The service provider network does not have visibility of the enterprise MDTs, MTI, and other mVPN components.

It is more likely—at least at the time of this writing—that multicast traffic will need to be tunneled across the WAN. Figure 9-17 shows this simpler scenario. The WAN edge routers have a LAN-facing MTI interface for MDT connectivity, a WAN-facing (regular) GRE interface, and run VRF-aware PIM. In mVPN terms, the CE-PE interface is a GRE tunnel that connects each site. This scenario allows for virtualized core networks to connect to nonvirtualized sites that run native PIM.

If the remote site is also virtualized, mVPN runs on all sites, as shown in Figure 9-18. The WAN edge routers use a different GRE tunnel for each virtual network. The remote site in Figure 9-18 uses hop-by-hop tunnels, or simply VLANs, to carry multicast traffic.

Figure 9-16 *mVPN Service*

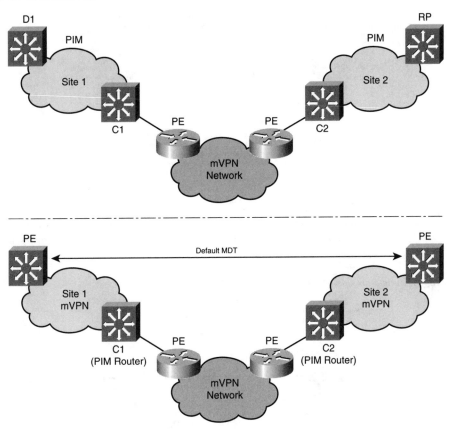

Figure 9-17 *Single-Domain-per-Branch Site*

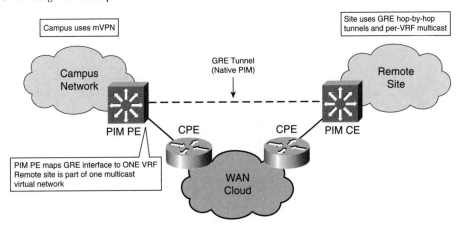

Figure 9-18   *Multiple-Domains-per-Branch Site*

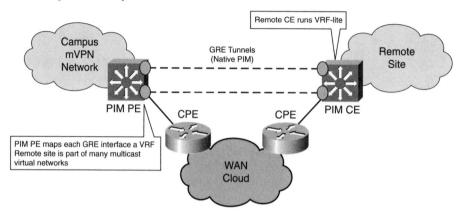

The final scenario, in Figure 9-19, shows each site as a different mVPN domain, where the CE of one domain is the PE of another. The tunnels are regular GRE and transport native multicast traffic across the WAN.

Figure 9-19   *Multiple-Domains-per-Branch Site*

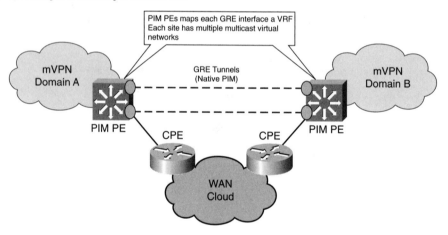

NOTE   In all cases, remember that RPF requires a unicast route to the multicast source (or RP). Routers in each site must have appropriate unicast routing information in every VRF; otherwise, multicast packets will be dropped.

Summary

This chapter discussed three main topics: basic multicast, managing multicast source and receivers across VRFs, and transport architectures.

A virtualized enterprise network is fully capable of carrying multicast traffic. The simplest case has source and recipients in the same VRF, in which case the design decision is whether to use p2p transport or mVPN.

The mVPN extranet solution addresses the case where source and receiver are not in the same VRF.

Standards work continues in this area. The references sections in Appendices C and D include texts for the interested reader to follow new developments.

CHAPTER 10

Quality of Service in a Virtualized Environment

The protocols used to virtualize campus networks have two effects on *quality of service* (QoS). First, they bring with them from their service provider origins several new mechanisms that might be useful in an enterprise environment. Second, they give rise to the basic question of how to implement QoS guarantees over a Virtual Network (VN).

This chapter attempts to cover both effects and starts by demystifying certain technologies, such as *differentiated services-aware traffic engineering* (DS-TE), before looking at which mechanisms can be applied (and how) in Virtualized Network.

QoS Models and Mechanisms: A Review

QoS is a continuation of network policy. Policy information is set at certain points, carried in protocol headers, and enforced throughout the network. The result should provide a predefined level of service for different types of traffic.

NOTE   You can also use QoS can to protect the network against certain types of security attacks, but that is beyond the scope of this discussion.

Many of the protocols used to virtualize network transport have fields dedicated to QoS, as summarized in the following list:

- **802.1q**—3 User Priority bits in the Tag Control Information field, used to set the *class of service* (CoS) value, commonly referred to as 802.1p bits

- **IP**—3-bit *Type of Service* (ToS) value or a 6-bit *differentiated services code point* (DSCP) value

- **MPLS**—3-bit *Experimental* [EXP] field on non-ATM links

- **L2TPv3**—No dedicated field

- **GRE**—No dedicated field

- **IPsec**—No dedicated field

On the device itself, the mechanisms used to effect policy should be familiar to readers of this book. In the interest of having standard definitions, the following list summarizes them:

- **Classification**—Selection of traffic for QoS processing. Selection criteria can be packet source interface, destination address, Layer 4 port information, or existing policy settings.

- **Marking**—Setting policy bits in a protocol header, such as IP DSCP or 802.1p.

- **Policing**—Limiting the bandwidth available to a category of (classified) traffic. Reasonable policers have multiple traffic limits: accepted aggregate rate, accepted bursts, and excess burst. How each category of traffic is treated depends on network policy. Policing discards or re-marks out of contract traffic. Shaping, on the other hand, queues out of contract traffic.

- **Queuing/scheduling**—Assigning traffic to ingress or egress queues based on classification. The number of queues on a device can vary wildly from 1 or 2 per port to several thousands on Service edge routers. Examples of queuing schemes include *weighted fair queuing* (WFQ), *weighted round robin* (WRR), and so on.

- **Congestion avoidance**—A set of schemes that discards data during congestion, thus reserving bandwidth for high-priority traffic at the expense of lower-priority traffic. Examples include *early packet discard* (EPD), *weighted random early detection* (WRED), or *weighted tail drop* (WTD).

- **Resource reservation**—The process of requesting and allocating link bandwidth for a category of traffic.

- **Link optimization**—Packet interleaving mechanisms that allow priority packets to meet latency or delay requirements.

QoS mechanisms detailed are deployed in support of a particular model or architecture. The initial Internet model was, of course, *point-to-point* (p2p) best effort. Other models include *integrated services* (IntServ), which uses the *Resource Reservation Protocol* (RSVP) to reserve bandwidth for flows of application traffic, and DiffServ. We review DiffServ in the next sections.

Differentiated Services

The DiffServ model is an architecture that allows scalable differentiation between data flows. With DiffServ, the majority of the labor-intensive QoS processing, such as classification, marking, and policing, is done at the network edge.

Traffic admitted to the network core is marked with a numeric value, a DSCP, which indicates to which class the packet belongs. The core devices process on a per-class (not per-flow) basis, and so they need to examine only the bits that carry the DSCP information (6 bits in the IP header) to know how to handle any particular packet.

DiffServ does not require state information or signaling of resource requirements, either on a flow or aggregate basis. Instead, each device is configured with certain administratively determined limits on the amount of resource per class. DiffServ is defined in RFC 2474 (*Definition of the Differentiated Services Field [DS Field] in the IPv4 and IPv6 Headers*) and RFC 2475 (*An Architecture for Differentiated Services*).

DiffServ introduces an important concept, namely *per-hop behavior* (PHB). PHB is the observable behavior of a device as it processes traffic. An end-to-end QoS service can be provided as long as the PHB is consistent across the network.

RFC 2474 defines two PHBs:

- **Default**—Simple best-effort class, with a DSCP value of 000000. Packets with no defined DSCP are mapped to the default class for best-effort service.

- **Class selector**—Provides for backward compatibility with 3-bit IP Precedence classes. Basically, it defines a DCSP of *XXX*000, where *XXX* represent the IP Precedence bits.

The two most significant PHBs that use DiffServ are *Assured Forwarding* (AF) and *Expedited Forwarding* (EF), which are both defined in separate RFC documents.

RFC 2597 defines AF, and RFC 2598 defines EF:

- **AF**—The AF PHB defines four different classes. Within each class, there are three drop probabilities: low, medium, and high. Classes are written as AF*ny*, where *n* is the class and *y* is the drop probability within the class. Lower values of *y* denote higher priority; so, for example, the AF11 has a lower drop probability (so a better service) than AF13. RFC 2597 leaves it up to network administrators to define which AF classes they want to use for different traffic types and to configure the routers to allocate resources appropriately. Similarly, RFC 2597 makes no recommendations as to how the PHBs should be implemented, leaving the choice up to vendors.

- **EF**—Offers a leased-line ToS, with strict guarantees for latency, jitter, packet delivery, and so forth. *Voice over IP* (VoIP) applications use the EF PHB.

It is important to apply the correct DSCP value to a packet. In a switched environment, there are typically two QoS domains (Layer 2 and Layer 3), and policy classifications must be correctly copied between each.

In a typical campus network, the access switch classifies traffic based on either the incoming interface or ToS settings (the latter is common when a PC is connected to a switch through an IP phone) and marks this information in the 802.1p bits on the VLAN trunks that connect to the distribution layer. On the distribution switch, these ToS settings are copied to IP DSCP bits.

Cisco provides guidelines for which Layer 2 and 3 values to use in an enterprise network. Table 10-1 gives the complete 11 DSCP values and corresponding PHB names, if defined.

Table 10-1   *Guidelines for 802.1p, IP Precedence, DSCP, and PHB Values in Enterprise Networks*

Application	Layer 3 Classification			Layer 2
	IP Precedence	PHB	DSCP	
IP routing	6	CS6	48	6
Voice	5	EF	46	5
Interactive video	4	AF41	34	4
Streaming video	4	CS4	32	4
Locally defined mission-critical data	3	—	25	3
Call signaling	3	AF31/CS3	26/24	3
Transactional data	2	AF21	18	2
Network management	2	CS2	16	2
Bulk data	1	AF11	10	1
Scavenger	1	CS1	8	1
Best effort	0	0	0	0

Information in Table 10-1 is taken from QoS SRND, available at http://www.cisco.com/go/srnd

The first settings column of the table lists the settings (limited to 7 classes) for IP Precedence rather than DSCP. Similarly, the last settings column shows the Layer 2 equivalence for each class.

The baseline QoS model is extremely granular, and it is often necessary to group different categories together (for example, in case you need to send data over a wide-area *virtual private network* (VPN) connection that supports only a limited number of classes, typically between three and five). This number is essentially determined by cost considerations in the wide-area provider's network.

However, the VPN protocols themselves can impose technical limitations. Of these, *Multiprotocol Label Switching* (MPLS) is the most interesting, not only because it is possibly unfamiliar, but also because it offers some valuable services not yet found with other the VPN transport protocols. The next section provides an introduction to MPLS QoS, but the interested reader is encouraged to consult some of the more specialized texts listed in the references at the end of the book.

MPLS Quality of Service

How does a network that uses a protocol with a 3-bit EXP field carry traffic transparently between customer sites that may need up to 11 different classes of service? VPN service offerings limit the number of classes of service available to customers, and MPLS is no exception. PE routers map customer-to-service provider traffic classes. However, the simple fact of crossing a service provider network should not impact how traffic is treated after it arrives at the remote site. In other words, the original traffic class information must not be lost by the MPLS network. To deal with this situation, MPLS has three different modes to carry customer DSCP settings in what are called pipes.

Before looking at pipes in more detail, we should address how DSCP values are mapped to MPLS EXP. The simplest way is to use the same model as for IP Precedence or 802.1p given in Table 10-1. MPLS vendors often have their own suggestions, such as AF31 to EXP3 and so on, but there is no actual standard to follow. Each MPLS network administrator is free to come up with whichever mapping works best for his applications.

Tunnels and Pipes

When IP packets are encapsulated in MPLS, the DSCP class settings can be copied to the EXP bits. The PHB across *label switching routers* (LSRs) is processed according to these EXP settings.

Because of *penultimate hop popping* (PHP), the last LSR on a *label switched path* (LSP) does not see the MPLS EXP field, so the QoS settings must be signaled in another way.

MPLS support for DiffServ (RFC 3270) adds different models to account for the various places that labels can be popped and how to relay marking information between domains. The following list qualifies the different kinds of LSPs used with the DiffServ model:

- **E-LSP**—An LSP where the PHB is defined by the EXP field only, for a maximum of eight classes.

- **L-LSP**—An LSP where the PHB is defined by both the EXP and Label fields. ATM MPLS networks use L-LSPs, which provide a dedicated VC per class (there is no EXP field). The rationale behind the added complexity of L-LSPs is that they offer more than the eight PHBs possible with the 3-bit EXP field.

Three different modes are found in MPLS networks. Each mode specifies the relationship between IP DSCP and MPLS EXP information:

- **Tunnel**—Changes to the EXP are copied to packet's DSCP.

- **Pipe**—Changes to the EXP are not copied to DSCP bits. Classification at the egress PE is done using the MPLS EXP value.

- **Short pipe**—A variation on the pipe mode, where the egress PE uses the packet's IP DSCP to apply PHB rather than the EXP.

NOTE	For further information, see Appendix B, "MPLS QoS, Traffic Engineering and Guaranteed Bandwidth," which contains an expanded explanation of MPLS QoS tunnel and pipe modes, traffic engineering, and guaranteed bandwidth (including examples).

MPLS Traffic Engineering and Guaranteed Bandwidth

Traffic engineering (TE) is one of the oldest arts in networking. It involves calculating and configuring paths through a network to use resources efficiently and provide the best traffic performance possible. RFC 2702 provides a useful definition:

A major goal of Internet Traffic Engineering is to facilitate efficient and reliable network operations while simultaneously optimizing network resource utilization and traffic performance. Traffic Engineering has become an indispensable function in many large Autonomous Systems because of the high cost of network assets and the commercial and competitive nature of the Internet. These factors emphasize the need for maximal operational efficiency.

Going beyond the commercial and competitive nature of the Internet, some concrete, operational problems can be solved with TE. Here, we concentrate on three: link congestion, link protection, and load balancing:

- **Link congestion**—A well-known issue in IP networks is that *interior gateway routing protocol* (IGP) best paths may be overused while alternative paths are either underutilized or not used at all.

- **Link protection**—If a path or device failure occurs along a primary LSP, routing protocols have to rerun the full (or incremental) *shortest-path first* (SPF) calculation before traffic can be forwarded again, which can take several seconds.

- **Load balancing**—Standard IGPs allow traffic to be balanced equally across only equal-cost paths. Unequal paths are ignored because the IGP will see them as longer routes to the destination.

MPLS TE gives network operators a way to solve the problems described in the preceding list. Basically, TE calculates shortest paths through a network, but within a given set of constraints. Because of this, TE is said to use *constraint-based routing* (CBR). The following list discusses how MPLS TE offers a solution to link congestion and protection issues introduced previously:

- **Link congestion**—Network administrators can build tunnels across less-used paths and route traffic along them. With less traffic on them, previously congested paths can become decongested.

- **Load balancing**—An added benefit of the Cisco IOS TE implementation is that there are 16 hash buckets for paths to a single destination. The buckets are allocated according to bandwidth and thus provide a proportional load-balancing capability.

- **Link protection**—With *fast reroute* (FRR) link protection, MPLS TE enables you to preconfigure a backup LSP at any point along the tunnel path, which the traffic will use if a link failure occurs on the protected LSR.

MPLS TE supports the notion of priority and preemption. Low-priority tunnels can be removed to free up bandwidth for higher-priority tunnels. Again, TE and FRR are discussed in more detail in Appendix B.

DS-TE and Guaranteed Bandwidth

You might now wonder, given the many advantages of MPLS TE, whether you even need to worry about QoS anymore. TE alleviates the problem of congestion by allowing traffic to be routed across underutilized links. Furthermore, a TE tunnel is created if there are enough resources along its path to meet its bandwidth requirements. However, MPLS TE is blind to class. You cannot build tunnels for different categories of traffic, just for different destinations.

DS-TE was developed (RFCs 3564 and 4124) to allow MPLS TE to be aware of traffic classes. However, as RFC 4124 points out, DS-TE is more than the simple equivalent of DiffServ on MPLS tunnels. Notably, DS-TE supports the concepts of preemption and explicit overbooking, neither of which are part of the standard DiffServ model, but are useful to service providers wanting fine-grain control of their bandwidth allocation and who need to provide strict, absolute guarantees for their service level agreements. DS-TE adds the concept of classes to TE. Simply put, LSRs now advertise pools of bandwidth and the RSVP and IGP processes are modified to check that adding a new tunnel does not affect tunnels using other pools.

The terminology of RFC 4124 refers to *Class-Types* (CTs), not pools (which is a Cisco IOS implementation term). A CT is defined as the set of aggregated traffic flows belonging to one or more classes that are governed by the same bandwidth constraints. Link bandwidth is allocated on a CT basis.

DS-TE is implemented with IGP extensions that advertise the bandwidth per CT available on a link. TE constrained routing calculation is run on a per CT basis, and RSVP extensions allow reservation requests to also be made per CT. DS-TE, just like regular TE, is a control-plane reservation mechanism. You still need to use queuing and discard mechanisms to enforce the traffic classes on the data plane. Please refer to Appendix B for additional details concerning DS-TE and Guaranteed Bandwidth.

At this point, you might be wondering when to deploy guaranteed bandwidth. For example, can standard DiffServ already support voice? Yes, but it relies on every hop along an end-to-end path enforcing the correct PHB, which is only possible as long as there are enough resources along that path. DiffServ offers no way to guarantee that this will be the case. DS-TE, however, can guarantee resource availability and thus provides for strict service levels without overprovisioning. As the name suggests, DS-TE relies on DiffServ at each hop to enforce the correct PHB required for the chosen bandwidth-allocation model.

Do I Really Need This in an Enterprise Virutal Network?

The decision to use any of the enhanced QoS mechanisms that are enabled by MPLS TE is independent of the decision to virtualize a network. In other words, the reason for deploying TE, FRR, or whatever should be in support of a business problem, such as guaranteeing application response times, or network availability. Many such justifications are perfectly valid. If none of these apply to your network, then, even if MPLS is the right technology for path isolation, there is no reason to use it with the other services it offers.

The central design issue when it comes to QoS in the context of a VN is how to enforce existing policies with all the new protocols making their appearance in the distribution and core network layers. This problem requires using hierarchical QoS strategies.

QoS Models for Virtualized Networks

Chapter 4, " A Virtualization Technologies Primer: Theory," broke down virtualization into link and device components. The preceding explanations discussed how link virtualization QoS can be provided, at least for networks using MPLS. However, there is some bad news at the device level. There is no concept of a virtual QoS mechanism on enterprise routers or switches. In our opinion, this work will have to happen; until then, the only option is to use per-VPN policies—hierarchical if needed, as discussed in the rest of this chapter.

One Policy per Group

A VN introduces an additional layer of hierarchy in the form of groups or segments, which gather together users or applications that have the same policy requirements. Designing QoS into a VN involves identifying whether each segment has a single or multiple QoS policies. We look at both cases.The network shown in Figure 10-1 uses Cisco QoS design recommendations and needs to introduce virtual segments for two user groups. The requirement is to maintain the same policy after the transition.

Two major parts of the network must be discussed. The LAN, or campus (composed of access, distribution, and core layers), with the traditional three-tier design, and the WAN connections to remote sites.The general rules in either case are as follows:

1 Set or enforce markings (at network ingress).

2 Copy markings between protocol boundary.

3 Police, queue, discard per class.

Figure 10-1 *VN QoS—Nonhierarchical*

Access

Distribution

Core

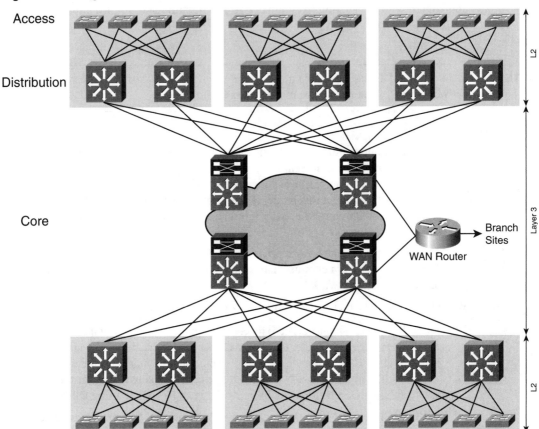

In the LAN, end hosts are deemed trusted or untrusted. In the first case, DSCP settings are maintained at the access layer. In the second, the switch sets QoS values (for example, EF for voice, AF31 for data, and so forth). As any good text on QoS will discuss in detail, you must consider many implementation dependencies, such as the number of egress queues and policer granularity. A low-cost, Layer 2 switch will—at best—be able to set 802.1p values, so the distribution layer would need to copy these settings to the IP layer. Although it is recommended to police untrusted traffic as close to the network edge as possible, because of the high interface speeds, congestion is uncommon in a LAN environment. If it arises, it is often cheaper to add more bandwidth than to fiddle with queues (you should still deploy queues to support VoIP).

The WAN is more complex because speed mismatches occur between connections, between sites, and with the LAN itself. Furthermore, if the enterprise is using a commercial IP VPN service, fewer classes will be available for inter-site traffic, so traffic must be re-marked with different DSCP values. Also, WAN routers are typically confronted with congestion, so you need to use queuing and discard and, possibly, shaping.

NOTE It can be useful to understand the models used when traffic is carried by a service provider between sites. Two nonexclusive models are as follows:

- **Point-to-cloud model**—The service level is defined between the enterprise *customer premises equipment* (CPE) and service provider network, regardless of destination. Customer traffic is policed on both ingress and egress to an agreed-upon rate. The advantage of this model is that provider and enterprise QoS policies can remain discontiguous and it is straightforward (for the service provider) to implement.

- **Point-to-service model**—A service level is defined between enterprise sites, just like Frame Relay or ATM circuits. Hard bandwidth guarantees require DS-TE in the service provider network.

We will consider two alternative designs: *hop-to-hop* (h2h) tunnels and MPLS VPN.

- **H2H IP tunnels**—For a packet to receive the appropriate QoS as it traverses the core, the DSCP value must be copied from the inner user IP header to the outer tunnel header. Figure 10-2 shows the QoS copy operation. The tunnel headend needs to use the Cisco IOS **qos preclassify** command to enable this behavior. After this is done, the switch's egress queuing and discard policy can be applied using DiffServ.

- **MPLS VPN**—The MPLS-VPN QoS model requires all per-VPN settings to be done at the PE, because that is the only place where the concept of a VPN exists. Cisco IOS automatically copies DSCP to EXP bits (the **set mpls experimental** commands allows different policy configuration). Apart from this change, and assuming the network uses the E-LSP model, policing, scheduling, and discard mechanisms are in essence the same as in the previous case; and regular DiffServ can be used to provide the service levels required by the different network segments, including voice.

  For traffic that is re-marked, MPLS provides the choice of using uniform or pipe models (see Appendix B for details) to determine whether inner DSCP changes if the EXP values do. This is something that can be decided only by network policy.

Figure 10-2 *QoS Recopy*

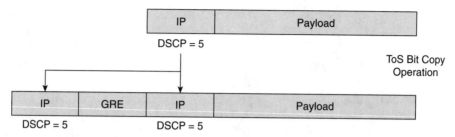

Note how we mapped traffic in a network segment to a DiffServ class and enforced QoS using standard mechanisms and design rules. All the link virtualization protocols already have the hooks needed to set DSCP (or 802.1p) values on incoming or outgoing traffic.

This solves many, but not all problems. A user in a particular segment may be infected with a virus and inadvertently send a flood of *Internet Control Message Protocol* (ICMP) messages to switches. The switch could conceivably become so busy processing ICMP packets that it could no longer guarantee the service level required by other VNs. This naive example (which ignores *network admission control* [NAC], *control-plane policing* [CoPP], scavenger class—all available to protect switches from this scenario) illustrates how traffic in one VN could adversely affect another. Logical routers (covered in Chapter 4) would not have this issue because dedicated hardware resources could be allocated to different VNs.

Why not use MPLS TE or DS-TE?

As discussed previously, MPLS TE addresses link protection, link congestion, or load balancing. None of these help here. Although excess traffic on a segment may result in link congestion, TE is not the appropriate tool.

DS-TE, on the other hand, allows class-based bandwidth allocation and could limit the virus-related traffic from one VN from starving other VN.

An alternative solution is to use network security mechanisms and aggressive packet discard at the edge to detect and dispose of excess traffic on any VN.

Multiple Policies per Group—Hierarchical QoS

The simple case described in the previous section might not be enough for certain situations where, for example, separate VNs exist for relatively large groups, each of whom want to run VoIP but who want to maintain traffic separation for all their applications. Figure 10-3 shows a sample network in which a single IT department creates VNs for two different engineering groups after a merger. The IT department does not control access switch ports, which are shared between groups, albeit with traffic in different VLANs.

Figure 10-3 *VN QoS—Hierarchical*

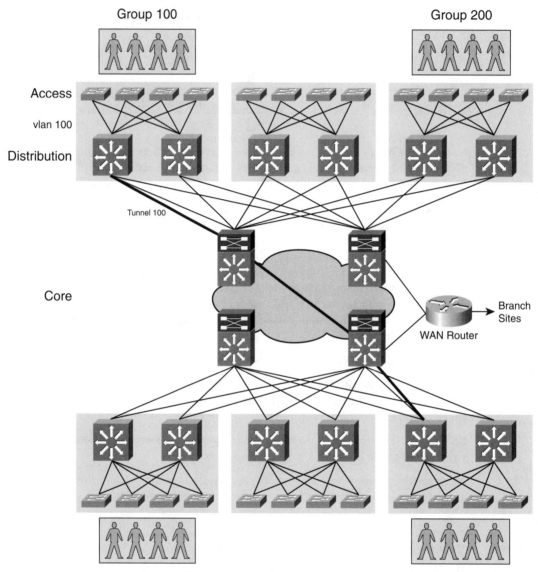

In this scenario, policy guarantees must be provided to different application flows within flows of user traffic, which requires hierarchical QoS mechanisms. The term *hierarchical* refers to the use of nested policy mechanisms. Hierarchical QoS allows for a parent group policy, and then child policies that belong to that group. For example, a department gets *x* Mbps worth of bandwidth (the parent policy), but within that there are different (child) classes of service for different applications.

When confronted with hierarchical QoS requirements, the recommended approach is to enforce per-VN differentiation at the edges of the network. Despite the more-complex policies, the usual design rules still apply when using hierarchy (for example, the combined link bandwidth allocated to voice should still remain under 33 percent, and 25 percent of link bandwidth should remain unreserved).

NOTE	The 25 percent rule is a basic design recommendation. Only 75 percent of the total bandwidth of any link should be allocated to major applications, leaving the rest for control traffic, link-layer encapsulation overhead, and unpredictable bursts of traffic.

Returning to our example, regardless of the multiple groups in which it runs, voice still needs to be marked as EF so that it is correctly queued in case of congestion in the core (here you have proof of the fundamentally democratic nature of networking: all voice is considered equal). As a consequence of this design approach, the network administrator is responsible for making sure that each VN, which may use different paths or devices, must be able to support *low-latency queuing* (LLQ) and, on slow WAN links, packet-interleave techniques such as *Link Fragmentation and Interleaving* (LFI), *compressed Real Time Protocol* (cRTP), and so on.

Our scenario requires that bandwidth of one of the engineering departments be limited to 100 Mbps (obviously the acquired company). Security policy requires that no single user exceed 10 Mbps. This policy should be enforced at the edge of the network in Figure 10-3 using hierarchical policing. The distribution switches would police the aggregate traffic in VLAN 100 to 100 Mbps, with a child policy that further limits any traffic flow within VLAN 100 to be less than 10 Mbps. The switches can still maintain a single set of queues for all traffic to guarantee priority for voice (policing is hierarchical, but queuing is not).

You might want to deploy hierarchical queuing on a tunnel interface. Remember that tunnel interfaces have no underlying hardware and so never congest and, therefore, will never queue traffic. If your network design needs a different behavior, you can use hierarchical policing and classes on both the tunnel and underlying physical interfaces. The reference section in Appendix C lists a document for further reading.

As usual, different products have different capabilities in this regard. Figure 10-4 shows one example: the ME3750 (from the 3750 Metro Ethernet white paper at Cisco.com).

Hardware support for hierarchical queuing, typically found in higher-end equipment, is costly, so be sure that a genuine requirement exists before specifying it.

Figure 10-4 *Hierarchical Queuing Scheme on the Catalyst ME3750*

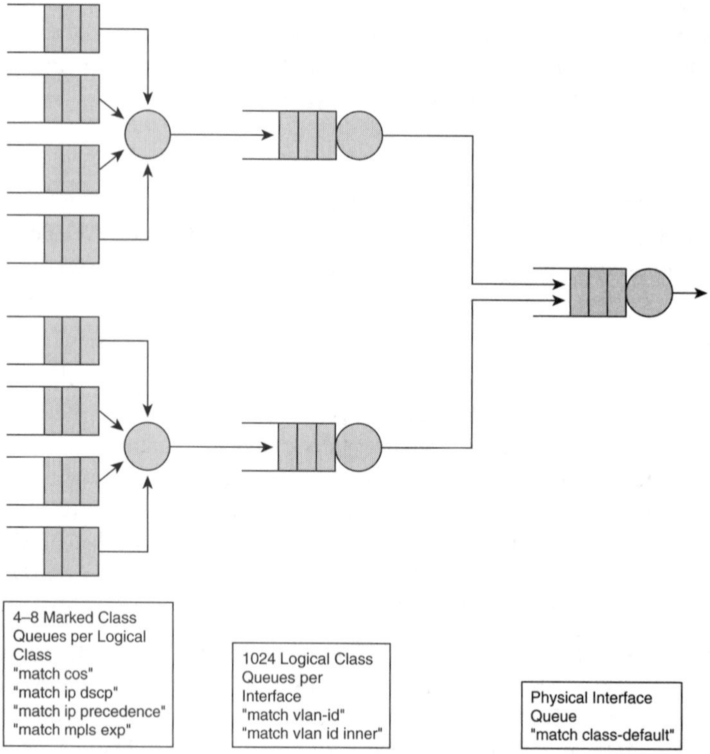

4–8 Marked Class
Queues per Logical
Class
"match cos"
"match ip dscp"
"match ip precedence"
"match mpls exp"

1024 Logical Class
Queues per
Interface
"match vlan-id"
"match vlan id inner"

Physical Interface
Queue
"match class-default"

NOTE   We owe a debt of gratitude to K. P. Mishra of Cisco Systems for his expert explanations of hierarchical service policies.

Summary

This chapter focused on QoS mechanisms available in virtualized networks and discussed some deployment considerations. The DiffServ model is just as applicable as before, as are the recommended QoS guidelines for enterprise switched and routed networks, with up to 11 different classes. If MPLS is used in the network, the number of classes should be reduced to less than or equal to eight.

MPLS TE and DE-TE are two powerful applications that enable network designers to improve link utilization and protection and to provide strict QoS guarantees without overprovisioning. The decision to deploy TE or DS-TE should be made independently of the decision to virtualize the network, because they address different problems.

At the time of this writing, QoS mechanisms have not been virtualized at the device level. Undoubtedly, they will be virtualized at this level in the future. Until then, we must use standard DiffServ mechanisms.

CHAPTER 11

The Virtualized Access Layer

Chapter 3, "A Basic Virtualized Enterprise," briefly described the typical multilayer campus architecture, with its traditional building blocks of access, distribution, and core. Other chapters looked at how the distribution and core must change to support virtualized services. Now it is time to look at the access layer.

The discussion is organized into three broad sections:

- A short section on the access layer to review the key features deployed in the wiring closet
- The issues of authentication and authorization
- A design example

Access Layer Switching

The role of the access switch is to physically aggregate user ports and switch user traffic both locally and to the distribution layer.

Figure 11-1 shows a wiring closet deployment. User-facing ports connect to end stations, such as servers, laptops, or phones, at rates of 10 Mbps, 100 Mbps, or 1000 Mbps. The uplinks are currently designed to operate at 1 Gbps, 10 Gbps, or as aggregated bundles of 1 Gbps, such as four 1-Gbps ports using EtherChannel. Access switches can be logically stacked into a group that can be managed as a single entity with one IP address and one configuration file. Stacked switches provide local switching capability across disparate physical chassis and can appear from the outside to function as a single device. Stacking implementation varies wildly, from highly sophisticated redundant ring-based interconnects to simple point-to-point connections cascaded from switch to switch.

In the classic campus design, each wiring closet switch has redundant connections to two different distribution switches and runs the Spanning Tree Protocol to select forwarding paths and provide redundancy in the Layer 2 domain. There are well-documented improvements to the original 802.1D standard, such as *Per VLAN Spanning Tree Plus* (PVST+) and *Rapid Spanning Tree Protocol* (RSTP), to cite just two examples. These have been incorporated into the IEEE specification as the 802.1D-2004 standard.

Figure 11-1 *Access Layer Switching*

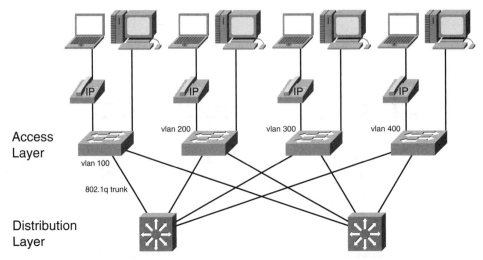

We greatly encourage network administrators to make sure they use current Spanning-Tree implementations and enable PortFast and UplinkFast on access and trunk ports, respectively. In addition, user-facing ports should be configured with the *bridge protocol data unit* (BPDU) Guard feature to prevent users from accidentally or intentionally adding a switch to the network (and playing havoc with spanning tree).

Figure 11-1 shows another recommended design practice, with one VLAN for each access switch. Spanning tree will select a trunk link to one of the distribution switches, with the other available for redundancy. It is possible to load balance traffic across the Layer 2 trunks. In the event that the network runs Voice over IP, the switches will also have a voice VLAN (also called the auxiliary VLAN). In this scenario, the wiring closet trunk interfaces will always carry at least two VLANs: a native VLAN for data and the auxiliary VLAN for voice.

VLANs limit broadcast domains; therefore, Cisco recommends no more than 512 devices in a wiring closet VLAN, which translates to 2 Class C IP subnets. Irrespective of the size, because of the recommendation of one VLAN per closet, there must also be least one different IP subnet for each closet, too.

The voice VLAN is on a different subnet than the data endpoints, and it is recommended to use an RFC 1918 subnet address for voice end systems. This is both for reasons of security and address management. Because data end stations might need to use a public IP address, you can conserve those addresses by using private ones for the voice VLAN. Also, a separate VLAN offers some protection from attacks or viruses originated on PCs. There is obviously more flexibility in smaller deployments than these hard numbers suggest.

Most access layer switches are pure Layer 2 affairs, with a single IP address for management purposes. However, in some cases it can make sense to deploy Layer 3 up to the edge of the network. In these cases, the wiring closet switches must run a routing protocol—*Enhanced Interior Gateway Routing Protocol* (EIGRP) or *Open Shortest Path First* (OSPF)—instead of the Spanning Tree Protocol on the uplinks.

At the beginning of this section, we mentioned stacking as a common feature on wiring closet switches. Be careful that you do not design out the redundancy from the access layer by tying the switches together with a half-duplex stack link. All the careful engineering of spanning tree, VLANs, and fast reconvergence cannot help if there is a single path of failure for the access switches in a closet. In addition, be careful that stacks do not add excessive latency to the end-to-end voice path. At high speed, this is unlikely, but congested switches can start queuing, and there is a well-defined time budget (150ms) available for voice packets to reach their destination. Distribution layer switches have sophisticated hardware, and there is a lot to be said for using it.

Access switches can deliver electrical power to end stations. This is useful to power wireless access points, small video cameras (for surveillance), and IP phones on an Ethernet network. Wiring closet switches sometimes have an auto-detection feature to recognize the type of endpoint connected to a port (Cisco devices use the *Cisco Discovery Protocol* [CDP] for this and auto-detect Cisco IP phones), which in turn allows them to send the correct amount of power over category 5 cable. The power budget of switches is not engineered to run all the ports at the highest power levels. End devices can negotiate predetermined, standardized power levels with the switch. Power over Ethernet is standardized as IEEE 802.3af.

The access layer is an important component in enforcing overall network security policy, especially the prevention of Layer 2 and Layer 3 spoofing. For example, the access switch should limit hosts to transmit only IP packets using the address allocated to them by DHCP. On a Cisco switch, you enable DHCP snooping (**ip dhcp snooping** command) to build a table of which Layer 3 / Layer 2 address combinations are allowed on which ports, and enforce the mapping using IP source guard (**ip verify source** command). IP source guard prevents a host from spoofing its IP address. When the switch has a trusted MAC-IP address database, such as the one provided by DHCP snooping, it can also prevent gratuitous *Address Resolution Protocol* (ARP). Using the dynamic ARP inspection feature, a switch looks at ARP replies generated by end stations and drops packets that purport to be from an IP address other than the one granted by DHCP on that port.

Port security, which we cover more extensively later, enables the administrator to protect the switch's *content-addressable memory* (CAM) table and limit the number of hosts allowed per port. Private VLANs are another security feature that prevents user ports from communicating directly with each other. End-stations can send traffic only to a selected trunk port. This is not applicable in the typical office environment (no matter how little you like your neighbor), but proves useful in shared public-space deployments such as airports, hotels, or universities, where most users only want to connect to servers or to the Internet. Private VLANs also prove useful between servers for infection containment.

The need to transport voice was the reason for *quality of service* (QoS) deployment in the access layer. To support VoIP, a switch, at the very least, must be able to differentiate between voice and data packets and mark each accordingly for appropriate treatment in the core. Chapter 10, "Quality of Service in a Virtualized Environment," discussed the QoS policy markings that the access layer must support. The access switch should also be able to rate limit incoming traffic on trunk ports to accommodate interface speed mismatches and traffic bursts.

On the user-facing ports, per-class marking and rate limiting are powerful security features. Excess burst traffic of the sort generated by viruses and worms can be marked and dropped aggressively to protect network bandwidth from being overrun. The access switch must also provide class-based low-latency queuing to guarantee timely voice packet delivery in the case that the trunk becomes congested.

The more advanced QoS features are expensive to implement in hardware, so they tend to appear correctly implemented only on higher-end products, despite some elaborate data-sheet claims.

The following list summarizes several of the more important access layer features:

- VLAN support, dot1q trunking
- Link aggregation: EtherChannel, LACP/802.3ad
- Spanning tree: 802.1w, 802.1s, PortFast, UplinkFast
- QoS: packet marking, classification, policing, and queuing
- Redundancy and fast convergence: 802.1w, EIGRP and OSPF optimizations, *Hot Standby Router Protocol* (HSRP)
- Layer 3: QoS and *access control list* (ACL) awareness, routing protocols for Layer 3 deployments
- Multicast: *Internet Group Management Protocol* (IGMP) snooping
- Inline power: 802.3af
- Security: dynamic ARP inspection, port security, DHCP snooping, and IP source guard, rate limiting, broadcast suppression

QoS underlines the access layer's role as the perimeter of the network trust boundary. In Cisco-recommended designs, policy should be applied and enforced as early as possible. Not only should the access layer discard noncompliant traffic, it should also prevent unwanted traffic from being put on the network in the first place. Sometimes, authorized users send unauthorized traffic, which can be dealt with by using a combination of QoS and ACLs, but those are coarse-grained tools when it comes to detecting unwanted or untrusted users in the first place. This brings us to the relatively recent requirement for access switches to be able to identify users and to authenticate them before accepting their data.

The next section of this chapter discusses authentication and authorization, which are the two components of access layer functionality that are affected by network virtualization.

The reason is simply stated as follows: Virtual Network membership is an aspect of overall network policy and, therefore, must be applied and enforced at the network edge. The access layers must place users into the correct Virtual Network as part of the authentication and authorization process.

That said, recognize that the access layer is already virtualized and has been for a long time! The switches use VLANs, and Ethernet frames are encapsulated in 802.1q as they traverse trunk links, with separate virtual networks for at least two applications (data and voice). As long as the access layer remains a Layer 2 environment, the existing mechanisms will continue to function just as before virtualization is deployed elsewhere in the enterprise network, with the possible need of supporting more VLANs on the network than before (if policy on a virtual network introduces new groups of users, there will need to be more VLANs at the access).

Implementing Dynamic Authentication and Authorization

Authentication means identifying a user, and authorization involves deciding what that user can do. Both are integral parts of an overall network security policy.

Network authentication and authorization are not new problems. IT departments the world over are making their users miserable by installing newer and "better" tools that make joining a network much more complicated than just plugging your laptop into the right port in a conference room. Of course, with regular security intrusions and threats, authenticated LAN access is, alas, a necessity. Virtualized Networks are no exception. In keeping with the general rule that what worked before virtualization must work after it, it must be possible to authenticate users but also—and this is new—to place them into the right network. To do this, there has to be a tie-in between the authorization and all the possible forms of tunnels being used for transport.

For example, an engineering company with an on-site contractor might want to limit network access to the LAN segment where that person will work, perhaps in a laboratory, and then revoke all forms of access when the contract expires. The network must therefore be able to do the following:

1 Identify the person (authentication)

2 Understand that the person belongs to a group of contractors

3 Place the contractor's laptop in a virtual network for lab access (authorization)

4 Place the employees with whom the contractor must work in the same Virtual Network (more authorization to place everyone in the right VLAN or *VPN routing and forwarding* [VRF])

5   Also allow the employees to connect to the rest of the company (routing and/or route-target configuration)

6   Allow contractor access to be revoked, either on demand or after a certain number of days (dynamic policy control)

In a virtualized environment, you will find the same authentication techniques as on a standard campus network, which is reassuring, because authentication needs to be based on something tangible: something you know, something you have, something you are. Authentication is an important, if difficult problem for today's administrator. It is, however, already part of to network virtualization. Thus, our interest lies in authorization.

Authorization is the link between a user's identity and the user's rights on a network. More specifically, authorization policy determines a user's network membership. In a Cisco environment, authorization manifests itself as Cisco IOS (or CatOS) commands applied to a user's traffic, usually at the interface level. In Virtual Network, these instructions contain VRF or VLAN names, or ACLs that determine which hosts or subnets are reachable for a user or group.

There are many different mechanisms to manage network membership. We need to pick one that allows the most flexibility and is the easiest to manage. To give away the element of surprise, the recommendation is to use 802.1x where available. But to understand the design trade-offs, it is necessary to see that network membership can be static or dynamic:

- **Static**—Guest Internet access at a company is an example. A user is unlikely to move between the guest and employee categories often.

- **Dynamic**—Some hotels and coffee shops provide wireless Internet access to subscribers. The network must therefore have two groups of users: those who have paid, who are free to surf; and those who have not, but who are invited to do so on a web page. Users can obviously move from one group to the other fairly often, which in turn, brings up the fact that authorization rules often must change.

The easiest way to allow regular change is to have a central policy store that all network devices consult before they forward user traffic. This in turn has implications for which mechanisms can be used to authorize users:

- If the type of media is important, authentication and authorization can be done per network device. One example is a specific policy for wireless users.

- If the user's status is important, say for billing purposes, the network needs to obtain a name, which can be checked against payment record.

- If the location of network connection is important, say a conference room, all hosts that connect to a certain network device and port (or interface) are authorized for a certain type of access.

You get the general idea. In each case, authorization is done using different data: *service set identifier* (SSID), username and password, MAC addresses, and so on. The authorization commands (such as VRF/VLAN name, ACL name) can be statically configured or downloaded dynamically.

Policy can quickly become complicated, often unduly so. The next sections discuss several of the different authentication and authorization options and their integration into the virtualized enterprise network. First, here is a final word on complexity. In our experience, it is better to keep things simple. Your network will work longer that way!

In a campus environment, authentication can be

- Clientless
    - Layer 2 clientless
    - Layer 3 clientless
- Client based

We will now look at each option in turn.

Clientless Authentication

The term *clientless* refers to the fact that no special software is required on host machines for them to access the network. The benefits of this are enormous: no special installation, no maintenance and upgrades, and no issues with compatibility. In LAN environments, a clientless solution involves using a network address as the user (or host) identifier.

Figure 11-2 shows a topology where hosts are authorized against their MAC address. When an end station is connected the first time, it sends a DHCP or *Address Resolution Protocol* (ARP) packet. The wiring closet switch intercepts the first packet and checks whether the source address is allowed to connect on this port. If so, the switch places the port into a VLAN and forwards all traffic thereafter normally.

Figure 11-2 *MAC Authentication*

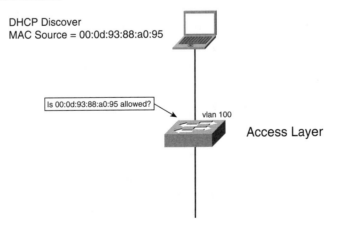

DHCP Discover
MAC Source = 00:0d:93:88:a0:95

Is 00:0d:93:88:a0:95 allowed?

vlan 100

Access Layer

All the different components come together in this simple example. Hosts are authenticated with their Ethernet addresses. The authorization policy simply grants or blocks network access and places the port in the appropriate VLAN.

Before looking at the implementation details, how good is this solution? The benefits include the following:

- **No client software**—Distribution and maintenance of software is an expensive recurring cost.

- **Not-PC centric**—Any host, be it a printer, card reader, or X-ray machine, can be accepted onto the network.

- **Multiple Layer 3 protocol support**—The solution is not tied to IP.

- **Supports virtualization**—VLAN names are statically configured on each port.

On the other hand, there are a number of obvious problems here. First, MAC addresses are not especially trustworthy because they can be changed. Malicious users can easily alter their Ethernet address. Innocent users can do the same thing when they replace a wireless adapter or change laptop. This brings us to the second problem: How does the switch know which addresses are allowed onto the network in the first place? There has to be a long list somewhere for the switch to query when an address appears on the network for the first time. Finally, static VLAN configuration is cumbersome if you expect to have a dynamic group membership environment.

The next section examines two different implementation alternatives of Layer 2 clientless authentication: a distributed approach using the port security feature found on Cisco switches, and a centralized one using *VLAN Membership Policy Server* (VMPS).

Static Clientless Implementation—Port Security

The port security feature configures switch ports to forward only traffic from a given MAC address. If another machine tries to use the port, all their traffic is dropped. The switch command needed to activate port security is as follows:

```
set port security 2/1 maximum 2
```

This example goes one step further by limiting the number of allowed MAC addresses on port 2/1 to just two.

In addition to just locking down each port with a set number of addresses, port security also lets you tell the switch to accept traffic either from only preconfigured addresses or from the first *N* addresses it learns.

There are multiple applications of port security. It allows protection against MAC address spoofing by preventing users from changing their address. It can also be used to lock down a port that belongs to a given user. For example, if network policy states that only one user can ever use a port in dormitory, port security can limit the MAC address accepted on the port to the first address learned after the port transitions to link up. After school starts, students connect their laptops to their ports and thus "burn in" their access rights for the year. This system is not perfect, of course, but it will work in a large number of cases, freeing up the support team to fix the unusual cases or problems.

What does this have to do with virtualization? Port security enables you to safely and statically bind ports to a VLAN. For example, a factory floor might have measurement and control systems running on Windows 3.1 (such scenarios exist!) that must be part of a virtual network used to manage production systems. Because of security risks, no unauthorized user can connect to the production network. The most pragmatic way to authorize such old software is to statically configure the VLAN names on the access ports.

This, of course, opens up the security risk that some other user physically might connect a different machine on one of the preconfigured ports. Port security mitigates this risk because it can be used to list the MAC addresses authorized on the ports.

NOTE   Admission control based on MAC addresses is always susceptible to spoofing. It is easy to change a MAC address on a laptop, for example. And it is common for MAC addresses to be labeled on PCs for inventory-management purposes.

The static, distributed approach makes sense when only a small number of ports need to be locked down (and when all other options fail). Despite the flexibility, it would be unwise to view port security as a general-purpose network-wide mechanism to map users to VLANs, because you need to correctly configure every MAC address on every port on every switch. There are better alternatives and, quite frankly, life is too short.

Instead, we need a central server where MAC addresses and VLAN mappings are configured just once and made available to all switches on the network. It so happens that there is centralized solution for MAC authentication: VMPS.

Centralized Dynamic Clientless Authentication—VMPS

VMPS was created by Cisco in the late 1990s to provide a way to dynamically assign MAC addresses to VLANs. Port security statically binds a host to a port (and, optionally, a VLAN). VMPS uses MAC addresses as a proxy for user identity and dynamically binds a MAC address to a VLAN. Under such a scheme, when a user connects to any port in the network, the switch will query a central server to find out which VLAN the host belongs to.

Figure 11-3 shows the main components of a VMPS solution. One of the switches in the network is the primary VMPS server that contains the canonical list of address-VLAN bindings.

Figure 11-3 *VMPS Solution*

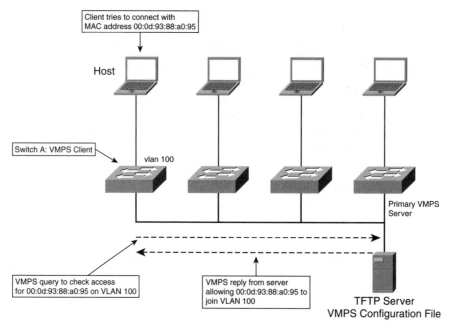

The server downloads the list from a TFTP server when it boots up. All other switches are VMPS clients and exchange query/responses (using UDP) to validate VLAN membership, as follows (the device names refer to Figure 11-3):

1   A host connects to switch A, which is configured for VMPS, and tries to send a packet.

2   Switch A sends a query to the VMPS server containing the host's MAC address.

3   The VMPS server looks up the address in its database. If VLAN mapping is allowed, it replies back to switch A allowing the port to be brought up in the corresponding VLAN.

VMPS has a number of features that allow a network administrator to control how the switch behaves when no match is found. The default behavior is to drop traffic from the address, but the client switch port can also be configured in secure mode, in which case it is shut down if authorization fails.

VMPS also supports the concept of a "fallback" VLAN. If the server does not find a VLAN name for the requested MAC address in its database, it can return a different VLAN name. The fallback feature is a simple way to create a guest VLAN—all known enterprise MAC addresses are stored in the VMPS database. All visitors, who have unknown addresses by definition, can connect but are placed in a fallback VLAN, which is only allowed Internet access. It possible to further refine VMPS policy by restricting VLAN membership to a particular port on a specified switch.

VMPS also supports IP phones, which require an additional VLAN per port, which must be statically configured. VMPS allocates the native VLAN name and makes sure that two different VLAN IDs are used for each VLAN.

The VMPS solution also has a graphical tool, called the *User Registration Tool* (URT), that enables administrators to easily edit VLAN membership on a Windows server and then make the resulting file available with TFTP to the VMPS primary and backup servers. The early versions of the product did no more, but URT has since been enhanced to integrate into an *Active Directory* (AD) structure. Now, in addition to host-based authentication, users can perform a Windows login to be able to connect to the network. These details are beyond the scope of this book and, for our purposes, it is enough just to know that there is a way to graphically administer the VMPS solution.

VMPS is a sophisticated clientless authentication and authorization system. It allows central administration, with options for different behavior when a client address is not found in the database and support for VoIP.

However, the trend today is definitely toward 802.1x, and we do not recommend VMPS as a general-purpose solution. After all, VMPS is proprietary and places an additional resource load on the wiring closet switches, which have to intercept packets, query servers, and so on—even as they forward other traffic at wire speed. As you will see, 802.1x has much stronger protocol security, albeit at the cost of putting software on the clients.

Before looking at 802.1x, we should point out that all the discussion so far has focused on Layer 2, but IP address-based authorization is also possible. It is not secure, but we review the pros and cons in the following section.

Layer 3 Clientless Authentication—Web Clients

Layer 3 clientless authentication can mean one of two things:

- Using a host's IP address as a credential to grant network access
- Providing an authentication scheme for hosts on routed interfaces

Consider the first option. Such a scheme makes sense when you need to restrict network access to entire subnets. For example, remote employees connect to a VPN concentrator and are allocated addresses from subnet 10.0.0.0/24. Network policy prevents these users from connecting to any lab machines (these network administrators are obviously inveterate control freaks, but that issue is beyond the scope of this book), so lab routers have an ACL rule, such as **access-list 1 deny 10.0.0.0. 0.0.0.255**.

NOTE   Because IP addresses are almost always dynamically allocated, it makes no sense to grant or refuse access at the port level using a host's source address in the way that we did with Layer 2. Otherwise, the network would have to allocate an IP address, and then decide whether the same address is allowed on the port the user was connected to when the user asked for the address in the first place!

Another example that has been deployed is to implement a simple walled garden (where users are restricted to certain content). Subscribers connect to the network and receive a 10.0.0.0 address and default gateway from DHCP. This 10.0.0.0 subnet is not routed to the rest of the network, so users can connect only to local servers.

Static or *policy-based routing* (PBR)-based VRF allocation are other (widely deployed) tools for Layer 3-based authorization. These are basically location-based policy setting schemes.

The second option listed at the start of the section is web-based authorization. This solves a different problem, where the network needs to know the identity of the user before deciding what to do with them. The web-based approach can seem appealing at first blush because the Layer 2 equivalent—802.1x—appears complex to deploy. The reasoning here is that every host already has a web browser, and every user knows how to enter a name and password on a web page, so there is no need to deal with supplicants. However, web-based authentication is more expensive than it first appears.

Figure 11-4 shows the setup. Before the user can authenticate, she needs to have an IP address to get to the registration server. However, we do not want her to be able to access the entire network yet, so she is limited to the 10.0.0.0 subnet, which allows her to reach the web server and nothing else (all this could be in a registration VRF, of course). After she authenticates, we need to move the user into the 192.168.1.0 subnet, which allows full access to the rest of the network. Here is where things get complicated because there is no way to tell an Ethernet host to return their IP address to get a new one.

Figure 11-4 *Web-Based Authentication*

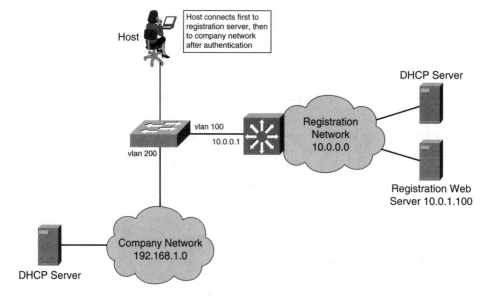

A second complication is how to get the user to the registration server in the first place. You cannot expect users to remember an IP address, or even a name. So, the network has to intercept all HTTP traffic, and redirect *Domain Name System* (DNS) requests so that a standard browser will display the registration page correctly. The redirection mechanism must then be removed after the user is authenticated.

To summarize:

1 The user connects to the network and requests an IP address.

2 The DHCP server returns an address from pool 10.0.0.0 and default gateway 10.0.0.1.

3 The user brings up a web browser and goes to some random site.

4 The network intercepts the DNS request, returning the address of the registration server at 10.0.1.100.

5 The network intercepts the HTTP request and sends it to the registration server.

6 The server presents the web page.

7 The user logs in.

8 The network allocates a new address to the user.

9 The user can connect to the website requested in Step 3.

The problem with the preceding simplified list is that there is no standard way to accomplish Step 8. However, there are workarounds such as scripts that telnet to the switch to reset the port, short DHCP lease times, DHCP reconfigure (RFC 3203), proprietary control protocols running between the server and switch to trigger VLAN or VRF changes, time-based TCP redirection, and *Network Address Translation* (NAT). These solutions are beyond the scope of this book.

Web-based authentication schemes do exist and are popular at public access points such as conferences or hotels. Cisco offers multiple implementations. *Building Broadband Service Manager* (BBSM) is a Windows NT server-based solution designed for hospitality environments. Cisco *Internet Services Group* (ISG) is a service provider class solution that is integrated into high-speed edge routers. However, to date, we believe that there is no web-based alternative for general deployment in the enterprise access layer that is as efficient as 802.1x, which is our next topic.

Client-Based Layer 2

Client-based access has a long history in dialup and *digital subscriber line* (DSL) networks, where a PPP client implements authentication and authorization and allows the service provider fine-grain control over who can access their networks, what they can do there, how long they can stay, and so on. The similarities between public-access networks and enterprise LANs is striking because the problem we are grappling with is that it is no longer possible to know a priori whether a machine that connects to a LAN port is trustworthy or even whether it should be there. Service providers have long had to deal with people who should not try to connect to their network.

In the late 1990s, the choice of PPP for DSL was not automatic because it involved distribution costs. Few operating systems at the time had a *PPP over Ethernet* (PPPoE) client, so the service provider had to send CDs to their customers with software stacks and provide support for installation and updates. Of course, this issue tends to dissipate with time as native implementations appear on the usual suspects of residential connectivity (Microsoft, Apple, Linux, Linksys, Netgear, and so on) and as the protocol definition stabilizes enough to mitigate incompatible implementations. For this same reason, client-based software was not an obvious choice for Ethernet authentication.

However, as discussed in the section that covered clientless authentication, there is not much choice. The Ethernet protocol does not have enough hooks to provide strong access control. That is what the IEEE proposes to deliver with the 802.1x standard.

802.1x provides an authentication and authorization mechanism for Ethernet networks. The switch, called the authenticator, blocks all network access until the client, called a supplicant, successfully authenticates.

Figure 11-5 shows the roles played by networked devices in an 802.1x environment.

Figure 11-5 *802.1x Roles*

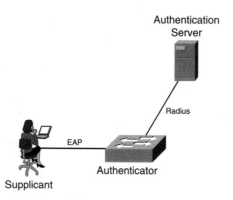

A definition of each role is as follows:

- **Supplicant**—The client that asks to be authenticated.

- **Authenticator**—The network perimeter that blocks access until the supplicant is authorized.

- **Authentication server**—The brains behind the entire operation that decides, based on the information forwarded by the authenticator, whether the supplicant should be admitted to the network. The 802.1x authentication service is often part of a RADIUS server.

The 802.1x standard defines protocol details and state changes that determine how the switch access port is allowed to move from a state where it accepts only 802.1x frames to one where the supplicant can send traffic normally.

802.1x is important to us because it allows access ports to be dynamically placed into VLANs. This single feature means that it is a key component to a virtualized network, which still run VLANs between access and distribution layers.

Next, we review some of the protocol-level details and discuss the interactions between 802.1x and the rest of the access layer functionality (for example, with DHCP).

802.1x Protocol Details

802.1x has protocols nested within protocols similar to a Russian matryoshka doll. 802.1x uses a transport mechanism (encapsulation frames and so on) to carry the *Extensible Authentication Protocol over LAN* (EAPOL) protocol between supplicant and authenticator. EAPOL, in turn, is the EAP protocol running over LANs. EAP comes to us from PPP, where it was created as an extensible—and standardized—authentication mechanism that did not require IP. You can think of EAP as an extension to PPP whose purpose is to avoid the spread of proprietary authentication methods above and beyond the well-known *Password Authentication Protocol* (PAP) and *Challenge Handshake Authentication Protocol* (CHAP).

EAP is defined in RFC 3748 as a framework for exchanging messages until the supplicant is either authenticated or denied access:

[a] Lower layer. The lower layer is responsible for transmitting and receiving EAP frames between the peer and authenticator. EAP has been run over a variety of lower layers including PPP, wired IEEE 802 LANs [IEEE-802.1X], IEEE 802.11 wireless LANs [IEEE-802.11], UDP (L2TP [RFC2661] and IKEv2 [IKEv2]), and TCP [PIC].

[b] EAP layer. The EAP layer receives and transmits EAP packets via the lower layer, implements duplicate detection and retransmission, and delivers and receives EAP messages to and from the EAP peer and authenticator layers.

[c] EAP peer and authenticator layers. Based on the Code field, the EAP layer demultiplexes incoming EAP packets to the EAP peer and authenticator layers. . . .

[d] EAP method layers. EAP methods implement the authentication algorithms and receive and transmit EAP messages via the EAP peer and authenticator layers. . . .

EAP offers a duplicate-free, reliable transmission channel. Different authentication methods (item [d] in the RFC definitions), which are often written as EAP-SOMETHING (such as EAP-TLS, EAP-TTLS, and so on), are multiplexed over EAP allowing the endpoints to choose from a list of methods. Network administrators must select the methods that are the most appropriate and choose supplicants and servers that support them. Figure 11-6 shows the list of supported authentication methods on a modern operating system.

Figure 11-6 *EAP Authentication Methods*

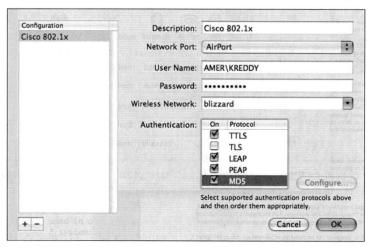

Because EAP was originally written with PPP in mind, an encapsulation was required to transport it over Ethernet. Figure 11-7 shows the EAPOL format (from IEEE 8021x-2001).

The most relevant field is the Packet Type, which can have one of the following values:

- 0 EAP-packet
- 1 EAPOL-Start
- 2 EAPOL-Logoff
- 3 EAPOL-Key
- 4 EAPOL-Encapsulated-ASF-Alert

You can see from the list that EAPOL adds only four messages to EAP semantics.

EAPOL frames are sent to a reserved group address, 01-80-C2-00-00-03, called the PAE group address. This address is taken from the 16 reserved *bridge protocol data unit* (BPDU) addresses in the 802.1D standard. No switch should forward packets with this address.

Figure 11-7 *EAPOL Frame Format*

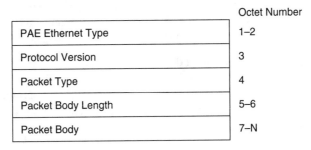

	Octet Number
PAE Ethernet Type	1–2
Protocol Version	3
Packet Type	4
Packet Body Length	5–6
Packet Body	7–N

```
PAE: EtherType code for PAE
Protocol Version: set to "0000 0001" for current version
Type:
        0 EAP-packet     1 EAPOL-Start     2 EAPOL-Logoff
3 EAPOL-Key      4 EAPOL-Encapsulated-ASF-Alert
Body: Present for types 0, 3 and 4
```

After all that background explanation, it is time to see how a client can actually gain access to a network. Figure 11-8 shows the protocol interaction between the different 802.1x roles.

Figure 11-8 *802.1x Protocol Exchange*

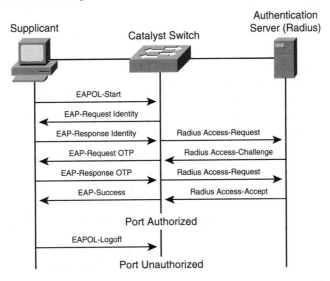

Before the supplicant connects, the switch port is in the unauthorized state. The client sends an EAPOL-Start message, and the switch (playing its authenticator role) replies with an EAP-Request Identity message. The supplicant's reply is relayed to the RADIUS authentication server, which then issues a challenge to which the supplicant must reply correctly. The supplicant can also issue a challenge to the authentication server, in the case of the mutual authorization scheme. When all parties have been authenticated, the RADIUS server sends the ACCESS-ACCEPT packet, which is relayed by the authenticator as the EAP-Success message. 802.1x events such as logon, authentication fail, and re-authentication are logged in RADIUS accounting messages.

In reality, the implementation details can vary quite a lot from the description in the previous paragraph. Cisco Technical Marketing Engineering teams have done extensive testing that characterize some of the major differences and provide detailed design recommendations. Our own 802.1x-related recommendations are based on this in-depth research and excellent documentation.

dot1x Implementation

Example 11-1 shows the Cisco IOS configuration needed to run 802.1x on a Cisco switch. The configuration is simple, with a global command to enable 802.1x and per-port activation using the **dot1x port-control** command. CatOS syntax obviously differs, but it is equally simple to configure.

Example 11-1 *802.1x Cisco IOS Port Configuration*

```
dot1x system-auth-control
interface gi2/1
  switchport mode access
  dot1x port-control auto enable
  spanning-tree portfast
```

When activated, the switch sends EAP-Failure on link up, followed by EAP-Request/ Identity frames. The supplicant should send EAPOL-Start, and then authentication can start. When the 802.1x process completes successfully, the switch puts the client MAC address in the CAM table so that it can always access the network, thus overriding any port security configuration that might be present on the port.

Many client protocol stack implementations do not assume that they will run in an 802.1x environment, so they send out DHCP Discover packets before sending EAPOL frames. These are discarded by the switch, and the client will have to resend them after authorization completes. Supplicants also behave differently when users log on and off. Some send EAPOL-Logoff events so that the switch can put the port into unauthorized state and send EAPOL-Start when a new user logs on. Others do not, in essence reducing 802.1x to host, not user, authentication. Of course, that is acceptable on a network where user authentication is done using other mechanisms such as Kerberos, but it has some implications for network accounting that we discuss later.

The basic configuration assumes a single host per port (and the IEEE documentation reinforces this by referring to point-to-point Ethernet links). Furthermore, 802.1x is intended for access ports and cannot be configured on trunks, *Remote Switched Port*

Analyzer (RSPAN), and so on. As a result, Ethernet frames with source MAC addresses other than that of the supplicant are discarded.

Cisco does not recommend connecting hubs to a 802.1x enabled port, but does provide two methods for dealing with such a scenario:

- **Multi-auth**—The switch forms 802.1x authentication relationships with multiple supplicants on a port. To do this, the switch unicasts EAP frames to the supplicant instead of multicasting. Not all supplicants support unicast communication. There are also a fair number of limitations with multi-auth mode, so a network administrator should consult the product documentation before use.

- **Multi-host**—The switch forms an 802.1x relationship with one supplicant on the port and then lets multiple MAC addresses send and receive traffic after the supplicant is authorized. If the supplicant disconnects (by sending a EAPOL-Logoff), the port transitions to the unauthorized state and the other hosts can no longer send and receive traffic. It is recommended to combine multi-host mode with the port security feature to limit the number of MAC addresses allowed per port.

Because of the Ethernet group addresses used by the supplicant and authenticator, it should be impossible to connect a switch between supplicant and authenticator because EAPOL frames are not forwarded.

When deploying 802.1x, you must decide which policy to apply to clients that do not, or cannot, successfully authenticate. It is not safe to assume that all clients have supplicants. Even those that do might not have the authentication method being used on the network. There are two basic options to manage such cases: MAC-auth-bypass and guest VLAN.

MAC-auth-bypass is a centralized approach for hosts with no supplicant (we call it centralized because the client MAC addresses can be stored in a central RADIUS server). The advantage is that the switch first attempts to use 802.1x before falling back on the less-secure method. MAC-auth-bypass is compatible with VoIP and applies only to the *port VLAN ID* (PVID) (the *voice virtual LAN* (VVLAN) is always authorized).

When the client fails to authenticate using 802.1x, the switch can try another method using the MAC-auth-bypass feature, which attempts to authenticate the learned MAC address using RADIUS (in other words, the switch does almost the same thing as it would have done if had detected a 802.1x supplicant). As shown in Figure 11-9, the client MAC address is used both as the username and password credentials in the RADIUS Access-Request packet. If the *authentication, authorization, and accounting* (AAA) server returns an Access-Accept, the client is allowed onto the network. For those who are familiar with *network access server* (NAS)-port authentication for DSL or dialup connections, this is analogous.

Figure 11-9 *MAC auth-bypass Runs After 802.1x*

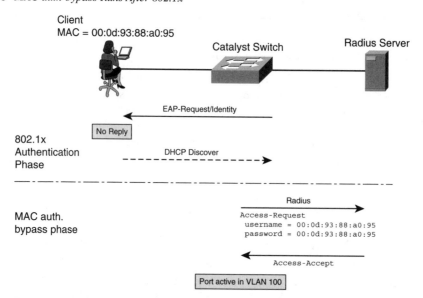

The guest VLAN was designed to allow graceful migration to 802.1x. The configuration of guest VLAN requires the **dot1x guest vlan** *VLAN* command on the access ports. Hosts that do not, or cannot, authenticate with 802.1x are placed in a named VLAN that the administrator can configure to have limited network access. The switch typically attempts to authenticate the supplicant three times before placing the port into the guest VLAN.

NOTE   Guest VLANs might require supplicant support to avoid a possible race condition. Recall that client protocol stacks often send DHCP requests before attempting to authorize with 802.1x. It is possible that a client is busy waiting for DHCP while the switch is waiting for EAPOL. The switch's 802.1x timers can time out, and the port can be placed in guest VLAN before client is ready to negotiate.

To avoid this, the switch 802.1x implementation should be able to remove clients from the guest VLAN if they receive an 802.1x frame and begin the authorization process anew (Cisco IOS has this "second-chance" feature). The supplicant should to be able to initiate EAPOL-Start (which is in accordance with spec) without seeing any EAP frames from switch. Some do, some do not.

The auth-fail VLAN is a special case of the guest VLAN where supplicants that fail to authenticate are placed. This differs from the guest VLAN, which can only contain supplicants that did not attempt to authenticate. In other words, auth-fail is for those who try, but fail; guest is for those who did not try at all. Only a single MAC address is allowed on any port in the auth-fail VLAN. The switch can be configured to put guest and auth-fail hosts into the same VLAN.

Incidentally, authentication failure can be defined as follows:

- No 802.1x after a configurable interval of time
- Access-Denied from RADIUS
- No reply to EAP-Request
- Incompatible authentication method

The network administrator needs to decide what policy to apply to the guest or auth-fail VLAN. The hosts can be directed to a server that allows them install or upgrade supplicant software, or the VLAN can simply allow Internet access. In either case, remember to provide a DHCP and DNS service for this VLAN, too.

Returning to switch setup, the other major configuration step is to enable RADIUS authentication for 802.1x supplicants, which requires the following commands:

```
aaa authentication dot1x default group radius
aaa authorization network default group radius
```

If you have worked with remote access, this part of the setup will look familiar.

The execution of the preceding commands assumes that a RADIUS server is already configured on the device. Remember that that the server must be reachable on ports that do not themselves need authentication. The **aaa authentication dot1x** command is the basic command to use RADIUS for port authentication, and the **aaa authorization network** command allows dynamic VLAN assignment.

The integration with RADIUS is the enabler for dynamic network selection. The authorization server sends the VLAN name in the RADIUS Access-Accept. The entire port is placed in the VLAN. The RADIUS attributes necessary for VLAN assignment are as follows:

- [64] Tunnel-Type=VLAN
- [65] Tunnel-Medium-Type=802
- [81] Tunnel-Private-Group-ID=VLANID or VLAN name

VLAN assignment can be combined with other per-user policies that have either dedicated RADIUS attributes or Cisco *vendor-specific attribute* (VSA)-pair support. For example, you can instantiate per-user access lists, or apply QoS policy using attribute 26,9,1 with a value such as **ip:inacl#1 = permit ip any any**.

Dynamic VLAN assignment appears to be a feature that every network should use without further thought. However, host software does not expect to change subnet when a user logs in. That is exactly what per-user VLAN assignment allows, however, so use it judiciously. Some operating system stacks that do support this feature attempt to ping the known default gateway (learned through DHCP during a previous user's session) every time 802.1x successfully authenticates. If there is no reply, it tries to renew its IP address. The DHCP relay forwards the packet to the (new) DHCP server, which can inform the client of the subnet change. The client then requests a new DHCP address.

If the client does not have some way to adapt to subnet changes, it is better to enforce per-user policy at a higher layer (consult Chapter 8 "Traffic Steering and Service Centralization" for more information).

As usual, the following question arises: What about voice? Just as with port security and VMPS, 802.1x works transparently with VoIP configurations. In the simplest scenario, phone ports are statically configured to bypass 802.1x authentication. On a Cisco network, it is possible to do a little better. If the switch detects a Cisco IP phone with *Cisco Discovery Protocol Version 2* (CDPv2), it allows the phone's MAC address to join the voice VLAN. The native VLAN port, called PVID in 802.1x jargon, is still deactivated until 802.1x successfully completes, so hosts connected behind the phone are still authenticated.

Figure 11-10 shows a typical deployment. A standard IP phone contains a three-port Ethernet switch, with one port connecting to the host, one to the on-board call processing logic, and the third to the LAN switch (because it is a switch, the phone really should not forward EAPOL frames, but it does anyway). If used, the RADIUS Tunnel-Private-Group-ID RADIUS attribute sets the native VLAN identifier, as you would expect.

Figure 11-10 *802.1x VoIP Scenario (No Phone on Supplicant)*

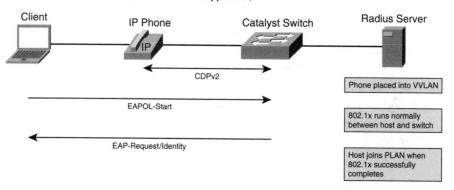

		CDPv2
	EAPOL-Start	
	EAP-Request/Identity	

Phone placed into VVLAN

802.1x runs normally between host and switch

Host joins PLAN when 802.1x successfully completes

NOTE There is a security risk here because any host that can spoof CDPv2 can in theory join the voice VLAN and attack the voice infrastructure (which should be protected, so the hole is not the end of the world, even if we would like to see it closed). The long-term answer is to put supplicants on IP phones, and this has started. Cisco high-end phones already have one, for example. Until then, many networks are open to unauthorized connection to the voice VLAN—the CDP solution is actually an improvement over the norm. Note that you cannot unplug an authenticated phone and connect a PC in its place. The switch will see the link state and address change and will deny access.

Just as for any supplicant, the phone's authentication can be easily monitored using a simple packet-capture program, which gives an attacker the ability to mount a replay attack using the captured packets. Strong password implementation is critical with tokens or public/private keys.

We have covered 802.1x in some depth and alternate Layer 2 and Layer 3 clientless schemes. 802.1x is the most complete and robust authentication and authorization solution available, irrespective of whether the rest of the network is virtualized. The next section examines a simple design and shows how to use 802.1x in support of network policy and how to tie the access and distribution layers so that users have access to the right virtual network.

Virtualizing the Access Layer

Having looked at different options for authenticating clients, we now attempt to pull together the various pieces with a design example.

The network shown in Figure 11-11 is migrating its core network to use Layer 3 virtualization with a combination of *generic routing encapsulation* (GRE) and *Multiprotocol Label Switching* (MPLS) tunnels. The distribution switches function as *provider edges* (PEs) and map incoming VLAN traffic to appropriate VRFs. Security is centralized in the data center, where traffic sent to and from the Internet and internal servers is cleansed.

Figure 11-11 *Virtualized Access Layer*

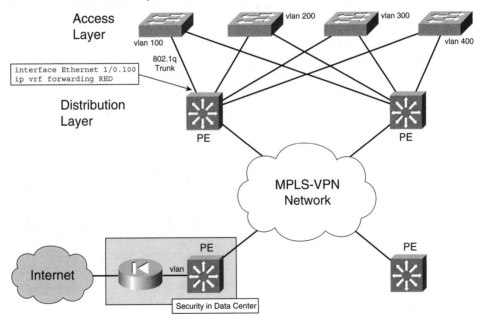

Because of a spate of security failures, the decision has been made to secure network access for all users and to enforce complete separation between employees and contractors, who need access only to lab networks.

Thus, there are two different groups allowed on the network:

- **Authenticated employees**—Employees who are allowed unrestricted access to the network. In case of authentication failure, employees should be allowed Internet access to update their host software and attempt to connect.

- **Non-employees (guests)**—Guests who are expected in shared spaces such as lobby areas, conferences rooms, and cafeterias. The network design must also allow for guests who connect to ports in employee areas. Guests are allowed Internet access, but their traffic must go through the cleansing device in the data center shown in Figure 11-11. Employees are not allowed to access corporate resources by running a VPN connection from a guest port back into the corporate network (the data center houses a VPN aggregator, which is not shown, to allow remote-employee connection).

Let's look at how to satisfy each of the design requirements in turn. The first decision is to use 802.1x for both network access security and dynamic group assignment. When available, Layer 2 authentication is easier to use than Layer 3. Layer 2 is well instrumented, secure, and transparent to almost all other features needed in the wiring closet.

The employee authorization is implemented with user profiles in a central RADIUS server. The right choice of authentication method is beyond the scope of our discussion here, but assume the use of EAP-TTLS. Every client, therefore, must have an 802.1x supplicant that supports this method. When authenticated, we have a choice of how to configure VLANs.

The first option is to bind access ports using RADIUS allocation. The access switch ports are configured as shown previously with the **aaa authorization network default group radius** command for dynamic VLAN allocation. The trunks between access and distribution carry dot1q traffic; and all employee VLANs are mapped to a VRF on the distribution layer using separate, routed logical interfaces for each physical trunk connection so that all traffic between closets is routed, not switched.

A consequence of using AAA to authorize user VLAN access is that it becomes cumbersome to allocate different VLAN names for every wiring closet because that involves using a different profile for any given user, based on where the user is sitting. It is possible to do this because the Access-Request comes with the IP address of the switch, and RADIUS servers allow scripts to be triggered to complete or change profiles dynamically.

There is another way. Because all VLANs are terminated at the PE on a Layer 3 interface and all inter-wiring closet traffic is routed (so the IP addressing plan has to support this— more on that later). As long as VLAN identifiers have local significance on the PE (in other words, the same VLAN ID can be used on two different interfaces), we can have the same VLAN name/ID for all employees, the wiring closets remain separate broadcast domains in accordance with best-practice LAN design.

Local VLAN significance is not universally available. Therefore, an alternative design is to use static configuration on the access switches so that each wiring closet uses a different VLAN ID (which is probably how they are set up already, so this approach eases migration). The PE terminates all employee VLANs into the same VRF. Remember that we can override the per-port configuration with 802.1x for dynamic, guest, and auth-fail VLANs, so we preserve the ability to have dynamic VLAN allocation should the need arise.

Employee DHCP requests are forwarded using the switch relay-agent function in the distribution layer to a DHCP server in the data center. The relay agent sets DHCP option 82 to communicate the physical port information to the DHCP server. The server allocates addresses from different IP subnets to each wiring closet by using the relay-agent information to select the right scope. In this way, we can guarantee Layer 3 routing between users connected to different wiring closets, no matter how the VLANs are named.

Employee peer-to-peer traffic is switched as early as possible, either at Layer 2 in the wiring closet for hosts on the same physical switch or Layer 3 in the distribution. The VRF route-target and routing configuration on the distribution switches forces all Internet- or server-bound packets through the data center's security center. See Chapter 6, "Infrastructure Segmentation Architectures: Practice," for information about how to configure the PE to do this. Figure 11-12 shows the inter wiring-closet traffic patterns for the Employee group.

Figure 11-12 *Permitted Traffic Flows for the Employee Group*

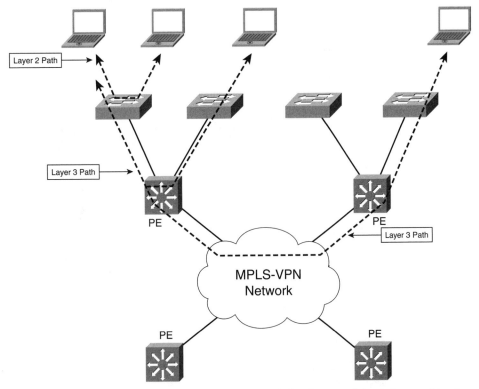

The second design requirement, guest access, is implemented through a combination of two methods. First, ports in public-access areas are locked down using port security to restrict access to the guest VLAN no matter who connects to them.

Second, on all other ports, a guest user group is configured using the per-interface command **dot1x guest-vlan** *VLAN ID*. The guest VLAN is again terminated on routed interfaces into a guest VRF at the distribution layer PE. Unlike the Employee group, the guest VLAN is a pure hub-and-spoke topology. All traffic must go to a data center PE. For this reason, a point-to-point tunnel, such as GRE, is a logical choice of transport protocol. See Chapter 4, "A Virtualization Technologies Primer: Theory," for more information about how to use route targets to do this in MPLS.

The data center PE forces all traffic through a virtual firewall context (also discussed in Chapter 4) and then on to the Internet. The firewall rules prevent all traffic from being routed back into the corporate network, including to the VPN aggregator. This satisfies the requirement of preventing employees from side-stepping 802.1x by building a VPN connection over the guest network and connecting back to the secure enterprise network (and, yes, people do this).

Figure 11-13 shows the allowed traffic flow for the Guest group. Obviously, there is configuration required on the firewall and data center PE, and on the distribution layer PEs, to do this correctly.

Figure 11-13 *Permitted Layer 3 Traffic Flows for the Guest Group*

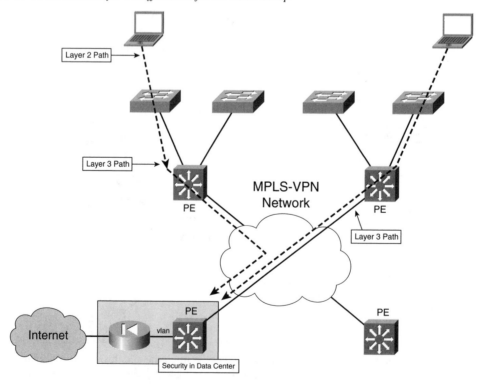

Guest VLAN members need a DHCP infrastructure. Because the core network is virtualized, there is no requirement to use different IP addresses from the employee network.

NOTE   In general, each virtual network needs its own policy infrastructure servers (DHCP, AAA, and so on), as this example shows. In other words, the network services must also be virtualized. No surprise there. There are—as usual—several options to implement this. You can deploy VRF-aware services that can maintain address pools and profiles for separate VRFs and support overlapping IP addresses. For example, Cisco has an elaborate per-VRF AAA feature set originally developed for service providers to do just this for RADIUS. The other option is to deploy virtualized servers with dedicated DHCP and RADIUS instances for each virtual network. Chapter 8 of this book reviewed how to connect virtual servers to VLANS and VRFs.

As discussed earlier in the chapter, the access switch moves a port into the guest VLAN if it does not receive EAPOL-Start or EAP replies after a configurable interval. Because clients could time out their DHCP requests before the switch moves their port to the guest VLAN, they might need to manually renew their request for an IP address. Expect support calls from users whose host software self-allocates the 169.254.0.0/16 subnet when they do not hear back from a server.

Recall from the requirements that employees who fail to authenticate must also have Internet access. We have the choice between setting up a separate auth-fail VLAN, which is a valid approach, or extending the Guest group semantics to include the tried-but-failed users. Cisco IOS allows the second option, so that is what we deploy in this design, using the **dot1x guest-vlan supplicant** global command.

Dynamic Groups

We have concentrated on static group definitions: employees or guests. In other words, the port to group binding can be dynamic, but group membership is static. Network reachability policy is similarly straightforward: authenticated users get everything; others get the Internet. Other deployment scenarios require more granular policy.

For example, on-site contractors in a restricted environment might be allowed to communicate with only a subset of the employee community. To implement this, we would like to set up a Virtual Network for this category of users. There are a couple of design options:

- **Layer 2**—Dynamically bind users in this group to a contractor VLAN. The distribution layer maps the VLAN to a MPLS VPN to allow routed communication between peers, but not with any other Virtual Network, creating a closed user group. The obvious disadvantage is that employees find themselves quarantined from the rest of the network. To solve this issue, create alternate 802.1x user profiles. For example, user/password allows full access to the network. A second profile, called user.restricted/password, has a Tunnel-Private-Group-ID attribute that forces the port into the contractor VLAN. The employees just need to log in with the right username for this to work.

- **Layer 3**—Create a separate VLAN and subnet for the contractors. On the PE, create an extranet VRF using MPLS route-targets that allows communication between the contractor subnet and one, or several, of the employee subnets. This approach makes certain assumptions about subnet allocation that will not apply to all cases. However, it is a good solution to allow both employees and contractors access to shared servers. For example, if the policy is that employees are allowed everywhere; but contractors have access only to their local LAN and a central server (say to upload reports), bind the contractor VLAN dynamically using RADIUS and map the VLAN to a VRF at the distribution as before. Then either download a per-user access list that restricts where contractors can go, or use route-targets on the PE to leak the route to the authorized server address and nowhere else. Employee configuration is unchanged.

The access layer of a virtualized network is atypical in that we have not introduced a new forwarding paradigm. As discussed at the start of the chapter, the Layer 2 access layer is already virtualized. The design examples concentrated on using 802.1x to map policy and group definitions to VLANs, which are mapped to VRF structures at the distribution. Note how, because there is nothing "new" in the forwarding path, there is no need to use VRF-aware features.

For the sake of completeness, the following is a quick review of the other major access layer features required for our design:

- **Security**—As previously discussed, dynamic ARP inspection, DHCP snooping, IP source guard, and port security should all be deployed in this scenario. Just because users are authenticated does not mean that they will behave themselves. RADIUS accounting is a valuable source of post-mortem data because it links IP address with user port with traffic statistics. You can combine this with NetFlow data from the core network to analyze who is sending what to whom and when.

- **QoS**—As discussed in Chapter 10, QoS internals are not virtualized. Use separate traffic classes for voice, regardless of the group it belongs to. You can choose to provide lower QoS guarantees to the Guest group, in which case those packets should be classified accordingly on the access ports. Remember, you can download per-user configuration in an 802.1x RADIUS profile. Finally, you can also use the scavenger class to aggressively discard excess-burst traffic on any port. Chapter 10 has the details.

- **Other access layer features**—This includes link aggregation, IGMP snooping, inline power, and so on.

Layer 3 Access

We have spent little time discussing Layer 3 wiring closet deployments as we have focused on the more traditional Layer 2 approach. This is because we currently recommend staying with a Layer 2 access layer when deploying virtual networks. To understand why, consider the following reasons:

- **Capital cost**—To support virtualization, the access switches must have VRFs, which represents an incremental hardware cost beyond what is required for a fully functional Layer 2 solution. Some access switches already support VRFs.

- **Feature support**—All the features deployed at the access layer must become VRF aware, especially authorization. Whether 802.1x allows dynamic VRF binding is implementation dependent, but if it does not, it becomes nontrivial to authenticate and authorize. Because all traffic on a port is already bound to a VRF, the 802.1x server must be reachable within that VRF. Distribution switches already have the required per-VRF features (and do not require 802.1x integration) and, though individually more expensive, there are fewer of them. Of course, Cisco and others do offer solutions with sophisticated access layer hardware that have the required per-VRF feature set for routing, security, QoS, and multicast.

- **Operational cost**—Turning on IP in the wiring closet multiples the number of routers in the network by a significant factor. Routing deployment will be more complex as a result, with more opportunity for error. However, removing spanning tree is not without benefit, and routed access limits broadcast domains to single ports, which mitigates against some categories of spoofing attack.

- **MPLS VPN**—In the case of a network using MPLS VPN, the logical architecture places the PE function in the wiring closet. This is not a good idea. RFC 2547 requires a *Border Gateway Protocol* (BGP) implementation beyond the scope of what you would expect to find on a wiring closet switch. Furthermore, each PE needs to be configured, so increasing their number creates more work and more opportunities for error (without the corresponding gain of removing spanning tree—routing took care of that already). Finally, PEs maintain a full mesh of LSP tunnels. If you increase the number of PEs, you must deploy BGP route reflectors to scale.

- **VRF instantiation**—Just as Layer 2 access has dynamic VLAN configuration, so would a Layer 3 solution have dynamic VRF binding. In this case, the user's RADIUS profile points to a VRF name rather than a VLAN ID. When successfully authorized, the user's port would be placed into the VRF. Sounds simple. However, the VRF must already be defined on the access switch with corresponding route distinguisher, route target, and BGP configuration (see Chapter 4 for more details). Also, to allow true user mobility, all possible VRFs must be preconfigured on every switch because any user might connect to any port. If the number of network-wide VRFs is small, this is not a major issue. Otherwise, it consumes switch resources (memory) for VRFs that might never have any attached interfaces. This is a well-understood problem for dialup and DSL access. The solution is to terminate subscriber sessions on a Layer 2 device and tunnel aggregate traffic to an external PE. In LAN terms, this means that Layer 2 access scales better.

For all these reasons, Cisco recommends using a point-to-point tunnel between access and distribution when Layer 3 is required or already deployed in the wiring closet. To reiterate, we do *not* suggest using MPLS in the wiring closet. Figure 11-14 shows the topology. Each group on the access switch is terminated into a VRF, which has a dedicated GRE tunnel to a corresponding VRF on the distribution switch, which—then and only then—label switches packets to other PEs.

Figure 11-14 *Layer 3 Access*

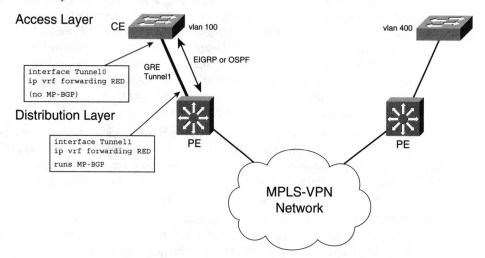

In Chapter 5, "Infrastructure Segmentation Architectures: Theory," we discussed hop-to-hop architectures. The Layer 3 access network in Figure 11-14 uses a Layer 3 hop-to-hop architecture (instead of the more traditional Layer 2 version—VLANs) to transport packets to the RFC 2547 PE in the distribution layer. It is not mandatory to terminate all the tunnels at the distribution. You can route GRE across the core to, say, a remediation server in the data center for *network access control* (NAC). Many such combinations are possible.

Summary

This chapter covered virtualized access layer design. The major impact of virtualization concerns authentication and authorization. Users are identified using either clientless or client-based solutions and bound to a VLAN.

Clientless authentication is based on MAC addresses in Layer 2 solutions. This has the advantage of being universal but is difficult to deploy efficiently on anything but the smallest network. Clientless Layer 3 solutions also exist, sometimes using web portals.

Our preference is to use 802.1x. The link to RADIUS is powerful and allows dynamic per-user policy instantiation, centralized management, accounting data, and more. The 802.1x protocol itself promises strong authentication, but the access layer should continue to use the fullest range of protection available to it to protect against spoofing, denial-of-service attacks, and excessive traffic from viruses.

We concentrated our discussion on a Layer 2 access layer for four reasons. First, that is the most deployed scenario. Second, migration to virtualized networks is easy because the wiring closet needs minimal change. Third, access switches do not offer the same features or performance as distribution devices, so turning them into PEs is not obviously beneficial. And, fourth, increasing the number of PEs in the network has an operational cost. The rest of the access layer feature set, which we reviewed in the first section, is unaffected by virtualization (or was already virtualized).

The design example at the end of the chapter showed how to implement network policy at the access layer and how to interact with the rest of the virtualized network.

We hope that you have found the information in this and previous chapters helpful as you choose what is best suited for your network.

P A R T III

Appendixes

L2TPv3 Expanded Coverage

Layer 2 Tunnel Protocol version 3 (L2TPv3) is an extension of regular L2TP that allows transport of data-link traffic other than PPP. The differences between version 3, defined in RFC 3931, and its previous incarnation are relatively minor and generally involve making the protocol less PPP specific. RFC 3931 lists the major differences from the original specification (RFC 2661, which we probably now need to refer to as L2TPv2):

Separation of all PPP-related AVPs [attribute-value pair], references, etc., including a portion of the L2TP data header that was specific to the needs of PPP.

Transition from a 16-bit Session ID and Tunnel ID to a 32-bit Session ID and Control Connection ID, respectively.

Extension of the Tunnel Authentication mechanism to cover the entire control message rather than just a portion of certain messages.

The L2TPv3 protocol consists of components to bring up, maintain, and tear down sessions. It can also multiplex different Layer 2 streams into a tunnel.

The RFC defines three different deployment models for L2TPv3, which are differentiated by the level of protocol processing on each tunnel endpoint. In all three cases, the deployment models refer to an *L2TP access concentrator* (LAC), which performs cross-connect function in the Layer 2 domain, and the *L2TP network server* (LNS), which terminates and processes Layer 3. The difference between the deployment models really concerns matching Layer 2 and Layer 3 across an L2TP tunnel. Figure A-1 should make this clearer.

The deployment models are as follows:

1 **LAC/LNS model**—This is the classic dial/DSL scenario, in which the LAC performs a Layer 2 cross-connect function and tunnels PPP traffic to an LNS. The LNS terminates the Layer 2 traffic and routes IP traffic. The PPP session is started by a client that connects to the LAC, and the LAC then begins tunnel and session setup with the LNS.

2 **LAC/LAC**—Each L2TP endpoint performs a Layer 2 cross-connect. This is the scenario for pseudowires. In this model, either endpoint can begin session establishment with its peer.

3 **LNS/LNS**—Two Layer 3 hosts use L2TP as a tunnel interface (for example, when a PC uses an L2TP client and begins a Layer 3 tunnel to another LNS over IP). This mode is also known as voluntary tunneling.

Figure A-1 *L2TP Deployment Models*

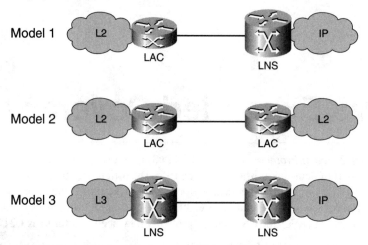

The L2TP protocol has a control- and data-plane stack, as shown in Figure A-2. The next two sections review each one in more detail.

Figure A-2 *L2TP Control- and Data-Plane Stack (from RFC 3931)*

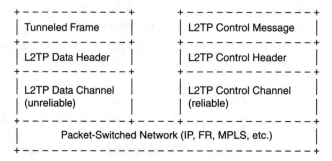

L2TPv3 Control Channel

L2TP has a reliable control channel and 15 different control message types. The major ones for the setup and teardown of the control channel itself are as follows:

- 1 (SCCRQ) Start-Control-Connection-Request
- 2 (SCCRP) Start-Control-Connection-Reply
- 3 (SCCCN) Start-Control-Connection-Connected
- 4 (StopCCN) Stop-Control-Connection-Notification

The major control messages for session setup and teardown are as follows:

- 7 (OCRQ) Outgoing-Call-Request
- 8 (OCRP) Outgoing-Call-Reply
- 9 (OCCN) Outgoing-Call-Connected
- 10 (ICRQ) Incoming-Call-Request
- 11 (ICRP) Incoming-Call-Reply
- 12 (ICCN) Incoming-Call-Connected

L2TP uses a three-way handshake to establish the control channel. The initiating endpoint sends an SCCRQ message to the remote peer. The peer replies with an SCCRP. The originator confirms the channel is open with an SCCCN. The peers can negotiate capabilities, such as a hello interval or window size. The two endpoints also advertise their respective control connection identifier, which is included in each control message and identifies the receiver.

Tunnel teardown is a little more abrupt. One of the endpoints sends a StopCCN message. There is no reply. The peers simply wait for all outstanding message acknowledgments. The StopCCN clears all the sessions in the tunnel.

Session setup also uses a three-way handshake. If a tunnel endpoint detects an incoming [L2] call, from a PPP client for example, it sends an ICRQ to its peer, which replies with an ICRP. The calling peer completes session negotiation with an ICCN message. Outgoing-call messages are used if the endpoint decides, for whatever reason, to originate a session.

Just as with the tunnel itself, the peers can exchange capability information for the session during the negotiation phase. The most important of these are the session ID and cookie.

The session ID is analogous to the control channel identifier and is a "shortcut" value that the receiver associates with the negotiated context for a particular session (for instance, payload type, cookie size).

The cookie is an optional, variable-length field of up to 64 bits. The cookie is a cryptographically random number that extends the session identifier space so as to ensure there is little chance that a packet is misdirected because of a corrupt session ID. Because 2^{64} is a large number (and as long as it is random), the cookie makes L2TPv3 impervious to brute-force spoofing attacks (that is, attacks in which the attacker tries to inject packets into an active session).

The control messages contain two 16-bit sequence numbers, Ns and Nr which are used to provide reliable delivery. The Ns field contains the sequence number of the message being sent. The Nr field contains the sequence number the peer expects to receive next. Each peer has a queue of outgoing messages. When a message is sent with a certain value in the Ns outgoing field, it is held (in another queue) until the remote peer acknowledges the message in its Nr field. The sender will resend if it does not receive an acknowledgment after a certain time interval (the RFC suggests 1 second with exponential backoff). If still no acknowledgment is seen from the remote peer, all the sessions and the control channel itself are flushed—because there is obviously a communication problem, there is no point sending more data to the peer under current conditions. When an L2TPv3 tunnel is closed, the peers wait for all message acknowledgments before tearing down the tunnel.

The L2TPv3 control channel also has an authentication mechanism. At the least, this requires a shared secret used on both peers to calculate a hash, or checksum. If an endpoint wants to authenticate its peer, it includes a random value, called a nonce, in a control message. When the remote endpoint sees the nonce, it must start authenticating all subsequent control messages. Authentication cannot be half on, so the remote peer must also send a nonce so that it can authenticate the local peer.

L2TP authentication is based on *Challenge Handshake Authentication Protocol* (CHAP, RFC 1994). An authenticated message contains a digest, or checksum, which can only be calculated by an endpoint that has certain information. The recipient of the message also calculates a digest, using the same information, and compares the result to the value it received. If they match, the message is genuine. If not, the message is discarded.

An L2TP endpoint computes a message value by applying a one-way hash function using a shared secret, its own and its peers nonce, and the contents of the control message itself. Obviously, the security of this system depends on choosing a good shared secret (the name of your company probably does not qualify) and on the random values (and the strength of the hash algorithm itself, currently *secure hash algorithm* [SHA] or *message digest algorithm 5* [MD5]). A third party would have to know both of these values to be able to modify the control message and compute a new, valid digest. The nonces themselves are sent to the remote tunnel endpoint as part of the control message. They are not encrypted.

Figure A-3 shows the L2TP control message header. The header contains the control channel ID and the Nr and Ns fields for retransmission. The meaning of all these fields has already been covered. The control message payload, which is not included in Figure A-3, is a variable sequence of *attribute-value pairs* (AVPs). There are AVPs for Message Digest, Connection ID, Receive Window size, and so forth.

Figure A-3   *L2TP Control Message Header (from RFC 3931)*

```
 0                   1                   2                   3
 0 1 2 3 4 5 6 7 8 9 0 1 2 3 4 5 6 7 8 9 0 1 2 3 4 5 6 7 8 9 0 1
+-+-+-+-+-+-+-+-+-+-+-+-+-+-+-+-+-+-+-+-+-+-+-+-+-+-+-+-+-+-+-+-+
|                       (32 bits of zeros)                      |
+-+-+-+-+-+-+-+-+-+-+-+-+-+-+-+-+-+-+-+-+-+-+-+-+-+-+-+-+-+-+-+-+
|T|L|X|X|S|X|X|X|X|X|X|X|   Ver |            Length             |
+-+-+-+-+-+-+-+-+-+-+-+-+-+-+-+-+-+-+-+-+-+-+-+-+-+-+-+-+-+-+-+-+
|                     Control Connection ID                     |
+-+-+-+-+-+-+-+-+-+-+-+-+-+-+-+-+-+-+-+-+-+-+-+-+-+-+-+-+-+-+-+-+
|              Ns               |              Nr               |
+-+-+-+-+-+-+-+-+-+-+-+-+-+-+-+-+-+-+-+-+-+-+-+-+-+-+-+-+-+-+-+-+
```

Finally, the control channel has a keepalive message that is sent periodically (the interval is configurable) between endpoints. Thus, communication problems can be detected independently of call management or data traffic.

L2TPv3 Data Channel

After a session is established through the control session, the L2TP endpoint is ready to send and receive data traffic, using the header shown in the top half of Figure A-4.

Figure A-4 *L2TP Data Message and Session Headers (RFC 3931)*

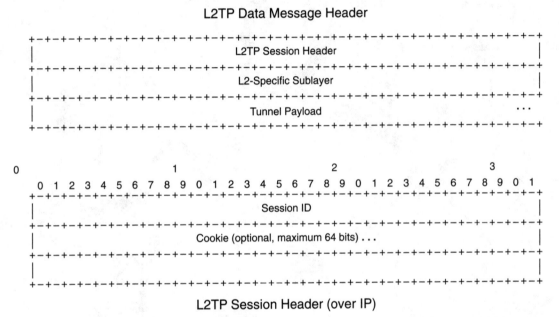

Each frame has a Session ID field in the session header, which is in the bottom half of Figure A-4. This field contains the session identifier value negotiated during setup (with an ICRQ/ICRP exchange, for example). No fixed mapping exists between data and control channels. A single data channel can carry frames belonging to multiple sessions. And, the session ID is used to multiplex different traffic streams onto the data channel. The Cookie field, also shown in Figure A-4, contains the cookie 64-bit value also negotiated during session establishment.

Although the data header has a Sequence Number field, the data channel is not reliable. The protocol can detect missing, duplicate, or out-of-order packets but does not resend. That is left to higher-layer protocols.

The RFC allows for the data channel to be set up either using the native control protocol or statically or using another control mechanism.

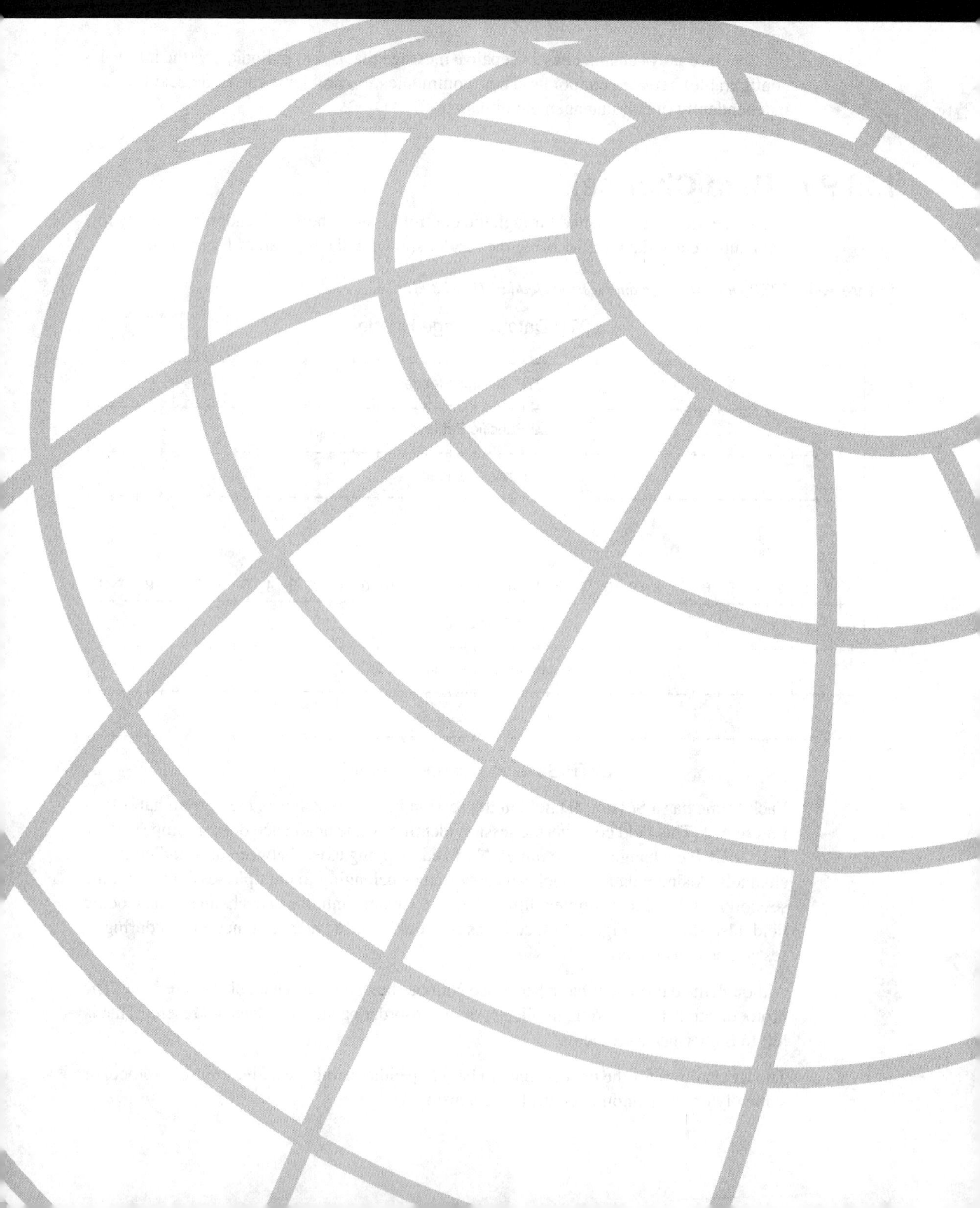

MPLS QoS, Traffic Engineering, and Guaranteed Bandwidth

This appendix covers topics related to *quality of service* (QoS) on *Multiprotocol Label Switching* (MPLS) networks in more detail than Chapter 10, "Quality of Service in a Virtualized Environment" (where they were originally presented). This appendix discusses the following:

* Uniform tunnel and pipe mode
* MPLS traffic engineering
* Guaranteed bandwidth

MPLS QoS—Uniform Tunnel and Pipe Modes

In uniform tunnel mode, any changes to a packet's *differentiated services code points* (DSCPs) are permanent, as shown in Figure B-1 and discussed in the following list:

1 A packet arrives at *link switched router* (LSR) A with a DSCP setting of 3. The switch policy determines that the appropriate *Expedited bit* (EXP) value for this class is also 3. The packet is forwarded across the core toward its destination.

2 LSR B reclassifies the packet into another class and sets the EXP to 4.

3 LSR C, the penultimate LSR, pops the MPLS label and egress LSR D sets the *Type of Service* (TOS) value to 4, to match the change in the MPLS core. If there is a label stack, the changes are propagated to the inner EXP field, and the next label would have its EXP set to 4.

4 Router E receives an IP packet with a DSCP setting of 4.

Figure B-1 *MPLS Uniform Tunnel Mode*

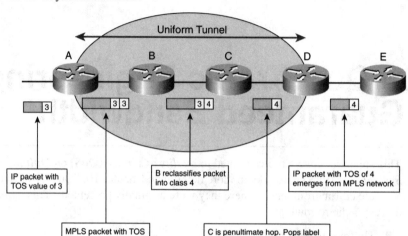

Pipe tunnel mode differs from uniform tunnels in two ways. First, changes to EXP are not copied to the internal DSCP. Second, the egress *provider edge* (PE) classification is done using the MPLS EXP value. Figure B-2 shows how pipe tunnel mode works, as described in the following steps:

1 A packet arrives at LSR A with a DSCP setting of 3. The switch policy determines that the appropriate EXP value for this class is also 3.

2 The packet is forwarded across the core toward its destination.

3 LSR B reclassifies the packet into another class and sets the EXP to 4.

4 When LSR D sends the packet, the DSCP setting is still 3. However, if there is a stack of MPLS labels, the changes are propagated to the inner EXP field. But, even in this case, the IP settings are never modified.

The pipe tunnel mode has a subtlety. LSR D ordinarily does not see the EXP values because of *penultimate hop popping* (PHP) on LSR C. However, because of the semantics of the pipe tunnel, LSR D needs EXP information so that it can apply the correct PHB for the packet. To reconcile this conflicting state of affairs, the egress LSR uses a concept called *explicit null*, which causes the penultimate-hop router to no longer pop the outer label when forwarding frames to its upstream neighbor. Explicit null labels are not needed if the egress LSR is going to receive a label anyway (for example, if there are two labels on the stack, even if the outer one is popped, the PE always receives a labeled packet).

A variation of the pipe tunnel mode is called short pipe mode; in this mode, the egress PE uses the packet's IP DSCP to apply *per-hop behavior* (PHB).

Figure B-2   *MPLS Pipe Tunnel Mode*

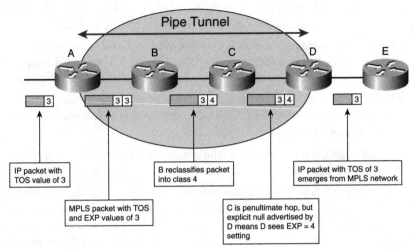

MPLS Traffic Engineering

As stated in Chapter 10, *MPLS traffic engineering* (MPLS-TE) addresses the following issues (also see Figure B-3):

Figure B-3   *Fish Problem*

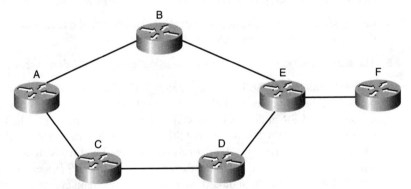

- **Link congestion**—*Interior gateway protocol* (IGP) best paths might be overused while alternative paths are either underutilized or not used at all. For example, in Figure B-3, the link between C and D is never used to forward traffic from A to F. All the packets go through B, which is the path with fewer hops. You can make the IGP use a different path by including bandwidth as one of the link metrics for *shortest path first* (SPF) calculation, but this is an approximate science and one that has no notion of congestion.

- **Link protection**—If a path or device failure occurs along the primary *link switched path* (LSP) in Figure B-3, routing protocols have to rerun the full SPF calculation before traffic can be forwarded again, which can take several seconds.

- **Load balancing**—Standard IGPs allow traffic to be balanced equally across equal-cost paths only. Unequal paths are ignored because the IGP sees them as longer routes to the destination, which is why the C-to-D link in Figure B-3 is not used in the first place.

MPLS-TE calculates shortest paths through a network, but within a given set of constraints using *constraint-based routing* (CBR). The operation is as follows (with the final result shown in Figure B-4):

1. All routers in the network run a link-state routing protocol with an extension that uses reservable link bandwidth as a metric.

2. The tunnel headend, Router A in Figure B-4, determines the best path to Router F based on available bandwidth, using a variant of standard SPF called *constrained SPF* (CSPF). CSPF prunes candidate paths from the SPF tree that do not satisfy some constraint (in this case, available bandwidth). In Figure B-4, the tunnel needs 40 Mbps. Router A finds the path to be A to C to D to E to F (perhaps because of slow or congested links elsewhere). The path appears as a dotted line in Figure B-4. As link-utilization conditions change, the CSPF algorithm will give different results for the same destination, which is the intended result.

3. After the path is found, the headend reserves a path through the network. Reservation is done using the *Resource Reservation Protocol* (RSVP) to signal label values. The headend sends a PATH message to the far end of the tunnel. The RSVP message follows the intended path of the tunnel, as defined by the CBR calculation.

4. Each LSR along the path checks whether it can allocate the requested bandwidth to the tunnel and updates the RSVP payload accordingly.

5. The remote endpoint sends an RSVP RESV message back along the tunnel path.

6. When it receives the RESV message, each LSR along the path reserves the bandwidth and allocates a label for the tunnel. The label data is communicated to the upstream LSR in the RSVP message. In more informal terms, the PATH message asks routers "please reserve this amount of bandwidth to this destination?" The RESV reply says "yes, I did so and here is the label to use to access the bandwidth I just set aside." Remember, though, that RSVP is a control plane reservation mechanism. Standard interface QoS mechanisms are required to implement policy.

7. After they are built, the tunnels, which appear as an IOS interface, still need to be included in the routing tables before a router can use them. You can do this with simple static routes on the headend router or by announcing it through the IGP as a directly connected path. Policy routing is a third option.

8. The tunnel is ready for use, with the label values defined at each hop along the LSP.

Figure B-4   *40-Mbps TE Tunnel Established*

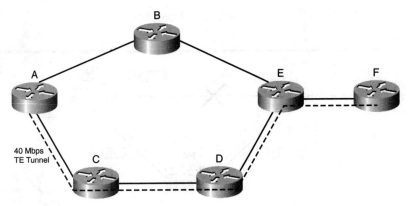

MPLS Fast Reroute

MPLS *fast reroute* (FRR) involves the following:

- FRR link protection enables you to preconfigure a backup LSP at any point along a tunnel path, which the traffic will use if a link failure occurs on the protected LSR. Without FRR, in case of a link failure, the tunnel headend must learn of the problem, run a new CBR calculation, and provision a new tunnel using RSVP before traffic can be forwarded again.

- Figure B-5 shows FRR in operation. The primary tunnel Tu0 is between R1 and R5. Suppose a link failure occurs between R2 and R3. R2 implements FRR by imposing a new label, 17, that corresponds to backup tunnel, Tu10, which goes through R4. Just as with a normal tunnel, the label is popped at the penultimate LSR, thus revealing the original label and allowing the packet to be threaded back into the original LSP, as shown in Figure B-5. R1 is notified of the failure by R2 and can provision a new LSP along an alternative path. If it does not, traffic is forwarded along the backup LSP. Note that R3 is unaware of the entire FRR operation.

FRR also offers node protection, which is more complex. Look at Figure B-6 and imagine that node R3 fails. Node R2 detects this and forwards traffic across the backup LSP, Tu10. However, the subtlety is that router R5 needs to see the same label as before the failure so that it can forward traffic along the correct LSP. R2 has to know which label R5 was expecting (16 in the case of Figure B-6) and push that value on the label stack as it sends the packet across the backup tunnel. In either case, if failure detection is quick enough, FRR can allow subsecond network reconvergence.

Figure B-5   *FRR Link Protection*

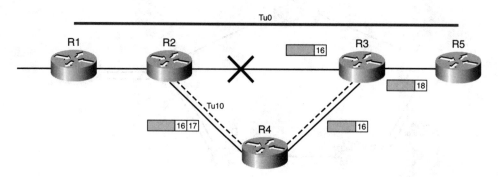

Figure B-6   *FRR Node Protection*

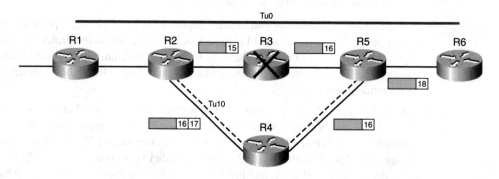

NOTE	Figure B-6 is a modification from the "Advanced Topics in MPLS-TE Deployment" white paper at http://www.cisco.com/.

Although we did not go into detail here, MPLS-TE supports the notion of priority and preemption. Low-priority tunnels can be removed to free up bandwidth for higher-priority tunnels.

Guaranteed Bandwidth

DiffServ-aware TE (DS-TE) was developed (see RFCs 3564 and 4124) to allow MPLS-TE to be traffic-class aware. DS-TE supports the concepts of preemption and explicit overbooking.

The terminology of RFC 4124 refers to *Class-Types* (CT). A CT is defined as the set of aggregated traffic flows belonging to one or more classes that are governed by the same *bandwidth constraints* (BC). Link bandwidth is allocated on a CT basis. BC is a generalized reference to the unit of bandwidth allocation, which can be percentage of link speed, absolute bit rate, latency requirements, percentage of free bandwidth, and so on. DS-TE implementations must be able to enforce the BCs for all the different CTs used on the network.

The relationship of different CTs to each other and to overall available bandwidth is defined in a bandwidth-constraint model. At least two models are currently defined (the normative RFCs, RFC 4125 and 4217 provide formal definitions). We explain them using examples (which are borrowed from the RFCs):

- **Maximum allocation model (MAM)**—Bandwidth is segmented into separate pools. Each CT is allocated its own pool of bandwidth. Figure B-7 shows the MAM model.

  For example, on a link of 100 units of bandwidth where 3 CTs are used, the network administrator might then configure BC0 = 20, BC1 = 50, BC2 = 30 such that

  — All LSPs supporting traffic trunks from CT2 use no more than 30 (for instance, voice <= 30).

  — All LSPs supporting traffic trunks from CT1 use no more than 50 (for instance, premium data <= 50).

  — All LSPs supporting traffic trunks from CT0 use no more than 20 (for instance, best effort <= 20).

- **Russian dolls model (RDM)**—Bandwidth is allocated from ever-increasing pools, where the bandwidth of each successive pool is inclusive of all the previous pools. Figure B-8 shows RDM graphically, which is easier to understand.

  For illustration purposes, on a link of 100 units of bandwidth where 3 CTs are used, the network administrator might then configure BC0 = 100, BC1 = 80, BC2 = 60 such that

  — All LSPs supporting traffic trunks from CT2 use no more than 60 (for instance, voice <= 60).

  — All LSPs supporting traffic trunks from CT1 or CT2 use no more than 80 (for instance, voice + premium data <= 80).

  — All LSPs supporting traffic trunks from CT0 or CT1 or CT2 use no more than 100 (for instance, voice + premium data + best effort <= 100).

Figure B-7 *Maximum Allocation Model (from RFC 4125)*

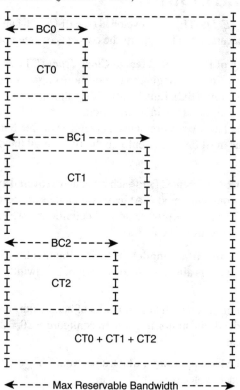

Figure B-8 *Russian Dolls Model (from RFC 4127)*

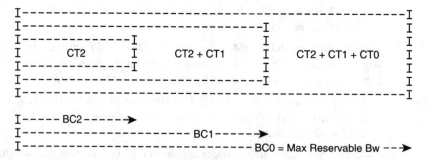

Each model has its own advantages. MAM, for example, has the property of class isolation: The bandwidth of any given class is independent of any other class, and this requires no preemption. However, MAM can be wasteful, because bandwidth allocated to CT1 cannot be given to CT0 if there is no CT1 traffic. RDM, on the other hand, does not have this last problem because CTs share bandwidth. However, RDM requires preemption for bandwidth constraints to be guaranteed.

DS-TE is implemented with IGP extensions that advertise the bandwidth per CT available on a link. TE constrained routing calculation is run on a per-CT basis and RSVP extensions allow reservation requests to also be made per CT. DS-TE, just like regular TE, is a control-plane reservation mechanism. You still need to use queuing and discard mechanisms to enforce the traffic classes on the data plane. To briefly review the implementation steps, consider a network requiring two classes: voice and data, where the voice class should be limited to 40 percent of the overall bandwidth, but QoS must be guaranteed. All other bandwidth is available for data.

- In DS-TE terms, there are two CTs: voice and data. Each CT should use its own DSCP value (for example, voice can be mapped to *Expedited Forwarding* [EF] and data to the *Assured Forwarding* [AF] classes).

- Use an appropriate queuing and discard scheme for each CT (for example, priority queuing for voice and *class-based weighted fair queuing* [CBWFQ] for data). Every interface on every hop used by the TE tunnels must also be configured with bandwidth pool values to effectively divide the bandwidth with a 60/40 ratio.

APPENDIX C

Recommended Reading

This appendix lists two types of reference material. The first category is the material used when we prepared the book. The second is material that covers in more depth some of the topics we introduced.

References to a small number of internal Cisco documents were particularly helpful or important (and for which no external equivalent existed). Obviously, these are not available to the general public (who should buy this book instead).

Chapter 1

http://www.cisco.com

"Campus Infrastructure"
"Cisco IP Communications for Enterprise Branch Architecture and Small Offices"

Chapter 4

http://www.cisco.com

"How to Choose the Best Router Switching Path for Your Network" (explanation of FIB and adjacency table structure)
"Configuring MPLS on the Optical Service Module" (where the IOS VFI configuration is from)
"L2TPv3 Enables Layer 2 Services for IP Networks"
"Configuring MPLS Basic VPN with RIP on Customer Side"
"OSPF Support for MultiVRF on CE Routers"
"MPLS VPN support for EIGRP between Provider Edge (PE) and Customer Edge (CE)"
"Managing Security Contexts"

Books

Doraswamy, N., and D. Harkins. *IPsec—The New Security Standard for the Internet, Intranets and Virtual Private Networks*. Prentice Hall, 1999.

Guichard, J., and I. Pepelnjak. *MPLS-VPN Architectures*. Indianapolis: Cisco Press, 2002.

Chapter 5

http://www.cisco.com

"Dynamic Multipoint IPsec VPNs (Using Multipoint GRE/NHRP to Scale IPsec VPNs)"

"Dynamic Layer-3 VPNs (RFC 2547) Support Using Multipoint GRE (mGRE) Tunnels"

"OSPF Support for Unlimited Software VRFs per Provider Edge (PE) Router"

"GRE Tunnel with VRF Configuration Example"

"Cisco Express Forwarding Overview"

"OSPF Design Guide"

"Scaling Inter-Domain Routing—A View Forward" (Geoff Huston, Telstra)

Inter-autonomous system MPLS VPN Configuration with VPNv4 eBGP Sessions Between ASBRs"

"Inter-Autonomous Systems for MPLS VPNs"

"MPLS VPN Carrier Supporting Carrier"

"Any Transport over MPLS"

"MPLS VPN Carrier Supporting Carrier IPv4—BGP Label Distribution"

"MPLS VPN Inter-AS IPv4 BGP Label Distribution"

Chapter 7

http://www.cisco.com

"MPLS VPNs over IP Tunnels"

"Dynamic Layer-3 VPNs (RFC 2547) Support Using Multipoint GRE (mGRE) Tunnels"

Chapter 8

http://www.cisco.com

"Cisco Services Modules Configuration Guides" (Firewall Services Module configuration guide)

Chapter 9

Cisco internal documents

Extranet VPN Functional Specification, http://www.cisco.com

Cai, Yiqun, "IP Multicast VPN Supporting Extranet," Cisco ENG-265179

Cai, Yiqun, "IP Multicast VPN—Extranet," http://wwwin-people.cisco.com/~ycai/slides/mvpn/e-mvpn.ppt
Implementing Enterprise MVPN (Cisco Internal. Source: author archives)
EPO mVPN Validation Test-lab (Cisco Internal. Source: author archives)

Public documents (http://www.cisco.com)

"IP Multicast Technology Overview"
"Configuring IGMP Snooping and MVR"
"IGMP Version 3"
"Multicast VPN Concepts"
"Multicast VPN Design Guide"
"Configuring Multicast-VPN"
"Multicast VPN IOS Feature Support"
"MultiVRF and IP Multicast"

Book

Apcar, J., J. Guichard, and I. Pepelnjak. *MPLS and VPN Architectures, Volume II.*
Indianapolis: Cisco Press, 2003.

Chapter 10

Device-specific QoS references (http://www.cisco.com)

"Catalyst 3750 Switch Software Configuration Guide" (Configuring QoS)
"Cisco Catalyst 3750 Metro Series IOS Release Product Bulletin"
"Catalyst 4500 Switch Software Configuration Guide" (Configuring QoS)
"Understanding Quality of Service on Catalyst 6000 Family Switches"
"QoS Policing on Catalyst 6500/6000 Series Switches"

Technology white papers (http://www.cisco.com)

"Implementing Quality of Service Policies with DSCP"
"DiffServ-aware Traffic Engineering"
"Implementing DiffServ for End-to-End Quality of Service Overview"
"Modular QoS CLI (MQC) Three-Level Hierarchical Policer"
"MPLS Traffic Engineering Fast Reroute Link Protection"
"MPLS Traffic Engineering—DiffServ Aware (DS-TE)"
"Advanced Topics in MPLS-TE Deployment"
"Quality of Service for MultiProtocol Label Switching Networks Q&A"
"Quality of Service Options on GRE Tunnel Interfaces"
"Reference Guide to Implementing Crypto and QoS"
"Fast Reroute Overview"

Books

Guichard, J., F. Le Faucheur, and J. P. Vasseur. *Definitive MPLS Network Designs*. Indianapolis: Cisco Press, 2005.

Osborne, E., A. Simha. *Traffic Engineering with MPLS*. Indianapolis: Cisco Press, 2002.

Szigetti, T., and C. Hattingh. *End-to-End QoS Network Design*. Indianapolis: Cisco Press, 2004.

Chapter 11

Cisco product configuration information (http://www.cisco.com)

"Catalyst 6500 Series Software Configuration Guide, 8.5" (Port Security, Configuring Access Control, Cat6K Configuring Dynamic Port VLAN membership with VMPS, mac-auth-bypass and much, much more)

"Configuring IEEE 802.1x Port-Based Authentication: IOS Configuration" (also has information about guest and auth-fail VLAN and voice and port security integration)

"Configure IEEE 802.1x Authentication with Catalyst 6500/6000 Running Cisco IOS Software"

"VPN Access Control Using 802.1X Authentication"

"User Guide for the Cisco Secure User Registration Tool Release 2.5"

"Cisco IOS Service Selection Gateway Configuration Guide" (web-based access solution)

"Cisco Building Broadband Service Manager" (web-based access)

"EAP-TLS Deployment Guide for Wireless LAN Networks"

Cisco design and technology references (http://www.cisco.com)

"Layer 2 Access Control: Cisco IOS Software 802.1x"

"Gigabit Campus Network Design Principles and Architecture"

"VLAN Load Balancing Between Trunks Using the Spanning-Tree Protocol Port Priority"

"Spanning Tree PortFast BPDU Guard Enhancement"

"Cisco StackWise Technology"

"Cisco Catalyst Integrated Security-Enabling the Self-Defending Network"

"Cisco IP Telephony Reference Guide for Call Manager 4.0 and 4.1—Network Infrastructure"

Internal documents (created by TMEs in Cisco Technology Systems and enterprise Systems Engineering teams)

"IBNS/802.1x Basic—Details of AAA attributes for 802.1x implementation"

"Application Note: 802.1x and DHCP—Interoperability of Clients, Supplicants and Cisco implementation"

"Deployment Guide: Authenticated Identity Information—DHCP Snooping, RADIUS Accounting"
"Deployment Guide: L2 Security Features and Port-Based Access Control"
"Cisco IBNS Multiple Authentication Techniques in Hub Environments"
"IBNS and IP Telephony Application Note: Deployment Guide"
"Application Note: Use of 802.1x Guest VLAN to Provide Guest Access"
"Routing & Switching VT, November 2004: Wireless and Wired Guest Access Solution" (by Max Ardica, Simone Arena, Alex Dolan)
"Routing & Switching VT, May 2005: Campus VPN for NAC Remediation and Guest Access" (by Max Ardica, Henry Carmouche)

Books

Kaza, R., and S. Asadullah. *Planning for Cisco IP Telephony.* Indianapolis: Cisco Press, 2005.

Reddy, K. *Building MPLS-Based Broadband Access VPNs.* Indianapolis: Cisco Press, 2004. (Discusses service provider solution for some of the access problems discussed here, such as per-VRF services, virtual home gateways for PPP to MPLS termination, RADIUS attributes, and so on.)

General technology references

"What is 802.1x?" by Joel Snyder, Network World Global Test Alliance http://www.networkworld.com
"Architecting Your 802.1x-Based WLAN Deployment Using Odyssey and Steel-Belted Radius" Funk Software, http://www.juniper.net
"802.1X Port Authentication with Microsoft's Active Directory," Foundry Networks, http://www.foundrynet.com
"802.1X Port-Based Authentication HOWTO," by Lars Strand, http://www.tldp.org/HOWTO/html_single/8021X-HOWTO/
"Examining 802.1x and EAP," by Peter J. Welcher, April 2004, http://www.netcraftsmen.net/welcher/papers/dot1x.html
"Switching: Campus Design," by Peter J. Welcher, January 2000, http://www.netcraftsmen.net/welcher/papers/switchdesign.html
"Switching: Dynamic VLAN's, VQP, and VMPS," by Peter J. Welcher, October 1999, http://www.netcraftsmen.net/welcher/papers/switchvmps.html
"Deploying Identity-Based Access Control," by Peter J. Welcher, May 2004, http://www.netcraftsmen.net/welcher/papers/dot1x-deploy.html
"Switch Integrated Security," http://ist.uwaterloo.ca/cn/security/switch.html
IEEE8021x-2001: IEEE 802.1x standard on http://grouper.ieee.org/groups/802/1/

RFCs and Internet Drafts

This appendix lists RFC and *Internet Engineering Task Force* (IETF) drafts that relate to the subject matter covered in this book.

Chapter 4

RFC 2784, *GRE*

RFC 3931, *L2TPv3*

RFC 2401, *Security Architecture for the Internet Protocol*

RFC 2402, *IP Authentication Header*

RFC 2406, *IP Encapsulating Security Payload (ESP)*

RFC 2409, *The Internet Key Exchange (IKE)*

RFC 3031, *Multiprotocol Label Switching Architecture*

RFC 3032, *MPLS Label Stack Encoding*

RFC 3036, *LDP Specification*

Chapter 5

draft-ietf-l2vpn-l2-framework-05.txt, *Framework for Layer 2 Virtual Private Networks (L2VPNs)*

draft-ietf-l3vpn-gre-ip-2547-03.txt

  Use of PE-PE GRE or IP in BGP/MPLS IP Virtual Private Networks

draft-ietf-l2vpn-requirements-04.txt, *Service Requirements for Layer-2 Provider-provisioned Virtual Private Networks*

draft-ietf-l3vpn-ipsec-2547-04.txt, *Architecture for the Use of PE-PE IPsec Tunnels in BGP/MPLS IP VPNs*

draft-ietf-l2vpn-signaling-03.txt,

Provisioning Models and Endpoint Identifiers in L2VPN Signaling

draft-ietf-l3vpn-ppvpn-mcast-reqts-00.txt, *Requirements for Multicast in L3 Provider-Provisioned VPNs*

draft-ietf-l3vpn-2547bis-mcast-00.txt, *Multicast in MPLS/BGP IP VPNs*

draft-ietf-l3vpn-rfc2547bis-03.txt, *BGP/MPLS IP VPNs*

draft-ietf-l3vpn-as-vr-01.txt, *Applicability Statement for Virtual Router-based Layer 3 PPVPN Approaches*

draft-ietf-l3vpn-vpn-vr-02.txt, *Network-based IP VPN Using Virtual Routers*

draft-ietf-l3vpn-as2547-07.txt, *Applicability Statement for BGP/MPLS IP VPNs*

draft-ietf-pwe3-control-protocol-17.txt, *Pseudowire Setup and Maintenance Using the Label Distribution Protocol*

draft-ietf-l3vpn-bgpvpn-auto-06.txt, *Using BGP as an Auto-Discovery Mechanism for Layer-3 and Layer-2 VPNs*

draft-ietf-pwe3-ethernet-encap-10.txt, *Encapsulation Methods for Transport of Ethernet Frames Over IP/MPLS Networks*

draft-ietf-l3vpn-framework-00.txt, *A Framework for Layer 3 Provider Provisioned Virtual Private Networks*

RFC 2547, *BGP/MPLS VPNs*

Chapter 6

RFC 1918, *Address Allocation for Private Internets*

RFC 2332, *NBMA Next Hop Resolution Protocol (NHRP)*

RFC 2547bis, *BGP/MPLS IP VPNs*

Chapter 9

draft-ietf-mboned-intro-multicast-03.txt, *An Introduction to IP Multicast Routing*

RFC 3376, *Internet Group Management Protocol, Version 3*

draft-rosen-vpn-mcast-05.txt, *Multicast in MPLS/BGP VPNs*

draft-ietf-l3vpn-2547bis-mcast-01.txt, *Multicast in MPLS/BGP IP VPNs*

draft-ycai-mvpn-experience-00.txt, *Experience with Multicast VPN*

Chapter 10

RFC 1633, *Integrated Services in the Internet Architecture: An Overview*

RFC 2475, *An Architecture for Differentiated Service*

RFC 2702, *Requirements for Traffic Engineering Over MPLS*

RFC 3270, *MultiProtocol Label Switching [MPLS] Support of Differentiated Services*

RFC 3564, *Requirements for Support of Differentiated Services-aware MPLS Traffic Engineering*

RFC 4124, *Protocol Extensions for Support of Diffserv-aware MPLS Traffic Engineering*

RFC 4125, *Maximum Allocation Bandwidth Constraints Model for Diffserv-aware MPLS Traffic Engineering*

RFC 4127, *Russian Dolls Bandwidth Constraints Model for Diffserv-aware MPLS Traffic Engineering*

Chapter 11

RFC 3748, *Extensible Authentication Protocol (EAP)*

INDEX

Numbers

A

forwarding, 245
RPF, 245
shared trees, 247
source trees, 246
VRF, 40, 45–47
definition of, 57
displaying, 58
FIB, 58–60
LR, 61
multicast, 250–255
multiple VRF on routers, 57–58
resource allocation, 60
RIB, 58–59
routing table information, 59
sharing routes between, 58
traffic processing, 60
VRF awareness, 62
VR, 61
forwarding plane, 41
FRR (fast reroute)
link protection, 279–280
MPLS, 333
fusion routers, 50
fusion-switch deployment model (MVR), 258

G

global space, multicast in, 255—259
global tables, leaking traffic (unprotected services), 217–218
globally significant code points, 44
GRE (generic routing encapsulation), 41, 66
configuration, 260
headers, 67
ISO configuration, 68–69
mGRE, WAN, 177
MPLS over (WAN, VN extensions over), 192, 194–195
P2P GRE, WAN, 176–177
peer-based L3VPN architectures,
  RFC 2547bis, 160
RP keepalives, 67
tunnel-based L3VPN architectures, 96–98, 141
failovers, 150
failure detection, 150, 152
hub configurations, 143

hub routes in hub-and-spoke mGRE overlays, 154–155
IGP, 153
load balancing, 149
OSPF, 153–154
overlays, 155, 259–260
resiliency, 149
spoke configurations, 143–144
VRF interconnections (WAN, VN extensions over), 200–202
guaranteed bandwidth, 335–337
guest access (networks), 7–8
guest VLANs, 308–309

H

h2h (hop-to-hop) architectures
ACL, 94
constrained routing, 95
IP tunnels, VPN QoS models, 282
Layer 2 solutions, 92
complexity of, 90
scalability of, 91
user groups, 93
VLAN, 90–91, 125–129
Layer 3 solutions, 129
ACL, 138–140
adding interfaces to VRF, 132
advantages of, 93
complexity, 92
converting core links to dotlq trunks, 133–134
creating VLAN, 132
creating VRF, 131–132
EIGRP address families, 137
hierarchy support, 93
network topologies, 130
PBR, 139–141
routed nodes, 93
scalability, 92
segmented campus networks, 130
static routing, 93
VLAN ID, creating for core data path virtualization, 134–135
VRF, assigning SVI to, 135–137
VRF-lite, 129

N

W

X – Y – Z

SEARCH THOUSANDS OF BOOKS FROM LEADING PUBLISHERS

Safari® Bookshelf is a searchable electronic reference library for IT professionals that features more than 2,000 titles from technical publishers, including Cisco Press.

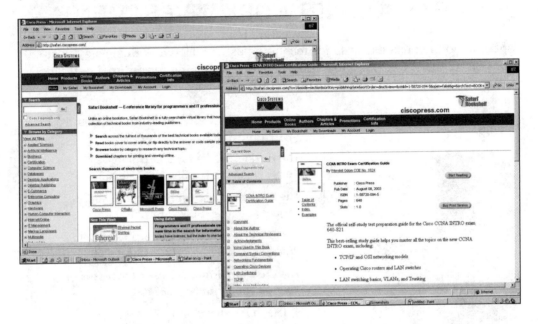

With Safari Bookshelf you can

- **Search** the full text of thousands of technical books, including more than 70 Cisco Press titles from authors such as Wendell Odom, Jeff Doyle, Bill Parkhurst, Sam Halabi, and Karl Solie.

- **Read** the books on My Bookshelf from cover to cover, or just flip to the information you need.

- **Browse** books by category to research any technical topic.

- **Download** chapters for printing and viewing offline.

With a customized library, you'll have access to your books when and where you need them—and all you need is a user name and password.

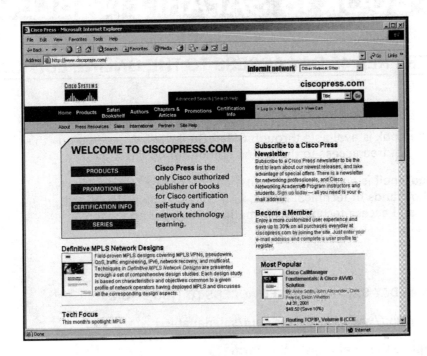
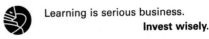

Safari
BOOKS ONLINE
ENABLED

THIS BOOK IS SAFARI ENABLED

INCLUDES FREE 45-DAY ACCESS TO THE ONLINE EDITION

The Safari® Enabled icon on the cover of your favorite technology book means the book is available through Safari Bookshelf. When you buy this book, you get free access to the online edition for 45 days.

Safari Bookshelf is an electronic reference library that lets you easily search thousands of technical books, find code samples, download chapters, and access technical information whenever and wherever you need it.

TO GAIN 45-DAY SAFARI ENABLED ACCESS TO THIS BOOK:

- Go to **http://www.ciscopress.com/safarienabled**

- Complete the brief registration form

- Enter the coupon code found in the front of this book before the "Contents at a Glance" page

If you have difficulty registering on Safari Bookshelf or accessing the online edition, please e-mail customer-service@safaribooksonline.com.